ONE NATION
UNDER SEX

ONE NATION UNDER SEX

HOW THE PRIVATE LIVES OF PRESIDENTS, FIRST LADIES AND THEIR LOVERS CHANGED THE COURSE OF AMERICAN HISTORY

LARRY FLYNT
& DAVID EISENBACH, PH.D.

palgrave
macmillan

ONE NATION UNDER SEX

Copyright © Larry Flynt and David Eisenbach, 2011.

All rights reserved.

First published in 2011 by PALGRAVE MACMILLAN® in the U.S.—a division of St. Martin's Press LLC, 175 Fifth Avenue, New York, NY 10010.

Where this book is distributed in the UK, Europe and the rest of the world, this is by Palgrave Macmillan, a division of Macmillan Publishers Limited, registered in England, company number 785998, of Houndmills, Basingstoke, Hampshire RG21 6XS.

Palgrave Macmillan is the global academic imprint of the above companies and has companies and representatives throughout the world.

Palgrave® and Macmillan® are registered trademarks in the United States, the United Kingdom, Europe and other countries.

ISBN: 978-0-230-10503-4

Library of Congress Cataloging-in-Publication Data

Flynt, Larry.
    One nation under sex : how the private lives of presidents, first ladies and their lovers changed the course of American history / Larry Flynt and David Eisenbach.
        p. cm.
    ISBN 978-0-230-10503-4
    1. Sex scandals—United States—History. 2. Political corruption—United States—History. 3. Politicians—Sexual behavior—United States—History.
4. Ethics—United States—History. I. Eisenbach, David. II. Title.
HQ18.U5F54 2011
306.770973—dc22

                                                                    2010042329

A catalogue record of the book is available from the British Library.

Design by Letra Libre, Inc.

First edition: April 2011

10 9 8 7 6 5 4 3 2 1

Printed in the United States of America.

CONTENTS

Eight pages of illustrations appear between pages 132 and 133.

To my wife Liz, my biggest supporter.

To my parents, Joanne and George Eisenbach.

ACKNOWLEDGMENTS

W e would like to give special thanks to Andrew Stuart, our dedicated literary agent, and Alessandra Bastagli, our talented editor. Thanks also to Destin Jenkins and Jacob Shapiro for their research assistance and to the Columbia University Library, the Library of Congress, the Franklin D. Roosevelt Library, the New York Public Library, the National Archives and the UCLA University Library. Thanks also to Alan Bradshaw, Alison Brod, Sarah Brown, Emily Carleton, George and Joanne Eisenbach, Stephanie Gangi, Charity and Kevin Keating, Adam Liebner, Roosevelt Montes, Melrose Phillips and Alyssa Quart.

INTRODUCTION

I pledge allegiance to my Flag and the Republic for which it stands, one nation, indivisible, with liberty and justice for all.

Pledge of Allegiance, 1892

During the Red Scare of the 1950s, Congress added the words "under God" to the Pledge of Allegiance in an attempt to link patriotism with religious piety and distinguish America from the godless Soviet Union. But there was a bigger point—that God played an essential role in guiding and shaping our nation. Leaving aside the dubious notion of a deity who favors one country above all others, we do believe there really is an all-powerful force that shaped our great nation. That force is sex. We have discovered that, far from being a purely private matter, the sexual activities of America's leaders affected pivotal events that altered the lives of millions. *One Nation, Under Sex* is the first history to explain how the personal lives of presidents, First Ladies and other notable Americans shaped the country we live in today.

Our tales of White House intimacy offer an entertaining mix of sordid and romantic, gay and straight, tragic and comical, titillating and horrifying. One of our goals is to offer readers eye-opening revelations involving people and events they have heard about their entire lives but never fully understood. We have been careful, however, not to automatically repeat the many salacious rumors and hearsay that have appeared in the media. Our extensive footnotes reflect the support for our historical accounts. We also take time to debunk myths about our leaders that have been passed down over generations. We are not out to dish gossip; we want to add a new dimension to American history.

Traditionally, historians have been squeamish about examining the sex lives of presidents because they do not consider private affairs to be a worthy subject of "serious" history. The result is that our leaders' lives have been so whitewashed that people think Thomas Jefferson and Abraham Lincoln were made of the granite of Mount Rushmore, not flesh and blood. Historians have been even more reluctant to delve into the private lives of First Ladies. We have discovered these influential women also had extramarital affairs and some were engulfed in scandals that had a major political impact. Other books have exposed the dirty laundry of historical figures and the steamy underbelly of American politics. We do that too, but we also explain how the sex lives of our national leaders affected elections, economics, international relations and even wars.

Our tales of love and sex also enable us to trace the changes in social mores throughout history. By deconstructing Dolley Madison's sex scandals we examine the place of women in the political life of the early Republic. Our look at President James Buchanan's 32-year-long relationship with Senator William Rufus King reveals how mid-nineteenth-century Americans handled the subject of homosexuality. The focus of our narrative may be on the private lives of political leaders, but in telling that story we also present a sweeping portrait of evolving sexual morality and gender roles in America.

Inevitably, we end up exploring the role of the media and the different ways reporters have treated political sex scandals throughout the course of history. We show that the freewheeling pamphleteers and printers of early America reveled in exposing the private affairs of politicians. Nineteenth-century newspapers also considered the sex lives of politicians fair game because a candidate's personal history was seen as a barometer of how he would behave in public office. Not until the early twentieth century did journalists adopt a professional code of ethics that prohibited reporting on the private lives of politicians. Suddenly, presidential liaisons were no longer considered a proper topic of serious journalism. Woodrow Wilson; Franklin and Eleanor Roosevelt; J. Edgar Hoover; John, Jackie and Bobby Kennedy; and Martin Luther King Jr. all benefited from the media's refusal to report on their personal lives. The rise of tabloid journalism and the end of the Cold War, however, freed the press to once again report on White House sex. Now, in the Internet age, anyone's private affairs can become news, no matter how crucial he or she is to the health and stability of the Republic. The media's current obsession with political sex scandals is actually not a new phenomenon but a return to the roots of the American political tradition. Bloggers are the new pamphleteers.

Gore Vidal, who wrote a novel about Abe Lincoln and was John Kennedy's friend, observed that "everything has so many chains of association in our unexpectedly Jacobean republic that nothing any longer surprises."[1] By ignoring the traditional rules of historical scholarship and directing our focus on the private lives of America's leaders, we have uncovered key connections between private acts and public affairs that other historians have missed. From the Revolutionary War to Monicagate and beyond, sex has played a crucial role in our nation's history. The story of America is truly one of the greatest and strangest stories ever told.

—*Larry Flynt, Los Angeles, CA*
David Eisenbach, New York City

CHAPTER ONE

FOUNDING FLIRTS AND FORNICATORS

T he first White House sex scandal erupted even before the building's construction was finished. Betsy Donahue, the wife of a carpenter working on the White House, opened a brothel for the construction workers in a shanty in President's Park. Federal commissioners did not care that the workmen gambled and drank, but when Mrs. Donahue began pulling her husband's coworkers off the construction site for afternoon quickies, that was too much. Betsy was arrested and her shanty was torn down on July 20, 1795.[1] Other than its location on White House property, Mrs. Donahue's sex business was not unique during the Revolutionary period, when prostitution was the full-time occupation of 1 in 25 women in America's cities.[2] Today we tend to imagine the people who built the early Republic to have been as dignified and composed as the historic documents they left behind. The Founders were indeed noble and gracious, but they were also earthy, lusty and as interested in sex and sex scandal as we are today. Like America's leaders throughout history, the Founders had vigorous sex drives and vibrant sex lives that played a major role in building our nation.

COLONIAL CASANOVA

The Founders might have declared independence on July 4, 1776, but unless they backed up their high-minded words and ideals with weapons and blood, the British army was sure to crush the great American experiment. In the first year of the war, the British invasion force outnumbered the rebels two to one. Since the Continental Congress had no money, no system of taxation and no credit to build an adequate fighting force, America desperately needed France's recognition and more importantly its army and navy.[3] Louis XVI hated the British and was willing to send covert arms shipments, but he did not like the idea of openly supporting a revolution against a fellow monarch and was certainly in no hurry to side with a loser.[4] The Continental Congress understood that the French government was not going to be won over with appeals to liberty or geostrategic interest; to win their full support, the French had to be courted and seduced. The trick was to find an ambassador who could charm the right French nobles and galvanize popular opinion in favor of the Revolutionary cause.

The Continental Congress looked for an ambassador who would be open-minded about French sensibilities, particularly their sexual mores, which appalled most Americans. John Adams said of eighteenth-century Paris, "There is everything here too which can seduce, betray, deceive, corrupt and debauch."[5] Paris at the time had over 14,000 legally registered prostitutes, an army larger than George Washington's Continental army.[6] To the average eighteenth-century American, all Frenchwomen would have looked like whores, with their cheeks painted in bright, round, three-inch-wide patches of rouge and their hairdos towering more than a foot high. To avoid messing their rouged cheeks, Frenchwomen greeted men by offering their necks to be kissed. According to Thomas Jefferson, Parisian women spent their days "hunting pleasure in the streets," while "our own countrywomen are occupied in the tender and tranquil amusements of domestic life." Jefferson reduced the difference between French and American women to "a comparison of Amazons and angels" and observed that Frenchmen "consider fidelity to the marriage bed as an ungentlemanly practice and inconsistent with happiness."[7] French visitors to America also noticed the stark cultural divide over sex. French politician Jacques Pierre Brissot de Warville noted in 1788 that almost all marriages in America "are happy and, being happy, are pure," because unlike Frenchwomen, American ladies were "entirely devoted to their households" and thought "about nothing but making their husbands happy and about bringing up their children well."[8]

If an ambassador to France was to be successful, he had to suspend his male chauvinism because French women ran the salons that were the center of political intrigue, social life and popular opinion.[9] The American ambassador needed to be able to win over the ladies, gain admittance to the salons and negotiate the delicate world of French influence, intrigue, innuendo and flirtation.[10] Looking over the professional and personal experiences of various candidates, Congress did not take long to choose Benjamin Franklin, already famous throughout the colonies for being a gossip, a libertine and a ladies man.

Ben Franklin was not the first American newsman to realize that sex sells, but he was a pioneer in pushing the envelope of what was acceptable in print.[11] When he entered the newspaper business in 1729, he attacked Philadelphia's only other newspaper for printing an article on abortion. Under the penname "Martha Careful," the 23-year-old Franklin condemned his rival publisher in the voice of an outraged woman: "If he proceeds farther to expose the secrets of our sex in that audacious manner we will run hazard of taking him by the beard in the next place we meet him." Thus Franklin manufactured the first recorded abortion debate in America. He did not really care about the issue; he just wanted to sell newspapers and undermine the competition.[12] A few years later, Franklin eliminated the rival newspaper and took control of the news business in America's largest city.

Franklin started America's first gossip column, which he called Busy-Body, in 1729. Although he admitted to his readers that Busy-Body's content was "nobody's business," he vowed that "if any are offended at my publicly exposing their private vices, I promise they shall have the satisfaction in a very little time, of seeing their good friends and neighbors in the same circumstances."[13] Franklin reported in 1731 how one unfortunate husband discovered his wife in bed with a man named Stonecutter. The cuckold tried to decapitate Stonecutter with a knife but only wounded him. Franklin ended the story with a pun on castration: "Some people admit that when the person offended had so fair and suitable opportunity, it did not enter his head to turn 'Stonecutter' himself."[14] The next issue reported on a constable who "made an agreement with a neighboring female to watch with her that night." Unfortunately the constable accidentally climbed into the window of a different woman, whose husband was sleeping in another room.

Franklin recounted that "the good woman perceiving presently by the extraordinary fondness of her bedfellow that it could not possibly be her husband, made so much disturbance as to wake the good man, who finding somebody had got into his place without his leave began to lay about him unmercifully."[15]

One of Franklin's most famous stories featured Polly Baker, who was put on trial for having her fifth illegitimate child. Polly argued in court that far from being punished she should be rewarded: "Can it be a crime (in the nature of things I mean) to add to the number of the king's subjects in a new country that really wants people? . . . I should think it a praiseworthy rather than a punishable action." Polly concluded, "In my humble opinion, instead of a whipping, [I deserve] to have a statue erected in my memory."[16] The judges were so moved by the speech that they acquitted her, and one of the judges married her the next day.[17] Franklin later admitted to Thomas Jefferson that he made up Polly's story and many others: "When I was a printer and editor of a newspaper, we were sometimes slack of news, and to amuse our customers I used to fill up our vacant columns with anecdotes and fables, and fancies of my own."[18] More than any other Founding Father, Franklin had a great appreciation for strong, sexually liberated, sassy women like the fictitious Polly Baker.

When readers complained about all the gossip in his newspaper, Franklin published an anonymous letter (written by himself, of course) defending gossip as "the means of preventing powerful, politic, ill-designing men from growing too popular. All-examining Censure, with her hundred eyes and her thousand tongues, soon discovers and as speedily divulges in all quarters every least crime or foible that is part of their true character. This clips the wings of their ambition." Franklin argued that gossip columns promote good behavior because, "what will the world say of me if I act thus? is often a reflection strong enough to enable us to resist the most powerful temptation to vice or folly. This preserves the integrity of the wavering, the honesty of the covetous, the sanctity of some of the religious, and the chastity of all virgins."[19] Of course, Franklin wasn't publishing gossip to protect the virgins; he was just out to sell newspapers.

He also invented America's first sexual and moral advice column. In 1731 he published an anonymous letter (which he wrote) asking, "Suppose a person discovered that his wife was having an affair with a neighbor, and suppose he had reason to believe that if he revealed this to his neighbor's wife she would agree to have sex with him, is he justifiable in doing it?" In the voice of the editor, Franklin self-righteously replied to his own letter, "Return not evil for evil, but repay evil with good."[20] In a 1731 treatise, "Advice to a Young Man on the Choice of a Mistress," Franklin recommended sex with older women, "because in every Animal that walks upright, the Deficiency of the Fluids that fill the Muscles appears first in the highest Part: The Face first grows lank and wrinkled; then the Neck; then the Breast and Arms; the lower Parts continuing to the last as plump as ever: So that covering all above with a Basket, and regarding only what is below the Girdle, it is impossible of two Women to know an old from a young one." Sex with a basket-covered older woman also avoided pregnancy. Franklin pointed out that "as in the dark all Cats are grey, the Pleasure of corporal Enjoyment with an old Woman is at least equal, and frequently superior, every Knack being by Practice capable of Improvement." "And Lastly," Franklin concluded, "they are so grateful!!"[21]

By attracting readers with salacious stories and an open discussion of sex, Franklin became the first American printer to make a profit from his newspaper. Other printers used their newspapers to advertise their other businesses—job printing and often a general store.[22] Franklin pushed ad sales and advised businessmen on the best ways to market their products in print. While other colonial newspapers crammed their ads onto the back page, he sprinkled his ads throughout his paper, making them harder to skip over. He plowed his fortune into funding other printers in cities up and down the seaboard and in return got a share of their profits and their big scoops.[23] By the age of 42, Ben Franklin was America's first media mogul, with his own news network, and so rich that he could retire in 1747 to concentrate on the passions that would make him famous: inventions, science experiments, politics and women.

Along with his racy writings, Franklin's unconventional personal life was well known to the Continental Congress. In his autobiography, he confessed, "[The] hard-to-be-governed passion of youth had hurried me frequently into intrigues with low women that fell in my way, which were attended with some expense and great inconvenience." One great inconvenience of sex with "low women" was venereal disease, "a continual risque to my health, . . . which of all things I dreaded, though by great good luck I escaped it."[24] One great expense of Franklin's running around was the birth of his illegitimate son William in 1730. A friend recalled that Franklin made "some small provision" for the mother, "but her being none of the most agreeable women prevented particular notice being shown, or the father and son acknowledging any connection with her."[25] Franklin had no use for the mother, but his son came in handy 20 years later when he needed someone to risk his life flying a kite in a lightning storm. Franklin had William perform the death-defying feat.[26]

Right after William's birth, the 24-year-old Franklin decided he needed a wife to look after his infant. His first choice turned him down after he insisted that her family mortgage their house to pay him a sufficient dowry.[27] Next he approached his ex-girlfriend, Deborah Read, whom Franklin called "a fat, jolly dame, clean and tidy."[28] The problem was that Read was still married. Although her husband, John Rogers, had run away, Pennsylvania law did not allow divorce for abandonment. If Read and Franklin married and Rogers returned, Deborah could be charged with bigamy, punishable by 39 lashes and life imprisonment. So six months after the birth of William, Deborah and Ben simply began living together in a common-law arrangement.

Franklin's love child became an issue during his run for the Pennsylvania assembly in 1764, when he was 58 years old. An opponent published a pamphlet claiming William's mother was a prostitute who later served Ben and Deborah as their maid until her untimely death and burial in an unmarked grave. Franklin's opponents also published a doggerel that mocked his wanton ways:

> *Franklin, though plagued with fumbling age,*
> *Needs nothing to excite him,*
> *But is too ready to engage,*
> *When younger arms invite him.*[29]

Even Franklin's best-selling *Poor Richard's Almanac*, first published in 1732, made clear his skepticism about marital fidelity: "Keep your eyes wide open before marriage, half shut afterwards."[30]

The Continental Congress knew Franklin liked to combine pleasure with diplomatic business. As an ambassador to London in the late 1750s he frequented the infamous Hellfire Club, which gathered members of parliament and influential aristocrats for sacrilegious rituals and orgies featuring prostitutes dressed as nuns. Participating in Hellfire high jinks enabled Franklin to win the trust of powerful club members who slipped him secret information on British negotiations with the colonies. There was rampant gossip in London that the 51-year-old diplomat was having an affair with his solicitous landlady, Margaret Stevenson. Franklin might have also been carrying on with her 18-year-old daughter, Polly.[31] One day a friend, famed artist Charles Wilson Peale, arrived unannounced at the Stevenson house and found "the Doctor . . . seated with a young lady on his knee."[32] Peale recorded the scene with a sketch of the two engaged in a lip-lock, while Franklin "cops a feel" and Polly plunges her hand into Ben's middle-aged crotch.

Far from disqualifying Franklin as an ambassador to France, his irrepressible sex drive, unconventional personal history and raunchy public writings made him the perfect choice.

Although he was 70 years old when he embarked on his mission to Paris, age had not withered his passion for the ladies. "I have marked him particularly in the company of women where he loses all power over himself and becomes almost frenzied," an amazed Thomas Jefferson wrote. "This is in some measure the vice of his age, but it seems to be increased also by his peculiar constitution."[33] Of all the Founders, only Ben Franklin could party and gossip with even the naughtiest French nobles and ladies.[34] And so the Continental Congress placed the fate of the Revolution in the hands of a paunchy, five-foot-nine colonial Casanova.

Franklin's way with women was on display as soon as he arrived in France on December 21, 1776. His fellow envoy John Adams observed, "My venerable colleague enjoys a privilege here that is much to be envied. Being 70 years of age, the ladies not only allow him to embrace them as often as he pleases, but they are perpetually embracing him."[35] One of the objects of Franklin's attention attributed the American ambassador's popularity to "that gaiety and that gallantry that cause all women to love you, because you love them all."[36] Franklin was a master of what the French called *amitié amoureuse,* or amorous friendship—a playful seduction involving teasing kisses, sly embraces, intimate conversation and rhapsodic love letters.[37]

Soon, stories about the lecherous old lover and his many mistresses spread from the streets of Paris to the colonies. Franklin tried to downplay the rumors in a letter to his niece in Boston: "You mention that kindness of the French ladies to me. I must explain that matter. This is the civilest Nation upon the Earth. Your first acquaintances endeavor to find out what you like, and they tell others. If 'tis understood that you like Mutton, dine where you will, you find Mutton. Somebody it seems gave it out that I loved ladies; then everybody presented me their ladies (or the ladies presented themselves) to be embraced, that is to have their necks kissed. The French ladies have however 1000 other ways of rendering themselves agreeable."[38] Adams sniped, "All the atheists, deists and libertines, as well as the philosophers and ladies are in his train."[39] What Adams did not understand was that activities and associations that ruined a reputation in Boston earned admiration in Paris.

So how did this balding, bifocaled old man, who called himself "Dr. Fatsides," become such a lass magnet? Franklin was famous in Europe even before he set foot in France. *Poor Richard's Almanac* had been translated into French as *La Science du Bonhomme Richard* and was a big hit. The French worshipped Franklin as an Enlightenment god whose famous kite-flying experiment debunked superstition by proving that lightning was nothing more than electricity.[40] People lined the streets to catch a glimpse of his entry into Paris. His portrait could be found on the walls of the most fashionable French homes. Franklin wrote his daughter, "The pictures, busts and prints (of which copies upon copies are spread everywhere) have made your father's face as well known as that of the moon."[41] After Comtesse Dianne de Polignac bored King Louis XVI with a long speech about Franklin's genius, the perturbed king sent her a porcelain chamber pot with Ben's face embossed inside.[42] Franklin was America's first international celebrity, and like any celebrity, his fame greatly enhanced his powers of seduction.[43]

One of the Frenchwomen on the receiving end of Franklin's *amitié amoureuse* was Madame Brillon, a rosy-cheeked, doe-eyed 33-year-old—the same age as his daughter. John Adams called Brillon "one of the most beautiful women in France."[44] She was the wife of a powerful politician and businessman who was 24 years her senior. While her husband amused himself with the family's governess, Franklin tried to bed Madame Brillon.[45] When she rebuffed his sexual advances, Franklin lewdly complained to her in a letter dated July 27, 1778, "My poor little boy, who you ought to have cherished, instead of being fat and jolly like those in your elegant drawings, is thin and starved for want of the nourishment that you inhumanely deny him."[46] Madame Brillon admitted that she was tempted, but, "You are a man, I am a woman, and while we might think along the same lines, we must speak and act differently. Perhaps there is no great harm in a man having desires and yielding to them; a woman may have desires, but she must not yield."[47] Instead, she dubbed him *mon cher Papa* and promised, "I give you my word that I will become your wife in paradise on the condition that you will not make too many conquests among the heavenly maidens while you are waiting for me. I want a faithful husband when I take one for eternity."[48]

Brillon became jealous when she heard about Franklin's more successful attempts at seducing other French ladies. "You ask me for the list of your sins, my dear papa," she pouted. "It would be so long that I dare not undertake such a great work. And yet you commit only one, but it has so many branches, it is repeated so often that it would take infinite calculations to assess its magnitude."[49] Franklin told Brillon she had no right to complain about his other women if she was going to "totally exclude all that might be of the flesh in our affection, allowing me only some kisses, civil and honest, such as you might grant your little cousins."[50] Brillon informed Franklin that everyone in Paris was talking about them: "Do you know, my dear Papa, that people have criticized my sweet habit of sitting on your lap, and your habit of soliciting from me what I always refuse?"[51] When John Adams came to pay court to the Brillons, two days after he arrived in Paris in 1778, he could not believe the host and hostess could tolerate each other's extramarital dalliances. He wrote in his diary, "I was astonished that these people could live together in such apparent friendship and indeed without cutting each other's throats. But I did not know the world. I soon saw and heard so much of these Things in other Families and among almost all the great people of the Kingdom that I found it was a thing of course. It was universally understood and Nobody lost any reputation by it."[52]

While Adams was repulsed by the French couple's loose morals, Franklin used his illicit courtship of Madame Brillon to win over her powerful husband, who was the receiver-general of trusts for the French parliament. Monsieur Brillon took pleasure in Franklin's courtship of his wife and teased the American ambassador, "You have surely just been kissing my wife, my dear Doctor, allow me to kiss you back."[53] Brillon served as a go-between for Franklin and French arms dealers and used his prestigious government position to push for direct military intervention against the British.[54]

After failing to score with Madame Brillon, Franklin moved on to the blue-eyed, 59-year-old widow Madame Helvetius, who was a relative of Marie Antoinette and ran the most influential salon in France.[55] The Helvetius salon gathered some of the greatest minds of the age, including Voltaire, Condorcet, Diderot, the abbé Galiani, former finance minister Turgot and David Hume. Although almost 60, Helvetius was still a looker. One regular at her salon complained that "because of her beauty, unusual wit and stimulating temperament, Madame Helvetius disturbed philosophical discussions considerably."[56] When the 99-year-old writer Bernard le Bovier de Fontenelle walked in on Helvetius in a state of undress, he exclaimed, "Oh, to be seventy again!"[57] Franklin begged Helvetius to go to bed with him: "If this lady is pleased to spend her days with Franklin, he would be just as pleased to spend his nights with her. And since he had already granted her so many of his days, of which he has so few remaining, she seems an ingrate for never having granted him a single one of her nights, which keep passing as a pure loss, without making anyone happy except Poupon [her cat]."[58] The widower Franklin fell so hard for Madame Helvetius that he proposed marriage twice, but she enjoyed her freedom and declined.

John Adams was shocked by his visit with the randy Brillons, but he was absolutely flabbergasted five days later when he visited Helvetius's salon: "Oh Mores! I said to myself. What absurdities, inconsistencies, distractions and horrors would these manners introduce into our republican governments in America. No kind of republican government can ever exist with such national manners as these. Cavete Americani."[59] Try as he might, Adams could not hide his contempt for the French nobles, who regarded him as a typical American prude. Adams complained to the Continental Congress that Franklin was wasting valuable time courting Helvetius, Madame Brillon and other French ladies instead of focusing on diplomatic business. What Adams did not understand was that his colleague's flirtations and love affairs were central to his diplomatic strategy.

The difference between how the two Americans courted the French came down to the fact that Adams was a puritan lawyer while Franklin was a free-thinking businessman. Adams thought the Americans could win French support by making a clear, logical case for an alliance against Britain. The problem with that approach was that Louis XVI and France's political elite had a visceral discomfort with openly assisting in the overthrow of a fellow monarchy. Franklin understood that the Americans were never going to win an argument with the French. To get them to form an alliance they had to be seduced and sold on the idea of America. Like any good salesman, Franklin first sold himself. His homespun fur cap and gossip about his love affairs generated a Romantic image of America that appealed to the French sensibility. To Frenchmen, the septuagenarian gallant was the embodiment of what they hoped to be at his age.[60]

Franklin inspired a popular movement in France in favor of military intervention against the British in America, and Louis XVI sent his army and navy to bolster General Washington's dwindling army. Unfortunately for Louis XVI, the 1.3 billion livres he spent backing the American Revolution bankrupted his kingdom. And when Franklin departed France in 1785, he left behind millions of people sold on the idea of liberty. After the French Revolution four years later, visitors to Parisian tourist shops could find statuettes of Franklin carved from "authentic" stones of the fallen Bastille.[61]

Ben Franklin's freewheeling approach to sex proved to be a huge asset when Frederick von Steuben approached the American ambassador in Paris to offer his services to the rebel army in 1777. Von Steuben had served with distinction in Frederick the Great's Prussian army during the Seven Years' War (1756–1763). But after the war, he was relieved of his duties and summarily discharged. Von Steuben found work as grand marshal to the court of the prince of Hohenzollern-Hechingen but had to flee after being accused of "having taken familiarities with young boys."[62] He spent years trying to join other armies, including the French army, but no one would pay for his services. Broke and disgraced, the 46-year-old von Steuben turned to Franklin to help revive his fortunes.[63]

While he was in France, Franklin had been desperately searching for an experienced military officer who could train General Washington's ragtag army of farmers. Although he heard rumors of von Steuben's fondness for young men, Old Ben didn't care. Franklin's favorite bathhouse in Paris, the Pot-de-Vin, was the city's premier gay pick-up joint.[64] In addition, with Washington's army on the brink of collapse, it was no time to get hung up on moral judgments. Rumors about von Steuben had to be countered with a cover story. American officials back home were told that the baron was leaving behind vast wealth and an exalted position in Europe out of an idealistic commitment to liberty. It is not known if Franklin, the master storyteller, concocted this tale, but in a letter to General Washington he did exaggerate von Steuben's military rank—promoting him to Frederick the Great's general staff.[65] We will never know if Franklin openly discussed the gay rumors with von Steuben; the most likely scenario is that Franklin didn't asketh and von Steuben didn't telleth.

Von Steuben was assigned in late 1777 to the winter quarters at Valley Forge, where he was horrified by the sight of soldiers starving and freezing to death. But he realized that if he could train such dedicated fighters properly, they could become the best soldiers in the world. He forged various colonial militias into a national army and devised a drill program that remained the official U.S. military manual until 1812. By the end of the war, von Steuben was one of the most famous men in America, and in 1783 George Washington wrote him a letter thanking him for changing the course of the war. Rumors about von Steuben's sexual proclivities reached the Continental Congress, however, and while the government rewarded other war heroes with large tracts of land, von Steuben received a gold-hilted sword and less than 5 percent of the reward money he anticipated. Von Steuben bought a shabby little farm in the wilderness of upstate New York, where he lived the remainder of his life with a male companion.[66]

AMERICA'S FIRST POLITICAL SEX SCANDALS

At the dawn of the Republic, two titans of the Revolution fought a fierce battle over America's future. George Washington's cabinet was divided between

Treasury secretary Alexander Hamilton and secretary of state Thomas Jefferson. Hamilton pushed for a powerful federal government with a national banking system that would stimulate economic activity and bring the Industrial Revolution to the United States. Jefferson, on the other hand, wanted to preserve a pastoral country populated with honest, incorruptible, independent farmers. Out of this ideological conflict emerged the young nation's first two political parties: Hamilton's Federalists and Jefferson's Democratic Republicans. The Founders did not originally intend for there to be political parties; they feared parties would corrupt elections with dirty tricks, force politicians to make decisions based on party loyalty rather than enlightened reason and debase political discourse with trivial scandal. The Founders were right—as soon as the new nation got its first political parties, it got its first political sex scandals. Neither Hamilton nor Jefferson could have imagined that their epic struggle over the destiny of a nation would thrust their shocking private lives into the public eye.

John Adams described Alexander Hamilton as "a man who's excessive production of secretions no number of whores could draw off" and who had "as debauched Morals as old Franklin who is more his Model than any one I know."[67] Everyone knew the "bastard brat of a Scottish pedlar," as Adams called Hamilton, had wedded the homely Betsy Schuyler for her family's money and political connections. Contemporaries also noticed that Hamilton's "wavy chestnut brown hair, classical nose, and deep-set violet eyes" attracted the attention of the ladies and how he shamelessly courted many, including his sister-in-law.[68]

During George Washington's first administration, in the summer of 1791, 34-year-old Hamilton was writing the "Report on Manufactures," a master plan for America's future industrial and commercial growth.[69] One summer afternoon a blonde-haired, blue-eyed 23-year-old beauty named Maria Reynolds showed up at the Hamiltons' home in Philadelphia, then the nation's capital, and asked to speak to the Treasury secretary alone. With his wife Betsy upstairs, Hamilton recalled that he "attended her into a room apart from the family."[70] Maria claimed her abusive husband had run off with another woman and left her penniless and friendless; she asked Hamilton for some money to travel back to her family in New York. Hamilton promised to deliver the money later that night at her lodgings. After his children were asleep, he told Betsy he had an errand to run and not to wait up. He grabbed a $30 bill ($700 today) and set off for his rendezvous with Maria.[71]

Hamilton described the scene: "I inquired for Mrs. Reynolds and was shown upstairs, at the head of which she met me and conducted me into a bedroom. I took the bill out of my pocket and gave it to her. Some conversation ensued from which it was quickly apparent that something other than pecuniary consolation would be acceptable."[72] And so Hamilton started consoling the young woman in distress in the same nonpecuniary way men have been consoling women throughout the ages. Over the next few weeks, Hamilton took breaks from writing the "Report on Manufactures" to rush over to Maria's house, always entering through the back door. When Betsy, pregnant again, took the children to Albany to escape Philadelphia's malarial summer, Hamilton began bringing Maria home to his own bed. At one point that summer, Betsy unexpectedly wrote Hamilton that she missed him so much she was going to come home early. Hamilton begged her to reconsider—Philadelphia was too hot, her health was too weak, he was too busy. "Much as I long for this happy moment, my extreme anxiety for the restoration of your health will reconcile me to your staying longer where you are. . . . Think of me—dream of me—and love me my Bestsey [sic] as I do you."[73] Even after Betsy returned in the fall, Hamilton continued to see Maria Reynolds.

Sometime that winter, Maria told Hamilton that her husband James was back in town and wanted to reconcile. She then introduced the two men, pretending that Hamilton was just a friend. James thanked the Treasury secretary for helping his wife and then asked for a job, something that paid well and didn't require much work.[74] Hamilton later recalled that he immediately suspected "some concert" between Mr. and Mrs. Reynolds in a blackmail scheme, "yet her conduct made it extremely difficult to disentangle myself" and so "the intercourse with Mrs. Reynolds, in the meantime, continued."[75] The plot thickened when Maria suddenly informed Hamilton that her husband had somehow discovered their affair. James then confronted Hamilton and demanded $1,000 ($23,000 today) or he would tell Betsy about Maria. Hamilton delivered the money and stopped seeing Maria. But James had hooked a big fish and wasn't about to let him get away. He wrote Hamilton, urging him to visit Maria as a "friend."[76] And so Hamilton was once again routinely having sex with Maria in the Reynoldses' bed, and James routinely asked Hamilton for "loans." The situation was simple: James was a pimp, his wife a prostitute and the Treasury secretary a gullible john.

Hamilton later attributed his folly to "vanity," a sense of entitlement that came with his immense power and achievement. After all, he was General Washington's aide-de-camp during the Revolutionary War, he wrote the Federalist Papers, he had created the National Bank, he founded the New York Stock Exchange and now he was formulating an industrial program that was going to build a bridge to the nineteenth century. For all he had done and was doing for his country, he deserved a little extramarital sex. Hamilton might have been the first statesman in the Republic's history whose vanity led him into a disastrous affair, but he was certainly not the last.

The convenient arrangement with the Reynolds couple soon turned sour, and Hamilton repeatedly tried to break it off. Every time, Maria would weep, moan and threaten suicide, and every time Hamilton returned to her bed. Hamilton also began to fear that if he cut off all contact, James would expose the affair. Even after the thrill was gone, the Treasury secretary made the calculated decision to keep up the arrangement and risk the chance of discovery rather than make a clean break and almost certainly get caught. Hamilton could not believe that he had got himself into such a pickle. He was the trusted friend of President Washington and the second-most-powerful man in America. Every day he did battle with Thomas Jefferson and always won. Yet sex had rendered him beholden to a hysterical woman and, in his own words, "an obscure, unimportant and profligate man."[77]

Finally, after 13 months, Hamilton summoned the courage to break off the affair for good. Miraculously, the demands for money ceased. His "Report on Manufactures" won widespread acclaim, and he was able to secure congressional approval for his plans to industrialize America. At 35, he was hailed as an economic genius and a visionary statesman. He had every reason to believe that soon people would be calling him President Hamilton!

The Reynolds affair might never have come to light had not James Reynolds and a partner in crime, Jacob Clingman, been arrested in 1792 for defrauding the Treasury Department of $400. Reynolds appealed to the Treasury secretary to drop the charges. When Hamilton refused, Clingman told Democratic Republican congressman Frederick Muhlenberg about the Treasury secretary's affair with Maria. Muhlenberg then shared the information with Thomas Jefferson's protégé, Senator James Monroe. Muhlenberg, Monroe and Virginia congressman Abraham Venable interviewed Maria, who affirmed that her husband could "tell them something that would make the heads of [government] departments tremble."[78] She also handed over several incriminating notes from Hamilton. The congressmen then confronted the Treasury secretary, demanding to know why he was giving money to James Reynolds and if he was involved in James's scheme to defraud the government. Hamilton copped to the payoffs but explained that he was paying the man only so he could have sex with his wife. The arrangement might not be conventional, but it wasn't criminal and in no way involved ripping off the federal Treasury. The three congressmen seemed satisfied with Hamilton's explanation and dropped the matter.

Although the three congressmen were Democratic Republicans who despised the Treasury secretary's economic program, they were gentlemen who believed a politician's sex life was not the proper subject for the political sphere.[79] Even though Jefferson and his fellow Democratic Republicans repeatedly tried to impeach Hamilton on trumped-up corruption charges, they never raised the Reynolds affair. For three years, Hamilton's enemies abided by the gentleman's code, and Hamilton left the Treasury Department in 1795 thinking that his record of service was unimpeachable and that he had set the nation on a course for greatness.[80]

The next year, Hamilton's fellow Federalist Vice President John Adams beat Jefferson in the 1796 presidential election to succeed George Washington. In the early Republic, the runner-up in the Electoral College vote became the vice president. So Jefferson found himself stuck in a Federalist administration in the constitutionally powerless office of vice president. Hamilton meanwhile was a private attorney but remained the leader of the Federalist Party and continued to direct the nation's foreign and domestic policies.[81] Jefferson began thinking that, for the good of the Republic, he might have to act less like a gentleman and more like a politician.[82]

After the election, the vice president leaked the Reynolds story to a hard-drinking Democratic journalist named James Callender. In a book blandly titled *History of the United States for the Year 1796*, Callender detailed Hamilton's cash-for-sex deal with Mr. and Mrs. Reynolds and claimed the arrangement was part of a bigger conspiracy with James Reynolds to defraud the government. "So much correspondence could not refer exclusively to wenching," Callender surmised.[83] The Jeffersonian press reveled in the Maria Reynolds scandal, which they presented as evidence that Hamilton's entire economic program was corrupt. Federalist banking and industrialization policies, after all, had always been closely associated with Hamilton's personal credibility and honest reputation.

Hamilton realized this highly publicized sex scandal imperiled not only his own political future but also his vision for America's future. He faced a huge dilemma: ignore the charges or tell the whole sordid truth. If he ignored the Reynolds story, his political allies and his wife would continue to dismiss it as a baseless smear, but his enemies would use the scandal to turn public opinion against his economic program.[84] It was a choice between personal humiliation and the public good. Hamilton furiously wrote a detailed 95-page booklet explaining that the arrangement with James Reynolds was just a private sex deal involving consenting adults and not a plot to defraud the government. "The charge against me is a connection with one James Reynolds for purposes of improper pecuniary speculation," Hamilton declared in the pamphlet. "My real crime is an amorous connection with his wife, for a considerable time with his privity and connivance, if not originally brought on by a combination between the husband and wife with the design to extort money from me."[85] Callender, the scandalmonger, famously summed up Hamilton's defense: "I am a rake and for that reason I cannot be a swindler."[86]

The Jeffersonian press pounced on the confession. Ben Franklin's grandson Benjamin Franklin Bache fumed in his newspaper *Aurora* that Hamilton "violated the sacred sanctuary of his own house, by taking an unprincipled woman . . . to his bed." Franklin's grandson also attacked Betsy for standing by her man: "Art thou a wife?, See him, whom thou has chosen for partner of this life, lolling in the lap of a harlot!"[87]

Although even Hamilton's allies thought his confession was too detailed, the lurid details gave a ring of truth to his denial of political corruption. Who could make up the Reynolds story? Hamilton's confession damaged his personal reputation but allowed him to remain a leader of the Federalist Party and a presidential prospect. One Federalist noted, "Hamilton is fallen for the present, but [even] if he fornicates with every female in the cities of New York and Philadelphia, he will rise again, for purity of character after a period of political existence is not necessary for public patronage."[88] By accepting personal disgrace, Hamilton prevented America's first political sex scandal from tainting his economic program and impeding the nation's entry into the Industrial Revolution.

Vice President Jefferson also hired Callender to write diatribes against President Adams.[89] After reading one of Callender's slanderous screeds, Jefferson crowed, "Such papers cannot fail to produce the best effect. They inform the thinking part of the nation."[90] Jefferson's bare-knuckle approach to politics was exactly what he and his fellow Founders had worried about when they hoped the Republic would not have political parties. The Reynolds scandal and the harsh attacks on President Adams provoked a backlash from the Federalists, who passed the Sedition Act in 1798, making it a crime to "write, utter or publish any false, scandalous, and malicious writing or writings against the government of the United States or the President of the United States with the intent to defame or to bring them . . . into contempt or disrepute."[91] Predictably, one of the first journalists to run afoul of the sedition law was James Callender himself, who was sentenced to nine months in prison and a $200 fine.

In 1800, while Callender was in jail, Thomas Jefferson was elected president, and the journalist figured he was a made man. Jefferson granted Callender a presidential pardon, but having won the presidency, he no longer needed the groveling scandalmonger and refused to give him a political appointment. Instead, Jefferson slipped Callender $50 and broke off all contact. The president would soon learn that hell hath no fury like a lackey scorned.

While in prison, Callender had heard a rumor that Jefferson fathered children with a mulatto slave named Sally Hemings.[92] Disappointed at no reward from Jefferson and desperate for cash to support his children and fund his drinking binges, in 1802 Callender published an exposé of the president's relationship with Hemings: "It is well known that the man whom it delighteth the people to honor, keeps and for many years has kept, as his concubine, one of his slaves. Her name is Sally. . . . By this wench Sally, our president had several children. . . . The African Venus is said to officiate as housekeep at Monticello." Callender declared that he would be happy to confront the president in a courtroom and debate the truth of Jefferson's relationship with "the black wench and her mulatto litter."[93]

James Callender, the man responsible for the young nation's first political sex scandal, topped himself with its second. The story was the scoop of a lifetime. The sitting president was having interracial sex and fathering his own slave children.[94] And he was doing it while he harped on Hamilton's affair with Maria Reynolds. Jefferson became the first in a long line of hypocritical politicians who exposed an opponent's sexual indiscretions to score political points and then watched their accusations rebound with twice the force. Abigail Adams ruefully taunted Jefferson about Callender: "The serpent you cherished and warmed, bit the hand that nourished him."[95]

Sally Hemings's son Madison told a reporter in 1873 that his mother became Jefferson's concubine in Paris in 1785, after the master of Monticello was sent to replace Ben Franklin as ambassador to France. Jefferson was still heartbroken over the untimely death of his wife, Martha, three years earlier, when he was 39 years old.[96] He had promised Martha on her deathbed that he would never marry again, and he kept his vow. But that didn't mean the still robust widower was going to remain celibate. Sally was a light-skinned 14-year-old known around Monticello as Dashing Sall. Another slave described her as "mighty near white" with "long straight hair down her back."[97] She was the daughter of Jefferson's father-in-law and a slave mistress, Betty Hemings, who had six children with her master. Sally was therefore the half-sister of Jefferson's beloved wife and no doubt reminded him of his lost love. And so at 43 years old Jefferson began a sexual relationship with his teenage slave.[98]

Sally's son Madison later said that when Jefferson was called back to the United States, his mother was pregnant with his child. Slavery was illegal in France, and Hemings knew that she and her child would be enslaved in Virginia. At first she insisted on staying in Paris, where there was a community of free blacks. But according to Madison, she agreed to return with Jefferson after he "promised her extraordinary privileges, and made a solemn pledge that her children would be freed at the age of twenty-three years."[99] Shortly after Jefferson returned home with Sally, he joined George Washington's cabinet as the first secretary of state and began his bitter battle with Alexander Hamilton.

Madison Hemings said his father "was not in the habit of showing partiality or fatherly affection to us children," but his mother and his siblings were given light tasks around the house and protected from the overseer's lash.[100] Jefferson and Sally continued to be intimate while he was president. In the last year of Jefferson's presidency, in 1808, Sally gave birth to her sixth and final child, Thomas Eston Hemings, who was born when Jefferson was 65.[101] The Hemings children were the only slaves Jefferson freed at his death, and his legitimate daughter assumed responsibility for Sally in her old age. For decades, Sally's descendents insisted they were Jefferson's progeny, but most historians, out of racial anxiety and squeamishness about sex in general, adamantly refused to accept that a Founding Father would have sex with his slave.[102] Finally, DNA tests in 1998 confirmed that Jefferson or someone in his family fathered at least one of Sally's children.[103]

The Hemings story did not surprise people who actually knew Jefferson. A visitor to Monticello wrote in his journal that he "was amazed to see children as white as I was called blacks and treated as such."[104] Jefferson's oldest grandson noticed at Monticello "[slave] children which resembled Mr. Jefferson so closely that it was plain that they had his blood in their veins." The grandson recalled, "A gentleman dining with Mr. Jefferson looked so startled as he raised his eyes from [Jefferson] to the servant behind him, that his discovery of the resemblance was perfectly obvious to all." Jefferson's grandson also noted that "Sally Hemings was a house servant and her children were brought up house servants—so that the likeness between master and slave was blazoned to all the multitudes who visited this political Mecca."[105]

Sexual relationships between masters and slaves were commonplace. "I can enumerate a score of such cases in our beloved Ancient Dominion," Jefferson's neighbor and cofounder of the University of Virginia, General John Hartwell Cocke, wrote in his diary. "Nor is it to be wondered at, when, Mr. Jefferson's notorious example is considered." Cocke knew of many "Mulatto Slave Mistresses" in Virginia and the South: "All Bachelors, or a large majority at least keep as a substitute for a wife some individual of their own Slaves. In Virginia this damnable practice prevails as much as any where, and probably more, as Mr. Jefferson's example can be pleaded for its de-fense."[106] One in five divorce cases granted by the Virginia legislature dur-ing the early Republic involved adultery across the color line.[107] John Adams said he did not believe the Hemings story but conceded "there was not a planter in Virginia who could not reckon among his slaves a number of his children." Adams believed the sexual exploitation of slaves was "a natural and almost unavoidable consequence of that foul contagion in the human character—Negro slavery."[108]

Federalists viewed the Hemings scandal as justified retribution for Maria Reynolds and filled their newspapers with stories about "Mr. Jefferson's Congo harem." The *Boston Gazette* offered a new set of lyrics to "Yankee Doo-dle," which were reprinted around the country:

> *Of all the damsels on the green*
> *On mountain, or in valley*
> *A lass so luscious ne'er was seen,*
> *As Monticello Sally,*
>
> *Yankee doodle, who's the noodle?*
> *What wife were half so handy?*
> *To breed a flock of slaves for stock,*
> *A blackamoor's a dandy*
>
> *When pressed by load of state affairs*
> *I seek to sport and dally*
> *The sweetest solace of my cares*
> *Is in the lap of Sally.*[109]

Jefferson refused to address reports about Hemings, but he could not ignore two of Callender's other charges. The journalist revealed in 1802 that Jefferson's former friend John Walker, now a staunch Federalist, had begun publicly accusing the president of repeatedly trying to seduce his wife over the course of a decade. It all began back in 1768, when the Virginia colonial government sent Walker on a mission to negotiate a land deal with Indian tribes in western New York. Walker asked his boyhood friend Jefferson, then 25 years old, to look after his wife, Elizabeth, and infant daughter during his absence. Elizabeth rebuffed Jefferson's advances while her husband was away. But Walker claimed that even after he returned home, Jefferson "renewed his caresses" toward his wife. According to Walker, when he and his wife visited Jefferson's home in 1769, Jefferson tucked into the cuff of Elizabeth's sleeve a note "tending to convince her of the innocence of promiscuous love." On another occasion, Jefferson and the Walkers were staying at the home of a mutual friend. After the ladies retired to their rooms, Jefferson suddenly feigned sickness and left John and the other men downstairs while he snuck into the Walkers' room where Elizabeth was undressing for bed.[110] Elizabeth shouted, and according to John, Jefferson "was repulsed with indignation and menaces of alarm and ran off." Walker also claimed that another time he caught Jefferson lurking in the wee hours outside Elizabeth's boudoir dressed only "in his shirt ready to seize her on her way from her Chamber—indecent in manner."[111]

Jefferson's friend Thomas Paine questioned Walker's story of the decade-long seduction: "We have heard of a ten year siege of Troy," Paine cracked. "But who ever heard of a ten year siege to seduce?"[112] Elizabeth allegedly hid Jefferson's advances from her husband because she feared John would have to challenge the writer of the Declaration of Independence to a duel. Regardless of the truth of the story, when Callender published an account of Jefferson's harassment of Elizabeth in 1802, there was intense social pressure on John Walker to duel the president. Federalists prodded Walker to issue a formal challenge; regardless of the duel's outcome, Jefferson's enemies would win. The notion of a president fighting a duel was not absurd at the time. In fact, two years later, in 1804, Jefferson's vice president, Aaron Burr, would shoot and kill Alexander Hamilton in a duel. Jefferson consulted with his U.S. attorney general, admitting, "I plead guilty to one of their charges that when young and single I offered love to a handsome lady. I acknowledge its incorrectness."[113] To avoid a duel, the president wrote a private apology to John Walker and urged his former friend to help him suppress newspaper accounts and "consign this unfortunate matter to all the oblivion of which it is susceptible."[114] Walker accepted the apology, and Jefferson escaped having to fight a duel that would have brought either infamy like Burr or death like Hamilton.

The president also had to address Callender's 1802 accusation that Jefferson paid for the Maria Reynolds exposé and the slanders against John Adams. Jefferson denied paying Callender to smear anyone and claimed that he gave him money only to be "charitable."[115] Harry Croswell, editor of a Federalist newspaper in Hudson, New York, published an article questioning the president's claims of charity and denounced him as "a dissembling patriot."[116] Having seen his name slandered one too many times, President Jefferson retaliated by having Croswell arrested under New York State's malicious libel law in 1802.

The story of Hamilton's and Jefferson's dueling sex scandals took an interesting turn when Croswell hired Alexander Hamilton to defend him in court. Hamilton's defense strategy centered on a simple legal principle—if a newspaper prints the truth, it cannot be guilty of criminal behavior. Hamilton knew only one man who could testify that Jefferson did indeed pay for Callender's slanderous missives, and that witness was James Callender himself. The Democratic press bashed Callender for being a drunk and threatened him. The *Richmond Examiner* envisioned his death by drowning: "Oh! could a dose of James River like Lethe, have blessed you with forgetfulness, for once you would have neglected your whiskey."[117] A few weeks before the trial, Callender was found floating facedown in the James River. Although a coroner's jury ruled his drowning an accident brought on by intoxication, many suspected Jefferson's supporters had murdered Hamilton's star witness and dumped his corpse in the river.[118]

At Croswell's trial in 1803, Hamilton gave a six-hour speech arguing that the freedom of the press to criticize public officials was necessary to protect the public from corruption: "How often the hypocrite goes from stage to stage of public fame, under false array, and how often when men attained the last object of their wishes, they change from that which they seemed to be."[119] Hamilton's defense of the press was so eloquent and passionate, according to an observer, that he "drew tears . . . from every eye of the numerous audience."[120] Although a Democratic Republican judge convicted Croswell, Hamilton's legal argument inspired a movement to reform New York State's libel laws. In 1805, a year after Hamilton's death, the New York legislature passed a law based on his defense of freedom of the press. A historic legal precedent was set: publishing truth about a politician, however scandalous, can never be a crime.[121]

THE QUEEN OF HEARTS

Dolley Madison is famous today for saving George Washington's portrait before the British burned down the White House, but in early America she was notorious for sleeping with three presidents, one vice president and a multitude of congressmen and diplomats. Although the tales of Dolley's rampant promiscuity are not true, the story of how they got started provides insight into how this one woman rocked the political world of the young Republic.

Dolley and James Madison were an odd couple. He was a dour, bookish man with a powdered comb-over and, at five foot four, the shortest commander in chief in history. Wags called him the pigmy president.[122] Although the original framework for the Constitution was Madison's brainchild, he was so shy he asked another member of the Virginian delegation to present his "Virginia Plan" to the Constitutional Convention. In the love department, Madison was no Ben Franklin. He did not even try to woo a woman until he was 31 years old—when he suddenly realized he needed to marry in order to be a successful politician. He courted a 15-year-old named Kitty, the daughter of a fellow congressman. Today that smacks of robbing the cradle, but at the time such a young bride was commonplace even among the nation's elite.[123] Kitty seemed to respond well to Madison's courtship until she abruptly dumped him for a 19-year-old medical student. The congressman was so humiliated he did not approach another woman for another 12 years, when at 43 he asked Senator Aaron Burr to introduce him to a 25-year-old widow named Dolley Payne Todd. Burr had become friendly with Dolley while lodging at her mother's boardinghouse in Philadelphia. His wife meanwhile was dying of cancer in New York, and rumors swirled that Burr was having an affair with Dolley and planned on asking for her hand as soon as he heard the news of his wife's death. Madison was able to pop the question before Burr and married Dolley months after their first date in 1794.

Dolley was three inches taller than the "great little Madison" and 17 years his junior. She was described as a "well proportioned" "fine portly buxom dame" with a "mouth which was beautiful in shape and expression."[124] Dolley was said to put men "in pouts" when she walked down the streets of Philadelphia. During an afternoon stroll, a friend noticed all the gawking fellows and chided, "Really Dolley, thou must hide thy face—there are so many men staring at thee."[125] The Madisons' odd matchup and the fact that they never had any children generated rumors that Madison's "lack of amorous passion" forced Dolley to get her kicks from other men, including George Washington and vice president Aaron Burr.[126]

One of Thomas Jefferson's first acts as president in 1801 was to appoint his protégé James Madison as secretary of state. The widower president also invited the Madisons to live in the President's Palace, as the White House was then known, and asked Dolley to serve as his hostess at state functions. The Madisons were so close to Jefferson that on a visit to Monticello, Dolley begged Sally Hemings for the privilege of naming her newborn child. Madison Hemings recounted that Dolley promised Sally a present for the honor and his mother consented. "Mrs. Madison dubbed me by the name I now acknowledge, but like many promises of white folks to the slaves she never gave my mother anything."[127] Jefferson's enemies knew the Madisons were living with the president and immediately began spreading rumors throughout the nation that the secretary of state was impotent and pimping his wife to his boss.[128] Six months after moving in to the President's Palace the Madisons moved out.

During Jefferson's first year in office, a diplomatic incident known as the Merry affair seemed to confirm the rumors about the president and Dolley. Jefferson was frustrated that the British were not abiding by the peace treaty that had ended the Revolutionary War; British troops remained in outposts throughout the Mississippi Valley, while the Royal Navy impressed American sailors into forced service. Jefferson chose to publicly display his displeasure with Britain during a welcoming ceremony for the new British ambassador, Anthony Merry. Instead of escorting the female guest of honor, Merry's wife, into the dining room, Jefferson took Dolley's arm. Dolley knew the president was violating diplomatic protocol and whispered, "Take Mrs.

Merry." A guest at the party immediately exclaimed, "This will be the cause of war!"[129]

The treatment of wives at diplomatic functions was very serious business. Women at the time were held as symbols of a nation in its purest form. Jefferson's snub of the ambassador's wife was interpreted on both sides of the Atlantic as an affront to British womanhood and a slap in the face of English honor. Even worse, Jefferson gave precedence at the party to Dolley's 19-year-old friend Betsy Patterson, who had just married Napoleon's younger brother Jerome Bonaparte. At the time, Britain and France were engaged in a war that would determine the fate of Europe, and British newspaper reports about Jefferson's party foul fed the anxieties of the besieged nation. Even after Jefferson tried to apologize, Merry had to wait for orders from London on whether to accept the apology. Dolley solved the diplomatic impasse by inviting the Merrys over for dinner, and tempers soon subsided. A French military attaché in Washington reported home, "Mrs. Madison has become one of America's most valuable assets."[130]

Meanwhile, Federalist newspapers spun the Merry affair as confirmation of rumors that Dolley served as the president's mistress with her impotent husband's approval. Newspapers also claimed Jefferson and his secretary of state pimped Dolley's equally vivacious sisters to foreign dignitaries and congressmen.[131] Ambassador Merry read the vicious newspaper attacks on the president and the secretary of state and reported back to London that the American Republic was on the brink of collapse. He advised his superiors not to accede to Jefferson's demands on military deployments and naval impressments; no need to appease a regime that was about to fall apart. When the United States declared war on Britain in 1812, many commentators at the time pointed to the Merry affair as the cause. Of course there were bigger factors, but the Jefferson-Madison sex scandal did influence Britain's refusal to address American grievances that served as the casus belli for the War of 1812.[132]

PETTICOAT POLITICKING

Toward the end of his second term, Jefferson decided to follow George Washington's example of a two-term limit and not run again in 1808. James Madison jumped into the ring and challenged sitting vice president George

Clinton for the Democratic Republican presidential nomination. Senator Samuel Latham Mitchill of New York predicted Madison would win because he "gives dinners and makes generous display to the members [of Congress]. [Clinton] lives snug at his lodgings, and keeps aloof from such captivating exhibitions." The crucial difference between the two candidates was Dolley. "The Secretary of State has a wife to aid his pretentions," Mitchill observed, while "the Vice-President has nothing of female succor on his side."[133]

The Founders did not originally intend for party politics to play a role in choosing presidents; they wanted to leave presidential elections up to a nonpartisan Electoral College. With the rise of the two-party system, congressmen from both parties began holding caucuses to choose their nominees for president. Men who wanted to be president in the early Republic could not openly campaign for office; they needed to appear uninterested in the presidency. A show of grand ambition was still perceived as a dangerous threat to the republican order. Madison was able to keep his ambitions hidden by dispatching Dolley to do the politicking at social gatherings she held for the Democratic congressmen.[134] Early nineteenth-century social events in Washington functioned as polls do today; a soirée well attended by key political figures was seen as a sign that the host had significant political support.[135] With the help of her vivacious sisters, Dolley threw parties that were always the best attended in town.

During the lead-up to the 1808 election, the Federalist presidential nominee Charles Pickney publicly accused Dolley of trading sexual favors for the support of the Democratic congressional caucus.[136] Federalist congressman John Randolph declared he was going to present evidence of Dolley's affairs that "will make the hairs of congress stand *erect* as porcupine quills."[137] Anti-Madison newspapers cried, "Can a woman, who thus acted with a worthy husband, love her country, be a republican and know anything about patriotism?" A Federalist newspaper in Georgetown ran an advertisement for a phony book, with a chapter titled "Love and Smoke Cannot Be Hidden," about a thinly disguised impotent politician and his oversexed, adulterous wife.[138] Dolley successfully countered the accusations by inviting her fiercest critics to her parties as if she had nothing to hide. After Charles Pickney lost the 1808 election he admitted he "was beaten by Mr. and Mrs. Madison. I might have had a better chance had I faced Mr. Madison alone."[139]

Madison inherited a fractured government with a fierce congressional opposition that challenged the very legitimacy of his presidency. He also lacked the public stature and personal loyalties of his predecessors. Washington, Adams and Jefferson were all heroes of the Revolution.[140] With zero charisma, Madison was much better suited to working quietly on congressional committees than leading a nation. Fortunately, he had Dolley.

The new president's 33-year-old wife became the public face of the administration. Washington buzzed over her French fashions: feathered turbans, rouged cheeks, a big wig of ebony curls, and her décolletage gowns that, according to one observer, revealed "the most beautiful . . . neck and bosom . . . I ever saw."[141] Most American women tucked handkerchiefs into their necklines to shield their cleavage; not Dolley. On one occasion, the president's wife raised a toast to a Quaker guest who was not wearing his traditional hat, "Here's to thy absent broadbrim, Friend Hallowell," to which he replied, "Here's to thy absent kerchief, Friend Dolley."[142] Dolley's fingers were stained with the snuff that she shoved up her nose, even in public.[143] In an age when it was inappropriate for a woman's name to appear in the press, her picture graced the cover of the famous literary magazine *The Port Folio.* American manufacturers gave her their products, hoping for an endorsement, and Dolley received a flood of gifts from ordinary Americans as well. One woman sent a handkerchief to "shad[e] her lovely bosom from the admiration and gaze of the Vulgar."[144] Dolley became Washington's chief tourist attraction; at all hours people showed up at the door of the President's Palace hoping to meet her. A ship was christened the *Lady Madison,* and she appeared as a character in novels. The *National Intelligencer* dubbed Dolley the "Presidentress." More and more people began calling her by a new semiofficial title, the First Lady.[145]

Although Dolley dressed distinctively different from the typical American woman, she did not act as though she was above the average folk. One who witnessed her "moving through admiring crowds, pleasing all, by making all pleased with themselves, yet looking superior to all," exclaimed, "She moves a goddess, and she looks a queen!"[146] A newspaper dubbed her "a queen of hearts" for her habit of hugging strangers and offering her lips when they asked to kiss her.[147] A friend observed that she was "not the least of a prude as she one day told a bachelor, and held up her mouth for him to kiss."[148] Her sweet and solicitous approach toward everyone, regardless of whether they were opposition congressmen or ordinary citizens, became the model for what was expected of future First Ladies.

As the president's hostess, Dolley threw parties that were the center of Washington social life. The capital was still a drab town of 3,000 people huddled in the middle of a swamp. With no theaters, no museums and few taverns to provide amusement, even the president's most fervent political opponents eagerly awaited invitations to Dolley's soirées.[149] Once the party started, "Queen Dolley" was sure to pull her husband's opponents aside and employ her ample charms to win their hearts and minds. At one such party, House Speaker Henry Clay exclaimed, "Everybody loves Mrs. Madison!" Dolley gamely responded, "That's because Mrs. Madison loves everybody!"[150] After attending one of Dolley's parties in 1809, Washington Irving, author of *The Legend of Sleepy Hollow,* wrote, "Mrs. Madison is a fine portly buxom dame, who has a smile and a pleasant word for everybody. Her sisters . . . are like the two Merry wives of Windsor. But as to Jemmy Madison—ah poor Jimmy! He is a withered little applejohn."[151] Everyone in Washington knew that Dolley used her parties to lobby for the president's programs, and her use of flirtation to win over political opponents became commonly known as "Petticoat Politicking."[152]

Dolley soon learned that playing the queen of hearts could cut both ways. One Federalist newspaper blamed her refusal to play the quiet, unassuming spouse on her impotent husband's inability to satisfy her in bed and on "the insatiability of democratic women" in general. The newspaper called Dolley "the leader of the ceremonious flock who carried with her, if not the thing itself, at least the appetites of the second of four insatiable things mentioned in the 30th chapter of Proverbs, verse 16"; in other words she had a barren womb "which never says, 'enough.'"[153] Soon a rumor circulated that the president was pimping out his wife and her sisters in exchange for congressional votes. When postmaster general Gideon Granger heard Federalist congressman Samuel Hunt repeat the rumor, Granger challenged Hunt to a duel. Seeing the makings of an unnecessary bloodbath and a national scandal, Dolley diffused the explosive situation by inviting Hunt to lunch in an open letter declaring that the congressman was "a great favorite with Mrs. Madison and sisters."[154]

Dolley was not only the heart and soul of her husband's administration, she was also her husband's eyes and ears around Washington. She led groups of ladies to sit in on Supreme Court hearings and congressional sessions. Washingtonians marveled that thanks to Dolley "the women here are taking a station in society which is not known elsewhere."[155] People also noticed that the presence of ladies at governmental proceedings forced congressmen and senators to tone down their hyperaggressive rhetoric and add "more flowers" and higher morality to their speeches. Dolley pushed a feminine civility into the federal political culture. The macho, violent, bare-knuckle, all-or-nothing approach to politics that dominated the battles between the Hamiltonians and the Jeffersonians gave way to a more conciliatory, civilized style of political debate that became the model for modern American politics.[156] Even before the War of 1812 made Dolley an American hero, she was one of the most famous, most beloved people in the United States.[157]

James Madison had no desire for war with the British in 1812, but the War Hawks in his party figured that since Britain was busy grappling with Napoleon, the United States could just swoop in and seize a lightly defended Canada. The invasion of Canada failed miserably, and the British took the opportunity presented by Mr. Madison's War to reclaim the American colonies. When British commander George Cockburn landed troops on the Chesapeake coast and began his march to the nation's capital, he sent word that he expected to be entertained by Mrs. Madison in her drawing room. In a display of defiance, Dolley refused to leave Washington, DC, and remained in the President's Palace while her husband inspected the city's defenses.

With British forces on the outskirts of the capital, Dolley ordered the staff to prepare a dinner for her husband, telling them that if she were a man she would post cannon in every window and fight to the bitter end. Only after she was informed that the British had broken through the American lines and were heading her way did she decide to flee, after making sure her slaves loaded George Washington's portrait into a carriage. When British troops arrived at the President's Palace, they discovered Dolley's dinner table brimming with wine, spits of meat, and saucepans. According to one British officer, the soldiers sat down at the table, drank a toast to "Jemmy's health," ate the president's dinner and "finished by setting fire to the house which had so liberally entertained them."[158] Before leaving, General Cockburn carried away a portrait of the famous Dolley Madison and grabbed a cushion from one of her chairs while remarking on the size of the First Lady's plump bottom.[159] There wasn't much left of Washington after the British burned down the Treasury, State and War departments and other public buildings, so Cockburn moved on to the siege of Baltimore and Fort McHenry.

Dolley and James returned to Washington four days later, and seeing the devastation, the president suggested that they consider moving the capital back to Philadelphia. Dolly adamantly insisted on staying, and every day she greeted troops as they stopped in front of the makeshift presidential headquarters set up in a friend's house. She gave impromptu patriotic speeches to the soldiers and DC residents, who responded with huzzas and hats tossed in the air.[160] Less than a month after the city was destroyed, she threw a big party to open up the DC social season.[161] The press loved Dolley's refusal to be bowed by the war. One newspaper declared that thanks to the First Lady "the spirit of the nation is roused."[162] Soon America acquired a new symbol of perseverance in face of devastation when the President's Palace was reopened with a fresh coat of white paint that gave it the more democratic name "the White House."

The burning of Washington, DC, was a devastating disaster for the nation, but newspaper reports of Dolley saving Washington's portrait gave the public an act of bravery to celebrate. Along with Andrew Jackson, who routed the British at the Battle of New Orleans, Dolley became a national hero at a time when people at home and abroad questioned the legitimacy of the Republic.[163] After peace was achieved, the legends of Jackson and Dolley helped make Mr. Madison's calamitous war popular.[164] Meanwhile, the public learned that the Federalists had hatched a treasonous wartime plot to lead New England out of the Union in a secession movement. With the Federalists discredited, Madison's popularity skyrocketed and voters rallied to the Democratic Republican Party, which dominated American politics for the next two decades.

As the Federalist Party disappeared from the political scene, the vicious backbiting and scandalmongering that plagued the first two-party system was replaced by a period of bipartisanship known as the Era of Good Feelings. *Port Folio* attributed the political peace to Dolley, arguing that Thomas

Jefferson might have said, "'We are all Federalists, we are all Republicans' but Mrs. Madison reduced this liberal sentiment to practice."[165] At the end of Madison's term, even Federalist stalwart John Adams conceded that "not withstanding a thousand faults and blunders, [Madison's] administration has acquired more glory, established more Union, than all his three Predecessors, Washington, Adams, and Jefferson, put together."[166] President Madison never could have done it without his First Lady, who was called an insatiable floozy in her time but became an American hero for all time.

CHAPTER TWO

SEX AND THE CIVIL WAR

"**S**trange! Wild! Infatuated! All for Jackson!" exclaimed a Cincinnati man when he heard Andrew Jackson was running for president in 1824.[1] The hero of the Battle of New Orleans was a true force of nature. One of his friends called him "the most roaring, rollicking, game-cocking, horse-racing, card-playing, mischievous fellow that ever lived."[2] He also enjoyed a good fight. When Jackson got into business disputes, he didn't sue; he dueled—no lawyers, just pistols at ten paces. Over a dozen men made the mistake of crossing Jackson and found themselves looking down the barrel of his dueling pistol.

Jackson squared off against sitting president John Quincy Adams, son of the second president, in the 1828 election. Jackson and Adams had been bitter enemies since the 1824 presidential election when they both entered a wide field of candidates including Henry Clay, William Crawford and John C. Calhoun. Jackson had captured the most popular votes and the most Electoral College votes. But he did not win a majority of the Electoral College, which is necessary to claim the presidency. As dictated by the Constitution, the election was thrown into the House of Representatives, where Speaker Clay handed his support to Adams because, in Clay's words, "I cannot believe that killing 2,500 Englishmen at New Orleans qualifies for the various, difficult and complicated duties of the Chief Magistracy."[3] Two days later, Adams announced that Clay would be his secretary of state, and

Jackson's supporters howled that Clay and Adams had entered a "corrupt bargain" to steal the presidency. Jackson's followers spent the next four years sabotaging President Adams's ambitious agenda to modernize the federal government, and the Era of Good Feelings came to an abrupt end. The stage was set for a final showdown between Adams and Jackson in the election of 1828—the dirtiest, most sexually charged campaign in American political history.

AMERICAN JEZEBEL

The Adams camp started the mudslinging. A pro-Adams newspaper shrieked, "General Jackson's mother was a COMMON PROSTITUTE, brought to this country by British soldiers! She afterward married a MULATTO MAN with whom she had several children, of which General JACKSON IS ONE!!!"[4] The Adams campaign also accused Jackson of adultery after Charles Hammond, editor of the *Cincinnati Gazette,* reported that "in the summer of 1790 Gen. Jackson prevailed upon the wife of Lewis Roberts [Robards] of Mercer County, Kentucky, to desert her husband, and live with himself, in the character of a wife."[5] The scandalous accusation was technically true.

Almost four decades before the 1828 election, Rachel Jackson's first husband, Lewis Robards, threw her out of their house in a fit of jealousy. The 19-year-old woman moved back to Nashville to live with her mother, who had taken on borders, one being a tall, wiry, blue-eyed, granite-jawed, 22-year-old lawyer named Andrew Jackson. Rachel's mother liked Jackson because he could handle a gun and protect her house from Indian attacks. Rachel liked him for a different reason. When a rumor reached Nashville in 1790 that Lewis was coming back to retrieve Rachel, Jackson ran away with her to Natchez in Spanish Florida. A year later, Rachel and Jackson returned to Nashville, where they lived together as common-law husband and wife in the mistaken belief that Robards had gotten a divorce. Divorce in the eighteenth century required an act of the state legislature and a judicial ruling. Robards got permission from the Virginia legislature to sue for a divorce in Kentucky, but he did not bother to bring the case to court. Two years after Rachel and Jackson moved in together, in 1793, Robards finally brought a divorce suit and won on the grounds "that the defendant, Rachel Robards, hath deserted

the plaintiff, Lewis Robards, and hath and doth still live in adultery with another man."[6] Legally, Rachel was guilty of adultery and bigamy.

Jackson and Rachel officially married a short while later but forever lived
under a cloud of vicious gossip that Old Hickory countered by dueling anyone who impugned his wife's honor. He even challenged Tennessee governor
John "Nolichucky Jack" Sevier to a duel after the governor said, "I know of no
services you have rendered to this country other than taking a trip to Natchez
with another man's wife!"[7] Three decades later, during the 1828 election, the
Adams campaign revived the Robards scandal. The *Daily National Journal*, an
influential Washington newspaper, denounced Jackson as a reckless adven-
turer who "spent the prime of his life in gambling, in cock fighting, in horse
racing," and who "to cap off all his frailties . . . tore from a husband the wife
of his bosom."[8]

Publicizing the sexual indiscretions of politicians had become common
practice by the 1820s for various reasons. A wave of democratic spirit moved
most states to adopt universal suffrage without property qualifications for all
white males. With the expansion of the vote, mass political parties arose with
their own newspapers that were dedicated not to reporting the news but to
promoting their candidates and assailing their opponents with rumor and innuendo. Widespread literacy and advances in printing technology put newspapers into the hands of Americans in all classes and in all corners of the
country. Newspapers competed for America's mass readership by featuring
sensational news stories like political sex scandals. The Founders had traded
in each other's sex scandals, but the election of 1828 generated the first truly
national debate about a candidate's private life.[9] A close examination of the
Robards scandal reveals why sex scandals have played such an important role
in the American political tradition ever since.

When Frenchman Alexis de Tocqueville visited the United States in the
1830s, he was shocked by how obsessed Americans were about the private
lives of their leaders. "To the European, a public officer represents a superior
force: to an American, he represents a right," Tocqueville observed. Americans did not defer to "their betters" as the Europeans did, because in the United
States even presidents were not "betters."[10] In *Democracy in America*, published
in 1835, Tocqueville condemned the tendency of American journalists to invade the privacy of politicians and "assail the character of individuals, to track

them into private life, and disclose all their weaknesses and their errors."[11] Tocqueville concluded that American journalists delved into the personal lives of politicians just to sell newspapers.

What the Frenchman did not comprehend was that America's fascination with political sex scandals had as much to do with democratic republicanism as crass sensationalism. European countries filled high political offices with men from the upper and noble classes. In America, political office was open to all white men regardless of class or background. The American voter could not assess candidates based on pedigree or family name. A candidate's personal history became an imperfect but useful barometer to predict how he would behave in public office. "The sentiment that a man pure and upright in his private character, is the only safe depository of public trust, is one that commends itself to the American people," the *Albany Argus* declared. "It is obvious that the vices and immoralities of private life will be carried into the public administration, and that one who has been notoriously immoral and reckless in his personal gratifications, cannot be less reckless and selfish in his public capacity."[12]

Nineteenth-century political candidates surrendered their privacy the minute they stepped into the public sphere. The *Daily National Journal* argued that by running for office Jackson "provoked if not invited an investigation of his character" and his private life.[13] The pro-Adams newspaper *We the People* charged, "If Gen. Jackson cannot withstand investigations of his character, or if his friends shrink from them and threaten violence to the hand that chalks out their imperfection, neither he, nor his party, is calculated for office, or to administer the laws to a republican people." The Robards scandal was "an affair in which the National character, the National interest, and the National morals, were all deeply involved," *We the People* insisted, and was therefore "a proper subject of public investigation and exposure."[14] In the nineteenth century, the personal life of a presidential candidate was regarded not as a private matter but as an issue of national significance.[15]

Another reason for the prominent role that sexual morality played in the 1828 election was the spread of evangelical Protestantism during the Second Great Awakening of the 1820s. The "Father of Modern Revivalism," Reverend Charles Grandison Finney, drew a direct connection between personal morality and the health of the American Republic: "If general intelligence, public and private virtue, sink to that point below which self-control becomes practically impossible, we must fall back into monarchy, limited or absolute; or into civil or military despotism. This is as certain as that God governs the world."[16] President John Quincy Adams understood that the evangelical movement had made voters much more focused on religion than they were in his father's day. His campaign used the Robards scandal as a way to contrast the adulterous Jackson with the president's image as a pious, self-disciplined, Christian gentleman.[17] Pro-Adams newspapers claimed, "Between the two candidates the difference is as wide as between paganism and Christianity," and predicted that if Jackson were elected, "two centuries would then be found to have been sufficient to carry us from puritanism to its antipodes."[18]

Adams's supporters also argued that the election of Jackson would set an example that would destroy the nation's moral values. Charles Hammond of the *Cincinnati Gazette* asserted that before the 1828 election America was a land "where no man can succeed to a place of high trust who does not respect female virtue: or who stands condemned as the seducer of other men's wives, and the destroyer of female character." Hammond asked his readers if they were willing to "give sanction to conduct, which is calculated to unhinge the fundamental principles of society? Let all inducements to the maintenance of conjugal fidelity be broken down: let all veneration for the marriage state and covenant be destroyed; and let me then ask, what there is in social life worthy of regard?" Hammond urged his readers, "Show to the world your abhorrence of a man, who disregards the laws which even savages revere." If Jackson won, Hammond warned, society would no longer be able to censure a man "who may seduce his neighbor's wife, and take her to live with him in adultery," because the stigma of fornication would be obliterated by "his being no worse than the president of the United States."[19] In Europe, churches and royal families set the moral example for their citizens. Since Americans looked to the First Family for a national standard of personal behavior, the private backgrounds of both the presidential candidate and his wife were fair game.

Pro-Adams newspapers saved their worst venom for Rachel Jackson, whom they called an "American Jezebel," a "profligate woman" and a "dirty, black wench!"[20] One newspaper asked, "Ought a convicted adulteress and her paramour husband to be placed in the highest offices of this free and

Christian Land?"[21] The *Massachusetts Journal* inquired, "Who is there in all this land that has a wife, a sister or daughter that could be pleased to see Mrs. Jackson . . . presiding in the drawing room at Washington. THERE IS POLLUTION IN THE TOUCH, THERE IS PERDITION IN THE EXAMPLE OF A PROFLIGATE WOMAN—'HER WAYS LEAD DOWN TO THE CHAMBERS OF DEATH AND HER STEPS TAKE HOLD ON HELL.'"[22]

Old Hickory could take the verbal jabs. He had been shot twice in duels and had a bullet still embedded in his body. But he could hardly stomach the printed attacks on his beloved wife. After all, he had killed men for saying less. Jackson knew Adams was baiting him with the assaults on Rachel. "It is evident that it is the last effort of the combined coalition to save themselves and destroy me," he told a friend. "They calculated that it would arouse me to some desperate act by which I would fall prostrate before the people." Jackson resisted his innate impulse to take dramatic action: "For the present my hands are pinioned." But he vowed, "The day of retribution and vengeance must come, when the guilty will meet with their just reward."[23]

Jackson's supporters retaliated by pushing an unsubstantiated rumor that when Adams served as U.S. ambassador to Russia he pimped his wife's maid to the czar and "attempted to make use of a beautiful girl to seduce the passion of the Emperor Alexander and sway him to political purposes."[24] President Adams condemned the "new form of slander—one of the thousand malicious lies which outvenom all the worms of the Nile, and are circulated in every part of the country in newspapers and pamphlets."[25] "In pamphlets, newspapers, handbills, stump-speeches and dram shop dialogues, throughout the union, . . . in the face of fifty refutations," the president raged, "the skunks of party slander have been for the last fortnight squirting [personal attacks on me] round the House of Representatives, thence to issue and perfume the atmosphere of the Union."[26] On the basis of a single unsubstantiated rumor, newspapers throughout the nation and congressmen in the Capitol building began publicly accusing the president of the United States of being the "Pimp of the Coalition."[27]

All the personal attacks on Jackson did not have much effect on the vote. Jackson won a landslide victory, and for a brief time he felt vindicated. But the president-elect's joy was short-lived.

Although Rachel had heard the slanders against her for decades, the presidential campaign brought national attention to her scarlet reputation. Rachel felt so humiliated she considered skipping the inauguration. Jackson's trusted friend John Eaton urged her to reconsider: "The storm has now abated, the angry tempest has ceased to howl. A verdict by the American people has been pronounced. If you shall be absent how great will be the disappointment. Your persecutors then may chuckle, and say that they have driven you from the field of your husband's honors."[28] Buoyed by Eaton's reassurance, Rachel went to Nashville to shop for an inaugural gown in late December 1828. While in town, she discovered a leftover campaign pamphlet printed by Jackson's supporters defending her against various charges. Throughout the campaign, Jackson had been very careful to insulate Rachel from the meanest newspaper attacks. Looking at the pamphlet, she saw the full range of slanderous accusations in print for the first time. She returned home in a state of shock and days later she was hit by a massive and lethal heart attack.

John Eaton wrote her epitaph: "A being so gentle and so virtuous, slander might wound but could not dishonor."[29] After Jackson buried his wife in the same gown she planned to wear to his inauguration, the president-elect avowed, "May God Almighty forgive her murderers, as I know she forgave them. I never can."[30] And he never did.

Jackson fell into a deep depression that lasted months. He snapped out of it just in time to assume his duties as president. He brought to Washington his dear friend John Eaton and appointed him secretary of war. Jackson had once told Rachel that Eaton "is more like a son to me than anything else; I shall as long as I live estimate his worth and friendship with a grateful heart."[31] Jackson's devotion to Eaton was soon tested by another sex scandal that divided the nation.

THE PEGGY EATON AFFAIR

Jackson's presidency is mostly known for crushing the National Bank, forcing tens of thousands of Native Americans to walk the Trail of Tears, and ushering in the age of the common man in American politics. But Jackson's most significant legacy may be the Petticoat affair, a juicy sex scandal that tore apart his administration and set the country on the road to civil war.

Peggy O'Neil Timberlake was the coquettish daughter of a Washington, DC, innkeeper who lodged many politicians, including John Eaton and Andrew Jackson. The high-spirited girl entertained her father's lodgers by singing and dancing and won a dance competition judged by her hero, Dolley Madison, who crowned Peggy the Carnival Queen. One of her many admirers described the teenager as having a "well-rounded, voluptuous figure, peach-pink complexion, large, active dark eyes, and full sensuous lips, ready to break into an engaging smile."[32] She was also an incorrigible flirt who exchanged dirty jokes and discussed politics with her father's powerful guests— scandalous behavior for a girl at a time when a popular women's publication, *Female Friend*, declared, "A female politician is only less disgusting than a female infidel."[33]

Like Dolley Madison, Peggy was the subject of lurid rumors, including a claim that she earned a small fortune as a teenager servicing the sexual needs of Capitol Hill's lonely congressmen and senators. She also was said to have left a long trail of broken hearts around Washington, not to mention at least one suicide and a few duels. A 39-year-old career navy man, John Timberlake, overlooked the 17-year-old's lascivious reputation and married her anyway in 1816. Twelve years later, while Timberlake was at sea, Peggy hit the town with Andrew Jackson's trusted friend Senator John Eaton of Tennessee. The capital was abuzz with gossip about the two. One rumor claimed Eaton had gotten Peggy pregnant and arranged an abortion.[34] No one knows if these stories reached her husband while he was in the Mediterranean serving on the USS *Constitution*, but in April 1828, on the deck of Old Ironsides, he ended his life by slashing his own throat.[35]

When word of Timberlake's suicide got back to Peggy and John, they decided to get married. The only thing stopping them was gossip. Eaton was Jackson's right-hand man and did not want to add another scandal to his friend's presidency. When he told President-elect Jackson about his dilemma, Old Hickory implored him, "Yes, get married and shut their mouths."[36] On New Year's Day 1829, six months after Timberlake's death, John and Peggy were married. Washington society was aghast; Senator Louis McLane sniped, "Eaton has just married his mistress and the mistress of eleven doz. others!"[37]

After Jackson assumed the presidency months later in March of 1829, he inadvertently fueled the gossip by appointing Eaton the secretary of war. Former president John Quincy Adams noted in his diary, "The character of the woman was notorious, so notorious that much opinion was made to the appointment of her husband. The private morals of the country were deeply outraged by the appointment of Eaton to an office of Cabinet minister." Adams added, "But what could be expected from a President of the United States himself an adjudicated adulterer!"[38] The attacks on Peggy reminded Jackson of his late wife's plight and hardened his support for the Eatons. "Mrs. Eaton is as chaste as those who slander her," he averred, "I would sink with honor to my grave before I would abandon my friend."[39]

The Petticoat affair began at the start of the Jackson administration in the spring of 1829 when the wives of the cabinet secretaries, led by Vice President John C. Calhoun's wife, Floride, refused to invite the Eatons to their parties. One of the ladies who attended the Inaugural Ball reported that Peggy was snubbed the entire night: "This New Lady never approached the party. She was left alone and kept at a respectful distance from those virtuous and distinguished women, with the sole exception of a seat at the supper table, where, however, notwithstanding her proximity she was not spoken to by them. These are facts and greatly to the honor of our sex."[40] While ostracizing the Eatons seems petty today, upper-class nineteenth-century ladies saw the public snubbing of a scarlet woman as part of their sacred responsibility to uphold society's sexual customs.[41] No respectable woman in Washington dared to socialize with Peggy. Secretary of State Martin Van Buren quipped that DC society seemed to be afraid of catching the Eaton malaria.

Haunted by his wife's death, the president tried to comfort Peg: "We know, here, that none are spared. Even Mrs. Madison was assailed by these fiends in human shape. . . . I tell you I had rather have live vermin on my back than the tongue of one of these Washington women on my reputation."[42] Jackson decided to take action: "I did not come here to make a Cabinet for the Ladies of this place, but for the nation."[43] He demanded that his cabinet members invite the Eatons to their parties, but the cabinet secretaries feared their wives more than the president of the United States and refused to welcome the humiliated couple.

Self-righteous ministers soon entered the fray. Jackson's own minister, J. M. Campbell, told the president that Peggy had a miscarriage while her former husband had been away at sea for a *year*. Reverend Ezra Siles Ely warned Jackson to shun Peggy because he heard someone say, "Mrs. Eaton brushed by me last night and pretended not to know me. She has forgotten the time when I slept with her."[44]

Outraged, Jackson hired private investigators to discover the truth behind the lurid allegations. During his first year in office, the president's investigations on behalf of the Eatons consumed more of his time and energy than any political, diplomatic or economic issue.[45] When his agents found no proof of Peggy's promiscuity, Jackson badgered the preachers, "Don't you see now that she is a good woman?" And he lectured, "Female virtue is like a tender and delicate flower. Let but the breath of suspicion rest upon it, and it withers and perhaps perishes forever."[46] He finally summoned both ministers to a meeting of his entire cabinet and laid out his evidence. One of the ministers started arguing with the president over "whether the Eatons had been seen in bed together or merely sitting on it" before they were married. The president finally reached his boiling point and halted the debate with a thunderous final judgment: "She is as chaste as a virgin!" When Jackson's nemesis Henry Clay heard about the president's statement regarding the chastity of the twice-married mother of two children, he gibed, "Age cannot wither, nor custom stale, her infinite virginity."[47]

After the cabinet meeting, John Eaton challenged Reverend Campbell to a duel. The good reverend promptly fled to Albany. Eaton also wanted to duel Secretary of the Treasury Samuel Ingram but decided to clear it with the president first. Jackson replied, "If he won't fight, you must kill him."[48] Peggy implored John to take her along so she could load his pistol. Much to her disappointment, Ingram also skipped town.[49]

The fuss was hardly over. Jackson started to blame the entire controversy on his vice president, John C. Calhoun. Calhoun was a powerhouse in Southern politics, and he had grand ambitions to be president. His political leverage enabled him to force Jackson to fill most of the cabinet positions with Calhoun loyalists. Jackson figured that because Eaton was not one of the vice president's puppets, Calhoun found "it was necessary to put him out of the cabinet and destroy him regardless what injury [it] might do me or my administration."[50] Since Floride Calhoun was leading the pack of cabinet wives against Peggy, Jackson began to view the Eaton malaria as Calhoun's plot to undermine his presidency.[51]

Secretary of state Martin Van Buren exploited Jackson's suspicions. Van Buren ran the New York state Democratic political machine and was so adept at turning out the vote that he was nicknamed the Little Magician. As a bachelor, Van Buren was free to make frequent visits to the Eatons' home and invited them to State Department dinners and receptions.[52] One of the cabinet wives sniffed, "If Mr. Van Buren, our secretary, persists in visiting her, our ladies will not go to his house."[53] Van Buren couldn't have cared less about Washington society; he wanted the presidency, and he knew his road to the White House would be paved by Andrew Jackson. His scheme worked. "I have found the President affectionate, confidential and kind to the last degree," Van Buren bragged. "I am entirely satisfied that there is no degree of good feeling or confidence which he does not entertain me."[54] Jackson began to sing Van Buren's praises: "I have found him every thing that I could desire him to be and believe him not only deserving my confidence, but the confidence of the nation."[55]

Former president Adams understood how the battle over Peggy Eaton's reputation was quickly becoming a power struggle with national implications: "The Administration party is split up into a blue and green faction upon this point of morals: but the explosion has been hitherto deferred. Calhoun heads the moral party, Van Buren that of the frail sisterhood; and he is notoriously engaged in canvassing for the presidency by paying his court to Mrs. Eaton."[56] At Van Buren's instigation, Jackson asked for the resignations of his entire cabinet in 1831. The *Washington National Journal* complained that the Jackson administration looked like that of "the reign of Louis XV when Ministers were appointed and dismissed at a woman's nod, and the interests of the nation were tied to her apron string."[57]

Thanks to the twelfth amendment, ratified in 1804, the vice presidency was no longer given to the runner-up in the presidential election. Instead, a separate election for the vice presidency was held alongside the presidential election. Since the parties controlled who was nominated for the vice presidency,

Jackson was able to dump Calhoun from the Democratic ticket in 1832 and replace him with Martin Van Buren. At the end of his second term in 1836, Jackson rewarded Peggy's lone supporter with the ultimate prize when he handpicked Van Buren to succeed him as president. The Little Magician was the big winner in the Petticoat affair. The biggest loser was the Union.

During Jackson's first administration, the dispute over Peggy mirrored a conflict in the cabinet over the tariff, which was one of the main issues dividing the nation. Like the slavery issue, the tariff debate divided North and South. Northern states supported a high tariff, Southern states opposed it, and no state opposed the tariff more than Calhoun's home state of South Carolina. In Jackson's original cabinet, Eaton and Van Buren supported the tariff, and Calhoun and his loyalists opposed it. After Jackson fired the cabinet at Van Buren's suggestion, many Southerners feared the New Yorker now controlled the nation's tariff policy.[58]

Congress seemed to confirm that fear in 1832 when it voted with Jackson's support to increase the tariff. In protest, Calhoun became the first vice president to resign. He returned to South Carolina to run for the Senate. Getting dumped from Jackson's 1832 ticket left Calhoun's presidential ambitions in tatters and freed him from having to appeal to a national audience. Senator Calhoun became the foremost advocate for states' rights and the nullification doctrine, which claimed a state had the right to nullify, or refuse to enforce, any federal law the state deemed unconstitutional. Nullification undermined the very notion of the Union. Calhoun was so fervent in his opposition to the Jackson administration and the tariff that he formed a new political party known as the Nullifier Party. Instead of becoming president of the nation, Senator Calhoun became the father of Southern secession.

Led by Calhoun, South Carolina announced that it would defy federal law and not enforce Jackson's tariff of 1832. Congress responded with the Force Bill, authorizing Old Hickory to use the military to compel South Carolina to obey. The president sent warships to Charleston harbor and threatened to hang Calhoun and anyone else who defied his authority.[59] Tensions finally eased when Senator Henry Clay brokered a compromise tariff that pulled the United States and South Carolina away from the brink of a mini civil war in 1832.

Over subsequent decades, Senator Calhoun was the leading voice of the proslavery extremists. While other Southern politicians excused slavery as a "necessary evil," Calhoun argued that slavery was a "Positive Good" for both master and slave. Until the end of his life, in 1850, Calhoun was the foremost firebrand of the Southern cause. When Abraham Lincoln was elected president in 1860, Calhoun's home state, South Carolina, was the first state to secede, and its militia fired the first shots of the Civil War at Fort Sumter in Charleston harbor. What would have happened if the Petticoat affair had not ruined Calhoun's shot at the presidency? Perhaps as president he would have worked to bridge the divide between North and South rather than becoming the father of Southern secession. The Peggy Eaton affair did not cause the Civil War, but it certainly played an important role in how it unfolded. On the eve of the great national tragedy in 1860, Jackson biographer James Parton wrote, "the political history of the United States, for the last thirty years, dates from the moment when the soft hand of Mr. Van Buren touched Mrs. Eaton's knocker."[60]

As for Peggy Eaton, after the Petticoat affair her life became even more colorful. At age 59, after John Eaton's death, she married a 19-year-old dance teacher who eventually stole all her money and ran off to Italy with her 17-year-old granddaughter. In her later years, Peggy would regularly visit John Eaton's grave, until one day in 1879, she told cemetery workers, "It is the last time. I shall never come here again till I come to stay. It is a beautiful place to rest in at last." That November, on her deathbed, the 80-year-old said, "I am not afraid of death but this is such a beautiful world to leave." Ironically, the height of Washington society, including the current First Lady, attended the funeral of this once-scarlet woman. President Rutherford B. Hayes felt it necessary to apologize for not being on hand to pay his respects. One newspaper report on Peggy's death noted, "So long as the history of American politics is written and studied, her name must be remembered."[61]

THE BLUE AND THE GAY

Historians consistently rank James Buchanan as the all-time worst president.[62] During his presidency, from 1857 to 1861, Buchanan encouraged proslavery forces in the lead-up to the Civil War and refused to crack down on Southern states when they began seceding at the end of his administration. It is clear why historians think Buchanan was a terrible commander in chief. The mystery is, why was he so proslavery? He hailed from Lancaster, Pennsylvania—a fervently antislavery area. His local church was so disgusted by his proslavery views, it refused to admit him. How did this son of the North become such a fervent defender of the South? In two words: gay love.

James Buchanan, the only bachelor president, fell in love with Alabama politician William Rufus King, the only bachelor vice president. Both men remained unmarried for life at a time when only three in one hundred American men stayed single.[63] They met in 1821 when Buchanan was a freshman congressman and King, who was five years older, was a senator. Before his presidency, Buchanan lived with the flamboyantly effeminate King for 16 years. They were so inseparable they were known around Washington as the "Siamese Twins." Andrew Jackson called the fastidious King "Aunt Fancy" and Buchanan "Miss Nancy" (common nineteenth-century terms for gay men).[64] Tennessee governor Aaron V. Brown referred to them as "Buchanan & his wife."[65] In a letter to future First Lady Sarah Polk, Governor Brown reported that "Buchanan and his better half" got into a tiff and "Aunt Fancy [King] may now be seen every day, trigged out in her best clothes & smirking about in hopes of securing better terms than with her former companion [Buchanan]."[66] They were an odd couple—King was a handsome, curly-haired dandy, while Buchanan had mismatched eyes (one blue, one hazel), a whiskerless face and features that one historian called "eunuchlike, endomorphic."[67] To top it off, Buchanan had myopia in one squinty eye that forced him to tilt his neck forward and cock his head sideways to see straight.

After Buchanan was elected president, his niece and King's niece tried covering up the nature of their uncles' relationship by burning most of their personal correspondence.[68] Fortunately, they missed a couple of letters that are extremely revealing. When King served as ambassador to France in 1844, he wrote longingly to Buchanan, "I am selfish enough to hope you will not be able to procure an associate who will cause you to feel no regret at our separation."[69] A lonely Buchanan complained in a letter to a friend, "I am so solitary and alone having no companion in the house with me. I have gone wooing to several gentlemen, but have not succeeded with any of them."

Buchanan continued in the same letter, "I feel that it is not good for a man to be alone; and should not be astonished to find myself married to some old maid who can nurse me when I am sick, provide good dinners for me when I am well, and not expect from me any very ardent or romantic affection."[70] Of course, Buchanan did not get married, and when King returned from France, the Washington power couple reunited. During the 1852 election, Buchanan selflessly refused the vice presidential nomination in favor of his beloved King, who served as vice president until his death one year later.[71]

Given all the gossip about Buchanan's relationship with King, one would expect his private life to have become an issue when he ran for president. After all, the nineteenth-century press loved political sex scandals and regularly printed unsubstantiated rumors about the private lives of presidential candidates. Yet when Buchanan ran for president, the press ignored all the gossip about "Buchanan & his wife." In an age when some states punished sodomy with the death penalty, this silence is strange.

The historian Jonathan Ned Katz explains that in the nineteenth century homosexual relationships were "unspeakable" and unprintable. Katz cites the press reaction to Walt Whitman's homoerotic poems in *Leaves of Grass*, published in 1855—a year before Buchanan ran for president. Although Whitman wrote more explicitly about gay sex than any previous American author, only one book reviewer, Rufus Wilmot Griswold, acknowledged the homoeroticism in the poetry. Griswold, however, could not explicitly articulate what he found so objectionable. His book review condemned "the vilest imaginings and shamefullest license" and the "degrading, beastly sensuality" in Whitman's poems, but only vaguely referred to "the horrible sin not to be named among Christians." Whitman was emboldened by the press silence on the homoeroticism of his poetry, and the following year he issued a second edition of *Leaves of Grass* with additional poems that were even more graphic.[72] Fortunately for Buchanan, the American press did not feel free to discuss homosexual relationships until the late nineteenth century, so during the election of 1856 the "skunks of party slander" turned a blind eye to his personal life.[73]

Like the journalists in Buchanan's day, today's historians are also squeamish about acknowledging the sexual nature of his relationship with King. Some claim Buchanan was straight because, when he was 30 years old, he proposed to a woman named Anne Coleman. After Buchanan abruptly broke off their engagement, Anne died of what her doctor diagnosed as "hysterical convulsions."[74] According to the story, Buchanan felt so guilty for breaking Anne's heart he never again considered getting married. In fact, when he was in his forties and running for the Senate, he talked about having another fi-ancée but never went through with the wedding. When he sought the pres-idential nomination in his 50s, he talked about marrying Dolley Madison's 19-year-old niece, but that didn't pan out either. Buchanan seemed to talk about getting married whenever he ran for higher office.

Buchanan's sexuality has long baffled historians. One Buchanan biogra-pher wrote, "He may have feared sexuality, or simply lacked a capacity for emotional intimacy. Buchanan's failure to connect closely with anyone, save possibly his long-time roommate in Washington, Senator R. King, con-tributes to the air of mystery about him that existed in his lifetime and exists today. It is also doubtless one reason why his motives were always subject to question. No one save Buchanan really knew what he was up to."[75]

The "air of mystery" around Buchanan could be easily cleared up by ex-amining his love affair with King. A slave owner, King was Buchanan's polit-ical mentor.[76] King believed the younger man had the makings of a president and was constantly advising Buchanan on how to put himself in position to win the presidential nomination.[77] King also instilled his protégé with a ro-manticized vision of the slave system and a deep sympathy for slave owners. According to Buchanan's 1868 obituary in the *Chicago Tribune*, he "regarded the south as peopled with a superior class of men, who could do no wrong."[78] Buchanan once asked rhetorically, "Who could for a moment indulge in the horrible idea of abolishing slavery by the massacre of the high-minded, and the chivalrous race of men in the South? For my own part I would, without hesitation, buckle on my knapsack, and march in defense of their cause."[79] King's romantic relationship with Buchanan would account for the future president's slavish devotion to the Old South.

Buchanan and King's 32-year love affair had tragic consequences for the na-tion. Throughout his career, Buchanan bent over backward to help the proslavery cause, even if his actions violated the law and divided the nation. When he was ambassador to Great Britain in 1854, he wrote the Ostend Manifesto, which declared that the United States should take Cuba by force if Spain would not sell its slave-rich Caribbean territory. Buchanan hoped to incorporate Cuba into the Union as another slave state and to feed the South's ravenous hunger for more slaves. Although Northerners denounced the Ostend Manifesto as a plot to extend slavery and the State Department disavowed the document, the damage was done: Buchanan had further divided the North and South.

After he was elected president, Buchanan used his influence to get the Supreme Court to rule in favor of the proslavery forces in the infamous 1857 *Dred Scott v. Sanford* case. The Court's decision in favor of Scott's owner asserted that the Founders intended for black people to always be regarded "as a subordinate and inferior class of beings, who . . . had no rights or privileges."[80] The decision also nullified all restrictions that Congress placed on the spread of slavery into the free territories of the West. The *Dred Scott* decision generated so much fear of political turmoil that the economy immediately plunged into a freefall known as the Panic of 1857. Many Northerners lost faith in the federal government, which they believed was hijacked by "slave power." President Buchanan lent further credibility to the antislavery conspiracy theorists by surrounding himself with Southern men in his cabinet and in his personal life.

He favored the proslavery forces during the Bleeding Kansas crisis (1854–1858), when the antislavery Jayhawk majority fought against proslavery radicals called Border Ruffians. He appointed Robert Walker, a Mississippi slave owner, as governor of the Kansas Territory. Although Walker was proslavery, he was committed to a free and fair election in Kansas over the slavery issue. When Governor Walker discovered that the Border Ruffians had stuffed ballot boxes, he threw out the votes. Buchanan was appalled by the governor's judicious approach and forced Walker to resign. The president then started bribing members of Congress to accept the fraudulent election and admit Kansas as a slave state.

In his 1859 annual address to Congress, Buchanan echoed John C. Calhoun when he claimed that the slaves were "treated with kindness and humanity. . . . Both the philanthropy and the self-interest of the master have combined to produce this humane result."[81] A year later, when the Southern states started seceding in the wake of Abraham Lincoln's election in November 1860, President Buchanan refused to use military force to preserve the

Union. "The South has no right to secede, but I have no power to prevent them," said the commander in chief.[82] He continued to rely on his Southern cabinet members for advice even though they were conspiring against the federal government and passing his plans to secessionist leaders. The *Chicago Tribune* called him "the first American Executive to keep traitors in his cabinet after they had shown their treason."[83] By the time Lincoln took office in March 1861, Buchanan had surrendered most federal military installations in the South except two small outposts and Fort Sumter. And he would have abandoned Fort Sumter had a few loyal cabinet members not intervened.[84] It was as if the South had planted a Manchurian candidate in the White House.

The previous time a Southern state had tried to secede was during the 1832 Nullification Crisis, when Old Hickory sent warships into Charleston harbor and threatened to hang Senator Calhoun along with the rest of the nullification leaders. Watching Buchanan dither three decades later, Americans cried out, "Oh for an hour of Jackson!"[85]

Buchanan's inaction gave the rebellious states valuable time to consolidate their forces before Lincoln took over the presidency. Had President Buchanan done his job and made an effort to nip the secession movement in the bud in 1860, hundreds of thousands of Americans might not have lost their lives over the next five years of bloody civil war. When Buchanan died in June 1868, the *Chicago Tribune* rendered a bitter final judgment on the bachelor president: "The desolate old man has gone to his grave. Fortunately he is the last of his race. No son or daughter is doomed to acknowledge an ancestry of him."[86] Looking at Buchanan's treasonous record as president, it is no wonder his motives still baffle historians. His decisions make sense only if one makes the connection between his devotion to the Southern cause and his romantic relationship with King.

THE ORIGINAL LOG CABIN REPUBLICAN

To explain the man behind the legend that is Abraham Lincoln, historians have offered up some pretty wild theories, from a chronic syphilis infection to a genetic heart disorder that caused him to grow freakishly tall. A recent book, *Lincoln's Melancholy,* claims to explain "how depression challenged a President and fueled his greatness."[87] Once again, an examination of a president's sex life can shed light on his life-long struggle with depression, on his famously volatile marriage and, perhaps, on his key role in the fight against slavery.

Lincoln's sexual orientation has been questioned for three reasons. First, he had consistently problematic relationships with women, particularly his wife. Second, the most intimate relationship of his life was with a slave owner named Joshua Speed. And third, Lincoln liked to sleep with men.

Contemporaries of young Abe were puzzled by his utter lack of interest in girls. Lincoln's stepmother recalled he "was not very fond of girls." Another friend, James Short, remembered "he didn't go to see the girls much. He didn't appear bashful, but seemed as if he cared but little for them." According to Short, when Lincoln craved companionship he "would just as lieve the company were all men as to have it a mixture of the sexes."[88] Another friend, John Hands said, "I never Could get him in Company with women: he was not a timid man in this particular, but [he] did not seek such company." Seven other friends of young Lincoln went on the record essentially saying that Abe "didn't like girls much."[89]

Lincoln also had trouble connecting with women as an adult. He proposed marriage to a few women, but none of his engagements went smoothly. When he was twenty-eight, Lincoln's friends in Illinois fixed him up with a visitor from Kentucky named Mary Owens who found Lincoln "deficient in those links which make up the chain of a woman's happiness."[90] Lincoln wrote that he "saw no good objection to plodding life thru hand in hand with her" and planned to marry her when she returned to Illinois for another visit. Owens did return three years later, and Lincoln still had no girlfriend, so Mary's friends and family assumed he would propose. Unfortunately, time had taken its toll on Mary. Lincoln described her new appearance in a funny letter to a friend:

> I know she was over-size, but she now appeared a fair match for Falstaff. I
> know she was called an "old maid" . . . but now when I beheld her, I could
> not for my life avoid thinking of my mother, and this, not from withered
> features, for her skin was too full of fat to permit its contracting in to wrin-
> kles; but from her want of teeth, and weather-beaten appearance in general,
> and from a kind of notion that ran in my head, that nothing could have

commenced at the size of infancy and reached her present bulk in less than 35 or 40 years; and, in short, I was not all pleased with her.[91]

Most men as repulsed as Lincoln was by this woman would have promptly shut down any prospect of marriage with her. But not Lincoln, who conceded, "I had told her sister that I would take her for better or for worse" and so "at once I determined to consider her my wife." Not the most romantic way to kick off a marriage, but typical of a man who did not see much hope in finding romance in marriage to any woman. Lincoln recalled, "I mustered my resolution and made the proposal to her direct."[92] To his great shock and relief, Mary Owens sensed his ambivalence and rejected his halfhearted proposal.

Abe had an even harder time going through with his proposal to another Kentuckian, Mary Todd. They had a stormy union from the beginning: she broke up with him and reconsidered, he dumped her and had second thoughts. At one point, he tried breaking off their engagement in a letter that he asked a friend to deliver. The 34-year-old Lincoln reluctantly reconsidered dumping Mary, and after three years of on-again, off-again drama, Mary and Abe got hitched. On the day of their marriage ceremony, Lincoln lamented to a friend, James H. Matheny, "Jim, I shall have to marry that girl." Matheny recalled that at the wedding "Lincoln looked and acted as if he was going to the slaughter" and that "Lincoln often told him directly and indirectly that he was driven into the marriage."[93]

Married life did not bring Mary much happiness either. One of the Lincolns' neighbors in Springfield said Mary "was seen frequently to drive him from the house with a broomstick." Another time Mary chased Abe around the backyard wielding a butcher knife.[94] She also seemed to enjoy humiliating her husband in public even when he was president. "Mrs. Lincoln repeatedly attacked her husband in the presence of officers," one army officer recalled. "He bore it as Christ might have done with an expression of pain and sadness that cut one to the heart, but with supreme calmness and dignity. He called her 'mother,' with his oldtime plainness. He pleaded with eyes and tones, till she turned on him like a tigress and then he walked away hiding that noble ugly face so that we might not catch the full expression of its misery."[95] A White House steward observed the First Lady assaulting the president: "Struck him hard—damned him—cursed him."[96] Mary also was a shopaholic whose obsessive shopping sprees burdened her husband with massive bills and became a national scandal when he was president.

Nine months after their wedding, Mary gave birth to their first child, so Abe's reluctance to commence their marriage did not entail a reluctance to consummate it. Still, plenty of closeted men have gotten married and fathered children, so the question remains, was Lincoln one of them? He certainly would not be the only closeted homosexual married to an irate, shopaholic wife.

Looking beyond Lincoln's ever-present beard—as in a wife who disguises the fact that her husband is in the closet—it is worth examining the more telling fact that Abe liked to sleep with men. At 22, Lincoln moved to New Salem, Illinois, where he met 19-year-old Billy Greene in 1831. Greene recalled that the moment he laid eyes on young Abe, he noted that "his thighs were as perfect as a human being could be."[97] Greene tutored the uneducated Lincoln in grammar and they also shared a cot so narrow, according to Greene, "when one turned over the other had to do likewise."[98]

After being admitted to the bar in 1837, the 28-year-old Lincoln moved to Springfield, the Illinois state capital. On his first day in town he met a handsome 23-year-old named Joshua Speed, who immediately invited the tall stranger to share his bed. Lincoln's law partner and first biographer, William Herndon, wrote that Speed became "the only intimate friend that Lincoln ever had" and that Lincoln "loved this man more than anyone dead or living" not excepting Mary Todd.[99] Speed himself said "no two men were ever more intimate."[100] Lincoln and Speed shared everything with each other over the next four years, including a bed.

Sharing beds was common in the nineteenth century, particularly on the frontier where beds were a luxury. Speed, however, was not poor. He was a store owner and an heir to a Kentucky plantation tilled by 70 slaves. Although Lincoln was a penniless lawyer and state legislator when he arrived in Springfield, the law practice he started was soon thriving, and he was more than able to afford his own lodging.[101] Lincoln and Speed simply liked to sleep together. As Lincoln biographer Carl Sandburg poetically wrote, "Providence had given these two men streaks of lavender, spots soft as May violets."[102]

After four years of living together, in January 1841 Speed suddenly announced he was moving to Kentucky. Lincoln immediately fell into a deep depression that left him bedridden and unable to attend legislative sessions. Speed later recalled, "Lincoln went Crazy—had to remove razors from his room—take away all knives and other such things—&c—it was terrible."[103] A suicidal Lincoln told Speed he was not afraid of death and would be more than willing to die except for the fact "that he had done nothing to make any human being remember that he had lived."[104] Lincoln described his own depression over Speed's departure in a letter to his law partner: "I am now the most miserable man living. If what I feel were equally distributed to the whole human family, there would not be one cheerful face on the earth. Whether I shall even be better I cannot tell; I awfully for[e]bode I shall not. To remain as I am is impossible; I must die or be better."[105] A concerned friend wrote, "Poor L! How the mighty have fallen! He was confined for about a week, but though he now appears again he is reduced and emaciated in appearance and seems scarcely to possess strength enough to speak above a whisper. His case at present is truly deplorable but what prospect there may be for ultimate relief I cannot pretend to say!"[106] A less polite friend said Lincoln "went Crazy as a Loon."[107] The local newspaper even joked about Lincoln's "indisposition."[108] After seven months of misery, Lincoln visited Speed in Kentucky, where he spent a month being nursed back to health.

Speed meanwhile was having his own emotional breakdown. He proposed to a woman shortly after moving to Kentucky, and over subsequent months he and Lincoln exchanged letters regarding both men's anxiety about getting married. Lincoln advised him, "If you went through the ceremony calmly, or even with sufficient composure not to excite alarm in anyone present, you are safe, beyond question."[109] The main object of Speed's anxiety was not the wedding ceremony but the wedding night.[110] The morning after his first night with the woman he finally married, in 1842, Speed sent Lincoln a report. Lincoln immediately wrote back, "I opened the letter with intense anxiety and trepidation; so much that although it turned out better than I expected, I have hardly yet at the distance of ten hours become calm. . . . You say that something *indescribably horrible and alarming still haunts you*. . . . Again you say you much fear that the Elysium of which you have dreamed so much is never to be realized."[111] Why were these men so fretful about Speed's wedding night? Historian Jonathan Ned Katz speculates that either the 30-something bachelors were virgins or their prior sexual experiences were limited to prostitutes. Katz writes, "Neither had experienced intercourse with a woman he considered 'good' and both seem to have dreaded the opportunity. . . . Far from yearning for sexual intercourse with a good woman, both men seemed deeply anxious about their ability to complete such copulation—no instinctual heterosexual desire here."[112] But there's more to this situation than performance anxiety.

After a few months of marriage, Speed assured Lincoln that he had become more comfortable with his wife. Lincoln wrote back, "That you are happier now than you ever were the day you married I well know, for otherwise *you could not be living.*" Lincoln then asked the big question: "Are you now in Feeling as well as judgment glad that you are married as you are? From anybody but me this would be an imprudent question . . . but I know you will pardon it in me. Please answer it quickly, as I feel impatient to know. *Yours Forever, Lincoln.*"[113] Lincoln was impatient to learn if Speed was still depressed and anxious about being married, because he was considering proposing to Mary Todd. Speed's response must have reassured him because shortly thereafter Lincoln popped the question.

Historians acknowledge Lincoln's indifference to girls as a youth, his extended bachelorhood, his intimate relationship with Speed, and his problematic dealings with his wife. But most historians still refuse to even entertain the possibility that Lincoln was gay. To explain how a straight man could remain unmarried until the age of 34 without entering a single significant female relationship, they point to a discredited story involving Ann Rutledge, who died during her supposed engagement to Lincoln.[114] Just as in the story of Buchanan and Anne Coleman, Lincoln was allegedly so emotionally crushed by the loss of his first soul mate that he could not bear to look for another.

Some historians also suggest that Lincoln turned to prostitutes for sex on the basis of a story reported by William Herndon. One of Abe's old friends told Herndon that one day a 30-year-old Lincoln announced he was "desirous to have a *little*" and asked, "Do you know where I can get *some?*" The friend told Abe about a prostitute he had frequented. Lincoln went to her house and "told his business and the girl, after some protestations, agreed to satisfy him." According to Abe's friend, "Things went on right—Lincoln and the girl stript off and went to bed." But before "any thing was done," Lincoln asked, "How much do you charge?" "Five dollars, Mr. Lincoln," said the girl. When Abe admitted, "I've only got $3," the girl assured him, "I'll trust you, Mr. Lincoln, for $2." Lincoln thought a moment and said, "I do not wish to go on credit—I'm poor & I don't know where my next dollar will come from and I cannot afford to Cheat you." He then got up out of bed, buttoned up his pants and offered the girl the $3.00, which she refused, saying, "Mr. Lincoln—You are the most Conscientious man I ever saw."[115] This story sounds like an R-rated version of George Washington chopping down the cherry tree. Yet this spurious tale is often presented as proof that Lincoln liked girls after all. And no one questions the source: the Lincoln friend who told Herndon the story about Honest Abe and the prostitute was Joshua Speed.

O CAPTAIN! MY CAPTAIN!

Marriage did not stop Lincoln from sleeping with men even when he was president. During the summer of 1862, Lincoln enjoyed spending time relaxing with the soldiers who guarded him at his presidential retreat on the grounds of a veterans' hospital about a mile and a half north of the White House. A rugged-looking, bearded guard attracted Lincoln's attention, and one Sunday morning the 53-year-old president requested an audience with the soldier.[116] The object of Lincoln's interest was 44-year-old Captain David Derickson of the 150th Pennsylvania Volunteers—nicknamed the Bucktail Brigade because of the fur pieces that decorated their caps. The president asked Derickson to ride along with him on his commute to the White House the next day, and according to Derickson, he and Lincoln spent every day together for the next four months.[117] They attended church and the theater together and, even though Derickson was a junior officer, Lincoln invited him to cabinet meetings. Much to the annoyance and envy of high-ranking officials, Derickson was free to drop by the president's office unannounced.[118] Lincoln also took Derickson with him to inspect the troops after the pivotal battle of Antietam. Famed war photographer Matthew Brady captured the inspection tour in a photo of the presidential entourage that showed Derickson standing off to Lincoln's right.

When the War Department ordered Derickson's unit to go to the front, Lincoln countermanded the order, saying that the unit "are very agreeable to me; and while it is deemed proper for any guard to remain, none would be more satisfactory to me than Capt. D. and his company."[119] Even Lincoln found his bro-mance with Capt. D. a little awkward and joked about it "with a twinkle in his eye," saying, "the captain and I are getting quite thick."[120] Thick indeed, because there was something else they did regularly together.

Virginia Woodbury Fox, daughter of a Supreme Court justice and the wife of an assistant secretary of the navy noted in her diary on November 16, 1862: "Tish says, 'there is a Bucktail soldier here devoted to the President, drives with him and when Mrs. L. is not home, sleeps with him.' What stuff!"[121] Preeminent Lincoln scholar David Herbert Donald dismisses the significance of Fox's comment: "Mrs. Fox's diary entry reports a rumor; obviously neither she nor her friend had any first hand evidence."[122] Donald is right; this rumor does not prove anything. But Fox's reaction to the rumor is significant. She is shocked by the thought of these men sleeping together "when Mrs. L. is not home." That her friend Tish and others were gossiping about Lincoln and Derickson indicates that people in the nineteenth century did not think it was normal for two men of means to share a bed. To Fox and her friends such intimacy between men was scandalous.

Although Donald dismisses Fox's diary entry, the Lincoln scholar has greater difficulty discounting a similar story found in an 1895 history of Derickson's regiment. Its author was Thomas Chamberlin, who was Derickson's immediate commanding officer and who had firsthand knowledge of Lincoln's relationship with Derickson. Chamberlin wrote, "Captain Derickson in particular advanced so far in the president's confidence and esteem, that—in Mrs. Lincoln's absence—he frequently spent the night at his cottage, sleeping in the same bed with him, and it is said, making use of his Excellency's nightshirt!"[123] Donald confirms that Chamberlin was an "honorable man" and that his dry regimental history is not filled with gossip. Donald also notes that no member of Derickson's regiment expressed objection to Chamberlin's story, including Derickson's son who served under his father during the summer of 1862. So what does Donald make of Chamberlin's account? "I think it is hardly surprising that [Lincoln] may on occasion have asked the congenial captain to share his bed; in those days, it was not unusual for men to sleep together."[124] Donald ignores the fact that the rumor of Derickson sleeping with the president was sensational to Virginia Fox and her friend Tish, "What stuff!"[125] The historian Mark Epstein also denies a sexual dimension to their relationship: "These rumors seem more sensational now than they did in 1862 when it meant little more for men to share a bed than that they had only one bed, or they were cold, or they fell asleep while they were talking."[126] Epstein ignores the fact that Lincoln's summer retreat was a mansion with plenty of beds, that Derickson and Lincoln could not have been "cold" in the Washington, DC, summer, and that if they had somehow fallen asleep in bed together "while they were talking," then they had been talking in bed.

Lincoln's summer retreat is now a museum, and the bedroom where Lincoln and Derickson flouted social convention is now known as the Emancipation Room. In this room during the summer of 1862 Lincoln began writing the Emancipation Proclamation, which transformed the aim of the Civil War from the preservation of the Union to the liberation of millions. A person did not have to be gay to see the injustice of slavery and Lincoln was mainly motivated to issue the Emancipation Proclamation by military and political exigencies. But it is reasonable to assume that a man who felt trapped by the sexual and social mores of his time would have possessed an added sympathy for the enslaved.

So on the basis of all the evidence, was Abraham Lincoln gay or, in the terms of his day, a "sodomite" or "bugger"? We cannot definitively say. He seems to have enjoyed sleeping with men, but there is no record of him having sexual relations with them. What Abe and his sleep partners did in the sack is left to our imagination. We have only circumstantial evidence about his sexuality, such as Lincoln's difficulties connecting with women and his letters to Speed regarding both men's deep anxiety about Speed's wedding night. Lincoln does seem to have been anxious about having sex with women, and society's marital ideal certainly did not match his true personal desires. Repressed sexual desire certainly could explain Lincoln's lifelong bouts with depression along with his strange attraction to death.

During the war, Lincoln remained good friends with the slave-owning Joshua Speed. On one of Speed's visits to the White House in late 1862 Lincoln brought up the Emancipation Proclamation that he had issued a few months before. Speed later recalled that although Lincoln knew his friend opposed the proclamation, he "seemed to treat it as certain that I would recognize the wisdom of the act when I should see the harvest of good we would glean from it."[127] Lincoln then began reminiscing about how Speed's abrupt departure from Springfield back in 1841 threw him into such a deep depression that the only thing preventing him from suicide was a desire to "link his name with something that would redound to the interest of his fellow man." Speed recalled that Lincoln then said "I believe in this measure [meaning his proclamation] my fondest hopes will be realized."[128] Through the Emancipation Proclamation, Lincoln finally achieved his lifelong wish to make a historic contribution to humanity.

Six hundred thousand of our fellow Americans did not die in the Civil War because of sex. The Civil War was fought over slavery and secession. But we can certainly say that sex played a key role in how the war originated. Without Peggy Eaton's sex scandal, Andrew Jackson would not have destroyed John C. Calhoun's hopes of becoming president and turned him into a nullification firebrand and the father of Southern secession. If James Buchanan had not fallen in love with an Alabama slave owner, the secession movement would not have had such an encouraging dupe in the White House in 1860. And if Lincoln hadn't been so sexually complicated, he might not have become the Great Emancipator.

CHAPTER THREE

AFFAIRS OF STATE

Woodrow Wilson and his successor Warren G. Harding were two presidents who were definitely not gay. Reporters in the 1920s joked that the only difference between them was that Harding frequented whorehouses in Columbus, Ohio, while Wilson preferred fancy bordellos in Paris.[1] Actually these two did not agree on much. Wilson was a Progressive Era Democrat who oversaw a massive expansion of federal economic regulations, while Harding reinstituted a laissez-faire approach to big business. Wilson attempted to revamp the international order with his League of Nations; Harding returned the United States to an isolationist foreign policy. The two men did, however, have one thing in common—both hid sexual secrets whose revelation could have dashed their presidential hopes and rendered them insignificant footnotes of history. Fortunately for these presidential lotharios, American journalists in the early twentieth century had adopted a code of professional ethics that prohibited reporting on the sex lives of politicians. Reporters were free to joke among themselves about Wilson's and Harding's affairs, but they could not write about them.

PECK'S BAD BOY

Woodrow Wilson might have resembled a prim Sunday school teacher or, by his own description, "a rare bookworm . . . incapable of sentiment, smileless and given over to dead love."[2] But underneath his bowtie and button-down shirt lurked a raging libido. White House usher Ike Hoover attested that President Wilson was "no mean man in love-making when once the germ . . . found its resting place."[3] Wilson himself once bragged about his own "great capacity for loving the gentle sex."[4] Two women who were on the receiving end of Wilson's "great capacity" would shape the course of history.

Born the son of a Presbyterian preacher in 1856, Wilson grew up in Virginia with a passion for preaching to the masses. But instead of the pulpit, he was called to the college lectern and quickly worked his way up the academic ladder from professor at a women's college to president of Princeton University. With the same messianic fervor that would later guide his work as commander in chief, he fought epic battles against the Princeton faculty, administrators and students over everything from eliminating the college's exclusive dining clubs to building a graduate program. To escape the stress, in 1907 he embarked on a fateful monthlong vacation to Bermuda without his wife Ellen.

Over solitary meals in the hotel restaurant, the 50-year-old Wilson amused himself by casually watching the other diners. One evening he noticed a slender, elegant woman who stirred his heartstrings; he dubbed her "My Lady." Whenever she entered the restaurant he immediately rearranged his seat so he could gaze on her while he ate. The object of Wilson's infatuation was Mary Allen Hulbert Peck, a glamorous 44-year-old socialite, recently separated and known in Bermuda social circles for her "frank courting of susceptible males." Wilson's cousin described her as a "seductive" woman with an "absorbing way of listening to the words of wisdom uttered by a man."[5] One Bermudan society lady called Peck "a bewitching woman, and a snare for men folk," while another noticed "a little restless look of unfulfilment about her eyes and mouth that gave grounds for romantic speculation."[6] Dressed in fashionable shirtwaist tops tightly nipped around her corseted waist, Peck was a grand departure from Wilson's wife, who was described as "short, round-faced, round pompadoured, red-cheeked and not so becomingly dressed."[7] Seeing Peck alone in the lobby one afternoon, Wilson impulsively wrangled a dinner date. For the rest of the vacation, they dined together and took long walks on the beach every day, but Wilson never mentioned Peck in his letters to his wife back home.[8]

The next year he returned to Bermuda, again without Ellen, and as soon as the ship docked he rushed to see "my precious one, my beloved Mary."[9] Wilson later recalled their "delectable walks to the South Shore when you were like a gay child of nature, released into its native element, and I felt every quickened impulse of the blood communicated to me."[10] He credited Peck with delivering him from "all the abominable self-consciousness that has been my bane all my life and felt perfectly at ease, happily myself, released from bonds to enjoy the full freedom of my mind."[11] During long walks on the beach, Wilson counseled Peck on her marriage and advised her to seek a divorce. She, in turn, told him to follow his heart, get out of academia and get into politics.[12] Sitting on the beach, Wilson told Peck he would take her advice with his eye on the White House. But he predicted, "The next president of the United States would have a task so difficult as to be heartbreaking and that I'd probably sacrifice my life to it if I were elected."[13] Wilson's words would prove prophetic.

Wilson quit Princeton and successfully ran for governor of New Jersey in 1910. The governor exchanged letters with Peck nearly every week and secretly visited her in New York.[14] In one letter, Wilson wrote, "God was very good to me to send me such a friend, so perfectly satisfying and delightful, so delectable." Wilson later admitted to being "deeply ashamed and repentant" about his relationship with Peck, which he later characterized as "a passage of folly and gross impertinence, long ago loathed and repented of."[15] Rumors about the governor's affair soon spread, and Wilson acquired the nickname "Peck's Bad Boy."[16]

Ellen Wilson suspected there was something between her husband and Peck, and she told her trusted physician, Dr. Carey Grayson, that the "Peck affair" was the "only unhappiness her husband had ever given her."[17] Ellen seems to have confronted Woodrow about the affair in letters that he destroyed.[18] Regarding the affair, Wilson later wrote that he "knew and made explicit what it did not mean. [His wife], too, knew and understood and has forgiven."[19] During Wilson's presidential run in 1912, journalist David Lawrence recalled that rumors involving Wilson and Peck were "whispered about the corridors of the Democratic National convention."[20] At one point, Wilson's rival, House Speaker Champ Clarke, seemed to be winning the delegate count and Wilson's advisors suggested he withdraw his name. But Ellen insisted they continue to fight, and in the end the Democrats nominated Peck's Bad Boy for president.[21]

As the Democratic nominee, Wilson faced off against the incumbent, Republican William Howard Taft, and former Republican president Theodore Roosevelt, who ran under the newly created Progressive, or Bull Moose, Party. Two Princeton trustees who hated Wilson tried to sabotage his campaign by hiring detectives to shadow him and Peck. Journalists descended on Princeton to see if there was anything to the rumors of the affair. One reporter asked Professor William Magie for his reaction to the story that Wilson and Peck were seen dragging a plush rug to a secluded Bermuda beach screened by bushes. The sardonic professor replied, "Personally, I think he read her poetry."[22]

Three months before Election Day, Wilson heard that one of his letters to Peck had been shown to a judge in connection to her divorce proceeding. In a panic he told Peck, "No matter how completely discredited later, [the letter would] just at this juncture ruin me utterly, and all connected with me. . . . The mere breath of such a thing would, of course, put an end to my candidacy and to my career. It is too deep an iniquity for words."[23] Wilson did not have to worry. Someone offered President Taft's campaign "a sheaf of letters" from Wilson to Peck, but the Republicans declined to accept them. Roosevelt's campaign advisors wanted to publicize the Peck affair, but the Bull Moose would not stoop to slander. "What's more it won't work, those letters would be entirely unconvincing," Roosevelt insisted. "Nothing, no evidence would ever make the American people believe that a man like Woodrow Wilson, cast so perfectly as the apothecary's clerk, could ever play Romeo!"[24] Amazingly, neither Wilson's opponents nor the press printed a word about the Peck affair. On Election Day, Taft and Roosevelt split the Republican base and Wilson won the White House with 42 percent of the vote.

MA, MA, WHERE'S MY PA!

The hands-off approach taken by Taft, Roosevelt and the press to Wilson's dalliance marked a major change in American politics. In the nineteenth century, scuttlebutt about the sex lives of presidential candidates filled America's newspapers and was routinely used by both parties to discredit opposition candidates. As a young man, Wilson had witnessed a presidential candidate's sex life become the dominant issue of the 1884 campaign. A minister started the controversy when he informed the *Buffalo Evening Telegraph* that the Democratic nominee, Grover Cleveland, was "guilty of habitual immoralities with women," one of whom was a "beautiful, virtuous, and intelligent young lady" named Maria Halpin.[25] The minister claimed that when Cleveland was a lawyer in Buffalo he "won her confidence and seduced her" and that when she became pregnant, he not only reneged on his promise to marry the poor salesgirl but "employed two detectives and a doctor of bad repute to spirit the woman away and dispose of the child."[26]

The Republican Party pushed the Halpin story to undermine Cleveland's image as an honest, faithful statesman. Cleveland responded to the accusation by openly admitting he had had a fling with Halpin and halfway admitting he had fathered a child with her. "Whatever you do," he ordered his campaign operatives, "tell the truth."[27] The truth was complicated. Although Cleveland paid Halpin child support, he did not know if he was the father, because she was also sleeping with his friend and law partner, Oscar Folsom. Halpin did not know which man was the father either, and so she named her son Oscar Folsom Cleveland.

Newspapers throughout the nation embraced the Halpin story. One newspaper claimed Cleveland's "election would argue a low state of morals among the people, and be a burning shame and never-to-be-forgotten disgrace to the nation. No man with such a private character as is shown in respect to him is fit to fill any office in the gift of the people."[28] A famous political cartoon by Frank Beard depicted a portly Cleveland stomping his feet in frustration while Halpin holds a baby screaming, "I want my Pa!"[29] Republican political rallies featured operatives pushing baby carriages and chanting, "Ma, Ma, where's my Pa?" Democrats retaliated by circulating a rumor that the Republican nominee James Blaine had a child with his wife just three months after they were married. The Democratic newspaper the *Indianapolis Sentinel* declared, "There is hardly an intelligent man in the country who has not heard that James G. Blaine betrayed the girl whom he married and then only married her at the muzzle of a shotgun."[30]

Despite all the charges and countercharges, Cleveland's most effective weapon was honesty. The voters appreciated his forthright admission of paternity and rewarded him with the White House that November. Joyous Democrats across the nation could be heard chanting, "Ma, Ma, where's my Pa? . . . Gone to the White House, ha, ha, ha!"

Given how quickly the Cleveland sex scandal became such a major issue in the 1884 campaign, why, just a few decades later, did the Peck affair not spark a similar brouhaha? In the intervening decades a sea change had occurred in how journalists approached the private lives of politicians. While nineteenth-century newspapers were openly affiliated with political parties, early twentieth-century news publications began to pride themselves on independence and objectivity. Throughout the 1910s and 1920s nearly every guide to professional newspaper practice frowned on exposing the private lives of politicians. The American Society of Newspaper Editors declared in 1923, "A newspaper should not publish unofficial charges affecting reputation or moral character without opportunity given to the accused to be heard." Furthermore, "a newspaper should not invade private rights or feelings without sure warrant of public right as distinguished from public curiosity."[31]

Journalists began to conceive of themselves as gatekeepers responsible for distinguishing between, in Walter Lippmann's words, "giving the public what it wants" and "giving the public what it should have."[32] George Harvey, editor of *Harper's Weekly,* told an audience at Yale University in 1908, "To protect the people from themselves, to point out their errors and to urge rectification, is the true mission of journalism." Harvey congratulated his fellow journalists for no longer exposing the private lives of politicians: "The asperities of to-day seem innocuous when compared with those of the good old times . . . when [John] Jay was anathematized as a scoundrel and Jefferson as an atheist and a satyr."[33] Unlike nineteenth-century newspapermen, journalists in Wilson's day had become part of the establishment and had assumed the tasks of controlling the mobbish emotions of the masses and of shielding the private lives of America's leaders from the public eye.

Politicians in the twentieth century also started to take legal action to suppress journalists still willing to expose political sex scandals. The California legislature in 1900 banned the publication of "any caricature of any person residing in this state, which caricature will in any manner reflect upon

the honor, integrity, manhood, virtue, reputation, or business or political motives of the person so caricatured, or which tends to expose the individual so
caricatured to public hatred, ridicule, or contempt."[34] Similar statutes were
passed in New York in 1897, Pennsylvania in 1903, Indiana in 1913, and Alabama in 1915. The sponsor of the Pennsylvania law argued that "the Com-
monwealth is interested that those who render her service should be treated
with deference and respect, so that when they go forth in performance of her
functions those to whom they are sent may feel that they are vested with authority."[35] By the time Wilson ran for president, journalists were beholden to
professional standards and laws that forced them to ignore the sexual peccadilloes of politicians.[36]

LOVE AND WAR

While the outbreak of World War I in August 1914 sent Europe into the
trenches, President Wilson was hit by a terrible tragedy of his own. On August 6, First Lady Ellen Wilson died of an incurable kidney ailment. Wilson
was crushed but didn't take long to rebound. Just a few months later, he was
courting a new girlfriend. "How I love to make love to you!" the president
wrote to Edith Galt, whom he called his "delectable comrade" and "dear chum
of my mind and heart."[37]

White House physician Dr. Carey Grayson was responsible for intro-
ducing Wilson to his new love interest. Grayson had gained the president's
confidence while treating Ellen, and after her death he focused on helping
Wilson overcome his deep depression. Grayson described the president's condition to his friend Edith Galt: "When I went in to see him, tears were
streaming down his face. It was a heart-breaking scene. A sadder picture no
one could imagine."[38] Relief was soon on its way in the form of love. Not
long after Grayson described the president's misery to his lady friend, he took
Wilson out for a drive around DuPont Circle, where they happened to see
Edith. Wilson perked up and asked, "Who is that beautiful woman?"[39]

At five foot nine, with black hair, deep blue eyes, and a Rubenesque figure, Edith traced her ancestry all the way back to colonial Virginia and was
related to Thomas Jefferson, Martha Washington and Pocahontas. She had
a talent for marrying well. Her first husband, Norman Galt, owned the most

opulent jewelry store in Washington, DC, and when he died she inherited a fortune.

Dr. Grayson had introduced the 42-year-old widow to Wilson's cousin Helen Bones. After the two women took a walk in Rock Creek Park one day in March 1915, Bones invited her back to the White House. At first Edith declined: "I couldn't do that. My shoes are a sight and I should be taken for a tramp."[40] Helen assured her that Wilson was out golfing with Grayson, but when they arrived at the White House they bumped into the smitten president, who insisted that they all have tea together. Edith later wrote, "This was the accidental meeting which carried out the old adage of 'Turn a corner and meet your fate.'"[41] White House usher Ike Hoover observed that the "impressive widow" entered Wilson's orbit under circumstances "most natural and yet no doubt with intentions that might lead to anywhere." By the end of the evening Wilson was love struck and, according to Hoover, "the ice was broken and from that time on it was a continuous automobile ride for this lady."[42]

Over the next month, Wilson visited Edith so often the Secret Service assigned her a code name, "Grandma." Secret Service agent Edmund Starling, who frequently escorted Wilson to Edith's house, said the president behaved as though a young boy in love and sometimes did a little jig after leaving her home. One night, Wilson departed Edith's house and was seen skipping through the streets of Washington singing, "Oh you beautiful doll, you great big beautiful doll!" Starling was ordered to keep the president in his sight at all times and had to resist the desire to look away when Wilson and Edith canoodled during their walks in Rock Creek Park.[43] A scandalized White House staff still loyal to Ellen began carping about "the President and Pocahontas."[44]

Within weeks of meeting Edith, Wilson was pouring his heart out: "I need you. I need you as a boy needs his sweetheart and a strong man his helpmate and heart's comrade." He confessed to Edith that he loved her "with a sort of fierce devotion compounded of every masculine force in me."[45] When she was away he wrote of his "unutterable longings and delights" and how he lay awake in his bed pretending to whisper endearments to her although his arms were empty.[46] He also complained that in her absence his lips "can speak nothing worthwhile all day long for lack of your kisses."[47] While Wilson was enraptured by Edith's kisses, she was turned on by his power: "Much as I love your delicious love letters, I believe I enjoy even more the ones in which you tell me what you are working on, for then, I feel that I am sharing your work and being taken in to partnership, as it were." She reminded the president, "Please don't forget to tell me about the Democratic Committee Matter when we are together."[48]

The press soon began to speculate on the relationship. *Town Topics* reported on August 5, 1915, that "Mrs. Galt's home is in a smart quarter of the city. It has an attractive interior and she entertains in good style. A frequent guest at her board is the president, who wisely ignored the tradition that the Chief Executive should not visit private houses and goes unannounced wherever and to whoever he pleases to the confusion of his guards."[49] The *Washington Post* created a stir when it reported that on one of their theater dates "rather than paying attention to the play the President spent the evening entering Mrs. Galt." The *Post* meant to print "entertaining." Dr. Sigmund Freud would have loved that slip and could have cited it in his essay "Thoughts for the Times on War and Death" (1915), which blamed World War I on subconscious sexual repression.[50]

When Edith expressed concern about the press coverage, Wilson assured her, "If we keep within bounds, as we shall, and give them no proofs that they can make use of, we can and should ignore them." Wilson understood that the press of his day, unlike previous eras, would not openly question the propriety of a president's relationship. And anyway, he explained to her, far from being a distraction from his duties, their relationship was a "matter of efficiency" for his work as president. "I am absolutely dependent on intimate love for the right and free and most effective use of my powers and I know by experience what it costs my work to do without. And so we are justified in taking risks."[51] Although the press coverage of the president's relationship with Edith was benign, much of the public was horrified by the president's behavior so soon after his wife's death. Rumors and innuendo about the couple spread throughout the country, including a suggestion that Ellen Wilson died of a broken heart over Wilson's affair with Edith. Wilson impulsively decided to counter the gossip by making their relationship official. After knowing Edith for less than two months, Wilson asked for her hand in marriage on the south portico of the White House. The president's proposal shocked Edith, and much to his disappointment and distress, she said she needed to think about it.

While the 58-year-old president pursued his new flame like a young man in the heat of passion, the deadliest war in human history was raging in Europe. The British blockaded Germany and began hiding weapons shipments on passenger liners departing from America. The Germans countered by unleashing their U-boats against British passenger liners. Although Wilson was committed to keeping the United States neutral, every day brought news that threatened to drag America into the war. The president turned to Edith, more than anyone, for support.

On May 2, 1915, despite Germany's warnings to Americans not to travel on British passenger liners, 1,924 people departed New York on the *Lusitania,* bound for Liverpool and with a secret cargo of 173 tons of ammunition and shrapnel shells. Four days later, a German U-boat torpedoed the *Lusitania,* the largest ship afloat, killing 1,198 passengers, including 128 Americans. News of the attack put Wilson under intense pressure to declare war. But even in the midst of a major national security crisis, he was not distracted from his romance.

After the *Lusitania* sank, Wilson isolated himself for three days. When he emerged, he visited Edith briefly and then hopped on a train to Philadelphia to make his first public statement on the crisis. In his speech Wilson urged his fellow Americans to resist the knee-jerk desire to retaliate: "The example of America must be the example not merely of peace because it will not fight, but of peace because peace is the elevating and healing influence in the world and strife is not." Then came his historic words: "There is such a thing as a man being too proud to fight. There is such a thing as a nation being so right that it does not have to convince others by force that it is right."[52] Wilson's speech on the need for the United States to avoid being drawn into the horrors of World War I has gone down in history as one of the greatest speeches ever given by a president. But he had not planned on saying those legendary lines. He later told Edith that, after seeing her that day, he was in such a whirl of distraction he did not know if he was in Philadelphia or New York and that when he stood to speak he did not know what he was going to say or what he had said once he sat down. The infatuated pres-

ident was just winging it. "It must have been because love had complete pos-
session of me," Wilson later gushed to Edith. "I knew that I had left the
speech in your hands and that you needed me as I needed you."[53]

The next day, Wilson composed a letter to Germany demanding that
they restrain their U-boats. But his thoughts kept returning to Edith: "And
oh I have needed you tonight, my Sweet Edith! What a touch of your hand
and a look into your eyes would have meant to me of strength and steadfast-
ness as I made the final decision as to what I should say to Germany. You
must have felt it. You must have heard the cry of my heart to you and known
in every fiber of you that I needed you."[54]

On May 28, 1915, Wilson received Germany's response to his demand.
Not only did the Germans defend the sinking of the *Lusitania,* they refused
to curb their U-boat attacks. Wilson knew his next letter to Germany could
determine the fate of millions. Either he could challenge the kaiser's position
and risk a rupture in diplomatic relations or he could take a conciliatory tone
that would invite more U-boat attacks. Either option could push America to
the brink of war. Despite this monumental dilemma, Wilson was consumed
by Edith's refusal to accept his marriage proposal. He canceled all his ap-
pointments on May 28, including a cabinet meeting and a get-together with
newly elected senator Warren G. Harding. He then retreated to his bedroom
where he wrote, not to the kaiser, but to Edith: "For God's sake try to find out
whether you really love me or not." Wilson reminded her that he was president: "I need strength and certainty for the daily task and . . . I cannot walk
upon quicksand." In spite of the president's desperation, Edith still refused to
accept his marriage proposal. But she did pledge her love, and the president
was temporarily satisfied. After reading Edith's declaration of love, Wilson
sighed, "After many hours of inexplicable illness, deep depression and exqui-
site suffering, the light had dawned."[55]

Having dealt with Edith, Wilson could now deal with the kaiser. He
wrote Edith, "When I see your eyes alert tonight with the sweetest, holiest
thing in all the world, and hold you close in my arms and kiss you, with
pledges as deep as my soul, I shall be made fit for that [responding to the
Germans] and more."[56] He told Edith that while he organized his thoughts
on his letter to the kaiser, he could not stop thinking about her "gentle caresses
and the precious kisses."[57] Wilson invited his sweetheart to read a draft of

the letter. She told him to revise it: "There was nothing of you, yourself, in it and therefore it seemed flat and lacking color . . . you must put some little of yourself in it."[58] Wilson worked late into the night and sent Edith a second draft with his assurance that he had brought it nearer to her standard. After reading the second draft, Edith gave the president the green light: "I am quite content with the paper as it now stands."[59]

Edith would later tell Wilson, "I am always with you and love the way you put one dear hand on mine, while with the other you turn the pages of history."[60] She also turned the pages of history. She edited his diplomatic letters to Germany, and the president sent her official documents as if she were a cabinet member. Wilson assured her, "Whatever is mine is yours, knowledge of *affairs of state* not excepted, and that without reserve, except that, as you know, there may be a few things that it would not be wise or prudent to commit to writing."[61] Wilson called their relationship a "whole divine partnership transforming everything, the constitution of the United States itself included."[62]

Secretary of State William Jennings Bryan was furious when he read the letter to Germany that Edith and Wilson had composed. Bryan thought the letter was too harsh and wanted a more evenhanded approach to the European conflict. Bryan threatened to resign on June 7, 1915, but that day Wilson told Edith he was more disturbed by *her* news that she had invited a friend to move in with her. Wilson whimpered that the new housemate would monopolize her attention "to the inevitable exclusion of the man who loves you as, I believe, few women were ever loved before."[63] Edith's friend did not move in, but Bryan did resign.

"Hurrah! Old Bryan is out!" Edith gloated. "I could shout and sing that at last the world will know just what he is." When Edith read Wilson's conciliatory note accepting Bryan's resignation she complained that it was "much too nice. . . . Why was I not allowed to see it before publication?"[64] Wilson loved her fierce loyalty: "My how I like you, Edith, my incomparable Darling. And how you can hate, too. Whew!"[65] When Edith heard that Henry Ford planned to give Bryan $10 million to finance a peacemaking expedition to Europe, she told Wilson that the former secretary of state's "impertinence passes understanding, and that should he embark on even an American vessel for Europe and get blown up" she would award "our highest commendation and decoration to the commander of the submarine."[66]

Wilson worked with Edith on another letter to Germany in July 1915, informing the kaiser that any further U-boat attacks would be regarded as "deliberately unfriendly."[67] Wilson told Edith this letter was "so direct and emphatic and uncompromising" that unless Germany relented it would signify a final departure from neutrality.[68] Although America was now on the edge of war, the president's thoughts once again returned to love. On the same day that he worked on a final draft of the pivotal letter to the kaiser he wrote Edith, assuring her that his message went along the lines they had discussed and then pronounced, "You match and satisfy every part of me, grave or gay, of the mind or of the heart,—the man of letters, the man of affairs, the boy, the poet, the lover."[69] But he remained frustrated that Edith still had not accepted his proposal.

As if Wilson needed another distraction from the *Lusitania* crisis that summer, Mary Peck asked him to bail out her indebted son by buying the mortgages on some shabby properties in California. Wilson agreed and sent her son a check for $7,500 ($165,000 today). This act of generosity would come back to haunt the president and Edith.[70]

Wilson's closest advisor, Colonel Edward House, resented the president's becoming so engrossed in Edith that he relied on her advice instead of his.[71] Dr. Grayson complained to House that Wilson was so infatuated he was neglecting important state business. House recorded Grayson's complaint in his diary and cryptically noted that the doctor said other things too disturbing to write down.[72]

House and members of the cabinet feared that if Wilson announced an engagement so soon after his wife's death, voters would turn on him in the upcoming 1916 election. The cabinet secretaries held a meeting behind the president's back to discuss Edith in early September 1915. The postmaster general suggested that Wilson's oldest friend in the cabinet, secretary of the navy Josephus Daniels, talk to Wilson about postponing any nuptials until after the election. Daniels declined the job, which he called "the difficult and perhaps dangerous high and exalted position of Minister Plenipotentiary and Envoy Extraordinary to the Court of Cupid on a mission in which neither my heart or my head was enlisted and in the performance of which my official head might suffer decapitation."[73]

Action was finally taken by the ambitious secretary of the Treasury, William Gibbs McAdoo, who was married to Wilson's youngest daughter.

Having his own presidential ambitions, McAdoo had the most to lose if his father-in-law lost the election. McAdoo had heard that the president gave Mary Peck $7,500, and on the basis of that information, he told Wilson that Peck was so jealous over Edith that she threatened to publish their letters if he went ahead with the marriage. McAdoo hoped his lie would fool the president into delaying or perhaps canceling the wedding.[74]

Immediately after hearing McAdoo's tale, Wilson wrote to Edith on September 18, 1915, "with a heart too full for words" asking to see her immediately at her home.[75] There is no record of Wilson's words to Edith that evening, but she later referred to his revelation as "a rocket from the unseen hand of an enemy" and "the awful Earthquake of Saturday night that has caused doubt of the certainty of anything."[76] The next morning Wilson apologized for the "mortification and having thrown a new shadow about her" and wrote of feeling "stained and unworthy."[77] Edith assured him that, after spending the night struggling with his revelation, on Sunday morning she could see "straight—straight into the heart of things," and was ready to follow him "where love leads" and stand by him "not for duty, not for pity, not for honor—but for love—trusting, protecting, comprehending love."[78]

Fearing that any day the Peck affair would become public and, in Wilson's words, "make the contemptible error and madness of a few months seem a stain upon my whole life," he adopted Grover Cleveland's honest approach: "Whatever you do, tell the truth." Wilson typed up his own press release about his relationship with Peck:

> These letters disclose a passage of folly and gross impertinence in my life. I am deeply ashamed and repentant. . . . But none of this lessens the blame or the deep humiliating grief and shame I suffer, that I should have so erred and forgotten the standards of honorable behavior by which I should have been bound.[79]

McAdoo's deceitful attempt to sabotage the president's relationship completely backfired. Edith assured Wilson that "love was still on the throne, but pale and bleeding trying to smile through his tears—and say the blow did not really hurt."[80] And despite the possible fallout, she unequivocally agreed to accept his marriage proposal. Inspired by Edith's bravery, Wilson publicly announced the engagement and set the wedding date for December 18, 1915.

News of the proposal generated a lot of off-color jokes like the following:

"What did Mrs. Galt do when the president asked her to marry him?"

"She fell out of bed."

Edith now had even more power over Wilson's scheming advisors. She confronted Colonel House, who confessed that he and McAdoo had invented the story to dissuade the president from marrying her. McAdoo told Edith it all was the colonel's idea. Edith never mentioned their conspiracy to her husband. But House and McAdoo were on notice to never again cross the new First Lady.

All sorts of rumors about Mary Peck and Edith arose during the next year's presidential campaign.[81] Senator Harding told his mistress, "You must hear the late intimate gossip of this town relating to the big Chief and his affairs of the heart. I cannot tell you the truth they contain, but they are highly diverting. When we last discussed the affair (you and I) made the correct guess. There was a triangular tangle," between Peck, Galt and Wilson.[82] Not since Dolley Madison had a First Lady been the subject of such racy gossip. Another false rumor that spread during the 1916 campaign involved Wilson appointing Louis Brandeis to the Supreme Court as payoff for the lawyer's success in quieting Mary Peck with $100,000 in hush money.[83] The press, however, filtered such gossip from the campaign coverage. Wilson was reelected, and Edith became the first First Lady to stand beside her husband when he took the oath of office.

Now living in the White House, the president's closest confidante involved herself even more in the affairs of state. She assumed the task of encoding and deciphering her husband's covert wartime communications. She had access to the desk drawer where Wilson kept America's top national security secrets, and she insisted on attending the president's meetings with political leaders and foreign ambassadors. America's ambassador to Germany noted how, during the five hours he spent updating the president on the war, Edith "asked pertinent questions showing her deep knowledge of foreign affairs."[84] She even met with the secretary of the navy to discuss how to secretly arm American ships to repel U-boat attacks.[85] As pressures mounted on Wilson during the lead-up to America's entry into World War I, Edith began screening his mail and deciding who could meet with the president and who could not. Edith was essentially serving as the president's chief of staff at a time when women did not even have the right to vote.

THE PETTICOAT GOVERNMENT

After America entered the war, Edith helped Woodrow develop his strategy to make sure World War I would be the war to end all wars. Wilson issued a Fourteen Point Plan for the final peace that included setting up a league of nations to settle future international conflicts diplomatically. When the war ended with an Allied victory, Edith was by Wilson's side as he worked tirelessly in Europe negotiating the inclusion of the League of Nations into the Treaty of Versailles.

According to the U.S. Constitution, treaties must be ratified by a two-thirds vote in the Senate. Some isolationist senators, known as Irreconcilables, refused to vote for the treaty under any circumstances. But Massachusetts senator Henry Cabot Lodge led a large number of Republicans who were willing to support the Treaty of Versailles and the League of Nations if they could add a series of alterations, or "reservations," to the treaty. Wilson was determined to have his treaty ratified without any changes. He embarked on a road tour of the United States in the fall of 1919 to speak directly to the people about why the treaty had to be ratified without any alterations. Wilson warned that if the treaty did not get ratified and the United States did not join the League of Nations, there would be a second world war "sometime in the vengeful providence of God . . . in which, not a few hundred thousand fine men from America will have to die, but as many millions as are necessary to accomplish the final freedom of the peoples of the world."[86]

At each stop, the exhausted president grew weaker and shorter of breath. After traveling 8,000 miles by train and giving 37 speeches in 22 days, Wilson began to weep uncontrollably and complained of a splitting headache. The tour was canceled and the presidential entourage rushed back to Washington. Edith later described her thoughts during the long train journey home: "As I sat there watching the dawn break slowly I felt that life would never be the same; that something had broken inside me; and from that hour on I would have to wear a mask—not only to the public but to the one I loved best in the world; for he must never know how ill he was, and I must carry on."[87] On September 27, 1919, the *New York Times* reported, "The President Suffers Nervous Breakdown," but in fact the president had suffered a stroke. And the worst was yet to come.

On the morning of October 2, 1919, Edith Wilson walked into her husband's White House bedroom and found him collapsed on the floor. She immediately summoned Dr. Grayson, who helped her lift the paralyzed president into his bed.[88] White House usher Ike Hoover recalled that Wilson "was just gone as far as one could judge from appearances."[89] Neurological experts were brought in that evening to examine the president. After reviewing their notes 70 years later, a modern neurologist concluded that the stroke left Wilson "so seriously disabled, both in the medical and constitutional sense[, that] neither Wilson's thought process nor his conduct in office would ever be the same again."[90]

The Constitution says, "In case of the removal of the president from office, or of his death, resignation, or inability to discharge the powers and duties of the said office, the same shall devolve on the vice president." But Edith did not inform the vice president, high-ranking members of Congress, or the press about the president's condition. Instead she decided, in her words, to assume a "stewardship" of the presidency.[91] According to Hoover, an "air of secrecy" enveloped the White House, and Edith embarked on "the beginning of the deception of the American people."[92] When Vice President Thomas Riley Marshall showed up at the White House to inquire about the president's health, he was turned away.[93] Marshall had to rely on the newspapers for updates on the president's health, and the newspapers had to rely on Edith and Dr. Grayson.

At an emergency meeting of the cabinet four days after Wilson's collapse, Grayson claimed the president was alert and even annoyed that they were meeting without him. The *New York Times* reported that Grayson informed the cabinet the president's condition was "encouraging, but suggested that only urgent matters be brought to his attention in order that his rest be made as complete as possible."[94] Grayson told the cabinet that Edith would be the sole conduit between the president and the rest of the government. Cabinet members and congressmen had to send Edith their memos and questions for the president, and she responded with notes declaring Wilson's supposed decisions. "The only decision that was mine was what was important and what was not," she later wrote, "and the very important decision of when to present matters to my husband."[95]

The reality was that Wilson was in no condition to make any decisions. White House usher Ike Hoover described Wilson's typical day: woken at 10 AM, the president was put in a wheelchair and wheeled into another room or the porch, where he would spend an hour until Hoover put him back to bed. Wilson was never allowed to ride in the rear seat of the car, because he would have slid down or toppled over. Hoover said the president had gone from "giant to pigmy."[96] Four months after his stroke the president still could not focus and would break off in midconversation and stare off into space as if in a trance.[97] But the press continued to deferentially report Grayson's sham pronouncements about Wilson's "temporary exhaustion." Hoover said, "Never was deception so universally practiced in the White House as it was in those [press] statements being given out from time to time."[98]

When Wilson failed to make a public appearance after two weeks, the press began to speculate about his real condition. On October 14, 1919, the *San Francisco Bulletin* commented that "the secrecy and even the deception practiced by court physicians in the case of a monarch similarly afflicted have no place in the procedure of an orderly republic. We are a grown-up people and if told everything, will be better prepared to face the worst if there is really no hope for an improvement." On October 25, 1919, *Harvey's Weekly* condemned Grayson's cover-up as "flagrantly stupid from the beginning" and "an impropriety, an injustice so gross and at the same time so stupid as to defy temperate description." Some senators tried to convince Vice President Marshall to declare Wilson incapacitated and assume the presidency. Marshall respected Wilson to a fault and refused to challenge his authority.

In the 30 days after Wilson's stroke, Congress passed 28 bills that became law by default because the president failed to respond. Wilson has been credited with vetoing the Volstead Act, the bill prohibiting the sale of alcohol (the veto was later overridden). In reality, a presidential aide wrote the veto message with Edith's approval, and it is possible the president knew nothing about it. By December 1919, Washington was rife with rumors about the president, including that his signatures on bills were forged. The press even began to refer to Edith as the "Presidentress" and called Woodrow the "First Man." Republican senator Albert Fall erupted in a Senate speech, "Mrs. Wilson is President!" Dolley Madison had been celebrated in the press for her petticoat politics. Peggy Eaton had scandalized Washington with the Petticoat affair. Now Senator Fall and others were accusing Edith Wilson of installing a "Petticoat Government."[99]

Although Wilson was bedridden and unable to focus for extended lengths of time, he had recovered the ability to hold short conversations. Fearing that public pressure might force Congress to remove Wilson, Edith agreed to a visit from two senators, Democrat Gilbert Hitchcock and Republican Albert Fall. On December 5, 1919, Edith and Grayson staged what Ike Hoover called the "Great Camouflage."[100]

They dimmed the lights of Wilson's bedroom so that it was impossible for someone coming from the well-lighted hallway to see anything clearly. They arranged his blankets to cover his paralyzed left side and strategically placed papers on the nightstand near his good arm so he could pick them up and pretend to talk about them as if he had read them. Edith stood at the foot of the bed in case anything went wrong. Toward the end of the visit, one of the senators said to her, "You seem very much engaged madam." "Yes," she icily replied, "I thought it wise to record this interview so there may be no misunderstanding or misstatements made."[101] The ruse worked, and the senators reported that Wilson was capable of performing his duties as president.

Although the president could fool the two senators with polite banter, his mind at the beginning of 1920 was still so addled that he was incapable of comprehending and adjusting to shifting political realities. Like many stroke victims, Wilson did not sense the seriousness of his illness and did not recognize that he was thinking abnormally.[102] He was also in an information bubble, with Edith as his sole connection to the outside world. As the Senate debate over the Versailles Treaty got under way, she oversaw the review of all the diplomatic papers instead of the secretary of state or another cabinet member.[103] Since Edith was under strict medical orders not to upset the president with any bad news that might agitate him and precipitate another stroke, she hid the mounting opposition to the Versailles Treaty from her husband.[104]

As the vote approached, even Edith understood that if Wilson did not compromise with Lodge, the Democrats would not have enough votes to ratify the treaty and the United States would not join the League of Nations. On January 23, 1920, she told journalist Ray Stannard Baker that she tried to convince her husband to compromise but she could not change his mind. Baker realized the secluded president did not comprehend the extent of the opposition in the Senate and "he simply did not want to hear what was going on."[105] Everyone except Wilson knew the only way the treaty would be passed was with Lodge's reservations. But the White House obstinately ordered the Democratic senators to vote only for the treaty in its original form. Five months after his stroke, the president was so mentally out of touch he was incapable of saving his noble crusade for world peace.[106]

The morning of the vote, March 19, 1920, Lodge was confident that his version of the treaty, with his reservations, would pass: "I am positive that I now have enough Democratic votes added to my Republican votes to make this possible."[107] Seeing that the only hope for ratification was to vote for Lodge's reservations, 21 Democrats broke with the White House and joined 28 Republicans to vote for ratification with the reservations. Voting in opposition were 23 Democrats and 12 Republicans; 12 senators did not vote. Lodge's version of the treaty received 49 yeas to 35 nays, but since ratification of a treaty requires a two-thirds majority, the treaty was defeated. Wilson's version of the treaty without Lodge's reservations lost by an even greater margin. Had the White House compromised with Lodge, 23 Democratic votes would have been gained instead of lost, and the treaty would have been ratified by an overwhelming majority of 72 to 12.

William Jennings Bryan called the Senate's failure to pass the treaty "a colossal crime against our country and the world."[108] Senator Warren G. Harding blamed Wilson for being "such a bullhead that he will have no hesitancy in risking the ruin of this country to carry his points in Paris."[109] Republican senator Frank Brandegee said Wilson "strangled his own child."[110] Lodge also blamed Wilson: "Just as I thought that I had everything settled and that my number of Democratic votes was ample in every way, a sinister, unseen hand came out from the White House and drew away many votes, and I could do nothing."[111] Edith blamed Lodge: "At his door lies the wreckage of human hopes and the peril to human lives that afflict mankind today."[112] But more than Lodge, Wilson or anyone else, Edith was to blame.

By the spring of 1920, during the final days of her husband's administration, the press began to acknowledge the extent of Edith's power. The Canton, Ohio, *Daily News* announced on March 12, 1920, "One of the foremost statesmen in Washington is a woman—Mrs. Woodrow Wilson."[113] *Collier's* called Edith the "executive by proxy" who "not only proved herself as a real mistress of the White House, but mistress of a situation unique in American political life."[114] A foreign newspaper, the *London Daily Mail,* on February 22, 1920, gave the most honest assessment of Edith's power: "Nothing more startling has been disclosed in this week of endless sensations at Washington, than the fact that the wife of President Wilson has for months past been acting President of the United States."[115]

Had Woodrow Wilson's "delectable comrade" not stood in the way of Vice President Marshall becoming president after Wilson's stroke, Marshall would have compromised with Lodge over the Versailles Treaty. The United States would have joined the League of Nations and would have played an active role in the international peace organization during the lead-up to World War II. According to Wilson's leading biographer, Arthur Link, "In a world with the United States playing a responsible, active role, the possibilities of preventing the rise of Hitler were limitless."[116]

THE SPY WHO LOVED HARDING

Warren Gamaliel Harding was the only president as shamelessly romantic as Woodrow Wilson. In one of his many love poems, he pined for his mistress:

> *I love your back, I love your breasts,*
> *Darling to feel, where my face rests,*
> *I love your skin, so soft and white,*
> *So dear to feel and sweet to bite,*
> *I love your knees, their dimples kiss,*
> *I love your ways of giving bliss,*

I love your poise of perfect thighs,
When they hold me in paradise . . . [117]

To the same mistress he moaned, "I want to weld bodies, unite souls, I want the divine embrace, the transcending union, the blissful affinity, and with them all the excruciating joy and unspeakable sweetness that I never did know and can only know when fastened by you."[118] And he pleaded, "You simply do not, cannot guess how I need you, and want you and ache for love's employments, as you inspire them."[119] Neither Harding nor the object of his adoration, Carrie Phillips, could have imagined that the affair they began when he was a lieutenant governor and she was a lonely housewife would end with him in the White House and federal agents accusing her of espionage. Theirs is a story of love, passion, espionage and sexual blackmail.

Harding once summed himself up as "a man of limited talents from a small town."[120] Before he entered politics he was an Ohio newspaper publisher who was mostly known for his garbled sentences. But he radiated a movie star quality that made people say, "He looks like a president!" William Allen White described his first impression of Harding: "He was a handsome dog, a little above medium height with a swarthy skin, a scathing eye and . . . the harlot's voice of the old-time political orator."[121] With the aid of his ambitious wife, Florence, Harding rode his imperious looks and gregarious personality into political office. His marriage to Florence, five years his senior, proved to be a great political partnership, but it was childless and sexless. To Harding's delight, plenty of women were willing to satisfy the needs of this "handsome dog."

As lieutenant governor in 1905, the 40-year-old Harding began an affair with a married neighbor, 30-year-old Carrie Phillips. With strawberry blond hair, pale blue eyes, and a high, round bosom, Phillips was frequently compared to the famously buxom Gibson Girl. She also had big ambitions, exceeding what Jim Phillips, her shop owner husband, could match. Her neighbor, the dashing leading citizen of Marion, Ohio, was much more to her liking.[122] Tragedy opened the door to their affair when the death of the Phillipses' two-year-old son sent Jim into a terrible depression. Harding suggested that Jim check in to the Battle Creek Sanitarium in Michigan and assured his friend that he would look after Carrie. While Jim was away in the sanitarium Harding repeatedly checked up on the lovely housewife. After an initial sexual encounter one afternoon in the Phillipses' bedroom, Warren and Carrie made use of the Phillipses' dinner table, their front porch and their garden for what Harding called "detours from the primrose path."[123]

After Jim returned, the two couples became so friendly they took vacations to Europe and Bermuda together. On one cruise, Jim and Florence went to bed early, while Warren and Carrie hooked up on deck just a few feet from the Hardings' cabin.[124]

Warren and Carrie also took their own trips together. Shortly before midnight one New Year's Eve in Montreal, they were having sex and simultaneously climaxed just as the cathedral bells rang in the New Year. A year later, Harding recalled "when the bells rang the chorus while our hearts sang the rapture without words and we greeted the New Year from the hallowed heights of heaven. Fate timed that marvelous coincidence. It was impossible for us to have planned, and . . . I count it to be the best remembered moment of my existence. . . . It thrills me, merely to live it over in recollection. No overwhelming enchantment ever compared to it in my life. The duet was attuned to the infinite—some higher realm at least, and souls stand in the loftiness of it, and the old year died in the fires of flaming hearts, and the light of the New Year shone with consuming ecstasy. Oh me! To live it again!"[125]

The affair had been going for six years when in 1911 Florence discovered one of Phillips's indiscrete letters. She immediately offered Harding a divorce, but he refused. He had no passion for Florence, but he did have a passion for politics. With his marriage intact, Harding was elected to the Senate in 1915. But higher office did not stop him from continuing his affair with Mrs. Phillips.

While the *Lusitania* crisis in May 1916 was drawing Edith Galt and Woodrow Wilson closer together, it threatened to torpedo Harding's 11-year relationship with Phillips. Ever since the Hardings and the Phillipses had taken a vacation together to Germany, Carrie had had an obsessive love for the German fatherland. She even moved to Germany during a separation from her husband. When war broke out, she returned to America and became a vocal supporter of the kaiser and a critic of Woodrow Wilson. After the sinking of the *Lusitania*, Harding infuriated Phillips when he spoke in favor of Wilson's aggressive response to Germany.[126] Before the Senate voted on the declaration of war two years later, Phillips warned Harding that she would reveal his letters to the press if he voted for war.[127] The Ohio senator voted to declare war on Germany anyway, and Phillips did not go through with her threat. Harding forgave her and continued seeing his pro-German mistress throughout World War I.

Phillips was such an outspoken critic of the American war effort that in the summer of 1917 she was placed under surveillance by the Bureau of Investigation, later known as the Federal Bureau of Investigation (FBI). Agents discovered that Phillips's teenage daughter Isabelle was engaged to the son of a German baroness who had been arrested in a hotel room with a young army officer carrying "papers of sufficient damaging character to cause her to be held a German spy." The agents also learned that the baroness had hosted Phillips and her daughter in New York.[128]

Bureau of Investigation agent Leonard Stern journeyed to Marion, Ohio, in March 1918 to interview people who knew Phillips. Everyone agreed she was a German secret agent, and they also revealed she was having an affair with Senator Harding.[129] According to agent Stern's report to the U.S. attorney general, Harding and Phillips "were found in a compromising position in a hotel near Marion, Ohio, and from that time until the present time it is common gossip in Marion that Mrs. Phillips is practically furnished with funds by Senator Harding." Stern reported that Phillips "secures information from Senator Harding, who secures the same from the Navy Department in Washington and gives this information to Mrs. Phillips; [and] that she then in some unknown manner relays this information to friends of the German Empire."[130] Agent Stern did not accuse Harding of being a spy, just a dupe. In the midst of the anti-German hysteria in America during World War I, even a casual association with a suspected German spy could get the average citizen fired. Here a U.S. senator, who was touted as a potential president, was carrying on an affair with a suspected spy and allegedly furnishing her with state secrets. Amazingly, the Justice Department did nothing to stop the relationship.

Someone did tip off Harding about the Justice Department investigation, and he immediately tried to caution Phillips that if she was not more careful she would be arrested. "The war situation, your attitude, my responsibility, all these lead to close observance. No one knows how many watchful eyes are following. You never leave home that it is not noted," Harding warned. "I cannot call or dine with you that it is not noted. I think much of this meddlesome watchfulness is aimed at me rather than you, but the point is that it exists, and we have to be governed accordingly."[131] When she failed to respond to his warnings, Harding brazenly turned to the cuckolded Jim Phillips: "I can't appeal very effectively. I wonder if you can command. Frankly I doubt it. Perhaps you can appeal. It takes more than tact. But it is really serious . . . save her from herself."[132] While Harding tried to muzzle Carrie, he curried favor with the White House by reversing himself on his previous criticisms of Wilson's war strategy.[133]

All relationships have their ups and downs. But Warren and Carrie's 15-year affair presented an unusual number of danger signs that would have convinced a reasonable man to break it off: his wife's discovery of their relationship, his election to the Senate, Phillips's blackmail attempt and the Justice Department's espionage investigation. Even though Harding knew federal agents trailed him and Phillips, he still found time during the summer of 1918 to sneak in at least two interludes with her. When it came to women, Harding was not a reasonable man. Fortunately for the aspiring president, the war ended without Phillips getting arrested for spying. But the official file detailing the senator's affair with the suspected spy remained in the hands of the U.S. attorney general. And that was just one of the many sex secrets that could have foiled his presidential run two years later.

THE PRESIDENT'S DAUGHTER

While Harding was carrying on with Phillips, he began an affair with a friend's daughter, Nan Britton, 30 years younger than the still-virile 51-year-old senator. Described by a contemporary as "a most attractive young woman, blond, fresh, vital," Britton became obsessed with Harding at the age of fourteen, when she covered her bedroom walls with his photographs.[134] "Nan wasn't interested in the movie stars; all she could talk about was Harding," her high school friend Ellen Metzger recalled. "I don't believe Mr. Harding encouraged her in any way. He didn't have to. Nan ran after him. He was so good looking, women chased him."[135] Britton covered her notebooks with

"Warren Harding—he's a darling" and when her teacher's back was turned, she wrote on the chalkboard, "I love Warren Harding." Britton was friends with Phillips's teenage daughter Isabelle and heard about Carrie's affair with Harding. "But this knowledge did not move me to condemnation of either Mr. Harding or Mrs. Phillips," Britton wrote a decade later. "The only thing I regretted was that I was not her age, and that I had not traveled in Europe, and that I was not 'in society' or in any kind of a position to attract his notice."[136]

Britton moved to New York after graduation from high school, and months after America's entry into World War I, she wrote Harding requesting a job. The senator informed Britton that he was coming to New York the following week and suggested they meet for an interview. The precocious 20-year-old knew what he really wanted: "Under the cordial phraseology of his letter, there was more than the mere desire to offer assistance to me."[137] Harding invited Britton to a hotel where he often stayed with Carrie Phillips and led her, arm in arm, into the reception room. After she revealed her school-girl crush, Britton later recalled that the middle-aged cad suggested they go up to his room "so we might continue our conversation without interruptions or annoyances. . . . We scarcely closed the door behind us when we shared our first kiss," she later wrote. "I shall never, never forget how Mr. Harding kept saying, after each kiss, 'God! God, Nan!' in a high diminuendo, nor how he pleaded in a tense voice, 'Oh, dearie, tell me it isn't hateful to you to have me kiss you!' And as I kissed him back I thought that he surpassed even my gladdest dreams of him."[138] Holding her in his arms, Harding admitted he had come to New York just to be with her; Britton admitted she was still a virgin and said that she would not have sex with him that night.

Days later, Harding invited Britton to join him on a speaking tour of the Midwest. Registering in hotel rooms as uncle and niece, they slept in the same bed, but she still refused to give Harding what he called "love's sweetest intimacy."[139] Harding begged, "Dearie, r' y' going to sleep with me? Look at me Nan; going to sleep with me dearie?" Britton was so naïve she still did not know how pregnancy worked. While they were making out in a private berth on an overnight train ride, she "experienced sweet thrills from just having Mr. Harding's hands upon the outside of [her] nightdress." She recalled that after this, her first orgasm, "I became panic-stricken. I inquired tearfully whether he really thought I would have a child right away." In the morning, she noticed Harding was tired and asked him why he had not slept well. "God sweetheart! What do you expect? I'm a man, you know."[140]

Harding finally took Britton's virginity months later in a second-rate Broadway hotel. As they lay in bed, the door burst open and two New York police vice squad detectives rushed in demanding to know Britton's age. Harding assured them she was not a minor, but the detective snapped, "You'll have to tell that to the judge." Then the other officer picked up Harding's hat and noticed "Senator Warren G. Harding" stamped on the sweatband. The detectives immediately dropped their bluster and became in Britton's words "not only calm but strangely respectful." Harding and Britton quickly dressed and the obliging officers snuck them out a side entrance and into a taxi. Harding slipped one of the cops a $20 bill and exhaled, "I thought I wouldn't get out of that for under a thousand dollars."[141]

Over the next year, Harding met Britton in New York once a week and she made regular visits to Washington, where they attended the theater and went out to dinner.[142] One evening in late January 1919 he brought her to his Senate office and asked her to disrobe so he could "visualize" her later during his workday. When he indicated he wanted to do more than visualize, Britton pointed out that they lacked "the usual paraphernalia which we always took to the hotels." Britton later observed, "And of course the Senate Offices do not provide preventative facilities for use in such emergencies." Before they proceeded to have unprotected sex on his office couch, Harding assured her he was sterile from a childhood case of the mumps. "But," Britton wrote, "he was mistaken."[143]

Britton recalled that after she informed Harding she was pregnant, the senator said, "We must go at this in a sane way," and gave her a bottle of "Dr Humphrey's No. 11 tablets," which he claimed his wife used to avoid pregnancy. He also assured her he had "ample funds" for an "operation," and given the choice between medicine and the knife, he would choose the latter. Britton refused: "I could not bring myself to destroy the precious treasure within me"; and on October 22, 1919, she delivered a baby girl. Harding suggested that she allow his sister to adopt the child, named Elizabeth Ann. Britton rejected the idea and moved in with her sister who lived in Chicago—site of the 1920 Republican National Convention.[144]

BLACKMAILING THE GOP

For 15 years, Carrie Phillips held out the delusional hope that Harding would quit politics, divorce his wife and marry her. Her great fear was that he would run for president—once in the White House divorce would be impossible. Harding assured her, "You need not be concerned about my [presidential] ambitions. I know how you feel about them, but you need not think of them—for there are none. I know myself pretty well, I know my insufficiencies, my incapacities and alas! My transgressions."[145] When Harding announced he was running for president in 1920, Phillips flew into a rage and told her husband about the affair. She then gave Harding an ultimatum: drop out of politics and divorce Florence, or watch her go public with their relationship.[146]

Harding responded by writing a letter to Phillips offering *her* an ultimatum. He could retire completely from politics "to avoid disgrace in the public eye" and never speak to her again, or he could continue to run for president and pay her big bucks. He promised, "I will pay you $5,000 [$57,000 today] per year in March each year, so long as I am in the public service."[147] Harding's salary as senator was $7,000. The president in the 1920s made $75,000. If he won the presidency, there would be plenty of money to cover Phillips's hush money payments. Harding's deal with Phillips became yet another incentive to become the commander in chief.

To figure out how to deal with the blackmail threat, Harding turned to Florence, who rallied at the challenge and was a key advisor through the primary races. On the eve of the Republican convention, Harding began to get cold feet and told Florence he was considering withdrawing his name from contention. She insisted they attend anyway. Harding's stenographer Kathleen Lawler observed that when Florence "threw the weight of her judgment, he consented to go to Chicago."[148]

Harding planned to arrive in the Windy City a day early so that he could visit Nan Britton and his daughter. Florence, however, put a tight leash on her husband and escorted him directly to their hotel. Only after the convention began and Florence became busy managing the delegate count was Harding able to slip out to see Britton. During the convention, he spent more time with Britton than he did winning over delegates.[149]

The nominating convention was deadlocked through the initial rounds of voting. Senator Frank B. Brandegee recalled that among the candidates there were no "first raters" but Harding was the "best of the second raters."[150] When the party bosses met in a smoke-filled room to discuss Harding, someone brought up his reputation as a rake. The party bosses confronted Harding the next morning when they found him wandering the halls of the hotel unshaven and hung over. He was taken to a suite where Republican operative George Harvey said, "We think you may be nominated tomorrow. Before acting finally, we think you should tell us, on your conscience and before God, whether there is anything that might be brought up against you that would embarrass the party, any impediment that might disqualify you or make you inexpedient, either as candidate or as President."[151] Harding asked for a few minutes to think alone.

Harding must have run though a long list: Carrie Phillips, Nan Britton and her child and untold other names lost to history. In addition there were the two New York vice squad detectives, the Justice Department officials involved with Phillips's espionage investigation, the attorney general and much of Marion, Ohio—hometown to Warren, Carrie and Nan. After ten minutes Harding rejoined the party bosses and declared, "Gentlemen, there is no reason in the sight of God why I cannot be president of the United States."[152] Later that day, with his wife watching from the spectators' gallery and Britton in the balcony, Harding won the Republican presidential nomination.[153] Three weeks later, Jim Phillips showed up at Harding's Senate office to begin negotiations for a big payout.[154]

Jim and Carrie knew the nominee had to pay up, and if he didn't have the cash, the Republican Party did. Harding went to the party bosses and told them the truth about Phillips—at least part of the truth. The party bosses were horrified. The election of 1920 was the first time women were guaranteed the right to vote. Twenty million new female voters would not ignore a sex scandal the way the all-male electorate did when Grover Cleveland was elected in 1884. GOP operatives assembled a slush fund that paid Carrie Phillips $25,000 ($286,000 today) upfront and promised a $2,000 ($23,000) monthly stipend for as long as Harding was in office.

The men who contributed to Phillips's slush fund anticipated a big return on their investment once Harding took over the government. Carrie Phillips became the first person in American history to successfully blackmail a major political party. But she was not the last. Harding's other mistresses soon learned about the arrangement and demanded their own cut from the slush fund. While the Republican Party paid off Harding's women, it churned out stories about his happy marriage, which the press dutifully parroted. One major magazine profile claimed the Hardings projected "a certain idyllic quality that happily married partnerships have."[155] Harding's most rabid critic, Professor William Chancellor, called the Republican whitewash of their nominee's personal life "the most deliberate lying of a continued and systematic kind that America ever saw in any Presidential campaign."[156]

To maintain Harding's image as a home-loving, home-staying family man, the Republican Party devised what they called the Front Porch Campaign. Instead of traveling the country, Harding stayed at home in Marion and greeted journalists and delegations of supporters from his front porch. The problem with the Front Porch Campaign was that Harding shared his hometown with Carrie Phillips and her angry husband. Kansas editor William Allen White observed that "every storefront in Marion was a giant bloom of red, white and blue; every storefront but one. And when the reporters asked about it, they heard one of those stories about a primrose detour from Main Street."[157] The only undecorated store in Marion was owned by Jim Phillips.

Professor Arthur Hirsch happened to be in Marion during the campaign and saw Carrie Phillips on Harding's front lawn chatting with the Republican nominee, who was sitting as usual on the front porch. "With one eye on him and the other on the front door of the residence, she would take one cautious step, then another, toward the porch," Hirsh recounted. "Suddenly, Mrs. Harding appeared. A feather duster came sailing out at Mrs. Phillips, then a wastebasket. Mrs. Phillips did not retreat. Next came a piano stool, one of those old, four-legged things with a swivel seat by which it could be lowered or raised. Not until then was there a retreat. She tossed a kiss and left quietly." Hirsch also recalled seeing Phillips at a campaign rally. "She sat quietly in the crowd, while Mrs. Harding was on the platform with her husband. . . . While he was speaking, [Florence] would get up and shake her fist at, I suppose Mrs. Phillips, get all excited, and sit down again. He seemed not to notice her."[158] The Republican National Committee realized Harding's rogue mistress put their Front Porch Campaign in daily jeopardy. To get her as far away from Marion as possible, the GOP put up $20,000 ($230,000 today) for Jim and Carrie Phillips to take an all-expenses-paid tour of China, Japan and Korea. Flush with cash, Carrie spent a year in Asia picking up a trove of diamond bracelets, earrings and necklaces.[159]

Harding's indiscretions were well known to the press corps covering the election. Journalist Ray Clapper recalled, "We did hear about the Marion Lady who had been sent off to China with her obliging husband so that during the campaign no tongues could wag." Clapper's wife, Olive, recollected, "The newspaper corps had uncovered a few stories about this handsome man's lady friend. Three newsmen, for instance, invited to dine at the home of one of Harding's widow neighbors, were, during the evening, taken upstairs by an innocent eight-year-old member of the woman's family and proudly shown Harding's toothbrush. Said the child, 'He always stays here when Mrs. Harding goes away.'"[160] Harding was very fortunate to run for president in an era when journalists embraced the code that the sex lives of candidates were private and had no place in political reporting.

Why didn't the Democrats expose Harding's affairs? Democratic nominee James Cox and his running mate—the young Franklin Roosevelt—fervently opposed Harding's conservative agenda, and a 1927 letter from Cox's campaign manager Francis Durbin to Cox reveals that the Democrats had dirt on Harding. Durbin complained to Cox, "The only regret I have is that in the 1920 campaign, when a few of us had the goods in regard to Mrs. Phillips and other disreputable things about the then candidate for President, the mask was not torn off and the American people told what kind of a man the Republicans had foisted upon them." Durbin blamed "a few selfish individuals like Joe Tumulty [President Wilson's personal secretary] and various other Democrats who had the goods and who felt like we were going to lose, for not telling the truth as they knew it to be. But they wanted to practice law in Washington and did not want to have the ill-feeling of the administration."[161] A mix of discretion and opportunism kept the Democrats from exposing Harding's affair with Phillips.

Harding actually took comfort in the Democrats' focus on Carrie Phillips because it distracted them from his illegitimate child. Nan Britton recalled that "it secretly amused him to realize . . . that the scandal . . . in which Mrs. [Phillips's] name and his were linked very frequently, was for us the greatest source of protection, for while the Democrats who were 'slinging mud' played with Mrs. [Phillips's] name they were not looking for mine or any other."[162] The Democrats missed a prime opportunity. One thing is certain: if the Democrats had won the 1920 election, President Cox and Vice President Roosevelt would have taken the country in a very different direction.

AN EMPTY SUIT WITH POWER

"I don't think I'm big enough for the Presidency. I can't make a damn thing out of this tax problem," President Harding once complained to William Allen White. "I listen to one side and they seem right, and then—God!—I talk to the other side and they seem just as right, and here I am where I started. I don't know what to do or where to turn. Somewhere there must be a book that tells all about it. My God! But this is a hell of a place for a man like me to be in."[163] Harding reverted to the orthodox Republican economic policies of deregulating business trusts and cutting taxes. In the short term, these policies contributed to the economic boom of the roaring 1920s, but in the long term, they helped create a bubble economy that burst with the stock market crash at the end of the decade.

In foreign policy, Harding was also at a loss. When Arthur Draper, the foreign correspondent for the *New York Tribune* stopped by after a trip to Europe, Harding called in his secretary Judson Welliver and said to Draper, "I don't know anything about this European stuff. You and Jud get together and he can tell me later; he handles these matters for me."[164] American foreign policy under Harding turned away from Wilson's internationalism at a time when Europe saw the birth of fascism with the rise of Mussolini in 1922. By the end of the 1920s, the foreign and domestic policies of three successive Republican presidents would leave a big mess for Franklin Delano Roosevelt.

Harding's tendency to delegate responsibility and not mind the store also resulted in his administration's record as the most corrupt in American history. He filled high-ranking positions with so many cronies from back home they became known as the Ohio Gang. Several took full advantage of their trusting, out-of-touch friend in the White House. Secretary of Interior Albert Fall became the first cabinet member in history to be convicted of a felony and sentenced to prison for accepting nearly $400,000 ($5 million today) from oil companies in exchange for the rights to tap the naval oil reserve in Tea Pot Dome, Wyoming. Director of the Veterans' Bureau Charles Forbes went to Leavenworth prison for embezzling millions from the illegal resale of supplies intended for veterans' hospitals, including painkillers for wounded World War I vets. U.S. attorney general Harry Daugherty, who had organized the Carrie Phillips slush fund, was indicted for accepting payments not to prosecute criminals. "My god this is a hell of a job," Harding erupted after hearing about yet another scandal. "I have no trouble with my enemies. But my damned friends! My goddamned friends they're the ones that keep me walking the floor at night."[165] Few things are more dangerous than an empty suit with power.

Being president didn't stop Harding from drinking alcohol with his friends despite the federal Prohibition laws, but it did impede his favorite pastime: chasing women. He whined to Nan Britton, "I'm in jail Nan and can't get out." Secret Service agents frequently snuck Britton into the White House even when Florence was home.[166] Britton recalled her first White House visit: "Mr. Harding said to me that people seemed to have eyes in the sides of their heads down there and so we must be very circumspect. Whereupon he introduced me to the one place where, he said, he thought we might share kisses in safety. This was a small closet in the anteroom, evidently a place for hats and coats but entirely empty most of the times we used it, for we repaired there many times in the course of my visits to the White House, and in the darkness of a space not more than five feet square the President of the United States and his adoring sweetheart made love."[167]

Harding ordered Secret Service agents to stand guard outside the little love closet while he and Britton cavorted. One time, five minutes after they entered, the First Lady appeared, arms akimbo and eyes ablaze, demanding that the guard get out of her way. When he refused to budge, she dashed around the corner to enter the closet through another door. The quick-thinking agent pounded on the door to alert the half-dressed lovers, who slipped out just in time. The agent hustled Britton out of the White House and into a waiting car while Harding ran to his office, where he pretended to be working when Florence finally caught up with him. Forty years later, John F.

Kennedy recounted this bit of presidential history to one of his girlfriends before they used the same closet for a quickie.[168]

Aside from Britton, Harding found little happiness in the White House. The stress of not knowing what to do as president got to him. Chief White House usher Ike Hoover, who had witnessed Wilson's stroke, said that Harding was so beset by constant anxieties that he paced the corridors of the White House restlessly day and night. Just like Woodrow Wilson, the burdens of office caught up with Harding during a cross-country speaking tour when he died of heart failure on August 2, 1923, at the Palace Hotel in San Francisco. Although Harding had been suffering from heart disease for years, false rumors about his "strange death" made their way into print in the 1920s and 1930s, including one book that claimed Florence poisoned him in retaliation for his affair with Nan Britton.[169]

After the president's death, the Harding family made the mistake of cutting off financial support for Britton and her child. Britton had no choice but to write America's first kiss-and-tell autobiography, *The President's Daughter*, published in 1927. Even if the book had not featured scandalous revelations about an adulterous president, it would have ignited controversy with its frank discussion of illicit sex, birth control and abortion. At the request of the New York Society for the Suppression of Vice, the police seized the unreleased copies of the book and the printing plates. Britton sued and won the right to publish her book, which became an instant bestseller.

Britton's irreverent tale of illicit love with the president of the United States hit the bookshelves at an appropriate moment in American history. In the wake of World War I, a Lost Generation of writers including Ernest Hemingway and F. Scott Fitzgerald was challenging the false idols and ideals of the prewar era. Sigmund Freud was revealing the raging sexual libido in everyone's subconscious. Flappers were kicking up their heels dancing the Charleston and revamping traditional notions of what it meant to be a lady. Margaret Sanger was promoting the diaphragm as a way for women to fully enjoy sex, free from the fear of unwanted pregnancy. And Prohibition made breaking the law a commonplace activity. *The President's Daughter* perfectly fit the rebellious, louche, "Anything Goes" zeitgeist of the Jazz Age and marked the waning of Victorianism and the emergence of modernity.[170]

While the public reveled in Britton's revolutionary book, the press either ignored or disparaged it. The few reviews that made it to print dismissed the book's importance and validity. Even the iconoclastic H. L. Mencken wrote, "This tale, I confess, does not interest me greatly."[171] One of Britton's book reviewers explained the reluctance of journalists to cover any of Harding's indiscretions: "The majority feel . . . that it is not only beneath their dignity but a breach of their patriotic integrity to notice such terrible statements about a dead ex President of the United Sates and other officials."[172] When Congressman John Tillman denounced Britton's book on the floor of the House of Representatives, he insisted that suppressing news of presidential adultery constituted "a matter of nation-wide interest and importance. It is a non-partisan question."[173] In a review of Britton's book, the former editor of *Collier's* Richard Child proposed, "Commandment no. 11: Thou shalt not whisper falsely against thy President." Child argued, "American citizenship owes it to [presidents and other statesmen] to reject the word-of-mouth story and the whispered slander."[174] Nineteenth-century journalists held no such qualms about slandering the private lives of Presidents Jefferson, Madison and Jackson. But twentieth-century journalists assumed responsibility for shielding the personal lives of presidents from the public in the interest of propriety and national security. As America's leaders confronted the great struggles of World War II and the Cold War, the press became even more determined to insulate presidents from sex scandals. Over the next half century, the cozy relationship between the press and the White House would have a major impact on the most powerful nation on earth, for better and for worse.

CHAPTER FOUR

THE BALLAD OF FRANKLIN AND ELEANOR

F ranklin and Eleanor Roosevelt had the most complicated marriage in the history of the presidency. Their love story involves a series of subplots with a cast of characters: Lucy, Missy, Nancy, Marion and a butch lesbian reporter nicknamed Hick. America's oddest First Couple certainly benefited from the cozy relationship between politicians and the press of their era—and so did the nation. Over the course of four decades, Franklin's and Eleanor's extramarital affairs transformed them into the dynamic team that led America through the dark days of the Great Depression and World War II. To tell this complicated love story, we must journey back to the very beginning. . . .

KISSING COUSINS

Franklin Delano Roosevelt was born into the elite air of American aristocracy in 1882. He was the scion of the wealthy Roosevelt clan that traced their Hudson Valley roots back to New Amsterdam. Young Franklin had the best tutors and was sent to the finest private schools. He also had the constant affection of his adoring yet overprotective mother, Sara. The boy meant *everything* to her. According to one story, when FDR caught scarlet fever while away at boarding school, Sara disobeyed doctors and the schoolmaster and climbed a ladder to her son's dormitory window so she could sneak in and look after him.[1] Under Sara's obsessive mothering, Franklin grew up a master of his universe with a beaming personality and a burning ambition to follow in the political footsteps of his distant cousin, President Theodore Roosevelt.

Although Eleanor was also a Roosevelt—Theodore's niece and Franklin's fifth cousin—her upbringing in New York City during the 1880s was the polar opposite of her husband's. Her mother, Anna, constantly instructed the homely, dour little girl, "You have no looks so see to it that you have manners." Anna nicknamed her "Granny," explaining to visitors, "She is such a funny child, so old-fashioned."[2] Eleanor's son James wrote, "She had been beaten down by her mother, and she was too aware of her plain appearance, buck teeth and curved spine which compelled her to wear a brace when she was young."[3] One of Eleanor's earliest memories was going for a walk in New York City with her alcoholic father, Elliot. As they passed the Knickerbocker Club, Elliot said he was going in for a minute and left little Eleanor to fend for herself on the city sidewalk. Eleanor waited outside the club for six hours, until the bar staff emerged carrying her father, who had passed out drunk.[4] When Eleanor was eight, her brother died of diphtheria; at nine, she lost her mother to the same disease. A year later, her father jumped out of a window in a failed suicide attempt and then died of a seizure. Her cold, distant grandmother Mary Ludlow Hall raised the abandoned child, who grew into a shy, awkward and insecure young woman—the exact opposite of her future husband. After Eleanor accepted Franklin's marriage proposal in 1904, she predicted to a relative that she would not be able to hold on to Franklin. "He's too attractive," she sobbed.[5]

When Franklin announced their engagement, his mother begged him to break it off and keep looking. But Franklin felt a kinship to Eleanor. He said, "She possesse[d] what every member of the Roosevelt family seems always to have, a deep and abiding interest in everything and everybody."[6] On March 17, 1905, the cousins married. President Theodore Roosevelt gave away the bride and congratulated the groom, saying, "Well Franklin, there's nothing like keeping the name in the family." If the newlywed cousins felt a kinship, it did not extend to the bedroom. Eleanor later told her daughter, "Sex, my dear, is something a woman must learn to endure."[7] Eleanor certainly learned to endure sex, and within a year of their wedding, she was pregnant with the first of six children. It was the other woman in Franklin's life who would ultimately test Eleanor's powers of endurance.

THE LOVELY LUCY

After Woodrow Wilson defeated Teddy Roosevelt in the 1912 presidential election, he appointed his predecessor's 31-year-old nephew, Franklin, to be the assistant secretary of the navy. FDR, who had been a Democratic New York state senator, eagerly accepted the offer; 15 years earlier his uncle Teddy had used the same position as a springboard to the national political stage. Franklin loved the DC social scene and the nonstop dinner parties with congressmembers and lobbyists, but his introverted wife was overwhelmed by the frantic schedule and hired a buxom 23-year-old named Lucy Mercer to be her social secretary. Lucy had long, light-brown hair, sapphire blue eyes and a velvety voice that was said to mesmerize men.[8] Her cousin observed that "every man who ever knew her fell in love with her."[9]

Lucy was the daughter of dissolute, high-living socialites who blew the family fortune and left her without a penny but with a pedigree in the Washington social register. Her insider knowledge of DC society was a major asset for Eleanor, who invited the former debutante to be the extra woman at dinner parties.[10] Eleanor soon gave Lucy more and more household responsibilities, including balancing the family checkbook and serving as a nanny to the Roosevelt children, who grew to love Lucy. Elliot Roosevelt recalled, "She was femininely gentle where Mother had something of a schoolmarm's air about her, outgoing where Mother was an introvert. We children welcomed the days she came to work."[11] Their father also welcomed the days when Lucy showed up for work, usually wearing a back ribbon modestly but fetchingly tied around her neck. Franklin once said, "Nothing is more pleasing to the eye than a good looking lady; nothing more refreshing to the spirit than the company of one."[12] Every morning FDR greeted Lucy with a warm sigh, "Ah, the Lovely Lucy!"[13]

The young woman could not have helped but notice Mrs. Roosevelt's flirtatious husband. British military attaché Arthur Murray said young

Franklin was "breathing health and virility."[14] A reporter pondered the looks of the assistant secretary of the navy: "The face was particularly interesting. Breeding showed there, cleanly cut features, a small, sensitive mouth, tiny lines running from nostrils to the outline of lips, broad forehead, close cropped brown hair, frank blue eyes, but above all the straight, upstanding set of the head placed on the man." Another journalist called him an "engaging picture of American manhood," and a Yale football coach said, "Mr. Roosevelt is a beautifully built man with the long muscles of the athlete."[15] Franklin's son Elliot observed that Lucy had "the same brand of charm as Father, and there was a hint of fire in her warm dark eyes. . . . I see it as inevitable they were irresistibly attracted to each other."[16]

When Eleanor took the children on summer vacations to Campobello or Hyde Park, Franklin stayed behind in Washington, and so did Lucy.[17] Franklin arranged weekend getaways with Lucy, sometimes inviting President Wilson's personal physician Dr. Cary Grayson and his wife to join them.[18] The affair was common knowledge among the DC power elite, who considered it customary for politicians to pack off their families for summer vacations to the mountains or the seashore while the "paterfamilias accumulated something attractive."[19] Teddy Roosevelt's daughter Alice once spotted Franklin and Lucy out on a weekend drive. "I saw you 20 miles out in the country," she told her cousin. "You didn't see me. Your hands were on the wheel but your eyes were on the perfectly lovely lady." "Isn't she perfectly lovely," Franklin proudly replied.[20] Alice provided a safe house for her cousin's trysts and even invited the two paramours to her dinner parities with the Washington powerbrokers.[21] When someone asked Alice how she could be so cruel to her cousin Eleanor, she quipped "Franklin *deserved* a good time. He was married to Eleanor."[22] Not content to merely humiliate Eleanor behind her back, Alice confronted her with the affair in 1917. Eleanor informed Franklin that Alice "inquired if you had told me and I said no and that I did not believe in knowing things which your husband did not wish you to know so I think I will be spared any further mysterious secrets!"[23] That same year, Eleanor used America's entry into World War I to justify firing Lucy as a wartime sacrifice, and she continued to live in denial about the affair. FDR meanwhile conveniently gave his mistress a job in the Navy Department.

Lucy Mercer was truly the love of Franklin's life and—he thought—the woman he should have married. Unlike Eleanor, Lucy enjoyed the outdoors, long drives in the country, listening to his stories and, most importantly, sex. Franklin even began to talk about leaving Eleanor and his six children and running away with Lucy.[24] He got his opportunity. After a two-month inspection tour of the European front in 1918, he returned home with a case of the deadly flu that was raging throughout the world. While he recovered, Eleanor unpacked his luggage and found a hefty packet of perfumed letters tied with a velvet ribbon and addressed to Franklin in a familiar hand. Reading letter after letter Eleanor could no longer deny the affair to herself. "The bottom dropped out of my own particular world," she later told a friend. "I faced myself, my surroundings, my world, honestly for the first time."[25] After 13 years of marriage, the letters confirmed her worst fear—Franklin was indeed "too attractive" for her. Just as it had been time and again throughout her childhood, someone she loved and trusted had abandoned her.[26]

Humiliated and furious, Eleanor immediately asked Franklin if he wanted a divorce. Although a divorce would have destroyed his promising political career, Franklin was tempted. First, however, he had to check with his mother. Sara immediately threatened to cut him off financially if he didn't stick with his marriage to Eleanor.[27] FDR's trusted political mentor, Louis Howe, also weighed in, telling him a divorce would completely destroy his political career and his dream of following in his uncle's footsteps.[28] Unwilling to trade money and power for love and happiness, Franklin begged Eleanor to remain married.

She would agree to take him back only on two conditions: one, that they would never again share the same bed, and two, that he would never again see Lucy Mercer.[29] FDR had no problem with the first condition, and the 34-year-old Eleanor, who had borne six children in ten years, never had another child. The second condition was much more difficult. Franklin broke up with Lucy by blaming Eleanor for refusing to grant him a divorce. He didn't mention that it was he who had chosen Eleanor—meaning money and politics—over their love.[30] Still, Franklin was heartbroken; this was the first major disappointment in what had been a carefree, graced existence.

FDR's son Elliot recalled how the Mercer affair altered his parents' relationship: "Through the entire rest of their lives, they never did have a husband-and-wife relationship, but . . . they struck up a partnership agreement. This partnership was to last all the way through their life; it became a very close and very intimate partnership of great affection—never in a physical sense, but in a tremendously mental sense."[31] Legendary columnist and Roosevelt relative Joseph Alsop wrote, "To begin with it is a reasonable surmise that his wartime love affair, profoundly and forever resented by Eleanor Roosevelt, caused their relationship to be transformed for good from a normal marriage into the highly successful working partnership many people will still remember." James Roosevelt noted, "After that father and mother had an armed truce that endured until the day he died, despite several occasions I was to observe in which he in one way or another held out his arms to mother and she refused flatly to enter his embrace."[32] Eleanor later told a friend, "I have the memory of an elephant. I can forgive, but never forget," adding, "I really grew up that year."[33]

Had FDR followed his heart and run away with Lucy, history would have been very different. With his marriage publicly intact, young Franklin remained the darling of the Democratic Party and continued his meteoric rise in national politics. Woodrow Wilson invited Franklin and Eleanor to join the presidential delegation to the Paris Peace Conference in 1919, along with Edith Wilson. In the 1920 race against Republican Warren G. Harding, FDR became the vice presidential nominee at just 38 years old. After Harding won a landslide victory, Roosevelt was seen as the bright, shining hope for the future of the Democratic Party.

That same year, Lucy Mercer married a 57-year-old widower named Winthrop Rutherfurd, one of the wealthiest members of East Coast society. More than twice Lucy's age, Rutherfurd never sparked the romance that she felt with Franklin.[34] More than a quarter century later, Lucy still longed for FDR's "beloved presence . . . his ringing laugh . . . all the ridiculous things he used to say" and a glimpse of "his extraordinarily beautiful head."[35]

And Franklin never stopped loving Lucy. According to Joseph Alsop, the breakup with Mercer had a profound impact on FDR: "His disappointment in a strong and strongly felt love [for Lucy] did much to banish the 'featherduster' side of Franklin Roosevelt, and to deepen, toughen and mature his character and personality even prior to his paralysis."[36] The loss of Lucy left Franklin more resilient, less frivolous and taught him for the first time how unfair and disappointing life can be—a lesson that was soon reinforced by the greatest challenge of his life.

MISSY AND FD

During the 1920 campaign, Franklin hired a pert five-foot-seven 22-year-old secretary named Marguerite LeHand. With ink-blue eyes and jet-black hair, LeHand charmed everyone with her cheerful sprit, throaty voice and contagious laugh. She also proved to be a highly efficient secretary. One of FDR's friends found her "a compound of cunning and innocence, forever baffling."[37] LeHand juggled the candidate's schedule and his children, who had such trouble pronouncing "Miss LeHand" that they called her Missy—the name stuck.[38] Missy was not the beauty Lucy Mercer was, but she did give FDR the fawning attention he craved. She called him FD, or "Effdee," something no one, not even Louis Howe, dared to do. After the election, Franklin asked Missy to stay on as his personal secretary.

The following summer, still smarting from the disappointment of losing the 1920 election, the 39-year-old Roosevelt decided to lift his spirits by visiting a Boy Scout camp on Bear Mountain. While camping with the scouts, FDR contracted polio, which paralyzed him from the waist down. In those days, a disability was considered a mark of shame. Franklin's mother assumed he would retire from politics and live the quiet life of a gentleman farmer with her in Hyde Park. Franklin, however, was determined not to let his disability turn him into an invalid. He was fitted with 10 pounds of metal braces that extended from his waist to his heels. He learned to use his arms to lift his braced legs out of his wheelchair, snap the braces in place, and with someone steadying him, lurch his shoulders forward with enough force to drag his lifeless legs an inch or two forward. Every day for years he would spend hours moving inches.

While the physical exertion was daunting, the psychological battle was worse. For people who have the use of their legs, it is impossible to truly comprehend the shock of paralysis. One day FDR was sailing his yacht and swimming for hours; the next day he needed someone to help him roll over in bed. It was especially difficult for him to be suddenly dependent on other people for even his most basic needs. If he dropped a pencil, someone had to pick it up for him. If he wanted something to eat, someone had to fix him a snack. Worst of all for a man famous for his "breathing health and virility," he was no longer the "engaging picture of American manhood." FDR not only lost the use of his legs, he lost himself. Winston Churchill aptly called this period of Roosevelt's life his Wilderness Years.[39] Fortunately for FDR and the world, Missy LeHand was by his side.

Franklin discovered that swimming was the one way he could escape the braces and the wheelchair and move unencumbered. He bought a 71-foot houseboat he called the *Larooco* and sailed off the coast of Florida in 1924. Eleanor spent just two weeks on the mosquito-infested boat and hated every minute, but Missy loved any place as long as FD was around.[40] For four months each winter between 1924 and 1927, Missy served as first mate and hostess on the *Larooco*. She mixed Franklin's cocktails, sat by his side while he fished and provided warmth and understanding when the frustrations of paralysis broke through his cheerful exterior. "There were days on the *Larooco*," Missy tearfully recalled, "when it was noon before he could pull himself out of depression and greet his guests wearing his light-hearted façade."[41] Missy understood that FDR needed an affectionate female companion who reassured him that he was still a virile Adonis; visitors to the *Larooco* would often find Missy sitting on FDR's lap.[42]

Eleanor hated Franklin's daily cocktail parties, partly because of her father's alcoholism and partly because she was bored by the chitchat and old stories that dominated FDR's casual conversations.[43] Missy knew that for Franklin storytelling was not just a matter of reliving the good old days. By recounting his stories, FDR could once again become that bold, young six-foot-two state senator standing up to the Tammany Hall bosses. Storytelling was FDR's therapy.

Missy also indulged FDR in one of his greatest pleasures—driving. He had a car specially made so he could operate it by hand levers instead of foot pedals. Roosevelt was a terrible driver and many people, including Eleanor, refused to ride with him, but not Missy.[44] She understood what it meant for him to be out on the open road. Most people take for granted their ability to change their scene at will just by walking away from their desks to get a cup of coffee. Driving was Roosevelt's way to break the mind-numbing monotony and take control of where he was going. Missy was always ready to ride shotgun, cozying up next to him and squealing with delight as he careened around hairpin turns.[45]

Of the 208 weeks between 1924 and 1928, FDR was away from home 116 weeks. During these absences Eleanor was with him for 4 weeks and his mother 2. The rest of the 110 weeks, day and night, he was with Missy.[46] Missy spent so much time with FDR that she started speaking with his Hyde Park accent. As her years with FDR slipped by, a friend asked Missy if she was concerned about getting married. "Absolutely not," she replied. "How could anyone measure up to FD?"[47] On a rare vacation by herself in Norway she found a flower on a glacier, pressed it and sent it to her boss with a note that read "I'm going to be so good when I get back and never get cross or anything. Isn't that wonderful?"[48] When FDR was away without her she wrote, "Gosh, it will be good to get my eyes on you again. This place is horrible when you are away."[49] Clearly Missy and Franklin were more than just friends, but were they having sex?

We know FDR was morally capable of having an extramarital affair; but was he physically capable? Although polio destroyed the feeling and movement in his legs, the rest of his body was unaffected. Years later, when he was running for president, FDR was examined by three eminent physicians who found him fit for office and discovered "no symptoms of *impotentia coeundi*," which means FDR could get an erection.[50] Franklin's friend Dorothy Schiff, publisher of the *New York Post,* once asked his doctor, "Is the President potent?" The doctor replied, "It's only his legs that are paralyzed."[51] FDR's son Elliot, who spent more time on the *Larooco* than any of the other children, thought his father and Missy were having sex. Another son, James, was not so sure, but he recognized that Missy "filled a need and made him feel a man again, which mother did not do."[52] When FDR was president, he appointed one of Missy's close friends, Joseph Kennedy, to be ambassador to Great Britain in 1938. For appearances' sake, FDR suggested Kennedy break off his affair with Hollywood screen siren Gloria Swanson. The brash Irishman promised he would if the president set an example for the rest of the administration and gave up Missy.[53]

Each winter, after spending four months cruising on the *Larooco,* Franklin and Missy relocated directly to a resort in Warm Springs, Georgia, that had attracted crippled patients and wealthy vacationers since the antebellum period.

John C. Calhoun and Henry Clay had journeyed to Warm Springs to enjoy the pools of 80-degree spring water that bubbled out of the ground.

FDR had heard that the magnesium-laced waters made polio victims walk again and took Eleanor on his first visit to Warm Springs. Eleanor hated it. So Missy was the one who remained by Franklin's side every day as he underwent a strenuous exercise regimen in the buoyant waters. FDR enjoyed Warm Springs so much, he decided to buy the resort and convert it to an aftercare facility for polio victims. For FDR, Warm Springs offered an opportunity to be in complete charge and rebuild his self-esteem. Dubbing himself "Old Dr. Roosevelt," FDR spent over half his time from 1926 to 1928 in Warm Springs, where he shared a cottage with Missy who constantly reassured him of his progress and encouraged his dreams of walking again.[54]

A pivotal moment came during a workout when he "almost made it." A friend recalled, "We had a substitute head nurse that day, a large woman. He braced himself against one wall in the living room, and the nurse walked backward in front of him. Slowly, ever so slowly, he forced his body across the room—one inch at a time, it seemed. He was so drenched with sweat that I was afraid he would collapse from exhaustion. I've always believed that something happened that day, that, while he pretended it was a triumph, the effort to simply inch his way forward was so monumental that this was the moment he knew he would never really walk again. . . . I remember looking at Missy's face while he was trying to walk. She was in tears." The friend noted, "It was not long after this, in fact, that he decided to return to New York and get back into politics, a decision that effectively brought an end to his physical recovery."[55]

FDR had not planned on running for governor of New York in 1928. But sitting governor Al Smith was running in that year's presidential election and needed a strong Democratic contender for governor to pull New York's Electoral College votes into the Democratic column. When Al Smith telephoned Warm Springs to beg FDR to run, Missy pleaded, "Don't you dare! Don't you dare!"[56] Missy wanted FDR to stay focused on his exercises and, more selfishly, she did not want to lose her monopoly on his time and attention. But when the New York state Democratic Party voted to draft FDR for the 1928 gubernatorial race, he felt he had no choice. After he got the nomination, Eleanor sent a telegram: "REGRET THAT YOU HAD TO ACCEPT BUT KNOW THAT YOU FELT IT OBLIGATORY."[57] Everyone who loved Franklin thought the gubernatorial run in 1928 was premature. "Well I've got to run for governor," Franklin shrugged. "There's no use in all of us getting sick about it!"[58]

The years Roosevelt spent trying to walk were not wasted. His exertions bulked up his upper body so much he bragged about having a chest expansion greater than heavyweight champion Jack Dempsey.[59] His upper-body strength enabled him to lurch his heavily braced legs forward in a walking fashion. Photos and carefully edited film gave the impression he just had a bad limp. The press also helped shield his paralysis from the public. During his run for governor, when newsreel cameras began filming as he was lifted from his car, Roosevelt admonished the cameramen with his famous grin, "No movies of me getting out of the machine, boys." If a photographer tried to snap the candidate in his wheelchair, another reporter might "accidentally" knock his camera to the ground or block his view. In political cartoons, both positive and negative, FDR was constantly portrayed as a running, jumping, soaring superhero.[60] When he died, most Americans were shocked to find out their four-term president was paralyzed.[61]

The same press corps that shielded Franklin's disability from public view also ignored his extramarital relationships with Lucy Mercer and Missy LeHand. Journalist Raymond Clapper wrote in his diary in 1933 that gossip about the Mercer affair "buzzed around Washington," yet Clapper and other reporters obeyed the era's rules of journalistic ethics and never wrote about it.[62] Journalists did report on FDR's special connection to Missy when he was governor. The *Saturday Evening Post* remarked, "Missy is attuned to his moods, knows how to keep him company with conversation and with silence." *Newsweek* commented, "She knows when he is bored before he realizes it himself. She can tell when he is really listening . . . and when he is merely being polite—which no one else can—and she sometimes even senses when he is beginning to disapprove of something that he still thinks he likes."[63] But the press never suggested there was anything more to their relationship than deep mutual understanding.[64] Reporters, editors, civil servants and even political rivals gossiped and joked about FDR's paralysis and his extramarital affairs, but nothing was ever publicized.

The Great Depression hit while FDR was governor. He confronted New York State's 32 percent unemployment rate by creating the Temporary Emergency Relief Administration. For the first time, down-on-their-luck citizens could turn to the government instead of relying on charities for food, clothing and shelter.[65] "Old Dr. Roosevelt" was on his way to becoming "Old Dr. New Deal." As the 1932 election approached, the Democratic governor of the nation's most populous state was in prime position to unseat incumbent president Herbert Hoover.

It has become a truism that FDR's paralysis transformed him into a great leader with a unique capacity to sympathize with the downtrodden. But his son James rejected the "theory that Father would not have been a great man and a great public figure had he not gone through his personal Gethsemane. . . . I believe it was not polio that forged Father's character, but that it was Father's character that enabled him to rise above the affliction."[66] James Roosevelt was right. FDR became a great leader in spite of his paralysis, not because of it. Paralysis was not a blessing in disguise, it was a horrific challenge that FDR overcame through the force of his will and character, along with the daily encouragement of the loving Missy LeHand.

LOVE NEST ON THE VAL-KILL

The Lucy Mercer affair and Franklin's therapeutic vacations freed Eleanor to go on her own personal odyssey. When Franklin was first struck with paralysis, FDR's political mentor Louis Howe knew he was in no shape physically and emotionally to remain involved in the political scene. Howe urged Eleanor to become actively involved in party politics and instructed her to serve as Franklin's avatar, speaking to audiences and networking in New York State while her husband recuperated. Eleanor was not up to the task. She was deathly afraid of public speaking; she was self-conscious about her looks; stressful situations gave her migraines; she didn't think she was smart or tough enough to enter the rough-and-tumble world of politics. After all, she had been brought up her entire life to be a quiet, supportive spouse while her husband mounted the public stage. Howe was crestfallen—unless Eleanor got over her deep-seated inhibitions and her Victorian sensibilities, FDR's brilliant political career would be over.[67]

Fortunately, in 1921 Eleanor befriended a lesbian couple, Elizabeth Read, an accomplished lawyer, and Esther Lape, a successful publicist who taught English at Swarthmore and Barnard. Eleanor, who never held a job in her life, was impressed by these two career women, saying, "If I had to go out and earn my own living I doubt if I'd even make a very good cleaning woman. I have no talent, no experience, no training for anything." During the early 1920s, Eleanor spent at least one night a week at Read and Lape's Greenwich Village apartment having dinner, reading poetry aloud to each other and dreaming together of a world refashioned through progressive ideas.[68] Still smarting from the Mercer affair, Eleanor turned to Read and Lape as role models for how she could explore her own talents and establish an identity outside of her husband's.[69] Read and Lape also opened a door to another world of sexuality. Eleanor later wrote, "I have for years thought that Providence was particularly wise and farseeing when it threw these two women together, for their gifts complement each other in a most extraordinary way."[70] In her personal journal she wrote, "No form of Love is to be despised."[71]

Eleanor soon made friends with another lesbian couple, Nancy Cook and Marion Dickerman. Nancy was a tough-looking, 38-year-old liberal firecracker who headed the Women's Division of the New York state Democratic Committee. Eleanor was impressed that Nancy was also a potter, jeweler, photographer and carpenter, and she praised her as "an attractive woman who had distinct artistic ability and could do almost anything with her hands."[72] Eleanor became so close to Nancy that she ordered twin brown-tweed knickerbockers suits, which they wore on outings together. Nancy introduced Eleanor to her lover, Marion Dickerman, a soft-spoken teacher who was the first woman to run for legislative office in New York.[73] Marion's opponent called her the "Escaped Nun."[74] The couple had shared a Greenwich Village apartment for 13 years in what was then called a "Boston marriage," a common term for the arrangement of two unmarried woman living together.[75] Both women had been involved in the struggle for women's suffrage, the pacifist movement and the fight against child labor. Nancy and Marion welcomed Eleanor into their lives and worked hard to extricate her from her shell. They took her hiking, swimming and horseback riding and even taught her how to drive a car.[76] Eleanor wrote to Nancy and Marion, "I feel I'd like to go off with you and forget the rest of the world existed."[77] When she was stuck on the

Larooco with her husband and Missy, Eleanor wrote, "Much love to Nan and to you, life is quite empty without your dear presence."[78] Thanks to Marion and Nancy, Eleanor grew confident and outgoing. All of her previous relationships were marked by reserve and formality. She began calling Marion "Dickie," and they called her "Muddie."[79] They kissed and hugged each other publicly and had pillow fights at night. In just two years under Nancy and Marion's guidance, Eleanor shed her overinflated sense of her own limitations. She began addressing audiences on the need for political reform and workers' rights.[80] Just as Louis Howe had hoped, Eleanor became a major force in New York politics and was able to keep her husband's name in the political mix while he recovered from polio.

FDR and Howe jokingly called Nancy and Marion "Eleanor's squaws," "she-men" and "she-males," while the acid-tongued Alice Roosevelt called them "female impersonators."[81] But Franklin developed a great affection for Nancy and Marion. After all, they made his wife happier than he had ever seen her, and her relationship with the two lesbians alleviated his guilt over Missy LeHand. Of course he also saw how they transformed his wife into a political powerhouse who kept his ambitions alive while he and Missy were off on the *Larooco* and in Warm Springs. He called his wife's lesbian friends "our gang," and they returned the affection. Marion said, "Never in my life have I met so utterly charming a man."[82]

One late summer afternoon in 1924, Eleanor, Nancy, Marion and FDR were picnicking on the banks of a stream called Val-Kill, two miles east of the Roosevelt house in Hyde Park. Eleanor wistfully remarked that it was probably going to be their last picnic of the summer. "But aren't you girls silly?" Franklin interrupted. "I bought this acreage myself. And why shouldn't you three have a cottage here of your own, so you could come and go as you please? If you'll mark out the land you want, I'll give you a life interest in it, with the understanding that it reverts to my estate upon the death of the last survivor."[83] A deed was drawn up, and FDR hired a contractor: "My Missus and some of her female political friends want to build a shack on a stream in the back woods."[84]

FDR presided over the construction of the Val-Kill "shack," which turned out to be a fieldstone cottage built in the traditional Hudson River Dutch style. FDR teasingly christened it the "Honeymoon Cottage," which was not far off the mark. Eleanor, Marion and Nancy slept together in the single bed-room. The furniture and silverware were inscribed with the women's initials, EMN. Eleanor embroidered the linens and towels with "EMN," and the three women received housewarming gifts monogrammed with their three initials. To celebrate the opening of the Val-Kill cottage, which they named Stone Cottage, FDR gave Marion Dickerman the book *Little Marion's Pilgrimage*, inscribed, "To my little pilgrim, whose progress is always upward and onward, to the things of beauty and the thoughts of love, and the like—From her af-fectionate Uncle Franklin, on the occasion of the opening of the love nest on the Val-Kill." He also gave them a copy of one of his favorite speeches, in-scribed "Another first edition for the library of the Three Graces of the Val-Kill."[85] It was in the security of Stone Cottage that one night Eleanor finally opened up to Nancy and Marion about the deep wound of Franklin's affair with Lucy Mercer.[86]

When Franklin slept at his mother's house in Hyde Park, Eleanor stayed with Nancy and Marion in Stone Cottage. Franklin's mother was confused by Eleanor's relationship with the two women with their close-cropped hair-cuts, neckties and mannish suits. Sara asked one of Eleanor's friends, "Can you tell me why Eleanor wants to go over to Val-Kill cottage to sleep every night? Why doesn't she sleep here? This is her home. She belongs here."[87] But even Sara began to appreciate her daughter-in-law's special friendship with the Graces of Val-Kill. Soon after Stone Cottage was built she wrote to FDR, "Eleanor is so happy over there that she looks well and plump, don't tell her so."[88] New York and Washington social circles soon began gossiping about Eleanor and her friends. Alice Roosevelt was heard bellowing in a fashion-able Washington restaurant, "I don't care what they say. I simply cannot be-lieve that Eleanor Roosevelt is a lesbian."[89]

In 1925 Eleanor, Nancy and Marion founded the newsletter *Women's Democratic News* to galvanize liberal female voters in New York.[90] The fol-lowing year they bought the Todhunter School, an academy for girls, and moved it to Stone Cottage. Marion was the principal, and Eleanor served as the assistant principal and taught courses on American history and literature. Eleanor took her students on field trips to New York City courts and tene-ments. "I would like them to see the worst type of old time tenement. They need to know what bad housing conditions mean," she later wrote. "All this made the government of the city something real and alive, rather than just words in a textbook."[91]

Eleanor was also learning. Under Marion and Nancy's tutelage, her political and social views underwent a sea change. Back when FDR served in the New York state senate, she opposed women's suffrage and the equal rights amendment.[92] By the late 1920s she was one of the nation's most prominent voices for women's rights. Five years before she met Nancy and Marion, she resisted attending a party for the financier Bernard Baruch because she figured many Jews would be present. "I'd rather be hung than seen," she declared. She went anyway and found "the Jew Party appalling. I never wish to hear money, jewels and . . . sables mentioned again."[93] But by the mid-1920s, she was regularly addressing Jewish organizations around New York State. Thanks to Nancy and Marion, Eleanor abandoned her Victorian prejudices and was on the road to becoming the great civil rights advocate that we know her as today.

By the time FDR was elected governor of New York in 1928, the Roosevelts had one of the most unconventional marriages in the history of American politics. Franklin got his daily dose of adoring female affection from Missy, while Eleanor was free to pursue her own life with Nancy and Marion. When a reporter asked for Eleanor's reaction to her husband's election as governor of the most populous state in the Union, she answered, "I don't care. What difference does it make to me?"[94] She then explained that she would spend a few days in Albany for the inauguration and then return on Sunday night to Val-Kill so she could teach her Monday morning classes. In the governor's mansion, Franklin got the master bedroom with an adjoining doorway to Missy's room. Eleanor chose a smaller bedroom around the corner from her husband and Missy.[95] What was happening in the governor's mansion was a nightly ménage à trois, although who was the other woman was not easily discernible.[96]

HICK DEAREST

During FDR's campaign for president in 1932, another woman entered Eleanor's life—a strapping, five-foot-eight, 200-pound, 40-year-old Associated Press reporter named Lorena Hickok. Dressing in plaid flannel shirts and boots, Hick had hulking shoulders that slumped forward, so she didn't walk so much as trudge.[97] According to family legend she was descended from Wild Bill Hickok—she certainly had the spirit of a rugged gunslinger. The only other woman working in the Associated Press's New York office, Kay Beebe, recalled that Hick "was a big sort of masculine type, and she could play poker and swear and smoke and drink with the best of 'em." Hick's male colleagues didn't mind that she wasn't ladylike—in fact, Beebe said, "*Everybody* liked Lorena."[98] But Lorena didn't like everybody; as a male colleague noted, "Hick had a tendency to fall in love with women."[99] "She made for me," a frightened Kay Beebe recalled, "She wanted to hug me, and it wasn't good."[100]

Raised in rural Wisconsin by a sexually abusive father, Hickok was a survivor her whole life. Recalling the abuse she endured, she wondered, "Why my mother, who was a grown-up, too, and just as big as my father, let him do the things he did."[101] She found her escape though writing, and got a job working at the *Minneapolis Tribune,* where she fell in love with a petite, fairhaired society page reporter named Ellie Morse. The two lived together for eight years, until Ellie abruptly dumped Hick and eloped with an old boyfriend. Hick bounced back and moved to New York, where she busted through the glass ceiling of the male-dominated journalism world. She was the first woman to have her byline appear on the front page of the *New York Times,* and at 35 years old she became bureau chief of the Associated Press in New York City.[102]

During the last weeks of the 1932 presidential campaign, a 39-year-old Hick was assigned to cover Eleanor. "You'd better watch out for that Hickok woman," FDR warned his wife, "She's smart."[103] FDR did not have to worry. The 48-year-old Eleanor charmed Hick, and the two quickly bonded over their traumatic pasts. Hick opened up about her sexually abusive father and Ellie's betrayal. Eleanor shared tearful memories of her alcoholic father and Franklin's affair with Lucy. The reporter became Eleanor's buddy and began presenting the American public with depictions of the aspiring First Lady as a modern day superwoman with "the energy of a dynamo" and "an outstanding civic and welfare leader."[104] Hick violated every rule of journalistic ethics by sending her dispatches to be reviewed by Louis Howe before she submitted them to her editor.[105] Within weeks of meeting Eleanor, the hardnosed reporter completely surrendered her professional integrity and became a mouthpiece for the Roosevelt campaign—such is the power of love.

At Franklin's inauguration on March 4, 1933, Eleanor wore a sapphire and diamond ring that Hick had given her for Christmas. Eleanor later wrote Hick, "I want to put my arms around you . . . to hold you close. Your ring is a great comfort. I look at it and think she does love me or I wouldn't be wearing it."[106] After the inaugural festivities, Hick returned to New York and was separated from Eleanor for the first time in months. The night she left Washington on March 5, 1933, the new First Lady wrote, "Hick my dearest, I cannot go to bed without a word to you. I felt a little as though part of me was leaving tonight, you have grown so much to be a part of my life that it is empty without you even though I'm busy every minute."[107] During a phone conversation with Hick the next day, Eleanor realized her son James was within earshot and later complained in a letter, "I couldn't say *je t'aime et je t'adore* as I longed to do but always remember I am saying it & that I go to sleep thinking of you & repeating our little saying."[108] Three days later Eleanor wrote, "My pictures are nearly all up & I have you in my sitting room where I can look at you most of my waking hours! I can't kiss you so I kiss your picture good night & good morning! . . . My dear, if you meet me [in public] may I forget there are reporters present or must I behave? I shall want to hug you to death."[109] Two days later on March 9 Eleanor wrote, "Oh! I wanted to put my arms around you in reality instead of spirit. I went & kissed your photograph instead & tears were in my eyes. Please keep most of your heart in Washington as long as I'm here for most of mine is with you!"[110] Despite the whirlwind excitement of her first week in the White House, Eleanor's thoughts always returned to Hick.

Marion Dickerman and Nancy Cook were jealous and had good reason to be.[111] In November 1933 Eleanor reported to Hick that she and a friend had been cleaning and decorating a house in upstate New York: "Sunday morning we worked till 1 AM but slept well. Tiny & I in her big double bed which was comfortable in the guest room, only I wished it was you."[112] Hick wrote Eleanor on December 5, "I remember your eyes, with a kind of teasing smile in them and the feeling of that soft spot just northeast of the corner of your mouth against my lips. I wonder what we'll do when we meet—what we'll say."[113] After a weekend away together, Hick wrote, "Each time we have together *that* way—brings us closer, doesn't it?"[114]

Eleanor and Hickok exchanged thousands of letters over the course of their 30-year friendship, but in 1936 Hick began burning hundreds—most dating from 1933 when the relationship was most intense. Hick explained to Eleanor's daughter Anna why she burned them: "Your mother wasn't always so very discreet in her letters to me."[115] The most revealing evidence of what Eleanor and Hick did sexually probably went up in flames.[116]

Being separated from Eleanor became so painful for Hick that she quit her prestigious job at the Associated Press in the summer of 1933 and moved into the White House, where she took a small room next to Eleanor's. The staff mocked Hick's bulldozer stride, gruff manner and butch garb. One maid sneered, "Put a seam down the middle of her skirt and I swear, old Hicky will be wearing a man's suit."[117] White House maid Lillian Parks said she never saw Hick and Eleanor "in a compromising situation, that is I never saw them in bed together. But I was at the White House on many occasions when Hicky, as we all called her behind her back, slept in the First Lady's bedroom suite, on the daybed in her sitting room. Supposedly, the reason was that there were so many guests."[118] Eleanor got Hick jobs with the Democratic National Committee (DNC) Women's Division and the Federal Emergency Relief Administration (FERA), but Hick's real job was companion to the First Lady. "What goes?" a White House staff member asked. "FDR was spending his evenings with Missy LeHand, while Eleanor Roosevelt was spending evenings with Lorena Hickok."[119]

Hick was aware of the raised eyebrows in the White House and was careful to hide from outsiders the fact that she lived there. One of her DNC duties was to escort female VIPs to the White House. "I had an understanding with the doormen and the ushers that when I arrived with one of my delegations there must be no indication that I ever entered the White House except on occasions such as these," Hick recounted in an unpublished memoir. The ushers "would greet me formally, along with the rest, take our names, and escort us to the Red Room, announcing us to the other guests assembled and waiting for Mrs. Roosevelt to come down. Mrs. Roosevelt would play the game, too, greeting me with, 'Why, how nice to see you!' as though she hadn't seen me for a month, although we had actually had breakfast together that morning!"[120]

Eleanor and Hick seemed to have been discussing a life together after the White House. After the First Lady visited an elderly friend, she wrote Hick, "It is sad to be helpless & poor and old, isn't it? I hope you & I together have enough to make it gracious and attractive." Thinking about furniture for their future home, Eleanor mentioned longing for a "corner cupboard . . . for our camp or cottage or house, which is it to be?" She wrote, "I've always thought of it in the country, but I don't think we ever decided on the variety of abode nor the furniture. We probably won't argue."[121] And she promised Hick, "We'll have years of happy times so bad times will be forgotten." The First Lady admitted to her lover, "I realize F.D.R. is a great man & he is nice to me but as a person, I'm a stranger & don't want to be anything else." But she also expressed resignation about her marriage, "I know I've got to stick. I know I'll never make an open break & never tell F.D.R. how I feel."[122]

Hick had a historic effect on the role of the First Lady. When Eleanor first entered the White House, she was depressed and anxious. She assumed she would have to abandon all the social and political activism she had begun with Marion and Nancy and take on the traditional role of White House hostess that all previous First Ladies had played—with the notable exception of Edith Wilson. Hick, however, recognized that Eleanor could use the prominent role of First Lady to make revolutionary changes for American women and the public as a whole. Hick worked behind the scenes, guiding Eleanor's decisions and activities that forever changed the role of the First Lady. She convinced Eleanor to become the only First Lady in history to conduct weekly press conferences, which enabled Eleanor to promote her liberal agenda unfiltered by her husband's political advisors. During her 348 press conferences, Eleanor championed everything from establishing a national minimum wage to enlarging the role of women in government, to funding public housing, to creating programs for the disabled.[123] Hick suggested Eleanor write for magazines about current affairs and came up with the idea for the First Lady to publish a running account of her daily experiences and political opinions, which became Eleanor's nationally syndicated column, My Day. Hick employed her writing skills editing Eleanor's articles before they were submitted. Eleanor wrote My Day from 1935 until she died in 1962, a total of 8,000 columns.[124] With Hick's encouragement, Eleanor signed a contract to deliver radio broadcasts for $3,000 a week. In an era when few women had professional careers, Eleanor became a public face of the New Deal and began her 30-year career as a pundit and activist.

Eleanor became such an asset for the administration that she was sent around the country in the 1930s to make personal appearances at coal mines, factories and labor meetings and assure workers her husband was fighting for them. When FDR needed a frank assessment of a New Deal initiative like the Civilian Conservation Corps, he dispatched Eleanor to inspect the CCC camps.[125] In the middle of World War II, FDR sent Eleanor to war-ravaged Britain. Newsweek reported, "The First Lady is receiving the greatest ovation ever paid any American touring Britain. Groups loiter about the American Embassy all day long hoping to catch a glimpse of her. There are spontaneous outbursts of cheers and clapping at stations when she unexpectedly appears."[126] Hick was thrilled by the press acclaim: "I'm simply delighted with the press you are getting. I'm awfully happy about it and so proud of you."[127] Hitler's propaganda chief Joseph Goebbels was less enthusiastic and ordered all German journalists to ignore "the hullabaloo about Eleanor Roosevelt."[128] Eleanor also ventured into the Pacific war zone on a 26,000-mile journey to visit the troops and comfort thousands of wounded servicemen. When ex-empress Zita of Austria-Hungary asked FDR if his wife's tour of the Pacific theater would exhaust her, he answered, "No, but she will tire everybody else."[129]

Lorena Hickok's support was key to Eleanor Roosevelt's emergence as a confident, fearless leader. For the first time, Eleanor found in Hick an adoring lover who was absolutely exclusive to her. Previously, she had always been the third wheel with various couples—Elizabeth and Esther, Marion and Nancy, even Franklin and his other women. But Hick was all hers. "Every woman wants to be first to someone in her life," Eleanor wrote, "and that desire is an explanation for many strange things women do."[130] For once, Eleanor knew that she—the homely, bucktoothed, sickly, shy girl—was the most important person in someone's life. The love of this one woman gave Eleanor the confidence to earn and embrace the love of millions.[131] "You taught me more than you know & it brought me happiness," Eleanor wrote

Hick. "You've made of me so much more of a person just to be worthy of you."[132] Lorena Hickok was the woman behind the woman.[133]

Hick went on vacations alone with Eleanor and, according to a White House staff member, always trailed behind the First Lady like a "St. Bernard." Newspaper reports usually identified Hick as Eleanor's secretary or even her bodyguard.[134] The *San Francisco Chronicle* remarked that the "plump, ruddy and hatless" Hickok "played the role of guardian in chief to the First Lady for several years."[135] When Hick complained to Eleanor about the gossip regarding their relationship, the First Lady reassured her: "Dear one, and so you think they gossip about us, they must at least think we stand separations rather well! I am always so much more optimistic than you are. I suppose because I care so little what 'they' say!"[136]

Hick was extremely worried about the press and was infuriated by a *Time* magazine cover story about her boss at FERA, Harry Hopkins. The article carried a particularly unflattering photo of Hick, and it suspiciously dwelled on her relationship with the First Lady. "His [Hopkins's] chief field representative and investigator is Miss Lorena Hickok. . . . She is a rotund lady with a husky voice, a preemptory manner, baggy clothes . . . [who] became fast friends with Mrs. Roosevelt. Since then she has been going around a lot with the first lady, up to Brunswick and down to Warm Springs."[137] Hick ranted to Hopkins's secretary, "I'm so fed up with publicity I want to kick every reporter I see. I suppose I am 'a rotund lady with a husky voice' and 'baggy clothes,' but I honestly don't believe my manner is 'preemptory.' Why the Hell CAN'T they leave me alone?"[138] Hick was most worried about the magazine's comments regarding her being "fast friends with Mrs. Roosevelt" and "going around a lot with the first lady." Having been a reporter, she knew that journalists deployed code words and suggestive phrases to say something without actually saying it. She also knew the president would accept his wife's unconventional relationship as long as it stayed within the White House walls, but not if it became a public scandal.

Hick noticed that after the article appeared, FDR started becoming testy toward her. White House maid Lillian Parks recalled, "When the Roosevelts first arrived in 1933, there was a short honeymoon stage around the White House when Hick was an open guest, welcomed by the President, joining the family for dinner. But eventually, so the sub rosa story went, he got the drift and feared the situation could give the White House a bad reputation. The President was heard raising his voice to Eleanor, telling her, 'I want that woman kept out of this house.'"[139] Parks also remembered one afternoon when the president was having a cocktail with Missy. Eleanor popped in to ask if she might bring in her female friends and Franklin shouted, "No you may not!" When Eleanor left, FDR exploded, "I can't stand those she-males." Parks noted, "That woman meant too much to Eleanor, and instead of keeping her out of the house, she simply kept her out of FDR's sight."[140]

Even worse for Hick than the president's displeasure was Eleanor's sudden emotional withdrawal. By mid 1934 the First Lady's demanding schedule left her little time or energy to devote to Hick. "No question that Hick helped Eleanor get her wings," a Roosevelt relative observed, "but once Eleanor began to fly she didn't need Hick the same way."[141] And that was a big problem, according to Roosevelt's granddaughter Eleanor Seagraves, because Hick "let herself slip into [a] role where she lost her old identity and became dependent on my grandmother."[142]

A moody, sullen Hick created a public scene during an August 1934 trip with the First Lady to Yosemite when dozens of tourists began taking pictures of Eleanor feeding chipmunks. Hick suddenly began stalking around as if a wild animal herself and shouting at the tourists, "Mind your own goddamn business," among other expletives. Hick recalled, "We had just started to feed them when I realized that we were completely surrounded by tourists, all pointing cameras at us. Bending over to feed a chipmunk is not a very dignified position . . . and I lost my temper." The First Lady had to "shush" Hick and pull her away from the slack-jawed vacationers.[143] Hick apologized for her behavior two weeks later: "Good night I hope you are having a happy, restful time at Camp—a happier, more peaceful time than you had with me. Oh, I'm bad, my dear, but I love you so. At times life becomes just one long, dreary ache for you."[144]

Eleanor and Hick became trapped in the vicious cycle that lovers often fall into during the initial stages of a breakup. As one demands more and more, the other pulls farther and farther away. Eleanor felt guilty about the situation: "I went to sleep saying a little prayer, 'God give me depth enough not to hurt Hick again.' Darling, I know I'm not up to you in many ways but I love you dearly."[145] Lorena asked Eleanor, "It would be so much better, wouldn't it, if I didn't love you so much sometimes? It makes it trying for you."[146] By 1934 Eleanor was writing, "Love is a queer thing, it hurts one but it gives one so much more in return!"[147] Eleanor certainly benefited from Hick's love; she became an internationally admired celebrity. Unfortunately, as Lorena explained to Eleanor in 1940, the First Lady's new fame got in the way of their relationship: "I'd never have believed it possible for a woman to develop after 50 as you have in the last six years. My trouble, I suspect, has always been that I've been so much more interested in the person than the personage. I still prefer the person, but I admire and respect the personage with all my heart!"[148] It seems that once Eleanor attracted the respect, adoration and love of the masses, she no longer needed Hick.

Hick tried filling the hole left by Eleanor's distance by having several flings. When Hick admitted a new love interest in June 1934, a jealous Eleanor snapped, "How hard for you to have a lady who is in love in her mind with you. Well if she is in love, you can tell her how to snap out of it!"[149] Hick became involved with Judge Marion Janet Harron of the U.S. tax court and brought the judge back to the White House so often that the guards stopped asking for Harron's identification. Despite her jealous words, Eleanor was actually relieved to see Hick move on. Ten years before, FDR had smiled on Eleanor's relationship with Nancy and Marion as welcome relief from the guilt of having Missy LeHand. Now Hick's new relationship was similarly sparing Eleanor the guilt of no longer needing the woman who sacrificed everything for her.[150]

THE SUBSTITUTE FIRST LADY

Everyone in the White House knew the First Couple were leading separate private lives. White House usher J. B. West said he "never saw Eleanor and Franklin Roosevelt in the same room alone together. They had the most separate relationship I have ever seen between a man and wife."[151] Harry Hopkins told a colleague, "Watch them, because they do all their communication with each other in public."[152]

While Eleanor was busy with her international acclaim and Hick, Franklin still had Missy. Missy's friend Barbara Curtis observed, "The president would work night after night, and she was always there working with him."[153] According to Lillian Parks, "Missy was somehow involved with everything FDR did for fun. Eleanor never showed any interest in FDR's stamp collection. Missy was an excited assistant collector, working on his collection with him and reminding him of where he had stashed some missing stamp." A White House staff member noticed, "Missy made sure to wear high heels that clicked along pleasantly instead of the low heels and sensible oxfords the First Lady wore."[154]

Missy began to wield authority in the White House. "When Missy gave an order we responded as if it had come from the First Lady," Lillian Parks recalled. "We really had two mistresses in the White House."[155] Missy was known to interrupt cabinet meetings to announce that it was time for the president to take his medicine or to remind him to put on his jacket because of a draft.[156] According to Parks, the entire White House staff concluded "that Missy was the substitute wife, and we honored her for it."[157] White House aide Ray Moley said, "There's no doubt that Missy was as close to being a wife as he ever had—or could have."[158] None of this was lost on Eleanor, who remarked, "He couldn't have lived without me but neither could he have lived without Missy." The First Lady figured, "If he had met her earlier, it would have been different."[159] "Missy alleviated Mother's guilt," Elliot Roosevelt noted. "Knowing Missy was always there allowed Mother to come and go as she pleased without worrying about Father or feeling she was neglecting her wifely duties."[160]

The substitute wife also became a key member of the administration. *Newsweek* proclaimed Missy "the President's super-secretary."[161] Sam Rosenman noted that "she was one of the few people who could say 'No' to the President and say it in a way he could take." During the 1936 campaign, Missy was on hand when FDR reviewed a boring financial speech with his speechwriters. As the president read aloud the turgid prose, Missy stood up and announced, "By this time the bleachers are empty and the folks are beginning to walk out of the grandstand." As she huffed out of the room, everyone cracked up and the draft was discarded.[162] FDR's advisors understood her special relationship with the president and began seeking her advice on when to approach him or when to put off a vexing matter until another day.

Missy's files contain numerous requests from the most powerful men in America asking her to intervene with the president on behalf of one important cause or another.[163]

Missy might have been FDR's substitute wife, but she was not the love of his life.[164] Despite the Herculean tasks that confronted Roosevelt during the Great Depression and World War II, the White House switchboard operators had standing orders to always put a certain Mrs. Paul Johnson right through to the president. "Mrs. Johnson" was really Lucy Mercer Rutherfurd.[165]

Over the decades since their heartbreaking split in 1918, Roosevelt had maintained contact with Lucy and occasionally saw her at Bernard Baruch's home in South Carolina. FDR provided her with tickets to his first inauguration, and she was present for his acceptance speech at the Democratic National Convention in 1936. After a severe stroke disabled her husband Winthrop in 1941, Lucy was able to regularly sneak visits with Franklin in Washington.[166] White House usher J. B. West described how the president would secretly meet with his wife's nemesis by ordering the Secret Service to take him for a drive in the Virginia countryside. Suddenly FDR would tell the driver to turn down a dirt road, remarking casually, "There seems to be a lady waiting along the road. Let us ask her if she needs a ride."[167] Standing next to her car would be the lovely Lucy, now 50 years old but still fetching and wearing a black ribbon around her neck just as she had when she first won FDR's heart 30 years before. After the president picked up Lucy he would order the driver to take a circuitous path to her destination. Sealed off from the driver by a glass partition, the two old friends reveled in each other's presence. One of FDR's guards, Mike Reilly, remembered that, after riding around with the "charming and beautiful woman," "the president would return to the White House much relaxed and happy."[168]

Lucy's visits to the White House were closely timed to avoid Eleanor—the First Lady would leave at four thirty and Lucy would be up in the presidential quarters by five thirty. Franklin Roosevelt Jr. once made a surprise visit while on military leave and popped in to FDR's study to find Lucy massaging his father's legs. The president blithely introduced her as his "old friend, Mrs. Winthrop Rutherfurd."[169] FDR also took Lucy to Shangri-La, a presidential retreat in a former Civilian Conservation Corps summer camp in the Maryland Catoctin Mountains, known today as Camp David.[170] Were Lucy and Franklin lovers at this point? The historian Doris Kearns Goodwin put it best: "It is impossible to know, though given the state of Roosevelt's health, doubt remains. Still, even if they did not share the same bed, it is reasonable to imagine that there was a pleasing sexuality in their friendship."[171]

Whether FDR was still having sex with Lucy would not have mattered to Eleanor. Even after two decades, the pain of the original betrayal was still raw. So the entire White House staff collaborated in covering up Lucy's visits; switchboard operators, Secret Service agents, government drivers, White House ushers, maids, secretaries and valets all participated in the conspiracy of silence. Of course, by 1941, ignoring secret visitors to the White House had become part of the routine of the Roosevelt years.

The press certainly was not going to expose a presidential sex scandal in the middle of World War II, when such an act would have bordered on treason. During the war, the commander in chief's whereabouts became a closely guarded national security secret. When FDR had his presidential train stop at Lucy's hometown in New Jersey on his way to Hyde Park, local newspapers wanted to report on his visit but had to ask the federal Office of Censorship for permission. All reports on the visit were suppressed.[172]

Lucy's visits could be kept from the national press and the First Lady, but shielding them from Missy LeHand was impossible. The day before one of Lucy's visits in 1941 Missy experienced the first in a series of strokes. Missy had had nervous collapses before: after the sale of the *Larooco* and after Franklin's announcement that he was running for governor in 1928. The events that preceded her nervous collapses were all threats to her monopoly on FDR's time and affection.[173] Franklin's grandson Curtis Roosevelt concluded, "I think it's not entirely speculative to tie Missy's eventual breakdowns to her frustration with the fact that she was in love with somebody who was probably not in love with her."[174]

Secretary of the Interior Harold Ickes said Missy's disability "constituted the greatest loss that the President has suffered since his inauguration."[175] Yet FDR seemed unfazed by Missy's sickness. "The strange thing," Elliot Roosevelt observed, "was that Mother was more protective and upset about Missy's illness than Father. He seemed to accept it and go through the loss without it affecting him nearly as much as I would have thought it would have affected him."[176] Visiting Missy in the hospital was unbearable for FDR, so Eleanor went to see her as much as she could. Economic advisor Elliot Janeway observed that "Roosevelt had absolutely no moral relation to Missy's tragedy. It seemed only that he resented her for getting sick and leaving him in the lurch. This was proof that he had ceased to be a person; he was simply the president. If something was good for him as president, it was good; if it had no function for him as president, it didn't exist."[177] Janeway's comment is not entirely fair. The heavy burdens of office combined with FDR's own declining health had left the president with little emotional currency to spend on caring for someone else. He was, however, extremely worried that Missy would not be able to afford her medical bills if he died before her, and he ordered his lawyer to revamp his will so she would receive half his estate. When his lawyer pointed out this change meant his children would get nothing, FDR insisted: "The children could care for themselves, but this faithful aide could not."[178]

On the evening of July 30, 1944, Missy and her sister went to the movies and saw a newsreel report on the president. Missy had not seen Franklin in person or even seen a recent picture of him for several months. "She was shocked at the way he looked and the way his voice sounded," one of Missy's friends recalled.[179] Seeing the images of the haggard president, Missy knew Franklin was approaching death. After the sisters returned home from the movies, Missy pored over old pictures of FD from their happy days on the *Larooco* and their first trips to Warm Springs until she fell asleep. That night, Missy was hit by a cerebral embolism and died at the age of 46.[180] Sam Rosenman called Missy "one of the most important people of the Roosevelt era" and concluded that "had she lived she could have so lightened his wartime burden that his own life would have been prolonged."[181]

CODA

Missy's absence from the White House left the president isolated and alone. "See who's home and ask them to stop in," he would tell an usher as he prepared his own cocktail. Many nights the usher reported back, "Sorry, Mr. President, there is no one home." FDR would then have a solitary meal on a tray and go to bed early.[182] Some of Missy's responsibilities were taken up by

Franklin's daughter Anna, recently divorced after a publicly scandalous affair with a married man. At her father's request, Anna secretly arranged for him to have desperately needed visits with Lucy Mercer Rutherfurd. Anna felt guilty for betraying her own mother, but after observing the two forbidden lovers, she recalled, "I realized Mother was not capable of giving him this: just listening. . . . Lucy was Father's emotion for life."[183]

FDR asked Anna to arrange another secret rendezvous with Lucy at Warm Springs in April 1945. Lucy invited the famed artist Madame Shoumatoff along on the trip to paint FDR's portrait. Seeing how gaunt her subject was, Shoumatoff decided to add bulk to his frame by having the president don a cape. As she was painting, with Lucy and FDR's cousin Daisy Suckley watching, Franklin suddenly complained of a terrible headache and slumped forward, his hand thrashing by his side. Daisy jumped up, asking, "Have you dropped your cigarette?" She recalled, "He looked at me with his forehead furrowed in pain and tried to smile. He put his left hand up to the back of his head & said, 'I have a terrific pain in the back of my head!'"[184] FDR then lost consciousness. At the age of 63, the president was dead of a cerebral hemorrhage.

Eleanor was sitting next to former First Lady Edith Wilson at a piano concert when someone whispered to her that there was an urgent call from the White House. As soon as she was told to return home immediately, she later recalled, "I knew down in my heart that something dreadful had happened."[185]

On the funeral train from Warm Springs to Hyde Park, Eleanor learned from Daisy that Lucy was with FDR when he died. She was furious with both her daughter and her dead husband. She later admitted having "an almost impersonal feeling at my husband's death, partly because much further back I had to accept the fact that a man must be what he is and that all human beings have needs and temptations."[186] "The act of being physically unfaithful seems much less important to the average man," Eleanor wrote in her memoir. Her husband "might have been happier with a wife who was completely uncritical. That I was never able to be, and he had to find it in some other people. Nevertheless, I think I sometimes acted as a spur, even though the spurring was not always wanted or welcome." In acknowledgment of the role that Lucy had played in her late husband's life, Eleanor requested that one of FDR's portraits be given to Lucy Mercer.[187]

We, like Eleanor, must acknowledge that FDR's extramarital affairs played a positive role in the success of the president, as well as the life of the man. Roosevelt craved the affection of women who—like his mother Sara—fuelled his self-confidence and gave him the kind of undivided attention that his hard-charging wife could not and would not. As Daisy Suckley observed, Eleanor simply "lacked the ability to give him the things his mother gave him."[188] And Franklin Delano Roosevelt's self-confidence was essential to his unique ability to rally the country during the Great Depression and World War II. By pumping up FDR, Lucy and Missy did the nation and the world a great service.

FDR's other women also freed Eleanor from having to attend to her needy husband and allowed her the space to explore her own sexuality. Most significantly, she was free to focus on her own historic fight for social and economic justice, becoming a political force in her own right. After her husband's death, Eleanor continued her crusade for women's rights and civil rights that she began with Nancy Cook and Marion Dickerson in the 1920s. President John F. Kennedy appointed her chair of the Presidential Commission on the Status of Women, and she lent her prestige and voice to the burgeoning civil rights movement. After she died on November 7, 1962, African American journalist Carl T. Rowen wrote in the *Boston Globe,* "Whether in praise or criticism, millions view Eleanor Roosevelt as one of the major reasons for the change in status of colored people, particularly American Negroes, during the last quarter century."[189] India's prime minister Jawaharlal Nehru said, "No woman of this generation and few in the annals of history have so well understood and articulated the yearnings of men and women for social justice."[190] Historians can debate the rankings of presidents but no one can dispute that Eleanor Roosevelt was the greatest First Lady.

After her death, someone discovered among the papers at her bedside a tattered, faded newspaper clipping of Virginia Moore's poem *Psyche:*

The soul that had believed
And was deceived
Ends by believing more
Than ever before.

Across the top of the poem, Eleanor had written "1918"—the year she discovered Franklin's affair with Lucy Mercer and began her journey of self-discovery that would make her a great humanitarian hero.[191]

Eleanor was laid to rest next to her husband in Hyde Park. Her funeral was attended by President Kennedy, First Lady Jackie Kennedy, Vice President Lyndon Johnson, and former presidents Truman and Eisenhower. After the sun went down and everyone had disappeared, a lone mourner slipped onto the grounds to bid a final farewell. Too distraught to attend the funeral, a 69-year-old Lorena Hickok secretly laid a wreath on Eleanor's grave in the dark of night.[192]

Famed artist Charles Wilson Peale produced this sketch after witnessing a middle-aged Franklin in a compromising position with 18-year-old Polly Stevenson in the 1750s. (Courtesy the American Philosophical Society)

Franklin's well-earned reputation as a ladies' man aided his effort to secure France's military assistance during the Revolutionary War. (Courtesy the Library of Congress)

A PHILOSOPHIC COCK

This 1804 political cartoon titled, "A Philosophic Cock," mocked President Thomas Jefferson's relationship with his slave Sally Hemings. (Courtesy the Library of Congress)

Dolley Madison may be famous today for saving George Washington's portrait but in early America she was notorious for sleeping with three presidents, one vice president, and a multitude of congressmen and diplomats. She was also well known for her cleavage. (Courtesy the Library of Congress)

Popular French dancer Madame Celeste entertaining President Andrew Jackson and his cabinet around the time a national sex scandal involving Peggy Eaton divided the cabinet and set the nation on a course to civil war. (Courtesy the Library of Congress)

Was Abe Lincoln gay? Members of Washington society gossiped about President Lincoln's wartime relationship with Army Captain David Derickson. An 1895 history of Derickson's regiment noted that "Captain Derickson in particular advanced so far in the president's confidence and esteem, that—in Mrs. Lincoln's absence—he frequently spent the night at his cottage, sleeping in the same bed with him, and it is said, making use of his Excellency's nightshirt!" (Courtesy the Library of Congress)

President Warren G. Harding's marriage to Florence, five years his senior, was a great political partnership, but it was childless and sexless. To Harding's delight, plenty of other women were willing to join him on what he called "detours from the primrose path." (Courtesy the Library of Congress)

President Wilson's girlfriend Edith Galt edited his wartime letters to the Kaiser and became his closest adviser after they married in 1915. After Wilson suffered a stroke in 1919, Edith took control of the White House. "Mrs. Wilson is President!" Senator Albert Fall fumed. (Courtesy the Library of Congress)

Franklin Roosevelt's affair with Lucy Mercer almost broke up his marriage and destroyed his political career in 1918. FDR continued to secretly meet with Lucy throughout his presidency and was with her on the day he died. FDR's daughter said, "Lucy was Father's emotion for life." (Courtesy the Franklin D. Roosevelt Presidential Library)

FBI Associate Director Clyde Tolson with J. Edgar Hoover. The two lifelong bachelors ate lunch and dinner together every night and took their vacations together. Meanwhile Hoover became a puppet master over the government by assembling secret files on congressmen, presidents, and Supreme Court justices. (New York Daily News Archive/Getty Images)

When John Kennedy was elected president in 1960 his speechwriter Ted Sorensen predicted, "This administration is going to do for sex what the previous one did for golf." The Kennedys were the perfect First Family for a nation on the cusp of the sexual revolution. (Courtesy the Library of Congress)

President Kennedy basking in the attention of Santa Monica beachgoers in 1962. JFK once admitted, "I get a migraine headache if I don't get a strange piece of ass every day." (Courtesy the UCLA University Library)

After JFK's assassination, Jackie moved into a house in Georgetown. Here she says good-bye to Bobby and his wife Ethel. It was during this period that RFK and Jackie began an affair that would have shocked the world. (Bettman/Corbis)

President Richard Nixon at his daughter's White House wedding in 1971. The FBI investigated his alleged affair with a Communist Chinese spy named Marianna Lui. (Courtesy the Library of Congress)

A 16-year-old Bill Clinton meets President Kennedy in the Rose Garden in 1963. When Clinton's mother saw this photo, she later recalled, "I knew right then that politics was the answer for him." (Arnold Sachs/Archive Photos/Getty Images)

More than three decades later, in 1995, President Bill Clinton greets 21-year-old intern Monica Lewinsky. When Monica's father first saw this photo he immediately noticed Clinton's "lascivious eyes. He looked at my daughter in a weird way." Monica called the president's undressing leer "the full Bill Clinton." (Getty Images News/ Getty Images)

CHAPTER FIVE

AMERICA'S SEX CZAR

During the Cold War, most Americans would have said the most powerful man on earth was the president of the United States, but Washington insiders would have said J. Edgar Hoover.[1] Presidents came and went, but not Mr. Hoover, who served as Federal Bureau of Investigation (FBI) director for 48 years. This unelected official became a puppet master over the three branches of government by assembling secret files on the private lives of congressmembers, presidents and Supreme Court justices. President Harry S Truman understood that Hoover used sex to threaten the constitutional order. "We want no Gestapo or Secret Police. FBI is tending in that direction," Truman wrote in 1945. "They are dabbling in sex life scandals and plain blackmail when they should be catching criminals."[2] But not even the commander in chief could stop Hoover, who revealingly christened FBI headquarters the Seat of Government.

KID NAPOLEON

Hoover was a snoop even as a little boy growing up in Washington, DC, during the waning days of the nineteenth century. At 11 years old he began meticulously recording the daily activities of his neighbors in his diary and supplemented his allowance by publishing a one-cent newsletter filled with neighborhood gossip called *Weekly Review*. The regimented youth led his high school marching brigade in Woodrow Wilson's inauguration parade. While attending George Washington University, Hoover got his first government job working at the Library of Congress. The uptight, orderly college student mastered the system for cataloging books—a system that he would later use to organize the FBI's files on tens of thousands of Americans.

During World War I, at just 23 years of age, Hoover became head of the Justice Department's Enemy Aliens Registration section, responsible for monitoring the activities of thousands of suspected saboteurs and dissidents. He failed to uncover any spies, but he did enjoy cracking down on anyone suspected of disloyalty. He once recommended that a German immigrant be sent to an internment camp for calling President Wilson "a cocksucker and a thief."[3] Hoover's superiors overruled the zealous young man, who promised himself that someday he would become the boss.

Hoover's big break came in 1919 when an anarchist suicide bomber blew himself up outside the home of U.S. Attorney General A. Mitchell Palmer. Palmer lived across the street from assistant secretary of the navy Franklin Roosevelt and his wife, who had just returned from a dinner party and narrowly missed the blast, which sent shards of glass and broken bricks into their car. The furious attorney general enlisted the 24-year-old Hoover to head the General Intelligence Division, which rounded up thousands of communists and anarchists. Hoover conducted this unconstitutional dragnet, known as the Palmer Raids, while President Woodrow Wilson was incapacitated by his stroke.[4] He ordered agents to spy on anyone who spoke out against him and his raids, including defense attorneys, journalists, college professors, religious leaders, judges and even senators and congressmembers.

The key to Hoover's power was information retrieval. His subordinates did the legwork of gathering information while he organized it all into his system. Scandals during Warren G. Harding's administration forced the resignations of Hoover's bosses, and by 1924 President Calvin Coolidge had named him director of the Bureau of Investigation, rechristened the FBI in 1935. At just 29 years old, the stocky five-foot-seven director was already known throughout the nation as "Kid Napoleon."

After the upheaval of World War I, cracking down on political dissidents fell out of vogue with a public yearning for what Warren G. Harding called "normalcy." So Hoover switched his focus to the new public outrage over the sexual liberation of the Roaring Twenties. Kid Napoleon launched a crusade against pornography and created a federal repository of obscene and improper materials called the Obscene File. Agents around the country were ordered to send to bureau headquarters pornographic booklets, leaflets and photos in sealed envelopes marked in capital letters "OBSCENE." The bureau soon boasted the world's largest collection of porn: stag movies, photographs, books, pamphlets, freehand drawings, comic strips and playing cards decorated with girly pictures.[5] Hoover also began strictly enforcing the 1910 White Slave Traffic (Mann) Act, which made it a federal crime to transport unmarried women across state lines for illicit purposes. Originally intended to break up prostitution rings, the Mann Act was soon used to prosecute unmarried couples who traveled to another state and had sex in hotels or private residences. Mann Act cases doubled under Hoover, a hero to conservative Americans who saw him as the last bastion of old-fashioned values in a modern world of sexual license.[6] In reality, a tiny percentage of Hoover's Mann Act investigations actually resulted in prosecutions; their real purpose was to provide the director with information about the sexual liaisons of powerful and influential Americans.[7]

Franklin Roosevelt bears the most responsibility for removing all effective restraints on Hoover's surveillance powers. With World War II on the horizon in the mid-1930s, Roosevelt gave the FBI permission to monitor suspected Nazi sympathizers, communists and subversives.[8] Even if there was no evidence that a group like the NAACP was infiltrated by subversives, the FBI kept it under surveillance on the grounds that it *might* become subversive.[9] FDR also began using Hoover to go after his political enemies.[10] Under Roosevelt's orders, the FBI opened files on hundreds of outspoken isolationists. For example, it worked to discredit Charles Lindberg by secretly informing the press that the source of his pro-Nazi attitudes was his German mistress.

Advances in wiretapping and microphone technology greatly enhanced the FBI's ability to peep into people's private lives. Roosevelt overrode existing law and authorized the FBI to wiretap and bug "persons suspected of subversive activities against the United States."[11] Breaking into someone's home to plant a bug became known in bureauspeak as a "surreptitious entry" or a "black bag job." But they were never called "burglaries," one former FBI assistant director explained, "because nothing was taken"—nothing except secrets.[12] The FBI particularly liked to plant bugs in hotels because they were the most likely places for extramarital sex. Agents got the full cooperation of Washington's Willard Hotel, the Waldorf in New York, Chicago's Blackstone Hotel, and the Holiday Inn and Hilton Hotel chains. Some hotels even assigned prebugged rooms to FBI targets. During World War II, the FBI bugged brothels in Washington and New York to catch foreign diplomats and turn them into informants. The FBI also caught several congressmen visiting cathouses and fed the dirt to President Roosevelt.[13]

During the 1940 presidential campaign, the FBI conducted more than 200 investigations into Roosevelt's political foes, including the Republican nominee Wendell Willkie.[14] When Hoover reported back that Willkie was having an affair with New York editor Irita Van Doren, FDR told an aide, "Spread it as a word-of-mouth thing, or by some people way, way down the line. We can't have any of our principal speakers refer to it, but the people down the line can get it out. I mean the Congress speakers, and state speakers and so forth. They can use the raw material. . . . Now, if they want to play dirty politics in the end, we've got our own people."[15]

FDR also used Hoover to protect his friends. Roosevelt had the FBI director investigate a rumor that his 45-year-old undersecretary of state Sumner Welles got drunk during an overnight train ride, exposed himself to several black porters and begged them to have sex with him. Hoover confirmed the story and reported that, one Christmas, Welles almost froze to death after stumbling into an icy stream while chasing one of the black workmen on his estate.[16] Hoover added that Welles once appeared drunk in a Parisian hotel accompanied by two male prostitutes and was frequently seen cruising public men's rooms for "coloreds."[17] FDR shrugged at the report: "Well, he's not doing it on government time, is he?" and assigned Welles a "bodyguard" to ensure he "did not endeavor to make propositions for such immoral relations."[18] Only after FDR's enemies threatened to open a congressional investigation into Welles's sex life did FDR force his undersecretary of state into an early retirement. Meanwhile, Hoover took a copy of the Welles file home with him and placed it in his nightstand for bedtime reading.[19]

Hoover's solid relationship with Roosevelt did not stop him from assembling a file on FDR's affairs with Lucy Mercer, Missy LeHand and even his cousin Daisy Suckley. The FBI file on Eleanor Roosevelt was particularly important to Hoover, who hated the liberal First Lady and called her "Old Hoot Owl" and "Horse Face."[20] Hoover liked to say that one of the reasons he never married was that "God made a woman like Eleanor Roosevelt."[21] Eleanor's support for civil rights particularly enraged the rabidly racist FBI director. "Whenever a black would speak out," said FBI assistant director William Sullivan, "he attributed it to Mrs. Roosevelt."[22] After the First Lady discovered that she was under FBI surveillance she wrote Hoover an angry letter on January 26, 1941: "This type of investigation seems to me to smack too much of Gestapo methods."[23] Hoover complained about Eleanor's criticism to FDR, who replied, "Well, Edgar, don't get excited. Just think about me. I have to live with her." Hoover told his aides, "The president says the old bitch is going through the change of life and we'll just have to put up with her."[24]

What remains of Eleanor's FBI file is 449 pages of fact and fiction. Lorena Hickok was under FBI surveillance throughout the Roosevelt years, and Hoover often joked about the First Lady's relationship with "bat breath."[25] Agents also reported that Eleanor had affairs with her chauffeur, an army colonel, her doctor and two leaders of the National Maritime Union. An FBI bug supposedly picked up one union leader complaining to the other, "Goddamn it, Blackie I've made enough sacrifices. Next time you service the old bitch!"[26] The FBI concluded that the union leaders were "servicing" the First Lady on orders from the Communist Party.[27]

The juiciest story in Eleanor's file involved a 30-year-old army officer, Joseph Lash. The First Lady became friends with Lash in 1939 when he was an outspoken student radical. During the war, the FBI and the army's Counterintelligence Corps (CIC) placed them under surveillance. The CIC even bugged Lash's hotel room and recorded him having sex with his girlfriend Trude Pratt. A short time later, in December 1943, Eleanor traveled to Chicago to visit Lash, and the CIC bugged her hotel suite. According to an FBI report, the CIC "recording indicated quite clearly that Mrs. Roosevelt and Lash engaged in sexual intercourse during their stay in the hotel room."[28] FBI agent George Burton reported to Hoover that the president listened to the recording during a White House meeting with the heads of military intelligence: "After this record was played, Mrs. Roosevelt was called into the conference and was confronted with the information and this resulted in a terrific fight between the President and Mrs. Roosevelt."[29] Burton noted that the next morning FDR ordered the chief of the Army Air Corps to "have Lash outside the United States and on his way to a combat post within ten hours. . . . It was learned that the president had ordered that anybody who knew anything about this case should be immediately relieved of his duties and sent to the South Pacific for action against the Japs until they are killed."[30]

Like many FBI files, the report on Eleanor and Lash is based on second- and third-hand information. The most likely explanation for the recording is that the CIC recorded Lash and his girlfriend having sex and later confused the tape with the one they made of Eleanor and Lash.[31] Hoover, however, was not interested in just the facts, he collected every rumor, no matter how implausible. Even completely innocent people were afraid of what was in their FBI files—and in Washington very few people were completely innocent.

Franklin Roosevelt was well aware of the FBI's outrageous charges against Eleanor. When the head of the American Federation of Labor, Robert Watt, complained to FDR that he was being investigated by the FBI, the president responded, "That's nothing to what J. Edgar Hoover says about my wife."[32] Not even the man who battled Adolf Hitler could stop Hoover from spying on his wife.

PERSONAL AND CONFIDENTIAL

By the 1950s, snooping into the private lives of government officials had become an institutionalized function of the FBI. Hoover knew that very few government officials were communists or spies, but he also knew that just about everyone had sex secrets. "The leadership of the Bureau knew exactly what he wanted," FBI assistant director William Sullivan said: "every bit of derogatory information on every congressman, every senator and on anybody else in Washington. He didn't have to make any requests—they'd feed it to him."[33] Former FBI agent Conrad Trahern said, "Hoover treated people wrong. He was a despot. He did everything to impose on people on Capitol Hill who were screwing broads and that sort of thing. . . . But the policy was to make J. Edgar Hoover happy, and I reported what I knew."[34] Hoover's goal was to find the dirt on anyone and everyone who might pose a threat to his power.[35]

To please the Boss, FBI agents cultivated DC prostitutes as informants.[36] In a 1960 FBI report to Hoover a call girl told agents that "Congressman XXXXXX" was a "weird one" because "he wanted her to perform unnatural sex acts with him" and "took nude photographs with a Polaroid camera."[37] Another agent reported to Hoover that "for two and a half years [a male informer] had received a great deal of money, possibly in excess of $3000 [$21,000 today], from a United States Senator for permitting the Senator to commit acts of oral sodomy on him."[38] A 1960 report detailed how a call girl got a request from a senator for a midmorning appointment. "Agents were advised when the Senator arrived and upon his departure, he was overheard XXXXXX 'It was wonderful.' After he had left the premises [the call girl] commented that the sexual ability of the Senator was pretty good."[39] If the FBI observed senators or congressmen with mistresses or prostitutes, agents warned them to be more careful. But the real warning was that Mr. Hoover now had a file that could destroy them.[40]

Chicago Tribune reporter Walter Trohan observed that "some of Hoover's overwhelming support on the Hill was due to what I can only call blackmail, polite blackmail."[41] "I learned a lot," Central Intelligence Agency (CIA) director Richard Helms said, "from fellows who had worked in Hoover's office before joining us. I used to hear how certain senators and congressmen would get caught in cathouses over in Virginia. When the report came in, Hoover would put it in his personal safe. If there was any problem with that senator, he would say, 'Don't worry, I've got those papers right in my safe. You don't have a thing to worry about.'" Former FBI agent G. Gordon Liddy said, "That's why when Hoover would go before the Appropriations Committee and say he wanted something, they'd give him anything. Anything, because they were afraid of what he had."[42] From 1924 to 1971 Congress did not hold a single public hearing on the FBI budget, and Hoover used his ample funding to create the world's most technologically advanced snooping organization.[43] For almost five decades, Hoover ran the largest and longest sexual blackmailing scheme in history.

Hoover used his files to shape public policy by influencing elections in favor of conservative candidates. "It was not uncommon," according to veteran FBI agent Arthur Murtagh, "to learn of some politically damaging information about some leading figure in politics as having been developed by the Bureau; and then, always at a time when it would be most damaging to the individual, the information would in some way show up in the *Chicago Tribune* or some other friend of the Bureau." Liberal senator Wayne Morse was so worried during his reelection campaign that he found himself crawling around his living room, peeping under furniture and looking up his chimney for microphones.[44]

Since FBI files were legally subject to congressional subpoena, Hoover created a secret filing system. While "Official and Confidential" files went into the main system, "Personal and Confidential" files were kept behind the desk of his trusted secretary. Files labeled "Do Not File" did not have serial numbers and so could be destroyed without a trace. The secret filing system allowed FBI agents to use illegal means to acquire information without fear of discovery.[45] Hoover always denied the existence of his secret files, but every senator and congressman knew he was lying.

Senators and congressmen knew the FBI posted informants in the Capitol building and bugged their offices.[46] The Judiciary Committee even called in experts to sweep the Senate corridors for bugs. When Senator Edward Long decided to hold hearings on the FBI's use of bugs, Hoover sent a couple of agents to present the senator with his Personal and Confidential file. Long's chief counsel Bernard Fensterwald recounted that "they handed [the senator] the folder, a fairly thin one, as I recall. And Long just sat there and read it for a few minutes. Then he closed the file, he thanked them and they went on their way. The next thing I knew we had orders to skip over the FBI inquiries and go on to whatever agency was next."[47]

Hoover threatened presidents, but he also protected them. When Hoover approached the federal government's mandatory retirement age, President Lyndon Johnson gave him a special waiver in May 1964. Hoover returned the favor a few months later when the Washington, DC, vice squad arrested White House aide Walter Jenkins for having sex with a retired military officer in a YMCA men's room. Johnson feared Barry Goldwater, his Republican opponent in the impending 1964 presidential election, would use the Jenkins matter to tar the entire administration with lax morals. So he asked Hoover to assemble a report on the personal lives of Goldwater's staff just in case. It is not known if Johnson used the report to intimidate the Goldwater people, but the Jenkins matter did not become a factor in the election, which LBJ won in a landslide.[48] The Senate Intelligence Committee discovered in 1975 that every president from FDR to Nixon had used the FBI to conduct illegal wiretaps and surveillance on his political opponents.[49]

Hoover wiretapped at least 12 Supreme Court justices, including chief justices Earl Warren and Frederick Vinson. When President Harry Truman considered appointing liberal justice William Douglas as chief justice, Hoover reported to Truman that Douglas "frequently becomes intoxicated at parties and has a habit of pawing women."[50] Truman ultimately decided to appoint conservative Frederick Vinson, who tipped the balance on the court to the right—much to Hoover's satisfaction.

Supreme Court justice Robert Jackson was one of the few people in government to speak out against the FBI. "I cannot say that our country could have no central police without becoming totalitarian. But I can say with great conviction that it cannot become totalitarian without a centralized national police," the justice famously wrote. Jackson explained how the FBI's snooping threatened American democracy: "All that is necessary is to have a national police competent to investigate all manner of offenses, and then, in the parlance of the streets, it will have enough on enough people, even if it does not elect to prosecute them, so that it will find no opposition to its policies. Even those who are supposed to supervise it are likely to fear it."[51] Hoover got the last laugh when Jackson died in his secretary's apartment, and the FBI director told reporters the Supreme Court justice croaked in the throes of passion with his mistress.[52]

In addition to the three branches of government, Hoover intimidated the Fourth Estate. When he learned that a magazine publisher was considering an exposé on the FBI, he sent rival magazines a plain brown envelope filled with photographs of the publisher's wife performing oral sex on her black chauffeur while parked in Rock Creek Park. The humiliated publisher killed the exposé and his magazine never printed a critical word about the FBI.[53]

Hoover obsessively monitored the private lives of celebrities: writers Tennessee Williams, John Steinbeck, Arthur Miller, John O'Hara, Aldous Huxley and E. B. White; scientists Albert Einstein and Jonas Salk; artists Georgia O'Keefe, Henry Moore and Pablo Picasso; and entertainers Elvis Presley, Bing Crosby, Jimmy Durante, Groucho Marx and Charlie Chaplin. Even

Mickey Mantle had an FBI file. Hoover especially enjoyed collecting dirt on Hollywood stars. He cultivated "friendly" actors, such as Ronald Reagan, to rat on their fellow actors.[54] The Los Angeles field office provided thousands of reports on stars and their drug problems, venereal diseases, homosexual encounters or interest in underage girls. A survey of the Personal and Confidential files reveals that celebrities of Hoover's era were just as drugged out and sexed up as today, the only difference was that the press back then did not report it.

The FBI director got a vicarious thrill reading about Hollywood sex secrets and reportedly took the files on movie stars home with him for his bedtime reading. He also loved socializing with the same celebrities he monitored; according to a top aide, "Hoover didn't associate with people unless he had something on them."[55] Most of all, Hoover enjoyed the power of immediately knowing what was happening in the private lives of celebrities. When Lucille Ball took a pregnancy test, a hospital employee reported the positive result to the local FBI office, which forwarded it to Hoover so quickly that the FBI director was able to call to congratulate Desi Arnaz before Lucy had a chance to tell him she was pregnant.[56] The FBI was the TMZ of Hoover's day.

Hoover was one of the first people to exploit the emergence of celebrity culture. Before the 1920s, the public assumed show folk led wild personal lives. But with the creation of mass electronic media, like radio and movies, entertainers became larger-than-life figures and household names. Advertisers began enlisting celebrities to sell everything from cigarettes to automobiles. Movie studios and PR firms carefully built and guarded their reputations. As movie stars became models of behavior and paragons of glamour and style, the gap between the real lives of celebrities and their public images presented an opportunity to Hoover. Suddenly knowledge of the sexual indiscretions of actors became a valuable commodity.

It is not a coincidence that Walter Winchell invented the modern gossip column at the same time that Hoover first began assembling files on celebrities. Winchell began publishing gossip in the tabloid *Evening Graphic* during the 1920s when American newspapers still refused to publish exposés on the private lives of public figures. By flouting the journalistic code of his day, Winchell acquired more influence and power than any other reporter. He became an international celebrity known for his irreverent reporting and his trademark fedora. He was also feared by everyone who was anyone in America—except of course J. Edgar Hoover. Hoover and Winchell formed a partnership and regularly exchanged scandalous scoops. They were frequently seen together at Winchell's specially reserved table at the Stork Club, where the two men basked in the fawning attention of the celebrities and millionaires whose careers they could destroy on a whim. Of course, Hoover opened a file on Winchell—eventually totaling 3,908 pages, it was one of the largest in the FBI system. The world's most famous gossip columnist never attacked Hoover's friends and was always ready to publish dirt on his enemies.[57] Winchell even endorsed Hoover for president in 1955.[58] But there was one big reason a presidential run was never an option for the FBI director.

JOHNNY AND CLYDE

While Hoover was investigating the sex secrets of thousands of Americans, he was hiding a big one of his own—Clyde Tolson, the number-two man at the FBI. When they first met in 1927, Hoover immediately offered a job to the strapping, dark-haired 27-year-old Tolson. In less than three years, Tolson went from being an agent-trainee to occupying the second-highest post at the bureau.[59] Tolson's dizzying rise to the highest echelons of government was unparalleled in the history of any federal bureaucracy.[60]

Over the next four decades, the two lifelong bachelors were virtually inseparable. Every weekday morning Hoover had his driver pick Tolson up at his apartment and then drop them off a few blocks from the Justice Department. The two G-men then walked lockstep the rest of the way. Hoover and Tolson had lunch together every afternoon at a reserved table in a remote corner of Harvey's Restaurant. They also dined together every evening at each other's house or back at Harvey's. Since Hoover did not like to be seen drinking in public, Tolson always kept the Boss's drinks hidden under his napkin.[61] Hoover insisted that if he was invited to a party, Clyde would also have to get an invitation.[62] "My alter ego is Clyde Tolson," Hoover liked to say, "He can read my mind." Clyde told anyone who would listen, "The Director is the Man of the Century."[63] Hoover called Clyde "Junior," while Clyde called Hoover "Boss" in public and "Eddie" in private, something no one else ever dared.[64] *Time* magazine noted, "Policeman Hoover has never been known to have had any woman-affair in New York City. A bachelor, he is seldom seen without a male companion, most frequently solemn-faced Clyde Tolson, his assistant." *Time* claimed that the reason Hoover eschewed the company of women was "his dread that someone, some day, somewhere, will plant a naked woman in his path, try to frame him."[65]

Nearly every weekend, Hoover and Tolson went to the racetrack, and they took all their vacations together. They spent Christmas and New Year's in Miami and every summer vacation at the Del Charro Hotel in La Jolla, California, where the owner built them a two-bedroom bungalow out back.[66] During one visit to the Del Charro, hotel staff reported hearing shouts and dishes breaking in Hoover's suite and then saw Tolson rush out, slamming the door behind himself. When Hoover and Tolson returned to Washington, Clyde called in sick for an additional nine days because, according to FBI sources, he was nursing a black eye and bruised lip from a well-flung ashtray.[67]

There is no hard evidence that Tolson and Hoover were lovers—no love letters or revealing diary entries. But there are dozens of adoring photos that Hoover took of Tolson, including several tender shots of Tolson sleeping. The eye behind the lens seems to have a deeply intimate and emotional involvement with the subject.[68]

Rumors were rampant about Hoover and Tolson during their lifetimes. One of Hoover's friends, Ethel Merman, said, "Some of my best friends are homosexual. Everybody knew about J. Edgar Hoover, but he was the best chief the FBI ever had." The owner of the Stork Club, Sherman Billingsley, called them "Mr. and Mrs. Hoover"—behind their backs of course. Truman Capote dubbed them "Johnny and Clyde" and claimed he spread rumors about them. "It got Hoover upset, that much I know," Capote said. "And got me—well about 200 pages in an FBI file."[69] FBI agents also exchanged stories about "J. Edna Hoover" and "Mother Tolson," and when one of Hoover's top aides, Louis Nichols, named his newborn son J. Edgar agents joked, "If it had been a girl, she'd have been called Clyde."[70]

In Hoover's era, homosexuality was considered a psychological illness. Given the sensitivity of Hoover's position as FBI director, any credible revelation of his homosexuality would have been grounds for immediate dismissal.[71] Hoover ordered FBI agents around the country to chase down all gay rumors about him.[72] When a Cleveland woman gossiped to her bridge club that Hoover "was a homosexual and kept a stable of young boys for his pleasure," word got back to FBI headquarters in Washington and, according to an FBI report, Tolson ordered the head of the Cleveland office to pay her a visit. FBI agents reported back that the woman agreed to "point out to each of those [who had been] present that her statement was not found on fact and that she was deeply sorry that she had made it and it should not have been made at all."[73]

According to FBI files, Hoover's agents also visited a Georgetown society matron and her hairdresser who were overheard gossiping that Hoover was a "sissy, liked men and was a queer."[74] An FBI agent assured the director that the hairdresser "fully realizes the seriousness of her accusations, and it is not believed that she will ever [again] be guilty of such statements."[75] A Detroit businessman who called Hoover gay was "scared to death" when FBI agents came knocking on his door. The interviewing agent warned the businessman that if he ever called Hoover a homosexual again the agent "might take care of him right there on the spot."[76] G-men also tracked down and intimidated a trucker who made a gay joke about Hoover in a New Jersey diner, a dance instructor who chatted about Hoover with a student, and a former CIA agent who mentioned Hoover's homosexuality during a dinner party. All retracted their statements under FBI interrogation, all were threatened and all entered the FBI file system.[77]

During World War II, a Kentucky man said he knew Hoover had a 17-year-old male lover. The head of the FBI field office in Louisville, M. W. McFarlin, tracked down the man and had him sign a statement saying that his statement was not true. McFarlin knew how to please the Boss and wrote a detailed report to Hoover on how he squashed the "vile and dastardly attack." "You may be assured," McFarlin assured Hoover, "that so long as there is a Federal Bureau of Investigation those associated with you will exert every means in their power to protect you from malicious lying attacks and throw the lies down the throats of those who utter them. It is a privilege to be associated with you in your great contribution to our country at war."[78] Hoover's anxiety about his sexuality was so great that his agents felt impelled to scurry around the nation cracking down on gay rumors and jokes even in the middle of a world war.

Hoover was gravely concerned about press reports on his personal life. When *Los Angeles Times* reporter Jack Nelson planned to write an article claiming Hoover was homosexual, the FBI director arranged a meeting with Nelson's bosses and sought to have him fired on the grounds of his excessive drinking. Nelson's editors spiked his story but refused to fire him, so Hoover placed the *Times* on the FBI's No Contact List, which meant agents were forbidden to help the paper on any stories.[79] Hoover also discovered that *American Mercury* publisher Lawrence Spivak was considering an article charging Hoover "with perversion." Clyde Tolson accosted Spivak in a restaurant, and FBI assistant director Louis Nichols pointed out that the "element of perversion" "infuriated" Hoover. Nichols reported to Hoover that Spivak apologized for even considering the article and praised the FBI's handling of the situation as "a wonderful demonstration of a free country, that had this occurred in any other country he would have been shot by now."[80]

Hoover was on the lookout for even the vaguest suggestion of his effeminacy in the press. Journalist Ray Tucker infuriated the director when he wrote in *Collier's*, "In appearance, Mr. Hoover looks utterly unlike the story-book sleuth. He is short, fat, businesslike, and walks with a mincing step. . . . He dresses fastidiously, with Eleanor blue as the favorite color for the matched shades of tie, handkerchief and socks."[81] Hoover immediately opened a file on Tucker. After the *Collier's* piece appeared, another columnist wrote, "Has anyone noted that the Hoover stride has grown noticeably longer and more vigorous since Tucker charged him with walking with mincing steps?"[82] Despite the hundreds of articles written about Hoover over the course of his five decades at the height of power, only a few even vaguely suggested he was gay. The press, like every congressman, senator, government official and president, knew not to upset the Boss.

So how did the press handle the fact that Hoover was a lifelong bachelor who lived with his mother until she died in 1938 and never seemed to have a woman in his life? The reporters repeated the awkward explanations typical for closeted men. Hoover told an interviewer, "I was in love once when I was young. I guess you'd call it puppy love." Another reporter claimed, "In [Hoover's] experience the women he wanted to marry were always involved with someone else." "Here is something I will confess," Hoover said in a 1939 interview, "if I ever marry and the girl fails me, ceases to love me, and our marriage is dissolved, it would ruin me. My mental status couldn't take it, and I would not be responsible for my actions." The phrase "mental status" was later deleted from reprints of the interview. The director continued in the same interview, "I have always held girls and women on a pedestal. They are something men should look up to, to honor and worship. If men would remember this and keep them there, married life would be better. I have had that idea about women all my life." Hoover also claimed his work took the place of women: "I became attached to the Bureau, and I don't think any wife would have put up with me."[83] That much was probably true.

Of course Hoover couldn't hide his deep desires from himself. The director reportedly became so troubled by his homosexual desires that in late 1946 he began seeing psychiatrists, including Dr. Marshall Ruffin. Ruffin's wife recalled, "Everybody then understood he was homosexual, not just the doctors." Her husband burned his case notes on Hoover before he died in 1984, but Mrs. Ruffin said Hoover "was definitely troubled by homosexuality and my husband's notes would've proved that."[84] The FBI director was trapped in a vicious cycle. His fear of being exposed fed his determination to assemble files on other people's sex secrets. But his files were daily reminders that he too could be exposed. Hoover was a pathetic, angry, little man whose anxiety about his own sexuality spurred him to become the most obsessed, most powerful and most dangerous sexual blackmailer on earth.

THE PINK SCARE

Hoover's anxiety about his sexuality grew during the Red Scare of the 1950s when a national panic arose about homosexuals in the federal government. The head of the Washington, DC, morals squad, Lieutenant Roy E. Blick, kicked off an antigay witch hunt in 1950 when he testified to Congress that 3,750 "perverts" worked in the U.S. government. A Senate report titled "Employment of Homosexuals and Other Sex Perverts in Government" warned that homosexuals were security risks because their "lack of emotional stability" and the "weakness of their moral fiber" made them "susceptible to the blandishments of a foreign espionage agent."[85] Hoover, who was always quick to exploit the latest public uproar, created the Sex Deviates Program in 1951 to investigate suspected homosexuals in government.[86] Hoover hounded out not only gay federal workers but also gay professors, teachers and police officers. Further, he used the Sex Deviates Program to expand his influence throughout the halls of government.[87] Agents would approach a gay public official and secretly agree to allow him to keep his job if he became an FBI informant. "In other words," according to one of Hoover's former aides, "if we found out that so and so was one, and most of them were quite covert about their activities, that person would be 'doubled' and would become a listening post for the FBI."[88] In a town where information is power, the Sex Deviates Program enabled Hoover to run a shadow government of closeted officials.

Senator Joe McCarthy was the first major politician to exploit the public's fear of gay government officials when he began accusing the State Department of being dominated by the "lace handkerchief crowd," "cookie pushers," and "striped pants diplomats with phony British accents." McCarthy told reporters that "if you want to be against McCarthy, boys, you've got to be a communist or a cocksucker."[89] McCarthy stumbled on a winning crusade against "pinks, punks and pansies" and milked it for all it was worth.

A onetime chicken farmer and high school dropout, McCarthy built his political career on lies, distortions and an exaggerated war record to become at 38 years old in 1946 the youngest man in the Senate. He quickly became known as the most dangerous politician in America, not for what he knew but for what he could accuse. Toward the end of his first term, Wisconsin voters began to see through his act and his popularity plummeted. Desperate for a crusade that could revive his flagging poll numbers, McCarthy got his hands on a four-year-old report that found "damaging information" on 205 State Department employees. One woman was put on the list because she entertained "Negroes and whites, both men and women, in her apartment."[90] Most of the people on the list had left the State Department by February 9, 1950, when McCarthy stood before the Republican Women's Club in Wheeling, West Virginia, and famously declared, "I have here in my hand a list of 205— a list of names that were made known to the Secretary of State as being members of the Communist Party and who nevertheless are still working and shaping policy in the State Department."[91] The senator's accusations immediately made headlines throughout the nation. At the next stop on his speaking tour, in Salt Lake City, McCarthy changed the number to 57, and when reporters brought up the discrepancy the senator—now intoxicated by fame and probably booze—barked, "Listen you bastards I just want you to know I've got a pailfull of this shit and I'm going to use it where it does me the most good."[92] McCarthy cared about headlines, not facts.

The senator's allegations about the State Department struck a nerve with a public that was already hysterical about homosexuals in the government. Right-wing syndicated columnist John O'Donnell praised McCarthy for exposing that "the foreign policy of the United States even before World War II was dominated by an all-powerful, super secret inner circle of highly educated, socially highly placed sexual misfits in the State Department, all easy to blackmail." O'Donnell claimed that of the first 2,500 letters McCarthy received in response to his campaign against the State Department, "only one out of four of the writers is excited about the red infiltration into the higher branches of the government; the other three are expressing their shocked indignation at the evidence of *sex depravity*."[93] A conservative Catholic newspaper praised McCarthy's exposure of "the presence of close to a hundred perverts in the State Department. . . . The time for being naïve about the substance of the McCarthy charges is long past."[94]

The idea that gays posed as much of a national security threat as communists was convenient for Red-baiting politicians. After all, there were few communists in government, but there were plenty of homosexuals. As McCarthy's crusade against pinkos and pansies transformed him from a bumbling, politically doomed senator into an all-American idol, Republicans nationwide began following his lead. After 18 years of being out of power, since Franklin Roosevelt won the presidency in 1932, the GOP had discovered a winning issue. One Republican fundraiser boasted, "Our party is finally on the attack and should stay there. And best of all, we may get rid of many Communist sympathizers and queers who now control policy."[95]

In an editorial, "The Aberrants" (March 17, 1950), the *Washington Post* tried to challenge the very basis of the Pink Scare: "There is, as far as we know, no reason for supposing that a person of homosexual bias is psychologically any more predisposed to the Communist ideology than a heterosexual person."[96] In a *Saturday Evening Post* article, Joseph and Stewart Alsop condemned McCarthy's attempt "to elevate the subject of homosexuality to the level of a serious political issue on the ground that sexual perversion presents a clear and present danger to the security of the United States."[97] McCarthy knew Joe Alsop was gay and countered with a veiled threat: "I can understand, of course, why it would be considered 'vulgar' or 'nauseating' by Joe Alsop."[98]

McCarthy knew he could not keep attacking the State Department without making substantial accusations against specific individuals. The problem was that he had no evidence to support his claims, so he turned to the one man who did—J. Edgar Hoover. McCarthy admitted to Hoover that he had made up his numbers and asked if the FBI could give him information to back up his charges.[99] Hoover saw McCarthy as a useful weapon in his efforts to undermine President Truman and ordered FBI agents to "review the files and get anything you can for him."[100] "The FBI kept Joe McCarthy in business," FBI assistant director Sullivan recalled. "We were the ones who made the McCarthy hearings possible. We fed McCarthy all the material he was using. I knew what we were doing. I worked on it myself. At the same time, we were telling the public we had nothing to do with it."[101] Hoover was the true creator of McCarthyism.[102] Soon McCarthy was hosting Hoover and Tolson for dinner and accompanying them to the racetrack on weekends.[103]

During the 1952 presidential campaign between Republican Dwight David Eisenhower and liberal Democratic Illinois governor Adlai Stevenson, FBI agents gave Eisenhower and McCarthy copies of Stevenson's Sex Deviates file. Police officers in Illinois and Maryland had told FBI agents that Stevenson had been arrested for homosexual offenses that were later expunged. A few Bradley University basketball players, under investigation for fixing games, reported that "two of the best known homosexuals in the state [of Illinois] were [Bradley University] President [David] Owen and Governor Stevenson, and that Stevenson was known as 'Adeline.'"[104] The FBI report added, "The basketball players were of the opinion that Stevenson would not run for President because of this."[105] Another FBI report claimed, "Stevenson and Owen were members of an elite homosexual group in New York."[106]

The Eisenhower campaign did not publish the gay rumors against Stevenson in its campaign literature, but it did circulate rumors that became so widespread the tabloid *Confidential* ran a story titled "How that Stevenson Rumor Started." *Confidential* reported that the Stevenson rumor "burned the ears of a nation" and was "the nastiest, most widely circulated hearsay in the annals of rumor mongering. By phone, on planes and trains, from the racket of factory assembly lines to the quiet of hospital rooms, from the big-town sharpies to unsophisticated villagers, it burned the ears of a nation."[107] Many FBI agents were disgusted by the bureau's interference with the 1952 presidential election. "There were a lot of us who were absolutely appalled by it," recalled a former agent, "but Mr. Hoover was determined to elect Nixon and Ike, and when he made up his mind to do something there was no changing it."[108]

Although the mainstream press refused to publish allegations about Stevenson, they could not ignore that the 1952 Republican Party platform implicitly raised the specter of homosexuality by condemning the Democrats for allowing "'immorality' among top policy makers."[109] The press also could not ignore Joe McCarthy, who repeatedly referred to Stevenson as "Adeline." Days before the election, McCarthy announced that he had bought airtime on 50 television stations and 550 radio stations to deliver a speech that would expose Stevenson "for the man he is." Rumors spread that McCarthy was going to call Stevenson a homosexual. In a preemptive strike, Stevenson's supporters contacted Eisenhower and threatened to expose his wartime affair with his driver Kay Summersby if McCarthy played the gay card. Someone in the Eisenhower campaign must have gotten to McCarthy, who disappointed his followers with a relatively innocuous speech against the Democratic nominee.[110]

When Stevenson challenged Eisenhower again in the 1956 election, Walter Winchell took the gay innuendo a step further in a national radio broadcast when he said, "A vote for Adlai is a vote for Christine Jorgensen." Jorgensen was an ex-GI formerly named George who had made headlines when he underwent a sex change operation in Denmark.[111]

Shortly after taking over the White House in 1953, Eisenhower signed an executive order listing "sexual perversion" as sufficient grounds for exclusion from federal jobs. Well into the 1960s, State Department officials made a yearly pilgrimage to Congress to reveal how many gay employees they fired that year. The annual rite had became a sad routine by 1968, when the *Washington Post* commented that just as "the ancient Aztecs or Mayas used to sacrifice virgins, annually, to propitiate the gods and to gain favors from them . . . the State Department sacrifices homosexuals, annually, to propitiate the

House Appropriations Committee, and to gain money from them."[112] During the Cold War, the State Department fired many more homosexuals than communists.[113]

McCarthy was playing a dangerous game, because rumors soon began to circulate about his own sexuality. His FBI file contained a claim by army lieutenant David Sayer that McCarthy had picked him up at a Washington, DC, hotel bar, got him drunk and "committed an act of sodomy on him."[114] A young Republican Party official told the FBI that McCarthy frequented the Bird Circuit, a number of gay bars around Grand Central Station.[115] "There were many files on Senator McCarthy," recalled a former Hoover aide. Fortunately for McCarthy, Hoover was a friend.[116]

One of McCarthy's enemies, nationally syndicated columnist Drew Pearson, began assembling his own file on the senator's sex life. By the early 1950s Pearson had become America's best-known political journalist thanks to his innovative column Washington Merry-Go-Round, which combined gossip, scandal and hardnosed political reporting. Critics slammed Pearson for violating the journalistic code that prohibited reporting on the private lives of politicians.[117] But he was also an admired muckraker whose exposés were credited with sending four corrupt congressmen to jail.[118] His column ran in more newspapers than any other in America and had an audience of forty million. Another twenty million listened to his weekly radio news show. Because his column was syndicated it was impossible for any one editor or publisher to censor him.[119] *Time* magazine called Pearson "the most intensely feared and hated man in Washington."[120]

Pearson did not think the gay rumors about McCarthy were substantial enough to print in his column, so he passed them to fellow McCarthy-haters, one being *Las Vegas Sun* publisher Hank Greenspun. When McCarthy accused Greenspun of being a communist during a radio broadcast in Nevada, the publisher retaliated with a shocking column in the *Sun:* "Joe McCarthy is a bachelor of 43 years. He seldom dates girls and if he does, he laughingly describes it as window dressing." Greenspun charged that during the Wisconsin state Republican convention "McCarthy spent the night with William McMahon, formerly an official of the Milwaukee County Young Republicans, in a Wausau hotel room, at which time, McCarthy and McMahon engaged in illicit acts with each other." Greenspun concluded, "It is common talk among homosexuals who rendezvous at the White Horse Inn [a Milwaukee gay bar] that Senator Joe McCarthy has often engaged in homosexual activities." Greenspun added, "The persons in Nevada who listened to McCarthy's radio talk thought he had the queerest voice. He had. He is." McCarthy complained to Hoover about Greenspun's accusations and asked if he should sue for libel. Hoover was well aware of McCarthy's FBI file and advised the senator to let the matter blow over.[121]

A year after the Greenspun article appeared, McCarthy married his secretary, Jean Kerr, in a ceremony attended by Hoover, Tolson, Richard Nixon and the Kennedy brothers. Willard Edwards of the *Chicago Tribune* "thought that Joe, nearly 45, consented to marriage only to quash stories that he was homosexual."[122] While the Pope sent his blessings to the McCarthys, Greenspun called the marriage "the biggest farce of the century."[123]

The Greenspun controversy taught McCarthy's enemies a valuable lesson. Even though they could not defeat the senator with facts and reason, he was vulnerable. To bring down McCarthy they were going to have to get into the gutter with him and play the gay card.

THE FALL OF JOE MCCARTHY

When Republicans took over the Senate in the wake of Eisenhower's 1952 landslide victory, McCarthy became chairman of the Senate Subcommittee on Investigations. He considered two candidates to fill the job as his chief counsel: 27-year-old Robert Kennedy and 25-year-old Roy Cohn. RFK's father was a major campaign contributor to McCarthy, who vacationed with the Kennedys in Hyannis Port and had dated two of Bobby's sisters. Cohn was the short, dark, abrasive son of a New York Supreme Court judge. When he was fresh out of law school, Cohn had wrangled a slot on the prosecution team at the Rosenberg trial in 1950. The young man's ruthlessness became legendary when it became known that he had secretly persuaded Judge Irving Kaufman to sentence Ethel Rosenberg to the electric chair.[124] J. Edgar Hoover was impressed by Cohn's intelligence and ferocity and appreciated the juicy stories about socialites, journalists and politicians in New York that the gossipy lawyer provided the FBI. Based on Hoover's recommendation, McCarthy made the fateful decision to hire Cohn instead of RFK as his chief counsel.

McCarthy grew to depend on Cohn for everything from organizing his schedule to plotting his next targets, but this dependence also made the senator vulnerable. Cohn was infatuated with David Schine, a tall, blond, 26-year-old heir to a theater and hotel fortune. One of Schine's contemporaries described him as handsome "in the style that one associates with male orchestra singers."[125] Cohn insisted in 1953 that McCarthy hire Schine to serve as an unpaid "chief consultant" to the Investigations committee. McCarthy was unimpressed with Schine, who was a Harvard dropout and did nothing of note except write an anticommunist pamphlet distributed in his father's hotels. But McCarthy needed Cohn, and Cohn wanted Schine. "Joe often told us that he had little use for Dave Schine," remarked a Washington reporter. "He kept him on, I think, out of loyalty to Roy. I guess he figured that one more guy around the office wasn't going to kill him. Of course, this guy just about did."[126]

The Cohn-Schine team baffled Washington insiders. "Schine seems to have the dominant influence, even though Cohn clearly outranks him in everything intellectual," one observer noted. "He seems to be fond of humiliating Cohn in front of strangers, quick in putting him into his place. He is most outspoken in his criticism of Cohn's mannerism and acts generally as if Cohn were his inferior."[127] Hoover liked Schine because his father allowed Tolson and Hoover to stay for free at his Miami hotel during their "working vacations." But that did not stop the FBI director from placing Shine and Cohn under surveillance.[128]

Questions about Cohn and Shine's relationship first appeared in the press when they took a whirlwind tour of Europe in the spring of 1953 to ferret out subversive literature from the shelves of U.S. Information Agency libraries. In Munich, reporters saw McCarthy's boys loudly demanding separate hotel rooms, awkwardly joking, "We don't work for the State Department!"[129] Drew Pearson repeated an eyebrow-raising story about Cohn and Schine bickering like newlyweds during their travels, and a London newspaper headlined "Cohn and Schine, the Two London Lovers."[130]

In November 1953, Schine was drafted into the army, and a distraught Cohn enlisted McCarthy in an effort to have Schine exempted from military service. When that failed, Cohn and McCarthy tried to have him commissioned as an officer. This too was denied because Schine was a college dropout. Cohn then began badgering secretary of the army Robert Stevens to give Private Schine special privileges during basic training. Stevens appeased Cohn, and the army issued Schine special equipment like mittens instead of gloves, special boots with straps and buckles, a fur-lined hood, a warm down sleeping bag and an air mattress. Schine was also allowed to leave the base on weekends "to work on committee business" with Cohn. In reality, Cohn picked up Schine from Fort Dix in a chauffeured Cadillac and headed straight to the Stork Club and other New York hotspots. According to a Defense Department document, the chauffeur later alleged the two "engaged in homosexual acts in the back of the car."[131]

After building a reputation slandering the State Department, McCarthy in the fall of 1953 moved on to the Defense Department by investigating communists in the signal corps research center at Fort Monmouth, New Jersey. When the army stonewalled McCarthy's investigation, he attacked secretary of defense George Marshall and even questioned President Eisenhower's commitment to internal security. Eisenhower baffled his supporters when he refused to respond to McCarthy's accusations, telling aides, "I'm not going to get into the gutter with that guy."[132] Many thought McCarthy intimidated the president, but the old general was just biding his time. In January 1954 Ike ordered the army to assemble a report on Cohn and McCarthy pressuring military brass to give special favors to Schine. If McCarthy could build a career on gay smears, he could be brought down by them.

Eisenhower was not disappointed by the report, which listed 44 counts of improper pressure, including Cohn's threat to "wreck the Army" and show it "in the worst possible light" if Schine did not receive special privileges. After reading the report, White House press secretary James Hagerty wrote in his diary, "It's a pip. Shows constant pressure by Cohn to get Schine a soft Army job, with Joe in and out of threats. Really bad report that could break this thing wide open."[133] Eisenhower ordered the army to release the report in March 1954. McCarthy and Cohn, believing that a good offense is the best defense, countercharged that the army was holding Schine "hostage" to dissuade them from going after communists in the military. To settle the matter the Senate convened nationally televised Army-McCarthy hearings on April 22, 1954. Two big questions hung over the hearings: What was the nature of Cohn's relationship with Schine? And why was McCarthy so enthralled to Cohn? The

New York Times observed, "The senator and his friends have now been truly hoist with their own petard."[134] Eisenhower's plan was coming together.

Two-thirds of all American households with TV sets tuned in to the hearings during the first week. News coverage of the hearings overshadowed the other historic events that spring, the *Brown v. Board of Education* decision and the fall of Dien Bien Phu.[135] Witnesses for the army fed the media frenzy with suggestive references to Cohn and Schine. Secretary of the army Stevens called Cohn's efforts to pressure the army a "perversion of power" and recounted that "Senator McCarthy said that one of the few things that he had trouble with Mr. Cohn about was David Schine." Stevens quoted McCarthy as saying, "Roy thinks that Dave ought to be a general and operate from a penthouse at the Waldorf Astoria."[136] Committee counsel Ray Jenkins asked Cohn, "You have been warm personal friends, have you not?" Cohn resisted the implication: "He is one of my many good friends, yes sir." Jenkins tried again: "Mr. Cohn, you and this boy David Schine, as a matter of fact, now, were almost constant companions, as good, warm personal friends, weren't you?" An army lawyer recalled gingerly asking Cohn, "What would happen if Schine got overseas duty?" Jenkins chimed in, "You mean you were breaking the news gently?"[137] Laughter filled the room while Cohn squirmed in his seat.

McCarthy claimed that Schine got special privileges because secretary of the army Stevens was personally fond of him. To prove Stevens's fondness for the young private, McCarthy's aides produced a photograph of Stevens and Schine standing next to each other smiling. The next day, the army's lawyer, Joseph Welch, revealed that McCarthy's people had cropped the original photo to remove a third man from the picture to give the impression that Stevens was smiling at Schine. Welch asked the McCarthy staffer who created the doctored photo, "Did you think this came from a pixie? Where did you think this picture that I hold in my hand came from?" McCarthy interrupted, "Will counsel for my benefit define—I think he might be an expert on that—what a pixie is?" Welch couldn't resist. "I should say, Mr. Senator, that a pixie is a close relative of a *fairy*. Have I enlightened you?" Knowing laughter roared forth from the hearing room. One journalist noted that Welch's "wicked thrusts" hurt not just Cohn but also McCarthy, who "looking down found himself dismembered." Welch received letters congratulat-

ing him on the fairy reference, which one observer thought really "fixed" Mc-
Carthy and his "pansy" friends.[138]

As Eisenhower had hoped, the hearings opened the door to a public discussion of McCarthy's relationship with his subordinates. Joseph and Stewart
Alsop wrote, "Certain suggestions as to the nature of the McCarthy-Cohn-
Schine relationship" might explain Cohn's "peculiar power" over his boss. Drew
Pearson claimed the "supposedly fearless McCarthy is deathly afraid of pint-
sized" Cohn because the young lawyer "knew all the secrets" including "extraordinary allegations" about McCarthy's "personal life which cannot be repeated
here."[139] When Pearson noted that Cohn was "unusually preoccupied with investigating alleged homosexuals" and that the relationship between McCarthy
and Cohn was "the biggest mystery in Washington," readers wrote letters urging the columnist to be less ambiguous about the homosexual angle to the
hearings.[140] Ex-senator William Benton wrote an aide, "These Cohn-Schine-
McCarthy rumors were everywhere. They are sweeping in on me. . . . Don't
you think this would be one of the most devastating things that could be
demonstrated—if true?"[141]

Senator Ralph Flanders took to the floor of the Senate and called the
Cohn-Schine relationship "the real heart of the mystery. . . . It is rational that
Cohn should wish to retain the services of an able collaborator, but he seems
to have an almost *passionate anxiety* to retain him. Why?" Flanders also asked,
"Does the assistant have *some hold* on the Senator? . . . Does the committee
plan to investigate the *real issues* at stake?" Flanders received thousands of letters thanking him for raising the issue "that had to be raised." One letter reported "the common gossip among servicemen and others is that Cohn is
determined to keep Schine from going overseas . . . because they are homosexuals." Another letter congratulated Flanders: "You are the first to put the
spotlight on the sordid relationship behind this tragic scene, a relationship
which must be evident to most people, but which, of course can't be stated
more specifically than you did."[142]

Since the hearings were broadcast live, the press could not filter the army's
suggestive testimony that riveted a nation. One television reviewer wrote,
"The absorbing attraction is to follow the testimony as it goes first one way
and then another, as first the Army and then Senator McCarthy make their
points. On TV it is the drama of *unrehearsed actuality* unfolding for everyone

to see at home."[143] The Army-McCarthy hearings were perhaps the first example of reality TV. Over the 36 days of live coverage, Americans saw constant shots of Cohn whispering into McCarthy's ear like a naughty schoolgirl—an iconic image that reinforced the notion that Cohn had a mysterious power over McCarthy and punctured the senator's image as a tough, honest straight shooter.[144] Cohn later wrote that McCarthy "came into American homes as humorless, demanding, dictatorial, and obstructive. With his easily erupting temper, his menacing monotone, his unsmiling mien, and his perpetual five-o'clock shadow, he did seem the perfect stock villain."[145] Army lawyer Joseph Welch played on the image of McCarthy as a bullying villain, famously admonishing the senator in front of the cameras, "Have you no sense of decency sir? At long last, have you no sense of decency?"[146]

McCarthy could see the hearings were becoming a disaster and once again decided to go on offense. He announced a plan to call members of the Eisenhower administration to testify whether the president ordered the report on Cohn and Schine to be compiled and released. Eisenhower did not want the world to know he was behind a gay smear campaign against a senator, so the White House invented the notion of executive privilege that enabled a president to forbid his advisors from having to testify before Congress on the grounds that "employees of the executive branch [must] be in a position to be completely candid in advising with each other on official matters."[147] Eisenhower's invention of executive privilege set an important legal precedent that presidents have claimed ever since.

The Army-McCarthy hearings forced Hoover to choose the side of the senator or the president; throughout the hearings the FBI quietly supplied the White House with briefings on how to counter McCarthy's accusations.[148] The public break between the senator and the director came when McCarthy tried to bring the focus of the hearings back onto the army's security failures by claiming he had a "carbon copy" of a "personal and confidential" letter from Hoover to the army warning of 34 security risks at Fort Monmouth. McCarthy broke Hoover's golden rule: never reveal the FBI as a source of confidential information. Hoover immediately sandbagged McCarthy by publicly denying that McCarthy had access to FBI files—which was true; Hoover provided McCarthy with memos based on the files, not the files themselves.

With both the president and Hoover against him, McCarthy was dead meat. In just four years he went from all-American hero to crude, creepy villain. After the hearings, Cohn resigned and joined a New York law firm. McCarthy was censured by the Senate on December 2, 1954, and three years later drank himself to death at the age of 48. Hoover, Tolson, Cohn, Richard Nixon and Robert Kennedy were among the vast crowd at his funeral.[149]

DWIGHT EISENHOWER AND KAY SUMMERSBY

Before his death, McCarthy tried to exact revenge against Eisenhower by dredging up Ike's wartime affair with his shapely brunette chauffeur Kay Summersby. An FBI file dated May 13, 1955, recorded that McCarthy aide Don Surine told agents that when Eisenhower was the supreme Allied commander, he asked the chairman of the Joint Chiefs, George Marshall, whether his army career would be jeopardized if he divorced his frumpy wife Mamie so he could marry Summersby. Marshall ordered Ike to stick with Mamie or surrender his command.[150] Surine's story was not news to the FBI. Washington had been gossiping about Ike and Summersby since the war. During the 1952 presidential campaign, Eisenhower's rival for the Republican nomination, Senator Robert Taft, tried to get copies of Ike's letters to Marshall. President Truman stopped "the Taft gang" by ordering the Pentagon to send him the letters, saying, "I don't think they should be used for dirty politics."[151]

Four months after McCarthy's aide reported Eisenhower's affair to the FBI, he tipped off agents that "Summersby had been staying at the [Washington] Shoreham Hotel for the last 30 to 45 days under an assumed name."[152] Hoover liked Eisenhower, but he was not going to miss an opportunity to gain leverage over the president. He immediately dispatched a pack of G-men to the Shoreham to find out if she was there for a liaison with the president. Agents staked out the hotel and checked the register but did not find her.[153]

Decades later, Kay Summersby was diagnosed with terminal cancer and decided to publish a candid memoir, *Past Remembering: My Love Affair with Dwight David Eisenhower* (1976). Summersby explained that they were deeply in love and talked of marriage. They tried to have sex three times but poor Ike could not get an erection.[154] Summersby provided a bittersweet account of their last attempt at sex during the final days of the war. "The fire was warm. The sofa was soft. We held each other close, closer. Excitedly. I remember thinking, the way one thinks odd thoughts at significant moments, Wouldn't it be wonderful if this were the day we conceived a baby—our very first time. Ike was tender, careful, loving. But it didn't work. 'Wait,' I said. 'You're too excited. It will be all right.' 'No,' he said flatly. 'It won't. It's too late. I can't.' He was bitter. We dressed slowly. Kissing occasionally. Smiling a bit sadly."[155]

HOOVER'S PUMPS

No discussion of J. Edgar Hoover is complete without examining the rumor that the FBI director was a cross-dresser. The story first gained credence when it appeared in Anthony Summers's 1993 biography *Official and Confidential: The Secret Life of J. Edgar Hoover.*[156] Summers based his claim on the recollections of Susan Rosenstiel, the fourth wife of Lewis Rosenstiel, a liquor industry magnate who made a bootlegging fortune during Prohibition. (Hoover was friendly with Lewis, who created the J. Edgar Hoover Foundation to fund anticommunist educational programs and publications.)[157] Susan Rosenstiel told Summers that in 1957 she attended a party hosted by Roy Cohn in a Plaza Hotel suite where she met Hoover clad in a fluffy black dress, lace stockings, high heels, false eyelashes and a curly black wig. Rosenstiel said that in the middle of the party, Cohn led everyone into a bedroom where "Hoover takes off his lace dress and pants, and under the dress he was wearing a little, short garter belt. He lies on the double bed, and the two boys work on him with their hands. One of them wore rubber gloves." Rosenstiel also said that, a year later, Cohn threw another party attended by Hoover with "a red dress on and a black feather boa around his neck. He was dressed like an old flapper, like you see on old tintypes. After about half an hour some boys came, like before. This time they're dressed in leather. And Hoover had a Bible. He wanted one of the boys to read from the Bible. And he read, I forget which passage, and the other boy played with him, wearing rubber gloves. And then Hoover grabbed the Bible, threw it down and told the second boy to join in the sex."[158]

Rosenstiel's story created a national sensation. *Tonight Show* host Jay Leno joked that when Senator Strom Thurmond first arrived in Washington in 1954, "J. Edgar Hoover was still walking around in a training bra." Leno added that the FBI director should have been called "Gay Edgar Hoover." President Bill Clinton and Republican Senate minority leader Bob Dole entertained the White House Correspondents Dinner with Hoover jokes. Clinton mentioned that he might have to replace the current FBI director but it would "be hard to fill J. Edgar Hoover's pumps." Senator Dole complimented the United Press International's Washington bureau chief Helen Thomas for her "lovely dress," surmising that it must have been "from the new J. Edgar Hoover collection."[159]

The story of a bewigged Hoover having sex with leather-clad boys in front of a room full of gawkers is mighty amusing, but it is probably not true. Hoover was terrified by even rumors about his sexuality. He would never have dressed in drag and engaged in a sex act in front of people he didn't know. Unfortunately the false stories about Hoover's cross-dressing have distracted from his truly scandalous acts as FBI director.

A congressional investigation after Hoover's death found that Hoover treated the public treasury as a personal bank account to live, in the words of a former deputy U.S. attorney general, "like an Oriental potentate."[160] The president had one chauffeur-driven, armor-plated, bulletproof car; Hoover had three, each of which weighed so much the FBI had to replace the tires and brakes every month.[161] Every summer during cost-free "working vacations" to California with Tolson, the FBI painted Hoover's house and performed renovations like installation of a lighted fishpond in his backyard and a front portico. FBI technicians hand made his living room furniture and installed a heated toilet seat that was invented in an FBI laboratory. Hoover decided the toilet was an inch too high and had the FBI replace it with a new one, cost free. When the rose-pattern wallpaper in his living room began to fade, the FBI Exhibits section created a paint that perfectly matched the pink roses and freshened up each flower by hand. When Hoover became upset after his lawn was not properly mowed, the FBI installed Astroturf.[162] Meanwhile wealthy friends lavished Hoover with gifts, investment tips, free dinners and free hotel stays. Hoover returned the favors by protecting them from criminal investigation.[163]

FBI agents also provided around-the-clock surveillance of Hoover's house. One morning Hoover discovered feces on his front stoop and suspected it was left by one of his political enemies. According to one agent, Tolson immediately arrived and started "going apeshit" and threatened to fire the guards. FBI forensic specialists rushed over to collect the mysterious turd to see if they could trace it to the perpetrator. They took it to the Smithsonian, where a zoologist noticed in it shells of berries that raccoons eat. After the agents assured Hoover that the suspicious crap came from a raccoon and not a nefarious enemy, Hoover ordered FBI technicians to build a raccoon trap and install it on his patio. The next morning Hoover woke up to find his neighbor's cat splattered on the side of his house.[164]

Hoover's handling of the raccoon turd could be a metaphor for his tenure at the FBI: an overblown, dramatic, futile waste. A congressional investigation after his death in 1972 found 19 percent of the bureau's total effort was still devoted to hunting "subversives." Criminal conduct was discovered in only 4 of 19,700 FBI investigations, and none of those involved espionage or terrorism. Even the FBI's vaunted number of convictions resulted from mostly inconsequential cases against car thieves and small-time bank robbers.[165] As for keeping Americans safe, Hoover was a bust. Although Hoover constantly hyped the threat of communism to the public, in an unguarded moment he admitted that the FBI had so many moles in the American Communist Party that without the dues from his spies the party would have gone belly up.[166] Hoover was good at outing communist professors, teachers, writers and actors but lousy at catching communist spies. While he ballyhooed the great job the FBI was doing protecting America's nuclear secrets, Los Alamos atomic physicist Klaus Fuchs and the Rosenbergs divulged those secrets to the Soviets. The atomic spies probably would have gotten away with it if a Soviet defector had not exposed their plot five years later.[167]

Hoover's most glaring failure was his passive approach to organized crime. He insisted that since "no single individual or coalition of racketeers dominates organized crime across the nation," the FBI as a federal agency did not have jurisdiction to go after the Mob.[168] Eisenhower's attorney general William Rodgers said Hoover had to be dragged "kicking and screaming" into a Mafia investigation.[169] The New York FBI field office had 400 agents working on communism in 1959 but just 4 investigating organized crime.[170]

Hoover had not always taken a hands-off approach to organized crime. He declared Dutch Schultz "Public Enemy Number One" in 1935 and said, "Racketeering is a problem which, if not solved, will destroy eventually the security of American industrial life and the faith of our people in American institutions." Yet by the 1950s the FBI's war on organized crime had become a low priority.[171] Hoover's refusal to investigate the Mafia became a national embarrassment and perplexed even his most fervent supporters.[172] Years after Hoover's death, former FBI agent Neil Welch was still baffled: "None of the usual excuses are convincing. Hoover and his top people knew of the existence of the mafia. They knew from the agents' reports that routinely referred to it, certainly all through the fifties. Hoover's attitude was so contrary to reality as to be a reason for great speculation. It's a mystery."[173]

Seymour Pollock, a close friend of Meyer Lansky, who was known as the Mob's accountant, claimed, "The homosexual thing was Hoover's Achilles' heel. Meyer found it, and it was like he pulled the strings with Hoover. [Hoover] never bothered any of Meyer's people." Pollock claimed that when Lansky's partner Bugsy Siegel opened the Flamingo in Las Vegas, "Hoover helped get the okay for him to do it" and "Hoover knew who the guys were that whacked Bugsy Siegel, but nothing was done." (Lansky approved the hit on Siegel in 1947.) Irving Ash Resnick, Nevada representative of the Patriarca family of New England, told journalist Pete Hamill that "Lansky had some pictures—pictures of Hoover in some kind of a gay situation with Clyde Tolson. Lansky was the guy who controlled the pictures, and he had made his deal with Hoover—to lay off. That was the reason, they said, that for a long time they had nothing to fear from the FBI."[174]

The CIA also allegedly had photos of Hoover and Tolson in a compromising position. Jon Weitz, an officer in the Office of Strategic Services (OSS; predecessor to the CIA), recalled a dinner party in the 1950s: "After a conversation about Hoover our host went to another room and came back with a photograph. It was not a good picture and was clearly taken from some distance away, but it showed two men apparently engaged in homosexual activity. The host said the two men were Hoover and Tolson."[175] The host of the party was probably CIA counterintelligence chief James Angleton, who was the basis for the main character in the 2006 film *The Good Shepherd*. CIA electronics expert Gordon Novel said Angleton showed him a "picture of

[Hoover] giving Clyde Tolson a blow job. . . . There was more than one shot, but the startling one was a close shot of Hoover's head. He was totally recognizable. You could not see the face of the man he was with, but Angleton said it was Tolson. I asked him if they were fakes, but he said they were real." According to Novel this photograph found its way into the hands of organized crime in 1946, a time when the OSS "was fighting [the FBI] over foreign intelligence which Hoover wanted but never got."[176]

We know that during World War II, the OSS worked with Meyer Lansky protecting the ports and gathering intelligence for the invasion of Sicily. We also know Hoover investigated the private life of OSS chief William Donovan. Did Donovan retaliate and share the goods on Hoover with the Mafia? We will never know for certain unless a photo emerges.

We do know that without a federal crackdown, the Mafia flourished throughout Hoover's long career, taking over Cuba and Las Vegas, hijacking major unions, corrupting numerous state and local governments, and flooding America's cites with heroin. Hoover might have built the world's most technologically advanced police force, but he refused to use it to protect America from the Mafia.

There was no public uproar over the FBI's devastating failure to contain organized crime, because Hoover intimidated America's most influential journalists and politicians with their sex files. Everyone in power simply turned a blind eye to the FBI's passive approach to the Mafia and its gross violations of civil liberties. Only after Hoover's death did the FBI finally begin aggressively fighting the Mob and obeying the Bill of Rights. FBI assistant director William Sullivan perfectly summed up Hoover's career: "He was a master con man, one of the greatest con men the country has ever produced."[177]

NIXON VERSUS HOOVER

Hoover had a big influence on Richard Nixon, who observed that "information was one of the primary sources of Edgar Hoover's power. He usually knew something about everything that was going on, and that knowledge made him as valuable to his friends as it made him dangerous to his enemies."[178] This was a lesson Tricky Dick learned all too well.

Hoover was responsible for Nixon's jump into the national spotlight in 1948, when the freshman congressman launched a crusade to prove that former State Department official Alger Hiss was a communist. Using Nixon as a pawn in his war against Truman, Hoover assigned agents to investigate Hiss and feed information to the young congressman. While Hiss was never proved to have been a communist in the courts, he was found guilty of perjury. Nixon instantly became the darling of the Right and was elected Eisenhower's vice president in 1952.[179]

Two decades later, Nixon was president and Hoover was still the director. Nixon wanted to intimidate the press just as Hoover did and asked the FBI director "for a run down on the homosexuals known and suspected in the Washington press corps."[180] Nixon also asked Hoover for permission to run his own illegal domestic spy operation out of the White House. Hoover rejected the president's spy plan, not because he cared about the violation of civil liberties, but because he wanted Nixon to have to go through the FBI for black bag jobs, or covert operations, as all his predecessors did. After the FBI director vetoed the president's spy operation, Nixon wanted to fire Hoover. "He should get the hell out of there!" But he feared the director "could leave with a blast," so he asked former FBI agent G. Gordon Liddy to write a report on how Hoover would react to being dismissed. Liddy, who later masterminded the Watergate break-in, warned Nixon that "Hoover could resist and *make good his threat* against the president." After reading Liddy's report Nixon said, "We may have on our hands here a man who will pull down the temple with him including *me*."[181]

It is possible that Nixon feared Hoover would expose his rumored affair with Marianna Liu, a cocktail waitress living in Hong Kong. When Nixon was a private attorney, he repeatedly met with Liu between 1964 and 1967 during business trips to Hong Kong. An FBI agent stationed there reported back to Hoover that Nixon and Liu were having an affair and that the CIA and British intelligence suspected Liu was a Chinese spy. Liu and Nixon were placed under surveillance and, at the behest of the CIA, British intelligence photographed Nixon through his hotel window with infrared cameras.[182] According to FBI assistant director Sullivan, Hoover "gleefully" read the report on Nixon and Liu and personally presented it to the president-elect before his first inauguration in 1969.[183]

After Nixon resigned in August 1974, an FBI source told the *New York Times* that while Nixon was president he pushed the immigration service to admit Liu, who moved to Whittier, California—Nixon's hometown. The *National Enquirer* and other tabloids reported in 1976 that Liu and Nixon had a "hot and heavy" romance. Liu adamantly insisted their relationship was platonic: "We had many opportunities to make love—we were alone in his hotel room at least six or seven times—but I wouldn't let it happen. He had an important career and a wife and family to think of."[184] When Liu was asked if she secretly visited the Nixon White House, she cried, "I'm not saying anything else about me and Mr. Nixon. Are you trying to get me killed?"[185] According to a 1976 *New York Times* report, the FBI never found firm evidence of a sexual affair between Nixon and Liu. But Hoover still could have threatened to expose Nixon's friendly relationship with a suspected Chinese spy, which certainly would have tainted Nixon's historic diplomatic breakthrough with China. Whatever Hoover's threat, Nixon chose to keep him around and wait for a higher power to remove the tenacious old man.

On May 1, 1972, a 77-year-old Hoover returned home from dinner with Tolson and a few hours later died of a massive heart attack, alone in his bedroom. After Tolson heard the news, he immediately ordered Hoover's secretary to secretly destroy all the Personal and Confidential files, and then he resigned—there was just no reason for him to continue at the FBI without Eddie around.

Nixon rejoiced when he heard the news, "Jesus Christ! That old cocksucker!"[186] Publicly, the president was a bit more somber: "All Americans today mourn the death of J. Edgar Hoover. He served his nation as Director of the FBI for 48 years under eight American presidents with total loyalty, unparalleled ability and supreme dedication. It can truly be said of him that he was a legend in his own lifetime."[187] Nixon ordered a state funeral with live television coverage on all three commercial networks. Hoover's body lay in state on the same bier that once had borne Abraham Lincoln and eight other presidents in the Capitol rotunda, where more than 25,000 mourners came to pay their respects.[188] Nixon also ordered that the new FBI headquarters bear J. Edgar Hoover's name in big gold letters.

Even in death, Hoover was determined to insulate himself from the outside world. His brass coffin was lined with lead and weighed over half a ton; two of his eight pallbearers were injured under the weight.[189] At Hoover's burial, Tolson was given the ceremonial folded flag—a public recognition of their special relationship. Hoover left his house and most of his million-dollar estate to Tolson, along with his two dogs. For the remainder of his days, Tolson lived as a recluse, emerging on rare occasions to visit his old boss's grave, and three years later he was buried steps away from Hoover. After 41 years of companionship, together forever.

CHAPTER SIX

THE NUDE FRONTIER

W hen John Kennedy was elected president in 1960 his speech-writer Ted Sorensen predicted, "This administration is going to do for sex what the previous one did for golf."[1] The sexy Kennedys, in stark contrast to the dowdy Eisenhowers, were the perfect First Couple for a country on the cusp of the sexual revolution. Jack was the dashing New Frontiersman, countering the Soviets and charming the ladies like a real-life James Bond. Jackie was an alluring beauty dressed in snug Oleg Cassini skirts and doing the Twist in the White House. Even JFK began calling Jackie "The Sex Symbol."[2] As Ted Sorensen predicted, the Kennedys reflected and accelerated America's move into the swinging sixties. But no one could have foreseen how sex would ultimately come to define the Kennedy era.

SEX AND THE PRESS

Even before Kennedy ran for president, his sexual conquests were legendary: Angie Dickenson, Kim Novak, Janet Leigh, Jean Simmons, Jayne Mansfield and Marilyn Monroe. During the 1960 presidential campaign, Kennedy aides debated whether rumors about their candidate's affairs with movie stars would hurt or help his chances in the fall. "Some people on staff said products are sold by star endorsement," Kennedy's media advisor Peter Summers recalled, "and that maybe a closeness [between JFK and female movie stars] of this nature will be a benefit to him getting elected. The other side was that you're not going to elect someone president who is perhaps ignoring his wife or cheating on his family." James Bacon, who covered Hollywood for the Associated Press, said of his friend Marilyn Monroe, "She was very open about her affair with JFK. In fact I think Marilyn was in love with JFK." Bacon did not write a word about the aspiring president and the silver screen goddess, because "before Watergate, reporters just didn't go into that sort of thing. I'd have to have been under the bed in order to put it on the wire for the AP."[3] Kennedy not only benefited from the journalistic code of ethics that prohibited reporting on any political figure's private life, he also charmed the press. His 22-year-old mistress Diana de Vegh observed, "The fact is a lot of reporters were very keen to spend time with him. I think he assumed they would not turn him in, and they didn't."[4]

In Kennedy's day reporters practiced what was called access journalism; the goal was not to nail politicians but to win them over to get access to big scoops. A newspaper columnist once sent a buxom brunette to the White House carrying a note he wanted delivered directly to the president. Kennedy later called the columnist to confirm: "I got your message—both of them."[5]

The Cold War also fostered a hands-off approach to the president's sex life because a scandal involving the commander in chief would have threatened the national security and been considered treasonous.[6] Kennedy knew that the press ignored his affairs and even camouflaged them with a steady stream of stories and images that depicted his marriage as the epitome of domestic bliss. The press enabled Kennedy to avoid having to choose between rampant sex and political success. Even under the intense scrutiny of the presidential campaign, he saw no reason to change his behavior. In fact, the more powerful he became, the more untouchable Kennedy felt—as he remarked to a friend, "They can't touch me while I'm alive and after I'm dead who cares?"[7]

INGA BINGA

The gap between reality and press reports on Kennedy's personal life helped him reach the apex of power, but it also left him dreadfully vulnerable to the one man who refused to look the other way—J. Edgar Hoover. As Vice President Lyndon Johnson put it to a few *Time* reporters, "J. Edgar Hoover has Jack Kennedy by the balls."[8] Although JFK's liberal supporters hoped he would oust Hoover as soon as he took over the White House, there was a good reason why Kennedy's very first act as president was to reappoint Hoover as FBI director.

Hoover opened his first Personal and Confidential file on Kennedy during World War II, when the 24-year-old navy ensign began an affair with a shapely, blonde Danish reporter named Inga Arvad. At the start of the war, Jack was assigned to the Office of Naval Intelligence in Washington where he spent his days writing intelligence reports and his nights painting the town red with the twice-married, 28-year-old woman he called "Inga Binga." Inga met Kennedy in 1941 when she interviewed him for a society column she wrote for the *Washington Times-Herald:* "The 24 years of Jack's existence on our planet," Inga gushed in her column, "have proved that here is really a boy with a future."[9] She told a fellow reporter that JFK was "refreshing" because "he knows what he wants. He's not confused about motives. . . . He's got a lot to learn and I'll be happy to teach him."[10] Jack was captivated by the sophisticated, sexually experienced older woman who was a welcome break from the debutantes, nurses and students he had been dating.[11] "What was it that enchanted Jack? Oh, sex," a mutual friend said. "She was totally woman. She wasn't handsome, she was gorgeous. Luscious, luscious is the word. Like a lot of icing on the cake."[12]

Trouble arose when one of Inga's envious colleagues, who harbored a crush on Kennedy, alerted the FBI that his new paramour might be a Nazi spy. Before the war, when Inga was a reporter for a Danish newspaper, the former Miss Denmark beauty queen became friendly with high-placed Nazi leaders, including Joseph Goebbels, Heinrich Himmler and Rudolf Hess. Hermann Goring invited Inga to his wedding where he introduced her to his best man, Adolf Hitler. Hitler was smitten and proclaimed Inga "a perfect example of Nordic beauty." He granted her two exclusive interviews along with an invitation to watch the 1936 Olympics from his personal box.[13] "I have enjoyed myself so much," the infatuated Fuhrer told Inga after a two-hour interview, "that I beg you to visit me every time you return to Berlin." Inga reported that Hitler "was not as evil as he is depicted by the enemies of

Germany. He is without doubt an idealist; he believes that he is doing the right thing for Germans and his interests do not go any further."[14] The FBI believed that Hitler appointed Arvad to be chief of Nazi publicity in Denmark. Hoover reported to U.S. attorney general Francis Biddle on January 21, 1942, that the woman who "captivated" Hitler had now "established close social and professional contacts with persons holding important positions in the government departments and bureaus vitally concerned with the national defense and in particular has become very friendly with several Naval ensigns," particularly John Kennedy who "made repeated visits to her apartment."[15]

Franklin Delano Roosevelt heard about the FBI's investigation into Kennedy's relationship with Arvad in January 1942 and interrupted his planning for the invasion of Africa and the Battle of Midway to personally urge Hoover to collect more information.[16] The commander in chief wanted the information because in 1940 Jack's father, Joe, then ambassador to Great Britain, had threatened to run against FDR for the Democratic Party nomination on an antiwar, isolationist platform. Although Roosevelt outmaneuvered Kennedy and secured the presidency, he relished the opportunity to use Joe's son for a little payback. After Pearl Harbor, Joe's isolationist stance made him suspect with the American people. If FDR could pin the ambassador's son to a Nazi spy, he could destroy the elder Kennedy once and for all.

At Roosevelt's request, Hoover had FBI agents intercept Inga's mail, tap her phone, plant microphones in her apartment and trail her night and day. FDR also had Hoover tip off Walter Winchell about the heated affair. Winchell ran with Hoover's tip in his nationally syndicated column: "One of Ex-Ambassador Kennedy's eligible sons is the target of a Washington gal columnist's affections. So much so she has consulted her barrister about divorcing her exploring groom. Pa Kennedy no like."[17] A day after the Winchell piece appeared, Jack was transferred out of Washington to a desk job at a naval base in Charleston, SC. The young JFK complained to a friend, "They shagged my ass down to South Carolina because I was going around with a Scandinavian blonde, and they thought she was a spy!"[18]

Much to Hoover's delight, however, Jack continued to entertain Inga Binga in Charleston. FBI agents planted bugs in Arvad's hotel rooms so they could provide their boss with lots of juicy details about the couple. One

FBI report on one of Inga's visits noted that "John Kennedy, Ensign, USN, spent each night with subject in her hotel room at the Fort Sumner Hotel, engaging in sexual intercourse on *numerous occasions*."[19] Although agents found absolutely no evidence that Inga was a spy, they did compile a 628-page file complete with steamy audio recordings that could have destroyed the political hopes of the Kennedy family.[20] JFK knew about FBI surveillance on Inga. "I'm afraid she's dangerous," he told a friend. "She certainly has connections with the Fascists in Europe, Germany especially. But as to being a spy, it's hard to believe she's doing that, because she's not only beautiful, but she's warm, she's affectionate, she's wonderful in bed. But you know, goddammit Henry, I found out that son-of-a-bitch Hoover had put a microphone under the mattress!"[21] Despite the threat Inga posed to his future, JFK could not quit her. Finally his father had to step in and pay Inga to quietly end the relationship.[22]

When Jack applied for overseas combat duty, his commanding officer in Charleston was at first reluctant to let such a competent intelligence officer go. But once he found out about Kennedy's affair with a suspected spy, he was happy to see Jack leave his department. Kennedy's commanding officer approved his transfer in July 1942, and soon Jack was training to become captain of a PT boat.[23]

After JFK rode his wartime heroism to a congressional seat in 1946, his friend Langdon Marvin recalled that "one of the things on his mind was the Inga-Binga tape in the FBI files—the tape *he* was on." When JFK was elected to the Senate, he vowed to use his new power to intimidate the FBI director. "That bastard. I'm going to force Hoover to give me those files."[24] But Hoover never surrendered Kennedy's files, and the randy young politician kept filling them with new material over the rest of his storied career.

JUDITH CAMPBELL AND THE STOLEN ELECTION

Kennedy campaign worker Langdon Marvin recalled that during the 1960 presidential run his boss would "dispatch me to a given town or city as a kind of advance man. I'd set things up for him. When he arrived, I'd pick him up at the airport. He'd clamber off the *Caroline*, the campaign plane his father had purchased for him, and he'd say to me, 'Where are the broads?'"[25]

Marvin was also responsible for hiring prostitutes to frolic with JFK right before his nationally televised debates with Republican nominee Richard Nixon. Millions of viewers witnessed what journalist Theodore H. White called a "calm and nerveless" Kennedy in sharp contrast to a "tense" Nixon.[26] JFK's cool, collected performance in those debates convinced many voters that the young senator could be a steady leader in a volatile world. Republican vice presidential nominee Henry Cabot Lodge exploded after watching Nixon in the first debate, "That son of a bitch just lost the election!"[27] The campaign cash that paid for JFK's pre-debate stress relief was certainly money well spent.

Sex played another important role in the success of the Kennedy campaign. On February 7, 1960, Frank Sinatra, who sang the Kennedy campaign song *High Hopes,* introduced the presidential candidate to a dark-haired, shapely brunette named Judith Campbell during a campaign break at the Sands Hotel in Las Vegas. Sinatra had dated Campbell until a certain evening when he invited a second woman to join them for a threesome. Campbell recalled how she "just absolutely froze. I went rigid; no one could have moved my arms and legs."[28] A year later Sinatra happily handed Campbell over to Kennedy, and, according to an FBI report, the Las Vegas police bugged a romantic interlude between them at the Sands.[29] Kennedy seemed to develop an instant affection for Campbell, and over subsequent weeks interrupted his campaign to call her almost daily to see what she was doing and whom she was meeting.

Weeks later, Sinatra invited Campbell to his show at Miami's Fontainebleau Hotel, where he introduced her to a well-dressed, middle-aged man in dark glasses: "I want you to meet Sam Flood." Later that evening, when Campbell mentioned to Kennedy that "Frank introduced me to Sam Flood," JFK said, "Oh yes, I know Sam Giancana."[30] We will never know for sure why Sinatra introduced Campbell to both the presidential candidate and the Chicago Mafia don. We do know Sinatra had been relaying information between the Kennedy camp and Giancana since the start of the campaign.[31] We also know that within weeks of Campbell's introduction to both men, this young woman found herself serving as their new go-between. Kennedy and Giancana obviously needed a less visible courier than Old Blue Eyes, but why tap a 26-year-old woman? In the highly unlikely event she betrayed her lover and the Mob boss, no one would believe her. Especially if she revealed the bizarre truth: that the Democratic Party nominee and the Mafia kingpin were plotting to steal the presidency.

Weeks before the election, Jackie Kennedy, pregnant with John Jr., went on vacation to Florida, and Jack took the opportunity to invite Campbell to stay at their Georgetown home. JFK had some important political business in mind. Looking at the Electoral College map, Kennedy knew the swing state of Illinois would be key to a victory over Richard Nixon; to win Illinois, Kennedy needed Giancana's help with the unions and Chicago's wards. According to Campbell, Jack asked if she would set up a meeting with the crime boss. A "little surprised," Campbell said, "Well yes. I'd be happy to. Why, or should I ask?" Kennedy replied, "Well, I think he can help me with the campaign."[32] He then pulled out a large satchel and asked if she would mind delivering it to Giancana. Although Campbell immediately accepted the mission, Kennedy said, "But I want you to know what's in it," and opened the satchel containing $250,000 ($1.8 million today) in $100 bills.[33] After an overnight train ride to Chicago, Campbell met Giancana, who snatched the bag from her hand without saying a word.[34] Right before the election, Kennedy asked Campbell to pass a second satchel of money to Giancana and set up a face-to-face meeting in her apartment. When the Democratic Party nominee met with the Mafia don, Campbell "went into . . . [her] bedroom and waited until they were finished talking."[35]

Campbell's contacts with Kennedy and Giancana quickly came to the attention of FBI agents, who reported to Hoover that she was sleeping with both men. Four days before the presidential election, agents from the FBI and the Internal Revenue Service arrived at Campbell's apartment to interrogate her about Giancana. "They treated me with such disrespect," Campbell recalled. "I gladly let them come into my home. And the way they were acting, I finally just told them to leave." As soon as they left, she called Kennedy, who offered "the same pat answer" whenever she complained about FBI surveillance. He would always say, "Don't worry about them," or "You have nothing to be afraid of. You've never done anything wrong in your life. You know Sam works for us."[36]

Sam's work paid big dividends on election night when Kennedy won Cook County by a suspiciously overwhelming 450,000 votes and squeaked out a victory in Illinois by fewer than 9,400 votes. FBI agents reported to Hoover that Chicago's returns were falsified.[37] With Giancana's help, Kennedy secured a slim victory in one of the closest presidential elections in American history. But Sam's work for the Kennedys was far from over.

KILLING CASTRO

Shortly before the inauguration in 1961, the president-elect asked Campbell "to take some information to Sam" and to Florida Mob boss Johnny Roselli regarding the "elimination" of Fidel Castro. Over the next year, Campbell made 10 or more trips to Giancana and Roselli with envelopes from Kennedy. Campbell said she and the president had a routine. After they had sex in the White House, they would have dinner and "Bobby would come in and bring the information in a manila envelope to Jack. And they would discuss a little bit about it. And Bobby often would put his hand on my shoulder and ask, 'Are you still comfortable doing this? We want you to let us know if you don't want to.'"[38] Campbell didn't hesitate in taking part in this conspiracy involving the president, the U.S. attorney general and the Mafia to assassinate a foreign head of state because she "was doing something for someone I loved dearly. It was as if my husband had asked me to do something for him, to carry some papers—if I had a lawyer for a husband and he wanted me to take some papers to a client. I never had the sense of just how serious all of it was. I was far too wrapped up in the fact that he trusted me. It just didn't register."[39] Such is the power of love.

Once again, in early 1962, Campbell came under the attention of the FBI when agents noticed Johnny Roselli's phone records registered frequent calls to Campbell and then discovered her phone records had dozens of calls to the president's secretary Evelyn Lincoln.[40] On February 27, 1962, Hoover sent RFK a memo about the suspicious phone records, benignly noting, "The relationship between Campbell and Mrs. Lincoln or the purpose of these calls is not known."[41] Hoover was much more candid about Campbell during lunch with the president on March 22, when he told Kennedy that he knew about their affair and warned the president that Campbell was also sleeping with Sam Giancana.[42] When lunch was done, Kennedy snapped to an aide, "Get rid of that bastard. He's the biggest bore." According to Campbell, Jack called that afternoon and told her to go to her mother's house and call him from there. "He said the phone in my apartment wasn't safe." Campbell "could feel his anger" over the telephone line. "He said that, at their meeting, Hoover had more or less tried to intimidate him with the information he had. He made it clear that he knew about my relationship with Jack, even that I'd been to the White House, that I was a friend of Sam and Johnny Roselli and that Jack knew Sam too. Jack knew exactly what Hoover was doing. Knowing that Jack wanted him out of office, he was in a way ensuring his job—by letting Jack know he had this leverage over him."[43]

Now that Campbell's cover was blown, Kennedy decided to dump her—which was probably going to happen anyway because their sex had begun to lose steam. "Slowly I began to feel that he expected me to come into bed and just perform," Campbell recalled. "I understood about the position he had to assume in lovemaking when his back was troubling him, but slowly he began excluding all other positions, until finally our lovemaking was reduced to this one position. . . . The feeling that I was there to service him began to really trouble me."[44] By the summer of 1962, Campbell had lost her value as sex object and secret courier. RFK found a new liaison to the Mafia and the president broke off the affair. But according to Campbell, during her last visit with JFK in August, she got pregnant. They agreed that she would get an abortion, and Campbell recalled "in our next conversation he asked, 'Would Sam help us?' I spoke to Sam and he said yes."[45] Giancana was appalled by how Kennedy treated such a trusting young woman, but the Mafia don now had even more leverage over the president, if he ever needed to use it.

Giancana might not have been the only outsider who knew about the abortion. On August 7, 1962, FBI agents on a stakeout of Campbell's apartment observed two young men scale the building to her balcony and slide through a glass door. Fifteen minutes later, the two left the apartment. The FBI agents did not stop them or report their crime to the police. Instead, the G-men tracked the license plate on the getaway car and found it was rented to a former FBI agent named I. B. Hale, who was head of security for General Dynamics, a military contractor. The FBI report to Hoover speculated that the two men were Hale's sons and that they broke into Campbell's apartment to install a bug or wiretap. Hoover did nothing to warn Campbell or confront

Hale because he did not want to expose his own surveillance of the president's girlfriend.[46]

Why was the General Dynamics head of security interested in Judith Campbell? In 1962 General Dynamics was heading toward financial collapse if it did not win a bid for a $6.5 billion ($46 billion today) military jet program known as the Tactical Fighter Experimental (TFX). Everyone familiar with the bids predicted that General Dynamics' main competitor, Boeing, would win the contract with its cheaper bid and better design that, according to the *Washington Post,* promised "longer flight range, more firepower, and shorter landing space requirements."[47] Four of the military's evaluation boards recommended Boeing's bid. But three months after the Hale boys broke into Campbell's apartment, secretary of defense Robert McNamara shocked Washington by awarding General Dynamics with the TFX program, the largest military aircraft contract in history. Suspicious senators opened an investigation into how the contract was awarded. The *Washington Post* editorialized, "In these circumstances the burden of proof that the TFX contract awarded to General Dynamics best serves the national interest clearly falls upon Secretary McNamara and his aides."[48] McNamara never had to answer fully for his decision because the Senate investigation was shut down after Kennedy's assassination.

The TFX program was plagued by delays and cost overruns that were appalling even by Washington standards. Six of the resulting planes, known as F-111s, were sent to Vietnam in 1968 for evaluation under real combat conditions. In little over a month, three of the six fell from the sky because of a malfunctioning horizontal stabilizer. Once again, McNamara's decision to award the TFX contract to General Dynamics came under fire, but by then the defense secretary had the much bigger problem of the Vietnam quagmire on his hands.

THE PLAYBOY PEACEMAKER

JFK once told British prime minister Harold Macmillan during a 1962 meeting that if he went too long without a new woman he suffered terrible headaches.[49] So as president, Kennedy always made space in his busy schedule for afternoon breaks with hookers, Hollywood starlets, a 19-year-old intern, or two secretaries who regularly joined him for orgies in the White

House swimming pool. The two secretaries were such fixtures in the presidential entourage that the Secret Service assigned them codenames—Fiddle and Faddle.[50] Secret Service files from the Kennedy years abound with background checks on airline stewardesses and models. Even Jackie joked that her husband's administration should have been called the "Nude Frontier."[51]

With so many women coming in and out of the Kennedy White House, it is surprising that none of them went to the press. One explanation for this can be found in the story of JFK's physical therapist, Susan Sklover, whom the Secret Service nicknamed "SK Lover." Sklover described Kennedy as "an ordinary lover" who insisted on fellatio but never reciprocated and then lay on his back and invited her to "climb aboard"—a ride that lasted a minute or two. "He wanted to be serviced," Sklover said. When she quit after six weeks, press secretary Pierre Salinger wrote her a check for $5,000 ($35,000 today), made her sign a confidentiality agreement and sent her off with a warning: "If you ever discuss the terms or details of your employment with the chief executive you'll never work again."[52]

The president's staff wasn't always able to protect their boss from himself. JFK's longtime friend Lem Billings observed that "it never occurred to Jack that some of these women might be considered dangerous. They were never searched, never questioned in depth." Billings recalled "an 18-year-old girl visiting from Ireland who wanted to meet the president. So he insisted they usher her straight into the Oval Office. It turned out she had a 15 inch butcher knife in her shoulder bag and had just been released from a mental hospital in Dublin." Having averted disaster, the White House quietly deported the girl back to Ireland.[53]

JFK's sexual taste ran the gamut from teens to senior citizens. One of Joe Kennedy's old flames, Marlene Dietrich, regaled friends, including Gore Vidal, with the story of one evening in 1963 when the president invited her for a drink at the White House. In Vidal's recounting, the 60-year-old grandmother arrived at six o'clock, an hour before she was scheduled to appear at an event honoring her wartime work aiding Jewish refugees. She was shown into the living quarters, where she found a bottle of German wine chilling on ice. Fifteen minutes later, the president walked in, kissed her, poured himself some wine and took her out on the balcony. "I hope you aren't in a hurry," he said. Dietrich explained that, actually, 2,000 people were waiting to give her an award in 30 minutes. JFK replied, "That doesn't give us much time, does it?"

He abruptly grabbed her glass and led her into the presidential bedroom. Dietrich described what happed next. "I remembered about his bad back—that wartime injury. I looked at him and he was already undressing. He was unwinding rolls of bandage from around his middle—he looked like Laocoön and that snake, you know? Now I'm an old lady, and I said to myself: I'd like to sleep with the President, sure, but I'll be goddammed if I'm going to be on top!" Remembering that she was supposed to appear on stage in fifteen minutes, Dietrich warned the president, "Don't mess my hair, I'm performing!" Dietrich recalled that after six minutes, Kennedy climaxed and fell asleep. "I looked at my watch and it was 6:50. I got dressed and shook him—because I didn't know my way around the place, and I couldn't just call for a cab. I said: 'Jack—wake up! 2,000 Jews are waiting! For Christ's sake get me out of here!' So he grabbed a towel and wrapped it round his waist and took me along this corridor to an elevator. He told the elevator man to get me a car to the Statler [Hotel] immediately—standing right there in his towel, without any embarrassment, as if it was an everyday event—which in his life it probably was." As Dietrich entered the elevator, Kennedy stopped her: "There's just one thing I'd like to know. Did you ever make it with my father?" "No, Jack," she answered, "I never did." A beaming Kennedy replied, "Well, that's one place I'm in first! I always knew the son of a bitch was lying."[54] Dietrich was the one who was lying, but she certainly made the president's day.

Given all the stories we now know about JFK's sexual high jinks, it's easy to see why many Americans view him as a reckless playboy. But judging President Kennedy by his private life ignores the remarkable job he did fulfilling the main responsibility of any president—keeping Americans safe. During the Cuban missile crisis of 1962, Kennedy resisted the warmongers and ideologues among the Joint Chiefs, the Congress and the press and chose diplomacy over war with the Soviets. Kennedy also learned an important lesson—if he did not act quickly to defuse the Cold War, the next superpower confrontation might result in a nuclear holocaust. JFK began secretly conspiring in early 1963 with Soviet premier Nikita Khrushchev and British prime minister Harold Macmillan to hammer out a Nuclear Test Ban Treaty that would open a new chapter in U.S.–Soviet relations.[55] Months later, he went public with his plans and boldly called for an end to the Cold War in his famous Peace speech at American University in June 1963: "Let us examine our attitude toward peace itself. . . . What kind of peace do I mean? I am talking about genuine peace. Not merely peace in our time but peace in all time."[56] The Peace speech was extraordinary because it challenged the ideological rigidity of the anticommunist mind-set by acknowledging that the world is not divided between black and white, good and evil. Kennedy put forth the revolutionary notion that compromise with the communists was possible and practical. But his mission to revamp the international order and secure a lasting peace faced a major obstacle from an unexpected quarter. During the summer of 1963, while the world watched JFK tour Europe and embark on détente with the Soviets, the president secretly worried about a prostitute who threatened both his peace plan and his presidency.

THE PROFUMO AFFAIR

The same month as the Peace speech, Prime Minister Macmillan, who played a key role in Kennedy's effort to end the Cold War, suddenly found his power threatened by a sex scandal. British newspapers began reporting in June 1963 that Christine Keeler, a 21-year-old showgirl turned prostitute, was carrying on simultaneous affairs with the British secretary of war John Profumo and Evgeny Ivanov, a Soviet intelligence agent stationed in London. The press speculated that Profumo revealed information about Britain's nuclear weapons during pillow talk with Keeler, who then shared the top secrets with her KGB lover. At the time there was absolutely no proof of bedroom espionage, but just the possibility was enough to threaten the government of Kennedy's friend and partner in peace, Harold Macmillan. JFK's close friend Ben Bradlee noted that from the moment news of the Profumo scandal broke, JFK "devoured every word. It combined so many of the things that interested him: low doings in high places, the British nobility, sex, and spying." Jackie recalled that her husband was "very depressed" over Macmillan's situation and "the prospect of what he considered to be a great hero brought down."[57] But Kennedy had another reason to be depressed by the Profumo scandal. Suddenly the sex lives of politicians were fair game for the press and the code of silence that shielded his peccadilloes from the public was no longer sacred. Even more disturbing for Kennedy were reports that Christine Keeler was part of a "V-Girl ring"— V for "vice"—that included two other women, bleach-blonde Czech Maria Novotny and Suzy Chang, a Chinese American beauty who was telling the British press that John Kennedy was one of her clients.

Chang's allegation caught the attention of J. Edgar Hoover. A day after JFK's Peace speech, Hoover ordered the FBI field office in London to launch Operation Bowtie—an investigation into the V-girl ring "with particular emphasis on any allegation that US nationals are or have been involved in any way."[58] Hoover had one particular U.S. national in mind.[59] After the FBI director received the Operation Bowtie report, he sent an ominous letter to U.S. attorney general Robert Kennedy on June 18, 1963: "In view of the president's forthcoming trip to Europe it is believed you would want to know of the following information which was obtained from a confidential informant who has furnished reliable information in the past." Government censors redacted the next two paragraphs of Hoover's letter before it was declassified, but Hoover closed it with a revealing suggestion: "In view of the extremely delicate and sensitive source providing this information, it is being furnished only to you with the belief you might want to *personally advise* the President concerning this information."[60] In his typical fashion, Hoover was simultaneously warning and threatening the president of the United States.

John Kennedy was so shaken by the FBI's interest in the Profumo scandal that four days after getting Hoover's warning he shared his concerns about Profumo with Martin Luther King Jr. The President knew Hoover was trying to discredit King by tarring him as a communist dupe. Under pressure from Hoover, Kennedy approved the wiretapping of King's advisor Stanley Levison in 1962. The FBI reported to the president that Levison and another King advisor, Jack O'Dell, were Soviet agents intent on using the civil rights movement to weaken America.[61] Kennedy probably did not believe the FBI's absurd allegations, but he knew that when it came to J. Edgar Hoover the truth did not matter. The White House had just announced its support for the civil rights bill in June 1963, and Kennedy anticipated a tough fight in Congress. Conservatives on Capitol Hill were already denouncing as a communist tactic King's idea for a march on Washington later that summer. After a meeting at the White House to discuss the civil rights bill on July 22, 1963, the president pulled King aside for a private stroll around the Rose Garden. King later recounted details of their conversation to his aides. Kennedy brought up Levison and O'Dell: "They're communists. You've got to get rid of them." Seeing that he was not getting through to King, the president then cautioned him, "I assume you know you're under very close surveillance." "You've read about Profumo in the papers?" Kennedy continued. "That was an example of friendship and loyalty carried too far. Macmillan is likely to lose his government because he has been loyal to a friend. You must be careful not to lose your cause for the same reason."[62] Kennedy finished with an ominous warning: "If they shoot *you* down, they'll shoot *us* down too—so we're asking you to be careful."[63] King eventually broke off contact with Levison, but by then Hoover had begun demanding permission to wiretap and bug King himself.

A day after his Rose Garden stroll with King, Kennedy flew to Europe where he was welcomed everywhere by adoring crowds, including a million West Berliners who greeted him with chants of "Kennedy, Kennedy." But while JFK inspired the free world with his Ich Bin Ein Berliner speech, back home one newspaper reveled in less exalted matters. On June 29, 1963, a right-wing Hearst tabloid, the *New York Journal American,* ran a front-page article titled "High US Aide Implicated in V-Girl Scandal" that quoted "London party girl" Maria Novotny saying that Suzy Chang, "a beautiful Chinese American girl," was a "former paramour of the [unnamed] American government official." The tabloid speculated that "one of the biggest names in American politics—a man who holds a very high elective office—has been injected into Britain's vice-security scandal."[64] It was one thing for the British press to speculate on John Kennedy's involvement with the V-girl ring, but now for the first time an *American* newspaper was hot on the trail of the president's sex life.

Something had to be done to contain the story. Attorney General Robert Kennedy, who was always responsible for cleaning up after his brother, immediately called the newspaper's publishers, who agreed to pull the explosive story after one edition. Two days later, on July 1, 1963, RFK yanked the reporters who wrote the article into his Justice Department office and demanded they identify the "government official" involved with the V-girls. According to the notes of FBI agent Courtney Evans, who attended the meeting, Bobby stared the reporters down with "those steel blue eyes" until they cracked and revealed that they were indeed referring to his brother.[65] Although the chastened reporters abandoned the story and no other newspaper picked it up, a dangerous precedent was set. American reporters were no longer going to automatically ignore stories about the president's sex life. The Kennedys had to be extra vigilant.

The next day, July 2, Bobby asked the FBI in a memo, "Have we learned what Christine Keeler and her friend did here in the US when they were here?"[66] The bureau responded that 28-year-old Suzy Chang had flown to New York many times and was seen on several occasions with John Kennedy, including a dinner at 21, one of his favorite restaurants.[67] Even more disturbing to the FBI was the case of Maria Novotny. Questioned by Scotland Yard in connection to the Profumo case, Novotny said she was 19 when she met JFK at a party hosted by the famous actor Vic Damone at a New York hotel. Novotny recounted how Kennedy took her into one of the suite's bedrooms for some midparty fun. She also said that after Kennedy's inauguration, his brother-in-law and Rat Pack member Peter Lawford recruited Novotny for something a bit more interesting for the president. Novotny recalled that, in a midtown apartment she shared with her television producer boyfriend Harry Alan Towers, she and two other prostitutes dressed as doctor and nurses and examined Kennedy, playing the role of patient. So far this was just another salacious tale for Kennedy's Personal and Confidential file. But the FBI also discovered that Novotny's boyfriend Harry Towers was a Soviet agent paid to dig up information that might be used to compromise powerful Americans. When Novotny returned to Britain in the wake of the Profumo scandal, Towers fled to Czechoslovakia.[68]

RFK must have panicked as he read the FBI report on his brother's activities with Chang and Novotny. He might be able to intimidate the press to avoid further investigation into his brother and the V-girls, but he knew the

FBI would be much more troublesome, especially with the espionage angle. The FBI was still investigating JFK's involvement in the Profumo case a year later, at the time of his assassination.[69]

THE QUORUM CLUB

The day the FBI informed the attorney general about his brother and the V-girls, Hoover read a July 2, 1963, editorial in the *Danville Virginia Register* suggesting the Kennedys wanted to fire him:[70] "Bobby and his big brother want to retire J. Edgar Hoover as FBI director and bring in a young man who will eagerly turn the respected agency into an enforcement arm—ready to enforce Bobby's orders everywhere."[71] After serving as FBI boss for 40 years, Hoover wasn't about to let the Kennedy boys push him out to pasture without a fight. His arsenal was stocked with a powerful weapon: sexual blackmail.

The next day, Hoover brought out the big guns when he told Bobby that an FBI informant claimed JFK had sex with a prostitute who might be an East German spy.[72] The woman of ill repute was Ellen Rometsch—a sultry 27-year-old brunette from East Germany with an hourglass figure, a beehive hairdo and a Cindy Crawford mole. Rometsch had been a member of a communist youth group and, according to the FBI, worked as a secretary for Walter Ulbricht, head of the German Democratic Republic government. She fled with her parents to West Germany and in 1955 married a German army officer who was later stationed at the Washington embassy. The FBI discovered that Rometsch was separated from her husband and working as a call girl whose high-profile clients included the president.

Ellen Rometsch had met John Kennedy in the spring of 1963 while working in a call girl ring run by Bobby Baker, one of Washington's most influential insiders. Baker had arrived in DC from Pickens, South Carolina, back in 1943, when he was 14 years old, to work as a congressional page. Thanks to his mentor Lyndon Johnson, he quickly rose through the ranks, becoming secretary of the Senate and a major player in Washington power circles. The key to Baker's unlikely success was his unique ability to provide DC movers and shakers with whatever they wanted, including women and whisky at his Quorum Club—run out of a smoky, dimly lighted bar at the Carroll

Arms Hotel on Capitol Hill. Ellen Rometsch worked as one of Baker's "party girls" for over two years and attracted a big fan club. One of Rometsch's many admirers recalled, "Everybody was in love with Ellen for about 20 minutes."[73] JFK was also a fan. After she visited the White House, Kennedy telephoned Baker with a report. "Mister Baker," the president roared, "that was the best blow job I ever had in my life."[74]

Reading over Hoover's report on Rometsch, RFK immediately understood its implications: America was on the verge of its own version of the Profumo scandal. On August 21, 1963, he ordered Rometsch summarily deported on an Air Force transport plane to Germany, where she regularly received large payments in cash.[75]

The story of JFK and the suspected East German spy might have ended there—with Rometsch joining a list of women whose silence was purchased with Kennedy money. But in late September 1963, Rometsch's procurer Bobby Baker came under investigation by Republicans on the Senate Rules Committee for influence peddling. While the world watched the president sign the Nuclear Test Ban Treaty with the USSR, the Republicans tried to dredge up anything that would tar his administration and the Democratic Party before the 1964 election. Republican Senator John "Whispering Willie" Williams, a gossipy puritan from Delaware, led the charge, demanding that Baker appear before his committee to answer questions about trading sex and cash for congressional votes at the Quorum Club. Rather than submit to Williams's grilling, on October 7 Baker drank four martinis and submitted his resignation as secretary of the Senate.[76]

The same day, an unnamed source, most likely from the FBI, tipped off investigative reporter Clark Mollenhoff about Rometsch's White House visits. Over the next two weeks, Mollenhoff sniffed out the steamy saga but did not publish a word. He knew his newspaper, the *Des Moines Register,* like every other reputable publication, shunned sex scandals unless they entered a court record or were the subject of an official investigation. On October 25, 1963, Mollenhoff shared the information he had gathered about Rometsch with Whispering Willie Williams and encouraged the senator to use his subpoena power to drag her back to the United States to testify about her contacts with high-ranking White House officials. As Mollenhoff hoped, Williams immediately agreed to subpoena the German call girl. The Rometsch sex scandal was now political news and Mollenhoff could publish his big scoop.[77]

RFK heard about Mollenhoff's article before it ran and tried to convince the publisher to spike it. But the next day, October 26, the *Des Moines Register* ran a headline report, "US Expels Girl Linked to Officials," about the interest of the Senate Rules Committee in allegations that senators were involved with "an exotic 27-year-old German girl" who was deported in August. The report noted, "The evidence is also likely to include identification of several high executive branch officials" and "some prominent New Frontiersmen from the executive branch of government" who attended parties with "the part-time party girl and prostitute." The article then ominously mentioned that "the possibility that her activity might be connected with espionage was of some concern to security investigators because of the high rank of her male companions." Even more disturbing to RFK was Mollenhoff's line that the "beautiful brunette" is "reported to be furious because her important friends did not block her expulsion."[78] RFK immediately dispatched a close friend, LaVern Duffy, who also had an affair with Rometsch, to fly to West Germany, track her down, pacify her and keep her from talking.[79]

The next day, October 27, 1963, the *Washington Post* carried an even more risqué article, headlined "Hill Probe May Take Profumo-Type Twist." The *Post* reported that in two days Senator Williams planned to hold a closed-door session of his committee on "an extremely sensitive and dangerous matter" involving "a spicy tale of political intrigue and high level bedroom antics" and featuring "a 27 year old German woman of alluring physical proportions." The article slavered over Rometsch's "vital personal statistics [that] included beauty contestant measurements of 35–25–34; five feet, six inches of height; 120 pounds of weight, and an attractive topping of dark hair."[80] John Kennedy's secretary Evelyn Lincoln described her boss's reaction to the Ellen Rometsch press coverage in a diary entry dated October 28: "The President came in all excited about the news reports concerning the German woman & other prostitutes getting mixed up with government officials, congressmen, etc." Lincoln noted that JFK "called [Senate majority leader] Mike Mansfield to come to the office to discuss the playing down of this news report."[81]

Bobby knew the situation would move beyond his control if just a few more newspapers carried reports about Rometsch. He ordered several Justice Department underlings to make repeated requests to have the FBI dissuade other journalists from picking up the story. After the fifth request, one of Hoover's underlings noted that RFK's aide "told me the President was personally interested in having this story killed."[82] Instead of helping the Kennedys squash the story, Hoover opened an FBI file on Mollenhoff's allegations, noting that "it was also alleged that the president and the attorney general had availed themselves of services of party-girls."[83] Robert Kennedy now found himself under FBI investigation, but that was the least of his troubles. If Senator Williams brought a disgruntled Ellen Rometsch back to testify before Congress, he and his brother would be ruined. Williams was scheduled to hold a closed-door Senate meeting on Rometsch in just two days. RFK had no choice but to turn to the only man who could stop the U.S. Senate: J. Edgar Hoover.

Usually, if the attorney general wanted to see the FBI director, he summoned Hoover to his office. But on October 28, 1963, just a day before Williams's meeting on Rometsch, RFK shuffled into the office of his ostensible subordinate to plead for help in shutting down the Senate investigation. Hoover toyed with his boss, claiming he could not do anything to stop the democratically elected Senate. But after Bobby sufficiently humiliated himself, Hoover went in for the kill and demanded two concessions in return for his help. First, the Kennedys had to confirm his job as FBI director, and second, the president had to host him for a White House lunch. A relieved Bobby Kennedy agreed, and a few hours later Hoover secretly assembled the leadership of the Senate, Democratic majority leader Mike Mansfield and Republican minority leader Everett Dirksen.[84]

Hoover began his meeting with the Senate leaders by spreading out the FBI files he had compiled on dozens of senators who had indulged themselves at Baker's Quorum Club. The director then implied that if the Senate opened an investigation into the president's personal life, he would expose the damaging files on their colleagues and unleash a Washington scandal unlike any in American history. It was a case of mutually assured destruction. Later that same day Senator John Williams made an announcement: questioning Ellen Rometsch was no longer on the Senate's agenda.[85]

A disappointed Drew Pearson condemned the Senate's decision to ignore the Rometsch scandal in a nationally syndicated column, "Senate to Keep Lid on Sex Rollicks." "The staid Rules Committee Senators now investigating the Bobby Baker case are sitting on a Pandora's box as far as sex is concerned. And they are determined not to open it up," Pearson fumed. "In the Pandora's box are the stories of high jinx not only on Capitol Hill but in the high places on Pennsylvania Ave. . . . The Senate Rules Committee will see no evil, hear no evil, speak no evil, as far as sex is concerned."[86]

Hoover meanwhile was so pleased with his ability to stop the Senate that he sent a memo to his subordinates bragging how he had intimidated the Senate leaders and how he got his precious lunch with the president.[87] During his previous White House lunch, in March 1962, Hoover had warned Kennedy that he knew about his affair with Judith Campbell. A year and a half later, on Halloween 1963, they were back together and getting along as though old chums, chatting about Ellen Rometsch and all the naughty senators. A few days later, Kennedy was feeling confident enough to joke about the Rometsch scandal with Ben Bradlee over dinner: "Boy the dirt he has on those senators you wouldn't believe it!" Kennedy also told Bradlee that with the onset of his 1964 reelection campaign he planned on inviting the useful FBI director over for lunch more often. Bradlee noted that JFK "felt it was wise—with rumors flying and every indication of a dirty campaign coming up."[88]

With the Rometsch scandal behind him by early November 1963, JFK had good reason to feel confident about his future. He had shown the American public he could steer the country around the threat of nuclear war during the Cuban missile crisis, and with the Nuclear Test Ban Treaty he had moved the United States and the Soviet Union toward greater cooperation. The economy was booming and his popular approval-rating hovered around 60 percent. Kennedy had every reason to believe he would be reelected the following year. But those high hopes were dashed a couple of weeks later in Dallas.

It is tempting to consider how different American history would have been if Hoover had not been able to stop Senator Williams from dragging Ellen Rometsch before his subcommittee in November 1963. What if John

Kennedy had been publicly connected to an East German prostitute? Rometsch was probably not a spy and Kennedy was certainly not spending his time with her discussing national security secrets. But just the allegation that the president was sleeping with an East German call girl would have been enough to bring down Kennedy, just as similar allegations had brought down John Profumo and Harold Macmillan. And what if Kennedy had had to defend himself during Whispering Willie's Senate hearings? It seems highly unlikely he would have been politicking down in Dallas on November 22, 1963. And so Hoover's ability to intimidate the Senate with their FBI files might have saved Kennedy from getting impeached over a sex scandal, but it had the unintended side effect of cutting short the president's life.

HOOVER VERSUS KING

The FBI escalated its war against Martin Luther King Jr. after he stood on the steps of the Lincoln Memorial in August 1963 and inspired millions with his nationally televised "I Have a Dream" speech. In a report on the "demagogic speech," FBI assistant director Sullivan declared, "We must mark [King] now, if we have not done so before, as the most dangerous Negro of the future in this Nation."[89] When Hoover read a memo reporting that *Time* magazine named King as the Man of the Year for 1963, the director scrawled in the margin, "They had to dig deep in the garbage to come up with this one."[90]

The Kennedys had initially resisted Hoover's request for permission to bug and wiretap MLK, but once the bureau acquired information about Ellen Rometsch, the brothers caved in.[91] On October 10, 1963, Robert Kennedy approved the FBI's request to conduct electronic surveillance "on King at his current address or at any future address to which he may move," that is, his hotel rooms.[92] RFK later explained to a friend that if he had not approved Hoover's request "there would have been no living with the Bureau."[93] Hoover did not really need permission to spy on King. But the U.S. attorney general's official approval insulated Hoover politically. If the public ever learned of the FBI surveillance campaign against King, the Kennedys would not be able to fire Hoover over it, because he could cite RFK's approval and everyone would blame the Kennedys.[94]

In early November 1963, the same week John Kennedy lunched with Hoover in the White House, the bureau installed wiretaps on MLK's home and office. Robert Kennedy was supposed to review the taps on King within 30 days—he never did. Over the next two years the FBI bugged King's hotel rooms on 15 occasions.[95] On Hoover's orders FBI assistant director Sullivan instructed agents in December 1963 to "keep close watch on King's personal activities. . . . Although King is a minister, we have already developed information concerning weakness in his character which is of a nature as to make him unfit to serve as a minister of the gospel." "We will," Sullivan vowed in the memo, "at the proper time when it can be done without embarrassment to the Bureau, expose King as an immoral opportunist who is not a sincere person but is exploiting the racial situation for personal gain."[96]

Martin Luther King Jr. was a man, not a saint. He admitted to a friend, "I'm away from home twenty-five to twenty-seven days a month. Fucking is a form of anxiety reduction."[97] On January 6, 1964, the FBI recorded King, several of his staff and a few women having an orgy at the Willard Hotel near the White House. "I'm fucking for God!" King shouted. "I'm not a negro tonight!" Agents recorded 19 reels of tape from the party and quickly transcribed them for the director.[98] Upon hearing the tapes, Hoover crowed, "This will destroy the burrhead!"[99]

Three weeks later Hoover ordered agents to bug King's hotel room in Milwaukee. At first the FBI agents in Milwaukee argued against the bug, explaining to the director that, since there was police protection on King that night, he would not be engaging in "entertainment." Hoover replied, "I don't share the conjecture. King is a 'tom cat' with degenerate sexual urges."[100] The Milwaukee bug failed to record anything of interest to Hoover. But a bug in the Hyatt House Motel in Los Angeles found more evidence of King's adultery and recorded him telling dirty jokes, including one that involved former First Lady Jackie Kennedy and her dead husband. Hoover immediately passed the information on to President Lyndon Johnson and Robert Kennedy. The director figured this information would "remove all doubt from the Attorney General's mind as to the type of person King is. It will probably also eliminate King from any participation" in an upcoming memorial for JFK.[101] The FBI also tried to prevent the Pope from granting King an audience during MLK's visit to Europe in September 1964.[102] Although the bureau dispatched an agent to brief Cardinal Francis Spellman on King's personal life, his visit with the Pope went forward as planned.[103] Hoover also tried to tarnish the glory of King's Nobel Peace Prize, which was announced on October 14, 1964. Bureau agents shared information about MLK's private life with the American ambassadors to Norway, Sweden, Great Britain and Denmark because, according to an FBI memo, "the Ambassadors might consider entertaining King while he is in Europe to receive the Nobel Peace prize."[104]

Hoover ordered FBI agents to assemble the King tapes into a highlight reel, which they mailed to King's home on November 21, 1964. When King and his wife, Coretta, returned from Oslo where he received the Nobel Peace Prize, Coretta opened the package containing the tapes and transcripts of MLK speaking lewdly and engaging in sex.[105] She also read the anonymous note that was enclosed in the package: "King, look into your heart. You know you are a complete fraud and a great liability to all of us Negroes. No person can overcome facts, not even a fraud like yourself. Lend your ear to the enclosure. . . . King, there is only one thing left for you to do. You know what it is. . . . You are done. There is but one way out for you. You better take it before your filthy, abnormal, fraudulent self is bared to the nation."[106] FBI assistant director Sullivan later claimed the purpose of the package was to cause "a break between King and his wife which would reduce King's stature and therefore weaken him as a leader."[107] King's advisor Andrew Young recalled, "I think the most disturbing thing to Martin was that he felt somebody was trying to get him to commit suicide."[108] When King played the tape for his closest aides, they all agreed it could only have come from the FBI.[109] King no doubt recalled JFK's warning in the Rose Garden about being under surveillance: "If they shoot *you* down, they'll shoot *us* down too." King told his friends, "They are out to break me. They are out to get me, harass me, break my spirit."[110] While King and Coretta were recovering from the shocking package, FBI agents tormented them further by reporting a fire in their home; fire trucks with sirens blaring rushed to their house in the middle of the night.[111]

Having failed to silence King, Hoover supplied members of Congress with information about King's private life and tried shopping the tapes to various news publications.[112] According to the editor of the *Atlanta Constitution*, Eugene Patterson, "Agents of the Atlanta FBI bureau visited us in our

office and alleged they had proof of Dr. King's involvement in extramarital affairs. . . . When I tried to explain we did not publish a peephole journal, and
told the agent a person's private life is not news, he hotly criticized *The Constitution* for supporting Dr. King's public leadership and binding its readers
to his private immorality."[113] Hoover was dumbfounded that every journalist
refused to expose King's private life. "I don't understand why we are unable to
get the true facts before the public," Hoover whined. "We can't even get our
accomplishments published."[114] Hoover's incessant harassment of King continued right up until MLK's assassination in 1968.[115] According to one FBI
agent, "The Director didn't exactly light any candles after King was killed."[116]

CHAPTER SEVEN

SEX, DEATH AND THE KENNEDYS

First Lady Jacqueline Kennedy once confronted the commander in chief with a pair of panties she had discovered under his pillow: "Would you please shop around and see who these belong to? They're not my size."[1] When a *New York Times* reporter asked her in 1962 what she thought her husband would do after his presidency, she deadpanned, "He'll probably take a job as a headmaster of an exclusive, all-girls prep school."[2] Clearly Jackie knew about her husband's rampant cheating; the question is, Why did she put up with it?

BLACK JACK

Jackie grew up adoring her father, John "Black Jack" Bouvier, a wealthy financier who was infamous in New York City and East Hampton, New York, for seducing his friends' wives.[3] In the summer of 1934, when Jackie was five, Black Jack invited one of his mistresses to watch his wife, Janet, compete in an equestrian show. After the competition the two women posed together sitting on a fence while Jack stood beside them. The next morning the *Daily News* published the photo, and Janet Bouvier discovered that while she was smiling for the camera, her husband and her friend were holding hands behind her back. Years later Jackie got ahold of the clipping and saved it. Senator George Smathers recalled that she "thought that picture was hysterically funny. In the White House, she would haul it out and point at it and just double over laughing. She had a randy streak of her own and thought her father's womanizing was sort of comical."[4] Her husband, who was featured in a 1953 *Saturday Evening Post* article, "The Senate's Gay Young Bachelor," no doubt reminded her of her charming, rakish father.[5]

Jackie also had the example of her mother, who refused to quietly tolerate her husband's philandering and sued Black Jack for divorce in 1940 when Jackie was 11. Divorce was still unusual enough at the time that the *New York Daily Mirror* reported on Janet's suit under the headline "Society Broker Sued for Divorce." The *Daily Mirror* gave a rundown of Black Jack's affairs with dates and photographs supplied by Janet's lawyer. The story was then reprinted in tabloids and newspapers across the country.[6] Jackie's younger sister Lee recalled, "It was, of all the divorces I've heard about and watched, I think probably one of the very worst because there was such *relentless* bitterness on both sides." Lee believed Jackie's experience with her parents' scandalous divorce gave her the capacity to shut out things that she did not want to hear. "Jackie was really fortunate to have or acquire the ability to tune out, which she always kept," Lee said. "I envied her so much being able to press the button and tune out."[7] Jackie's ability to tune out painful stories about the people she loved prepared her well for life with Jack Kennedy.

Divorce was never an option for Jackie. From the moment she married the 36-year-old senator in 1953, she planned on becoming First Lady. Over the next seven years she went out of her way to avoid a marital scandal that would destroy her husband's political career, even if he did not.[8] When JFK was elected president the stakes were even higher. "She cared about the country," explained Kennedy aide Richard Goodwin. "That feeling was at the sort of center of her life and it was important to her. She saw her husband as a great hero on the level of de Gaulle or Churchill. She was a fierce guardian of his presidential image in life as she was to be after his death."[9] Jackie was a pragmatist. She knew her private marital woes could become a major political scandal if they ever became public. She simply could not justify destabilizing the Republic in the middle of the Cold War over extramarital sex.

Money was another reason why Jackie tolerated her husband's cheating. While he enjoyed a free rein in the White House, she frequently traveled to New York and Paris for shopping sprees on Joe Kennedy's dime. The First Lady's secretary Mary Gallagher had the unenviable task of updating the president on Jackie's expenses. "My 'Battle of the President's Budget'—or should I say, his wife's—became so serious that I would take the long way around in the White House halls to avoid meeting him," Gallagher complained. "I just couldn't stand the reproachful look on his face." Jackie meanwhile joked, "The president seems more concerned these days with my budget than the budget of the United States."[10] Gallagher reported that Jackie's expenses for 1962 totaled $121,461 ($850,000 today), well above the president's $100,000 salary.[11] JFK also gave the First Lady money to build a horse farm in Atoka, Virginia, where she spent most weekends with their children while he entertained various sleepover guests at the White House.[12] The farm's annual expenses on veterinarians and animal feed cost almost three times the amount the Kennedys spent on their kids.[13]

Jackie's pride was the biggest reason she played the good wife. The only thing she asked was that Jack be discreet. "Jackie was not threatened even by Marilyn Monroe," Clare Boothe Luce said. "But if somehow word had gotten out, it would have upset her terribly. She could not bear the thought of being publicly humiliated."[14] Jack's friend Charles Spalding agreed, "She loved him and was obviously willing to put up with a lot. But she was very proud, and she could be very angry if her nose was rubbed in it." To avoid being humiliated, Jackie tried to never catch the president with his mistresses and always cabled to tell him exactly when she was returning from her vacations. "Jackie put up with the situation because she loved him. However she could not accept being humiliated," Gore Vidal observed. "And he was very careful that she *not* be humiliated. But when things started to leak out, when she became threatened, she sent him a message."[15] Jackie certainly knew how to send a message.

She might have grown up at a time when most women with cheating husbands had no choice but to quietly suffer the pain and humiliation. But she came of age at a moment when American women were beginning to experience a new level of sexual liberation and empowerment. The Food and Drug Administration approved the birth control pill in 1960, which empowered millions of women to control their own contraception. Two years later Helen Gurley Brown published the revolutionary bestseller *Sex and the Single Girl,* which argued that nice girls could be just as sexually active and aggressive as men. Meanwhile, Jackie lifted the strict limits on what a proper lady could wear. After *Women's Wear Daily* ran a photograph of the First Lady in a skirt cut three inches above the knee, women all across America began appearing in offices and at social events in increasingly shorter skirts, until the miniskirt appeared in 1964.[16] While Jackie was certainly a loving wife, she was also an alluring woman with needs of her own. According to her close friend Toni Bradlee, "She knew Jack was having affairs. She was pondering maybe doing it herself."[17]

REVENGE SEX

After JFK narrowly missed out on the vice presidential nomination at the 1956 Democratic National Convention, he decided to lift his spirits by yachting on the Mediterranean with his brother Teddy, Florida senator George Smathers, a few Scandinavian beauties and a Manhattan socialite who called herself "Pooh." Jackie, who was seven months pregnant, pleaded with her husband not to go. "I'm sure it was obvious to Jackie that he was going to have his share of female company on the trip," Smathers said. "She didn't want him to go and she let him know it, but in the end there just wasn't anything she could do about it. Jack just didn't have it in him to be monogamous."[18]

Jackie learned details about her husband's seaborne sex fest when the ship's captain gave a candid interview to a French journalist while in port. Two days later Jackie began experiencing severe stomach cramps and internal bleeding. She was rushed to the hospital, where doctors performed an emergency Caesarean to deliver a stillborn baby girl on August 23, 1956. It was Jackie's second miscarriage in as many years.[19] A hospital spokesman attributed the stillbirth to Jackie's exhaustion and nervous tension following the Democratic National Convention.[20] In reality, the cause was probably venereal disease. Jackie's failure to conceive a child in her first year of marriage had prompted JFK to get his sperm count tested. It turned out that her difficulty with childbearing had nothing to do with a low sperm count but with a chlamydia infection Jack had given her.[21]

Out on his floating bordello, the aspiring president was oblivious to the front page *Washington Post* headline SENATOR KENNEDY ON MEDITERRANEAN TRIP UNAWARE THAT HIS WIFE HAS LOST BABY.[22] He finally heard about his wife's miscarriage when his ship docked in Genoa three days later. At first he decided to continue the cruise: "If I go back there, what the hell am I going to do? I'm just going to sit there and wring my hands."[23] But Smathers told him, "You better get your ass back there right away if you plan on staying married—or getting to the White House."[24] Although Jack flew back to his wife the next day, their marriage was never the same.[25]

In the wake of the cruise Joe Kennedy feared Jackie would leave his son and destroy JFK's anticipated run for president four years later, in 1960. In the summer of 1956 Drew Pearson was the first to report on trouble in the Kennedy marriage, and in a follow-up article *Time* magazine claimed Joe offered Jackie a million dollars, a new house and a car to remain married.[26] During that year's Thanksgiving gathering at Hyannis Port, Joe told his son he didn't have to stop having affairs; he just had to be more discreet. "It's not *what* you are," Joe said, "it's what people *think* you are."[27]

Five months after the cruise, Jackie took her revenge on a 10-day trip to California with her friend Bill Walton, a gay artist whom JFK later appointed director of the White House Fine Arts Commission. While in Los Angeles, Jackie and Walton attended a dinner party where she met Hollywood's golden boy, actor William Holden, and his actress wife Brenda Marshall.[28] The next day Jackie invited Holden to go horseback riding, after which they had sex that Walton figured "was primarily driven by Jackie's desire to seek revenge on Jack." On the return flight to Washington Jackie raved to Walton how Holden was "an unselfish lover"—in sharp contrast to her husband. According to Walton, she told JFK about the fling with the movie star because "by flaunting it, Jackie probably hoped to reawaken Jack's romantic interest in her. I suppose she wanted to redefine herself as the kind of flirtatious woman Jack usually found irresistible."[29]

Jackie also retaliated over Marilyn Monroe. She first learned about her husband's affair with Monroe from her sister Lee. After Monroe died in August 1962, Jackie witnessed the Kennedy brothers swing into damage control. This was exactly the kind of humiliation that she couldn't bear. She immediately ran away with daughter Caroline to Ravello, Italy, to stay with Lee and her second husband, Prince Radziwill of Poland. George Smathers said the trip "was her way of telling [JFK] that he'd gone too far this time [with Monroe]. The possibility that she might be humiliated or embarrassed really got to her. She didn't like it not one damn bit."[30] The White House initially announced that Jackie would stay for two weeks, but *Time* magazine reported, "Jacqueline Kennedy had originally planned to stay at Ravello for two weeks. But two became three, and now they have stretched to four. She was having such a wonderful time that it almost seemed she might yet declare herself a permanent resident."[31] Rumors began to circulate that the First Lady was staying in Ravello for more than just the Italian sunshine.

During the trip Jackie enjoyed the company of one of Lee's other guests—the dashing, wavy-haired chairman of Fiat, Gianni Agnelli. When the Associated Press published photos of Agnelli and Jackie swimming together off the Fiat heir's 82-foot yacht, the president cabled his wife "A LITTLE MORE CAROLINE AND LESS AGNELLI." Jackie responded to her husband's request by scuba diving with Agnelli the next day—an outing that further titillated the hyperaggressive Italian freelance photographers, who had recently become known as the *paparazzi*.[32]

The term *paparazzi* came from the 1960 Federico Fellini film *La Dolce Vita*, which tells the story of Marcello, a jaded journalist played by Marcello Mastroianni, and his photographer sidekick, Paparazzo. The name "Paparazzo," Fellini explained, "suggests to me a buzzing insect, hovering, darting, stinging." After the American release of the film in 1961 *Time* introduced the American public to the word *paparazzi*, which the magazine defined as "a ravenous wolf pack of freelance photographers who stalk big names for a living and fire with flash guns at point-blank range." *Time* recounted that the Italian paparazzi "froze [actress] Anita Ekberg's bosom as it heaved in a wild dance at a private Roman orgy. When Katharine Hepburn passed through town recently, the paparazzi mounted Vespa scooters, putt-putted out to waylay her at Fiumicino Airport. Because Ava Gardner once called him a dirty name, Paparazzo Tazio Secchiaroli vengefully hid for hours in a cardboard box on a Cinecitta movie lot, finally got what he came for: an unflattering shot of Ava in an old bath towel, hair wet and stringy as a mop." American magazines soon began coupling their gossip reports with paparazzi snapshots. *Time* warned that, once freelance photographers started making $500 just by snapping a risqué picture of a celebrity, "no one is safe, not even royalty"— or the First Lady.[33]

George Griffin, an American consular officer in Italy, was "disillusioned" by the photos of Jackie with Agnelli: "She was the president's wife. Even the cynical Secret Service agents felt bad about it." The CIA also took notice. Undersecretary of state George Ball recalled, "An Agency official told me with some amusement that the CIA got a private message from Ravello to get Jackie's—what do you call it? Her diaphragm. They were ordered to fetch her diaphragm and send it over to Italy by the next plane."[34] The idea that Jackie would have asked the CIA to retrieve her diaphragm is absurd but that didn't stop such gossipy stories from making their way back to Washington.

When Jackie announced that she would remain a third week in Italy, 100 indignant women calling themselves the Concerned Citizens of America threatened to picket the White House and issued an open letter to Jackie: "Would you not better have served the nation and the President by remaining here at home by his side? We have honored you greatly with the position of First Lady of our land. We ask only that you not violate the dignity of that title."[35] Former First Daughter Margaret Truman speculated on the Agnelli imbroglio: "There was, I strongly suspect, a hidden drama being played out here, one that future biographers will explore at greater depth. Jackie was challenging Jack's attempts to control her—perhaps warning him that two could play the extramarital sex game."[36] JFK got the warning.

The Kennedy media image that shielded Jack's peccadilloes also protected Jackie, and neither one could divorce the other while in the White House. "We are like two icebergs," Jackie said: "the public life above the water, the private life submerged."[37]

THE GOLDEN GREEK

Mr. and Mrs. Kennedy were playing a dangerous game that almost caught up with them in the fall of 1963. At the same time that Ellen Rometsch came close to getting the president impeached, Jackie got herself into a public scandal with one of the world's most famous men, Greek shipping magnate Aristotle Onassis.

At five foot six, with a barrel chest and the face of a gangster, Onassis looked more like a hit man or a longshoreman than one of the world's richest men. But he had great success with the ladies, thanks to his combination of charm, power and, above all, generosity. One of his many mistresses, renowned opera singer Maria Callas, once said his "total understanding of women came out of a Van Cleef & Arpels catalogue."[38] Onassis frequently bragged that he could get any woman in the world, and he relished every opportunity to prove it. His sister said, "All of his life my brother loved meeting and making love to famous women. The more important or well known the woman, the more he loved to love her."[39] In the early 1960s no woman was more important or well known than Jackie Kennedy.

Onassis first became a public relations problem for the Kennedys in early 1962 when he began an affair with Jackie's sister Lee. At the time Lee was married to Prince Radziwill of Poland. Onassis compensated the cuckolded prince by appointing him director of his airline, Olympic Airways. Drew Pearson broke the story of Lee's affair with Onassis in his nationally syndicated column, "Does the ambitious Greek tycoon hope to become the brother-in-law of the President?"[40] The Kennedys couldn't care less about Lee's infidelity; Jack had also had an affair with her.[41] But they objected to Lee's relationship with "the Greek," as they called Onassis, because the Justice Department had indicted him in 1954 for criminal conspiracy to defraud the United States of millions of dollars. Onassis understood the situation: "The Kennedys could accept me as Lee's lover; that was personal. What they couldn't accept was the idea that I might actually marry her: that was politics."[42]

Onassis worried about how the president and the attorney general would punish him, until he discovered a way to counter their threats. His old friend Spyros Skouras, head of Twentieth Century Fox, revealed to him that both Kennedy brothers were sleeping with his studio's biggest star, Marilyn Monroe. When RFK called in early 1962 to pressure Onassis into dumping Lee, Ari countered, "Bobby, you and Jack fuck your movie queen and I'll fuck my princess."[43] Shortly after that conversation, the Kennedys dumped Monroe, who died of a drug overdose a few months later. The Kennedys realized they were powerless to stop Onassis's affair with Lee because he knew about their affairs with Monroe. Their troubles with the Greek, however, had only just begun.

In August 1963 Jackie gave birth to a premature baby named Patrick who died three days later. When Onassis heard about the First Lady's loss, he suggested that Lee invite her sister to escape Washington aboard his 325-foot yacht, the *Christina*. The ship had a crew of 58, a small orchestra, two Parisian hairdressers, three chefs (French, Italian and Greek), a sommelier, a Swedish masseuse and a steward and maid assigned to each of the nine staterooms. On deck was a five-seat, twin-prop amphibian airplane and a swimming pool with a mosaic bottom that could be raised to provide a dance floor. The interior boasted 42 telephones, El Greco masterpieces, fireplaces bedecked in lapis lazuli (which Onassis told his guests cost $4,000 a square inch [$28,000 today]), gold bathroom fixtures, and bar stools upholstered with the skin of whale testicles. Ex-Egyptian king Farouk called the *Christina* "the last word in opulence."[44]

Onassis's ship was also famous for something else. Asked about sailing on the *Christina*, actor Richard Burton recalled "the saline smell of ocean and sex."[45] John Kennedy, who was no stranger to sex-filled Mediterranean cruises, was enraged by the prospect of his wife yachting with Onassis. His secretary Evelyn Lincoln described JFK as "looking like thunder" after he heard about the cruise. But according to Lincoln, "Jackie had made up her mind, and that was that."[46]

FDR's son Franklin Roosevelt Jr., who had known Onassis for over 20 years and thought he was a "charming psychopath," asked Robert Kennedy what he intended to do about the invitation. Bobby darkly joked, "Sink the fucking yacht."[47]

Onassis was expecting the U.S. attorney general's phone call along with his usual threats. But this time, Bobby offered a deal. If Onassis canceled the cruise, the Kennedys would drop their objections to his affair with Lee and even allow a marriage. What the brothers didn't know was that Onassis had already cooled on Lee. When he rejected the Kennedys' high-handed offer, Bobby resorted once again to threats. "He said he would destroy me," recalled Onassis, who shot back, "My boy, you don't frighten me, I've been threatened by experts." "What's in the past, you Greek sonofabitch," RFK sneered, "will be nothing compared to what's in store."[48]

Still busy covering up his brother's fling with Ellen Rometsch in the fall of 1963, the attorney general suddenly found himself also having to cover for his brother's wife. In an attempt to lend an air of propriety to the cruise, he asked undersecretary of Commerce Franklin Roosevelt Jr. and his wife to chaperone Jackie.[49] "I'm not certain 'asked' is the correct term," Roosevelt noted. "I went on the cruise really at the command of the president who said he wanted someone who was his friend and whom he could trust to go along. We had a very good time, but I didn't really want to baby-sit for Jackie." According to Franklin's wife, Suzanne, "We were supposed to make it respectable so [JFK] had to be thinking up things for Franklin to be doing. He dreamed up a trade fair on Somalia for him to be there."[50] RFK instructed Roosevelt to keep Onassis as far away from Jackie as possible. With the Ellen Rometsch story still in the air, the Kennedys could ill afford another sex scandal. History had taken an ironic turn. During World War II, President Roosevelt tried to destroy Joe Kennedy by spying on Jack's affair with Inga Arvad. Twenty years later, President Kennedy was ordering FDR's son to keep his First Lady out of a sex scandal.

RFK directed the Secret Service to lay down a security blackout around Onassis's dock to prevent the paparazzi from snapping photos of Ari welcoming the First Lady onto the *Christina*. Roosevelt's wife recalled the "marvelously clandestine" trip from the hotel to the yacht in the wee hours of October 4, 1963. "It was all very cloak and dagger, Jackie had a code name: Lace." Onassis welcomed Jackie aboard by declaring he was "pleased that she had been able to come." Jackie coyly responded, "I never intended it otherwise, Mr. Onassis."[51] During a tour of the ship, the First Lady exclaimed, "So this it seems is what it is to be a king!"—quoting Alexander the Great upon entering the tent of his defeated nemesis, the Persian king Darius.[52] After Jackie retired to her stateroom, which Onassis called *Ithaca*, the golden Greek phoned his close friend and business partner Costa Gratsos, triumphantly proclaiming, "Lace has landed in Ithaca!" Gratsos replied, "I hope you're not going to regret it." "I'll make the waves, Costa," Ari said. "Let's see if Bobby Kennedy can walk on them."[53] No one could make more waves than the Greek shipping tycoon.

Although Onassis was 29 years older and three inches shorter than Jackie, the other guests soon noticed a chemistry between them. Jackie asked her host flirtatious questions such as whether he was romantic. "Of course I'm romantic!" Onassis declared, "You have no idea how romantic it is to make a million dollars."[54] After the other guests went to bed, Jackie stayed up with Ari, sitting under the stars listening to the stories of his life. At breakfast each morning the other guests gossiped about Jackie and their host and speculated that Ari reminded her of Black Jack Bouvier. During a long walk together on Ari's home island of Skorpios, Jackie said she wished her Greek idyll would never end.[55] Onassis also led Jackie on a tour of the island of Capri. He had often declared, "If a man cannot seduce a woman on Capri, he is not a man."[56] According to Onassis's biographer Peter Evans, the Greek and the First Lady had sex in her stateroom somewhere off the coast of Ithaca. One of the other passengers, Onassis's sister, later told Ari's daughter that he "seduced the President's *wife*, not his widow."[57]

When Onassis was in Jackie's stateroom he noticed her jewel case contained just a few pieces of jewelry that he deemed cheap. He immediately phoned Van Cleef and Arpels in Paris and told them to fly an impressive gift to the yacht. A few days later, much to Lee's shock and chagrin, Onassis presented her sister with a diamond and ruby necklace that cost $80,000 ($570,000 today). Once again Jackie was upstaging her little sister. Lee even complained in a letter to John Kennedy, "Ari showered Jackie with so many presents, I can't stand it. All I've got is three dinky little bracelets that Caroline wouldn't even wear to her own birthday party."[58] When Onassis was asked how he could blatantly snub his mistress in favor of her sister, he replied, "the Princess will get over it."[59] Gratsos worried that what had happened in Jackie's stateroom would cost a lot more than $80,000; "I kept thinking: This could be the most expensive fuck in the history of the world." Gratsos had good reason to worry.[60]

The Kennedys had been able to control the first news reports about the cruise by hiding the fact that Onassis was aboard. The initial report in the *Washington Post* vaguely mentioned that "the First Lady and her party would use the yacht *Christina* offered by Aristotle Onassis."[61] But the Kennedys could not control the European press, which carried daily reports on the cruise. Before each port of call, Onassis would tip off the paparazzi who were always waiting to snap photos of Jackie and him strolling through the narrow Mediterranean streets.[62] After seeing the photos in a Paris newspaper Maria Callas erupted, "Four years ago that was me by his side, being beguiled by the story of his life."[63] Drew Pearson cited the European reports in his column "First Lady's Cruise Causes Stir." "There's been a lot written in the European press about Jacqueline Kennedy's cruise on the yacht of the glamorous Greek shipping magnate, Aristotle Onassis, once indicted for cheating Uncle Sam and required to pay a whopping $7 million fine." Pearson then brought up Ari's complicated personal life, "Actually the publicity began long before Mrs. Kennedy arrived. It resulted from the fact that her sister, Princess Radziwill, spent most of the summer on the Onassis yacht, or as the guest of the big, brusque, and charming ship owner at his home. Onassis has been separated from his wife ever since Maria Callas, the famed opera star, left her husband for alleged matrimony with Onassis—which later cooled off."[64]

Republican congressman Oliver Bolton of Ohio used the cruise to score political points against the White House. On two occasions in October 1963 Bolton took to the floor of the House to officially condemn the First Lady and Franklin Roosevelt Jr. for demonstrating "poor judgment and perhaps impropriety in accepting the lavish hospitality of a man who has defrauded the American public." The *Washington Post* reported that the congressman added, "Why doesn't the lady see more of her own country instead of gallivanting all over Europe?"[65]

RFK advised his brother to order Jackie to return at once and that he "must not take no for an answer." The president pleaded with her over ship-to-shore radio, but Jackie refused. "But wouldn't that admit the critics were right?" she argued. "Why give the papers another headline? . . . Why emphasize something best ignored?" A White House insider speculated that "Jackie was making the president pay for all his screwing around." JFK had become a lame-duck husband.[66]

The cruise finally became a full-blown PR crisis when long-lens photos of Jackie sunbathing on Onassis's yacht made front page news around the globe.[67] United Press International's Merriman Smith suggestively wrote, "Touring with her sister, Lee Radziwill, Mrs. Kennedy allows herself to be photographed in positions and poses which she would never permit in the United States . . . she is almost a different person when traveling, as it were, on her own." An editorial in the *Boston Globe* asked, "Does this sort of behavior seem fitting for a woman in mourning?"[68] John Kennedy realized the Onassis cruise was becoming a greater PR fiasco than his wife's romp with Agnelli.[69]

Just a few weeks prior, America's newspapers and television networks were revering Jackie's dignity after the loss of her newborn; now she found herself engulfed in a media firestorm. For the first time Jackie had become a political liability for her husband. That week's Gallup poll showed the president's popularity had dropped to a new low.[70] With the start of the 1964 presidential campaign just months away, the Kennedys needed to do some damage control. Ben Bradlee noted at the time that Kennedy ordered Onassis not to enter the United States until after the 1964 election, which, in Bradlee's words, "was the best evidence that [Kennedy] thinks the trip is potentially damaging to him politically."[71]

Before Jackie's plane arrived home on October 17, 1963, RFK advised his brother to make a big show of family unity. The president showed up at the airport with John Jr. and Caroline in tow. One onlooker, Coates Redmon, noticed some awkwardness between the First Couple: "You could see them embrace, a very stiff, formal embrace."[72] But the press played along and presented the public with reassuring images of homecoming hugs and kisses. As usual, the press coverage of the Kennedy marriage was much different than the reality behind the scenes.

JFK undoubtedly noticed the $80,000 jewels Jackie brazenly wore when she got off the plane. When the First Couple returned to the White House they got into a blowout fight that ended with Jackie storming off to her Virginia horse farm. Evelyn Lincoln described the few hours the Kennedys spent together after Jackie's two-week vacation as "unpleasant, unpleasant; I would say very strained." The president's secretary figured that "Onassis fell for Jackie and then it turned out that he became *more than* just a friend."[73] Jackie's secretary Mary Gallagher also deduced from "the clues" she saw that "a significant relationship had been established" between Jackie and the Greek.[74] If even these two White House secretaries picked up on an affair, Onassis was probably right when he told Gratsos, "He [JFK] knows I've had Jackie."[75]

Evelyn Lincoln speculated that if Kennedy had not been assassinated, "the cruise would have been seen as a catastrophic wrong turn" that alerted the press to trouble in his marriage. "It [the cruise] would have exposed everything," and a second administration might have brought with it "the first divorce in the White House."[76] But only if JFK had won the next election. Even before the Onassis cruise, the Republicans were already planning to make the First Couple's suspected promiscuity a big issue in the 1964 campaign.[77]

After spending some more time in Virginia away from her husband, Jackie returned to the White House feeling guilty for causing so much political trouble and promised to dedicate herself to his reelection. "We'll just campaign," she assured her husband. "I'll campaign with you anywhere you want." Clare Boothe Luce assumed that "Jackie must have felt very guilty. Everyone knew how much she hated going out on the campaign trail with Jack." Weeks later at dinner with Ben and Toni Bradlee, JFK asked Jackie, "Maybe now you'll come with us to Texas next month?"

"Sure I will, Jack."[78]

A day after her husband was assassinated, Jackie invited Onassis to stay over at the White House for the funeral.[79] Presidential aide Ken O'Donnell recalled how Onassis's presence in the White House that weekend took everyone by surprise: "He wasn't exactly a Kennedy family favorite."[80] Mary Gallagher was shocked to see Jackie walking down a hallway on Onassis's arm.[81] The evening after the funeral, Jackie held a birthday party for John Jr., who had just turned three. Members of the Kennedy family and high-ranking administration officials attended the party along with Onassis. After the children went to bed, the adults continued the party. "The average American was at home crying in his mashed potatoes," one Secret Service agent observed, "but inside the White House that night it was party time." It was an Irish wake filled with old stories, booze and jokes, many of which were directed at Onassis. At one point RFK left the room and returned with a contract he had written for Ari to pledge half his fortune to the poor of Central America. Onassis played along with the gag and signed it, but he was not amused. "Bobby did everything he could to humiliate me tonight but I didn't take the bait," he reported to Gratsos; "the more I smiled, the madder he got."[82] After the party Jackie invited Onassis up to the yellow room of the family quarters for a private chat. JFK had been dead for two days.[83]

CAME-A-LOT

During the 10 years of her highly complicated marriage, Jackie learned from her husband and father-in-law the importance of managing the public's perception of reality. In the immediate aftermath of her husband's assassination, Jackie was the first member of the Kennedy inner circle to take up the task of spinning JFK's historical legacy. "What difference does it make whether he was killed by the CIA, the FBI, the mafia, or simply some half-crazed misanthrope? It won't change anything," Jackie declared. "It won't bring him back. What matters now is that Jack's death be placed in some kind of lasting historical context." Weeks after the assassination Jackie invited journalist Theodore H. White to Hyannis Port. "She knew I was writing a summation of the assassination for LIFE," White recalled, "and she wanted to discuss her husband's legacy—would I be willing to come up and talk to her?"[84] Jackie began their discussion by reciting the lines from the Broadway musical *Camelot:*

> *Don't let it be forgot*
> *That once there was a spot*
> *For one brief shining moment*
> *That was known as Camelot*

She then told White that "bitter old men write history. Jack's life had more to do with myth and magic than political theory or political science. History belongs to heroes and heroes must not be forgotten. If only for my children, I want Jack to be remembered as a hero. There will be great presidents again, but there will never be another Camelot." White knew portraying the Kennedy administration as a second coming of Camelot "was a misreading of history but I was taken with Jackie's ability to frame the tragedy in such romantic and human terms. There was something extremely compelling about it, particularly *since her marriage had been so problematic.*" White saw through Jackie's spin, but "under the circumstances, it didn't seem a hell of a lot to ask, so I said to myself, why not? If that's all she wants, let her have it. As a result, the epitaph of the Kennedy administration became Camelot—a magic moment in American history when gallant men danced with beautiful women, when great deeds were done, and when the White House became the center of the universe."[85] Jackie's Camelot myth came to define the Kennedy administration for a generation of Americans—a fitting reflection of Joe Kennedy's dictum "It's not *what* you are; it's what people *think* you are."

Humorist and columnist Art Buchwald laughed when he read White's article in *Life*. "I knew how compelling and earnest Jackie could be—and must have been—for Ted White to swallow all that Camelot business," Buchwald mused. "I'd known Jack and Jackie for years and had never heard either of them so much as mention Camelot. To be honest Jack couldn't stand Broadway musicals. He told me so himself. . . . The only connection between Camelot and JFK is that he *came a lot*. Now that made sense to me."[86]

Jackie soon found herself trapped by the Camelot myth she had created. In the public mind she was the keeper of the eternal flame, the devout widow in perpetual mourning, when in fact she was a sexually active woman still in her midthirties.[87] The press covered for Jackie in the months after the assassination by ignoring her romantic relationships. But in January 1964, on the basis of a tip from Onassis, Drew Pearson reported that the shipping tycoon visited Jackie's new home in Georgetown and insinuated that Ari was simultaneously sleeping with both Jackie and her sister Lee. After reading Pearson's column RFK complained to Pierre Salinger: "I've known that bastard Onassis for years. . . . He was a snake then, and he's still a snake. Other than his bankroll, I don't understand what Jackie sees in him."[88] RFK was bitter about Jackie moving on with Onassis for a couple of reasons. First, there was politics. Bobby needed to preserve the Camelot myth because he was about to run for a U.S. Senate seat in New York—a step toward recapturing the White House. If Jackie's affair with her sister's paramour became public, Camelot would be tarnished and his own political future damaged. But RFK also had a more personal reason for being upset.

JACKIE AND BOBBY

Months after JFK's assassination, in the spring of 1964, Jackie went on a vacation to Antigua with Lee, Prince Radziwill, Chuck Spalding and Bobby, whose wife, Ethel, stayed home in Virginia. Spalding remembered seeing "there was definitely something between [Jackie and Bobby]. You had to be dumb, deaf and blind not to sense it." Spalding "wondered why in hell Ethel Kennedy had sent her husband on vacation with Jackie while she remained behind. What could she have been thinking?"[89] "I knew Bobby and Jackie had grown close. I knew they vacationed in Antigua and that Ethel had not gone along," Arthur Schlesinger Jr. said. "What I didn't know is that there was apparently more to their relationship than I originally thought."[90]

When RFK moved to New York to pursue a Senate seat in the 1964 election, he chose a residence a few blocks away from Jackie's new Upper East Side apartment. Johnny Meyer, one of Onassis's fixers, said, "Ari was pissed when he found out that Bobby had followed Jackie to New York." Onassis exploded, "Bobby's going to fuck her, surest thing you know. Jack fucked her little sister, Jackie'll fuck his little brother."[91] Gore Vidal shared Onassis's suspicion but put it more elegantly: "As Lee had gone to bed with Jack, symmetry required her to do so with Bobby."[92]

Ethel knew about the affair, and when Jackie would visit Bobby, she reportedly registered her displeasure by jumping up and leaving the room. Ethel put up with Jackie, whom she called the "widder," along with rumors of RFK's other mistresses, including campaign staffer Mary Jo Kopechne and young starlet Candice Bergen. Just as Jackie had tolerated Jack's cheating, Ethel saw her husband's affairs as the price she had to pay to become First Lady.[93]

RFK and Jackie celebrated his election to the Senate in 1964 by taking a Christmas vacation to Palm Beach. Mary Harrington, who was staying next door to the Kennedy estate, recalled looking out her window one morning and seeing Jackie sunbathing topless in a black bikini bottom. A door opened and out popped RFK in white trunks. He knelt by Jackie's side, and "as they began to kiss he placed one hand on her breast and the other inside her bikini bottom. After a minute or so, she stood up, wrapped a towel around her breasts and shoulders, and walked toward the house. Bobby followed. I was shocked. It was clear that Bobby was sleeping with his sister-in-law." Harrington later admonished Kennedy for being so indiscreet. "You mean you were watching?" he asked. RFK then confessed the affair and to splitting his time between Jackie in New York and Ethel in Virginia. He explained to Harrington that he loved both women, who now needed him equally.[94]

RFK, in turn, needed both of them. Chuck Spalding credited Jackie with rescuing Bobby from his shock and depression in the wake of his brother's assassination. "For the first year or year and a half after Jack's death, Bobby was not very happy. But a few years after the assassination—from 1965 through 1968—he felt a sense of completion. [RFK] attributed his recovery to his relationship with Jackie. Bobby and Jackie were extremely close. I ought to know—I went on vacation with them. I was there with them." Longtime Kennedy family friend Morton Downey Jr. said, "Bobby Kennedy didn't need sex as a daily fix the way his brother Jack did, but he knew how to get it when he wanted it. Like his father and brothers, he could be rather brazen when it came to women. His relationship with Jacqueline Kennedy, however, was not solely based on sex. Unlike most of the other women in his life, he had deep feelings for Jackie."[95] Truman Capote described the affair as "perhaps the most normal relationship either one ever had. There was nothing morbid about it. It was the coming together of a man and a woman as a result of his bereavement and her mental suffering at the hands of her late, lecherous husband. In retrospect, it seems hard to believe that it happened but it did."[96]

The affair was so hard to believe that Jackie and Bobby felt free to be indiscreet. While Ethel remained at Hickory Hill with their children, RFK and Jackie enjoyed the fruits of New York City. "Everybody knew about the affair. The two of them carried on like a pair of lovesick teenagers," Franklin Roosevelt Jr. said. "People used to see them at Le Club, their torsos stuck together as they danced the night away. I suspect Bobby would've liked to dump Ethel and marry Jackie but of course that wasn't possible."[97] Although the press frequently commented on how close they had become and how much time they spent together, there was absolutely no suggestion that their relationship was anything more than two family members in mourning.[98] Jackie's biographer Sarah Bradford noted that the press protected Jackie as if she were "America's Queen." Newspapers and magazines never published photos of her smoking even though she was a chain smoker. If the press reported her dancing the Twist or the Frug, she always did so "in a dignified manner."

Jackie knew the media protected her and would often say, "Anybody who is against me will look like a rat unless I run off with Eddie Fisher." She also believed that after everything she had endured, she now deserved to be able to cut loose.[99] And she did.

Aside from her brother-in-law, Jackie carried on affairs with the designer of JFK's eternal flame memorial, Jack Warnecke; legendary venture capitalist Andre Meyer; and former undersecretary of defense Roswell Gilpatric. She also bagged Marlon Brando on a double date that Lee Radziwill arranged in February 1964. After dinner at Washington's exclusive Jockey Club, Lee and Jackie made a show of leaving the restaurant separately from Brando and Lee's date, movie director George Englund, one of her many lovers. The men soon rejoined the sisters back at Jackie's house. Lee and Englund canoodled on the couch, while Brando and Jackie drank and danced.[100] Brando recalled that after Jackie suggestively "pressed her thighs" into him, they sat down and began to "make out." "From all I'd read and heard about her, Jacqueline Kennedy seemed coquettish and sensual but not particularly sexual," Brando reminisced. "If anything I pictured her as more voyeur than player. But that wasn't at all the case." "She kept waiting for me to try to get her into bed. When I failed to make a move, she took matters into her own hands and popped the magic question: 'Would you like to spend the night?' And I said, 'I thought you'd never ask.'" A week later Jackie spent the weekend in New York, where she visited Brando in a small Sutton Place apartment. Brando noted "Jackie's boyish hips" and "muscular frame"; "I'm not sure she knew what she was doing sexually, but she did it well."[101] The sexual revolution and women's lib were in full swing, and the press regarded Jackie as yet another liberated woman freely indulging and enjoying her sexuality. Only the *National Enquirer* dared to report on Jackie's new lifestyle in a 1966 piece that was aptly titled "From Mourner to Swinger."[102]

While the national press, the New York and Washington social elite and even Ethel ignored Jackie's affair with Bobby, the FBI did not. At Lyndon Johnson's request, J. Edgar Hoover assigned FBI agents to spy on RFK during the 1964 Democratic National Convention. Johnson knew that John Kennedy had intended for his brother to succeed him in 1968 and that Bobby had urged the president to dump Johnson from the 1964 ticket. Now on the eve of his nomination, LBJ read a news report that Jackie would be attending the convention to urge delegates to draft Bobby for vice president.[103] "Let's face it," RFK told a close aide, "if Johnson had to choose between Ho Chi Minh and yours truly for the vice presidential slot, he'd go with Ho Chi Minh."[104] Special agent Courtney Evans, who served as the FBI's official liaison with the Kennedys, said, "If anyone seemed capable of perpetrating a 'dirty tricks' campaign it was President Johnson. Bobby always felt that if pushed to the wall, Johnson would leak the names of the women with whom John F. Kennedy, while president, had been romantically linked, including Judith Campbell Exner, Sam Giancana's girlfriend."[105] Thanks to the FBI, Johnson also had the goods on Bobby. FBI agents assigned to spy on RFK at the 1964 Democratic convention reported, "The subject seems to spend all his free time with Mrs. John F. Kennedy. Although it can't be confirmed at this time, they appear to be sharing the same hotel suite."[106]

The CIA might also have been spying on Bobby and Jackie. Back in 1963 when RFK first heard his brother was assassinated, he immediately called a high-ranking CIA official and asked, "Did your outfit have anything to do with this horror?" In the year after the assassination, Bobby used his contacts in the FBI, the CIA and his Justice Department to conduct his own investigation into his brother's murder. "He could talk about little else," said Ken O'Donnell. "He'd call me late at night and go through the multiple combinations and permutations that could have led to Jack's assassination. He had no faith in the newly formed Warren Commission's investigation, which is why he initiated his own."[107] According to Jack's old friend George Smathers, RFK believed rogue CIA agents orchestrated the assassination, but he decided not to push this avenue of investigation publicly because he feared the CIA would retaliate by publicizing his affair with Jackie. "At least, that's what Ted Kennedy told me," said Smathers. "Exposure in the media would have ruined any chance Bobby might have had of following in Jack's presidential footsteps. Frankly, between the CIA and Bobby's interlude with Jackie, it's a wonder that none of it had already been exposed in the press."[108] Whether the CIA actually orchestrated JFK's assassination, as RFK suspected, is certainly debatable. But it is clear that

Bobby's sexual relationship with Jackie made him so vulnerable to blackmail that he could not risk upsetting anyone who might have known about an alleged CIA assassination plot. Bobby had no choice but to ignore leads that he believed might solve the murder of his beloved brother and president of the United States.

Aristotle Onassis understood RFK's vulnerability. "I could bury that sucker," Ari said to Johnny Meyer, "although I'd lose Jackie in the process. But can't you just see the headlines." Instead Onassis rented an Upper East Side apartment near Jackie so he could compete with Bobby. He soon complained to Meyer, "She doesn't seem to mind Bobby Kennedy dropping in at all hours but when I visit her apartment, she tells me the doormen are talking."[109] Meyer was present during an argument between Onassis and Jackie over RFK. When Onassis exclaimed, "Your boyfriend's a little prick!" Jackie retorted, "Well that doesn't describe him anatomically."[110]

Jackie enjoyed playing these two powerful men against each other. Oil heiress Lilly Lawrence, who had known Onassis for years, observed that "Jackie was the most money-hungry woman I ever met. She and Ari had that much in common. She lusted after money and he possessed it." According to Lawrence, whenever Ari saw Jackie he handed her an envelope full of cash. "He was used to paying for sex," Lawrence said. "He enjoyed the company of call girls. Never one to mince words he used to say 'It's a straightforward transaction. There are no strings attached. You pay them and they spread their legs. If you want something special, you pay them a little extra.'"[111] While Jackie got Onassis to fund her lifestyle, she kept Bobby in line by threatening him with the possibility that she might marry Onassis.

Perhaps in revenge for stealing her megamillionaire, Lee invited both Onassis and Bobby to a dinner party she held in Jackie's honor in 1966. Other invitees included Mike Nichols, Leonard Bernstein, Sammy Davis Jr., Brooke Astor, George Plimpton, Kenneth Galbraith, Pierre Salinger and Franklin Roosevelt Jr. The room of luminaries fell silent when RFK and Onassis awkwardly greeted each other. Finally Franklin Roosevelt Jr. broke the tension, "I guess you boys know each other." The artist Larry Rivers recalled that "Jackie spent the rest of the evening attempting to divide her time and attention between her two pursuers."[112]

THE DEATH OF CAMELOT

In the wake of the January 1968 Tet offensive and a precipitous drop in Lyndon Johnson's poll numbers, RFK's advisors urged him to jump into that year's presidential race. When Art Buchwald asked Bobby if he intended to run, he said, "That depends on what Jackie wants me to do."[113] Kennedy advisor Jack Newfield recalled a meeting in Jackie's living room to discuss whether RFK should enter the race. Jackie said to Bobby, "Well there's a good deal of anti-Johnson sentiment out there. If I were you, I'd make a stand. But wait a few months before announcing. And when you do run, you must be authentic. You must be yourself. Don't try to be Jack." Newfield recalled, "It was as though the Oracle of Delphi had spoken. I'd heard many times from many people that they were lovers. I couldn't tell. But I could see they were extremely committed to each other. If she told him not to run, I don't think he would have. On the other hand, I believe she told him what she thought he hoped to hear. I'm not convinced she wanted him to run—she wanted him to do what she thought would make him happy."[114] RFK's presidential run certainly did not make Jackie happy. "Do you know what I think will happen to Bobby?" she asked Arthur Schlesinger Jr. "The same thing that happened to Jack. There is so much hatred in this country, and more people hate Bobby than hated Jack. That's why I don't want him to be president. . . . I've told Bobby this, but he is fatalistic, like me." Informed that Kennedy had hired a public speaking coach in preparation for his campaign, Onassis quipped, "The only thing JFK and RFK have in common is Jacqueline Kennedy."[115]

President Johnson was so disturbed by the prospect of Bobby taking the nomination from him that two weeks after RFK announced his entry into the race on March 16, 1968, LBJ shocked the nation and declared on national television, "I shall not seek, and I will not accept, the nomination of my party for another term as your President." With the incumbent president out of the race and Bobby leading in the polls, the Kennedy family gathered at Hyannis Port to discuss campaign strategy. According to a witness, Jackie was "more excited than I had seen her for years." In the middle of the discussion Jackie offered some encouragement, "Won't it be wonderful when we get back in the White House?" Ethel snapped, "What do you mean, *we?* You're not running. This is our moment in the sun." Jackie ran out of the house while the presidential candidate silently remained behind with his wife.[116]

That afternoon in Hyannis Port, Jackie realized she really had to move on from the Kennedys. She soon agreed to Onassis's marriage proposal but promised RFK she would hold off until after the November election. Onassis told Gratsos, "She's worth the wait. There's something mystifying about her. She's willful and provocative. She possesses carnal soul. She looks Greek but behaves like an American princess."[117]

Although Onassis might have been willing to wait for Jackie, he could not resist his need to one-up Bobby.[118] Tipped off by Onassis, Drew Pearson reported that the Golden Greek's relationship with Maria Callas was "on the rocks" and that Onassis was seen in "cozy company" with Jackie Kennedy. In the same column Pearson then accused the Warren Commission of "not doing its job" and claimed Robert Kennedy "dropped the ball" in failing to push for a full investigation of his brother's assassination. Pearson concluded his column with a provocative question: "If Lee Harvey Oswald was simply a patsy, as he claimed, then who murdered President Kennedy?" To the average reader the contents of Pearson's column seemed random: Onassis, Callas, Jackie, the Warren Commission, Bobby and Oswald. But RFK could have easily connected the dots. When Gratsos asked Onassis why he planted the article, Ari said he wanted Bobby to know "I'm still very much around—and I'm not going away."[119]

In the middle of the primary race, Onassis dropped another reminder that he could cause trouble for Bobby. On May 17, 1968, he told a reporter for the *Times* of London that "Mrs. Kennedy is a totally misunderstood woman. Perhaps she even misunderstands herself. She's being held up as a model of propriety, constancy, and so many of those boring American female virtues. She's now utterly devoid of mystery. She needs a small scandal to bring her alive—a peccadillo, an indiscretion. Something should happen to her to win our fresh compassion. The world loves to pity *fallen grandeur*."[120] RFK panicked when he saw Onassis's comments reprinted in every major newspaper, including the *Washington Post* and the *New York Times*. He feared the Greek was about to either announce his betrothal to Jackie or disclose RFK's affair with her. Either way the Camelot myth would be marred along with his shot at the presidency. According to Pierre Salinger,

Bobby immediately called Onassis and threatened to ban him and his oil tankers from the United States if he made another indiscreet comment about Jackie.[121] RFK then dispatched Ethel and Joan, Ted's wife, to meet with Jackie in her New York apartment to urge her not to marry Onassis until after the election. Ethel swallowed her pride and made the embassy to her husband's mistress. Despite Jackie's assurances that she would do nothing that would hurt Bobby's presidential hopes, RFK himself briefly abandoned the campaign trail to make a follow-up visit to Jackie's apartment. "For God's sake, Jackie, this could cost me five states!"[122] Again she assured him that she would not marry Onassis until after the election. After the visit, Salinger asked Bobby "what he planned to do about their nuptials should he win the presidency?" RFK responded, "She'll marry that man over my dead body. I'll deal with it when the time comes."[123] Those words proved prophetic.

Onassis wasn't stupid. He knew if Robert Kennedy won the presidency and restored Camelot in the White House, Jackie might reject his proposal or Bobby would use his vast power to stop the marriage. So Onassis decided to stop Kennedy from being elected president. He dispatched David Karr, the man who planted Ari's stories with Drew Pearson, to meet with Lyndon Johnson. According to the White House log on April 3, 1968, Karr and Pearson entered the Oval Office at 1:56 PM and left 50 minutes later. There is no record of what Karr and Pearson told LBJ. But shortly after Karr's visit, another presidential candidate, Senator Eugene McCarthy, met with Johnson and brought up RFK's candidacy. McCarthy described LBJ's reaction: "The president said nothing: instead he drew a finger across his throat, silently in a slitting motion."[124]

It is not known if Karr and Pearson told Johnson about Bobby's affair with Jackie. But if they did, LBJ certainly hated Kennedy enough that he would have exposed it before the 1968 Democratic nominating convention in Chicago. Right before the California primary in June 1968, Johnson leaked the story that RFK approved the FBI wiretapping and bugging of Martin Luther King Jr.[125] MLK had been assassinated that April and Johnson hoped the revelation would turn the black community in California against Bobby. It didn't work. Kennedy's overwhelming support among black voters carried him to victory in the California primary on June 4, 1968.

On the night of RFK's California primary victory, a Palestinian national-ist named Sirhan Sirhan gunned down Kennedy in the kitchen of the Am-bassador Hotel in Los Angeles. While RFK lay unconscious in a hospital bed, Jackie immediately flew from New York to be by his side. Ethel gratefully em-braced Jackie when she arrived and even left her alone to bid farewell to her dying lover. According to Kennedy speechwriter Richard Goodwin, "Jackie was the one who turned off the machines. She flew in and nobody else had the nerve. The poor guy was lying there, his chest going up and down—you know they have those machines that keep your body going forever—and he was brain dead and the doctors didn't dare pull the plug. Ethel was in no shape to do anything; she was lying on the bed moaning. Teddy was kneeling in prayer at the foot of the bed and finally Jackie came in and told the doctors they had to do it. It was the final seal for her."[126]

As soon as Onassis heard his rival was dead, he called Gratsos: "At last Jackie's free of the Kennedys. The last link has just broke." In a conversation with Johnny Meyer, Onassis gloated, "Somebody was going to fix the little bastard sooner or later."[127] Onassis flew immediately to New York to claim his prize.

In the wake of her lover's death, Jackie declared, "I hate this country. I de-spise America and I don't want my children to live here anymore. If they're killing Kennedys my kids are number one targets. I want to get out of this country and away from it all."[128] Onassis with his vast wealth and his own is-land was Jackie's quickest way to escape an America that killed the great loves of her life. Five months later, on October 20, 1968, the former First Lady mar-ried the Golden Greek on Skorpios. Newspapers around the world screamed headlines like JACKIE SELLS OUT! *Los Angeles Times;* THE REACTION HERE IS ANGER, SHOCK AND DISMAY, *New York Times;* JACKIE, HOW COULD YOU? Stockholm's *Expressen;* JACK KENNEDY DIES TODAY FOR A SECOND TIME, *Il Messagero.* A columnist for *L'Espresso* called Onassis "a grizzled satrap with liver-colored skin, a fleshy nose, a wide horsy grin—that's the lady's new husband."[129] The Vatican newspaper *L'Osser-vatore della Domenica* declared that Jackie's marriage to a divorced man was "in effect a renunciation of her faith," which made her a "public sinner."[130]

Jackie's new marriage did not go well. Forty-eight hours after the wed-ding, Onassis complained to a friend, "I've made some terrible mistakes in my life, but marrying Jackie might take the biscuit."[131] He told Johnny Meyer that Jackie "speaks incessantly of Bobby Kennedy. . . . All she's ever given me is the Kennedy clap."[132] By early 1969 Jackie returned full time to New York where she reignited her affair with Roswell Gilpatric.[133] Onassis resumed his relationship with Maria Callas and was in the process of filing for a divorce when he died in 1975.[134]

Jackie's marriage to Onassis in October 1968 was just the first in a series of events that undercut the Camelot myth. Months later, on July 18, 1969, Senator Edward Kennedy was on Chappaquiddick Island, near Martha's Vineyard, at a party for the "Boiler Room Girls," a group of young women who had worked on Bobby's presidential campaign.[135] Kennedy left the party with his late brother's mistress, 28-year-old Mary Jo Kopechne, and drove off a bridge over the Poucha Pond inlet. Kennedy escaped the submerged vehicle and then, by his own report, dove below the surface seven or eight times in a vain attempt to save Kopechne. Ultimately, he swam to shore and left the scene. He failed to alert authorities of the accident until the next morning, by which time Kopechne's corpse had been discovered. On July 25, Kennedy pleaded guilty to leaving the scene of an accident and was given a suspended sentence. The presiding judge at an inquest concluded that some aspects of Kennedy's account of that night were false and that negligent driving "appear[ed] to have contributed to the death of Mary Jo Kopechne."[136] Millions of Americans concluded that the senator used his wealth and power to escape jail time. The Chappaquiddick incident became a national scandal that dashed Ted Kennedy's presidential hopes and killed his family's final chance to restore Camelot to the White House.

The Senate Intelligence Committee in the 1970s conducted an investigation into John Kennedy's plot to kill Castro in the early 1960s with the help of Johnny Roselli and Sam Giancana. The Intelligence Committee issued a 1975 report noting that "a *close friend* of President Kennedy had frequent contact with the President" from the end of 1960 through mid 1962. FBI reports and testimony indicate that the *President's friend* "was also a *close friend* of John Roselli and Sam Giancana."[137] It didn't take long for the press to discover that the slain president's "close friend" was Judith Campbell. Two years later, in 1977, Campbell published a memoir, *My Story*, in which she admitted her affair with Kennedy, becoming the first of his many mistresses to come forward. Sam Giancana meanwhile was executed in his kitchen in 1975 before his scheduled appearance at the Senate hearing, and Johnny Roselli's legless torso was in a steel drum floating off the coast of Miami. For most Americans, revelations in the 1970s about the dark side of Camelot contributed to a general loss of faith in politicians and government in the wake of Vietnam and Watergate. An era of hope, belief and trust in the nation's leaders gave way to an age of pessimism, cynicism and suspicion.

CHAPTER EIGHT

THE FULL
BILL CLINTON

On the morning of July 24, 1963, John Kennedy cut short a meeting with the Joint Chiefs of Staff to address a group of high school boys. With all the pressures on the president that tumultuous summer of 1963—Berlin, Birmingham, Vietnam and Ellen Rometsch—the last thing he needed was another inconsequential photo-op on the south lawn. Nevertheless, at ten o'clock sharp, an elegantly tailored JFK strode out the south portico to say a few words to the eager teenagers. The speech over, Kennedy was about to head back to the West Wing when suddenly he changed his mind and turned to shake hands with the surging crowd. The first boy to grab the president's hand was a husky 16-year-old named Bill Clinton. Having muscled his way to the front row, the kid from Hot Springs, Arkansas, was determined to get a photo with the president. Bill's mother, Virginia, recalled, "When he came back from Washington, holding this picture of himself with Jack Kennedy, and the expression in his face, I knew right then that politics was the answer for him."[1]

Three decades later, in the summer of 1995, President Bill Clinton stood on the south lawn for a surprise forty-ninth birthday party attended by the White House staff. Dressed in snug blue jeans and a pink short-sleeved shirt, he quickly worked his way down the line of well-wishers until he came to a plump, full-lipped 21-year-old intern holding a sign that read "Happy Birthday, Mr. President." Like the young Billy Clinton three decades before, Monica Lewinsky had positioned herself right up front to catch the president's attention. As she stood under his lingering blue-eyed gaze, she felt his arm "accidentally" brush her ample breast as he reached for another hand.[2] A White House photographer captured the moment, and Lewinsky proudly sent the photo to her father. Bernie Lewinsky reacted to the photograph of his child's brush with history much differently than Virginia Clinton. "I, as a father and as a photographer, was really taken aback at the look in his eyes," Bernie recalled. "He has lascivious eyes. He looked at my daughter in a weird way."[3] Lewinsky called the president's undressing leer "the Full Bill Clinton."[4]

KENNEDY VERSUS CLINTON

No two presidents are more associated with sex than Kennedy and Clinton. Both radiated a powerful magnetism that stemmed from vigorous sex drives. "Some people are addicted to drugs. Some to power. Some to food. Some to sex," Clinton explained. "We're all addicted to something." Jack Kennedy never heard of sex addiction but he did admit, "I get a migraine headache if I don't get a strange piece of ass every day."[5] Clinton explained his hero's promiscuity, no doubt with a thought to his own: "He obviously was a man who thought he was ill, was in a hurry in life, grew up in a different time, was raised in a home where the rules were apparently different than most of us believe they should be now, and where the role of women in society was different than it is now."[6]

Kennedy and Clinton approached women differently. JFK rapidly consumed them, as if he could see the sand running through his personal hourglass; Angie Dickenson observed that sex with Kennedy "was the most exciting seven minutes of my life."[7] Clinton on the other hand savored his women. One of his mistresses, Gennifer Flowers, remarked that although Clinton was "not particularly well endowed," "his desire to please was astounding. He was determined to satisfy me, and boy did he! At times I thought my head would explode with pleasure."[8] Like Kennedy's, Clinton's sexual dynamism fueled his political success. A 1994 book, *Dreams of Bill,* compiled the nighttime fantasies that dozens of women had for their president, and Clinton won the support of 70 percent of unmarried women during his 1996 reelection campaign.[9]

There was one obvious difference between Kennedy and Clinton. One got away with untold numbers of White House affairs, while the other got impeached for just one. To account for this difference we need to look at the revolutionary changes in American society and politics between the 1960s and 1990s.

Between the Kennedy and the Clinton presidencies, access journalism was replaced by gotcha journalism. Ambitious journalists in the 1960s ingratiated themselves with politicians to gain access and get tips on stories. *Newsweek*'s Ben Bradlee and his wife regularly dined with Jack and Jackie Kennedy, while reporter Hugh Sidney caroused in the White House pool with the Kennedy brothers and their girlfriends. JFK's buddies in the press ignored the president's peccadilloes and got their biggest scoops in exchange.

Vietnam and Watergate destroyed the cozy relationship between Washington journalists and politicians. A survey of campaign coverage during the 1960 election found 75 percent of the press references to the candidates were positive; when Clinton ran in 1992, 60 percent of the comments about the candidates were negative.[10] Ben Bradlee, promoted to editor of the *Washington Post*, and two of his cub reporters, Bob Woodward and Carl Bernstein, exposed Watergate and inspired a generation of investigative journalists who looked to make their mark by bringing down politicians. Every president after Nixon knew the Washington press corps held their knives out looking for a vulnerable spot to dig in. By the time Clinton became president, the press had settled into an adversarial relationship with the White House; trust was lost, access denied, and uncovering conspiracies and cover-ups was the focus of reporting.

Since Kennedy's day, the government had also lost the trust of the people. The JFK assassination, the Gulf of Tonkin incident, the FBI's violations of civil liberties, the CIA-Mafia connection, Watergate, the Iran-Contra affair and a host of other real and imagined government conspiracies taught Americans to no longer give their leaders the benefit of the doubt. When it came to the federal government, Americans on both the Left and the Right assumed the worst.[11]

Clinton also had the misfortune of being president at the dawn of tabloid journalism. After the Supreme Court ended libel protection for "public figures" with the 1964 *New York Times Co. v. Sullivan* ruling, everyone in American public life became vulnerable to even the most outrageous, poorly sourced news stories. The rise of cable television in the 1980s and the creation of three 24-hour news channels made the news industry much more competitive. Increased competition forced major news outlets to give the masses what they wanted to know, rather than what they needed to know. Sales, advertising, subscribers and ratings were given priority over sourcing, credibility and responsibility. A new breed of celebrity reporter made the rounds of the news talk shows, filling airtime with rumors and predictions. The proliferation of news outlets made the media impossible to control by the 1990s. Thirty years earlier, Robert Kennedy could squelch scandalous stories about his brother by making angry phone calls to a half dozen editors and publishers. By the late twentieth century, the media industry had become uncontrollable.

In the 1980s Rupert Murdoch's News Corporation–Fox News empire pushed the networks and Cable News Network (CNN) to move into infotainment, the kind of sleazy but highly rated news programming featured on *Inside Edition* and *A Current Affair*. In the decade before Clinton's election, Americans watched nightly television news programs filled with salacious reports on televangelist Jim Bakker and Jessica Hahn, Reverend Jimmy Swaggart and prostitutes and John Wayne Bobbitt's severed penis. Editors and producers in Kennedy's day would never have run stories about oral sex in the Oval Office; in the Jerry Springer era no subject was taboo.

By the time Clinton came into office, Americans had seen a lot of DC sex scandals. The first modern American political sex scandal to make it to print came in 1974 when Washington police stopped a car carrying chairman of the House Ways and Means Committee Wilbur Mills and Fanne Foxe, a stripper known as the "Argentinean Firecracker." While an intoxicated Mills tried to explain to the cops why his face was covered in bloody scratches, Foxe popped out of the car and leaped into the Tidal Basin. Congress had its first gay sex scandal in 1989 when the *Washington Times* reported Massachusetts representative Barney Frank paid for sex with a male prostitute who ran an escort service out of the congressman's DC home.

The Supreme Court was not insulated from sex scandals either. During Clarence Thomas's nationally televised 1991 confirmation hearings, a former coworker named Anita Hill accused Thomas of complaining about a pubic hair in his can of Coke and inviting her to watch a porno movie starring the legendary Long Dong Silver. The media fell in love with political sex scandals, which always attracted more readers and viewers than stories about the budget or foreign policy.

Sex scandals entered the world of presidential politics in 1988 when the *Miami Herald* exposed Senator Gary Hart's affair with a leggy 29-year-old blonde model named Donna Rice. Heralded as the "new Jack Kennedy," Hart probably would have won the Democratic nomination had the *National Enquirer* not published a photo of Rice sitting on the delighted senator's lap. Late-night comedians had a field day with the picture of Rice and Hart, who was wearing a T-shirt emblazoned with the name of their party boat, *Monkey Business*.

At the time, Governor Clinton of Arkansas was mulling over a presidential run, and one of the state troopers on his security detail predicted, "Governor, you're gonna make Gary Hart look like a damned saint." "Yeah," Clinton replied, "I do, don't I?"[12] Beneath the bravado, Clinton was worried. "After the Hart affair," he wrote in his memoir, *My Life*, "those of us who had not led perfect lives had no way of knowing what the press's standards of disclosure were."[13] Clinton would soon learn that "standards of disclosure" were a thing of the past. The late-twentieth-century American media had come to resemble the nineteenth-century press, with no professional code of journalistic ethics to keep private affairs from becoming public scandals.

Like Hart four years before, Clinton began the 1992 presidential race as the frontrunner in a weak field of Democratic candidates. History seemed to repeat itself on the eve of the New Hampshire primary when the tabloid *Star* paid a five-foot-two, blue-eyed, bleach-blonde Little Rock nightclub singer named Gennifer Flowers to tell her story: "My 12-Year Affair with Bill Clinton."[14] Clinton had entered the race figuring he would probably lose and mount another run four years later with more experience and greater name recognition. The Flowers scandal suddenly turned a campaign that was about testing the waters into a do-or-die situation. If Clinton dropped out over a sex scandal as Hart had in 1988, he would never be president.[15]

The way politicians traditionally handled sex scandals was to deny the accusation and hope there was no evidence. That was not an option for Clinton, because Flowers had audiotapes of their intimate conversations. Like Alexander Hamilton after the Maria Reynolds scandal, Clinton had to save himself by giving a public confession. Instead of a pamphlet, Clinton used the confessional interview.

Thanks to Phil Donahue, Oprah Winfrey and Larry King, Americans had become accustomed to watching famous people rehabilitate their reputations by confessing their sins on national television. The Clinton campaign scheduled both Bill and Hillary to appear on *60 Minutes*. "We wanted them together, sitting next to each other," recalled political advisor James Carville.[16] The interview was set to air immediately after CBS's Super Bowl broadcast, the most watched television show in the world. The legendary *60 Minutes* producer Don Hewitt, who had produced the 1960 Kennedy-Nixon debates, knew the historic potential of the interview. Right before the cameras started rolling Hewitt assured Clinton, "It will be great television. I know, I know television. The last time I did something like this, Bill, it was the Kennedy/Nixon debates and it produced a president. This will produce a president too."[17]

Hewitt was right. The Clintons hit all the right notes. Bill managed to sound contrite without giving his opponents an explicit sound bite. "I have acknowledged wrongdoing. I have acknowledged causing pain in my marriage." He also assumed the role of media victim. "I have said things to you tonight that no American politician ever has. I think most Americans who are watching this tonight; they'll know what we're saying. They'll get it, and they'll feel we've been more than candid. And I think what the press has to decide is: Are we going to engage in a game of 'gotcha'?" Hillary then jumped in: "Are we going to take the reverse position now that if people have problems in their marriage and there are things in their past which they don't want to discuss which are painful to them, that they can't run?" When interviewer Steve Croft complimented the Clintons for staying together and reaching "some sort of understanding and arrangement," Bill gallantly cut him off. "Wait a minute, wait a minute. You're looking at two people who *love* each other. This is not an arrangement or an understanding. This is a *marriage*." Hillary added, "You know, I'm not sitting here, some little woman standing by my man like Tammy Wynette. I'm sitting here because I love him, I respect him, and I honor what he's been through and what we've been through together, and you know, if that's not enough for people, then heck, don't vote for him."[18] Far from looking peculiar or unconventional, the Clintons came across as a typical married couple with their fair share of betrayal and disappointment.

An estimated 34 million people watched the interview and 50 million more saw highlights on other news programs. Overnight, Bill and Hillary Clinton acquired national name recognition without spending a dollar. "The country and the media [were] riveted on us. Our name recognition skyrocketed," Carville crowed. "We were the only game in town. A southern babe, a Rhodes scholar presidential candidate, a compelling wife, a sexy tabloid, sex, lies, audiotape—how could you care about another candidate?"[19] A national poll taken by *ABC News* found 80 percent of respondents thought Clinton should stay in the race.[20]

The Gennifer Flowers scandal actually helped Clinton win the Democratic nomination by showing primary voters that he had the poise and resilience to take the hits from the Republican attack machine. The Big Dog was not going to be another punching bag like the previous three Democratic nominees, Carter, Mondale and Dukakis. James Carville's girlfriend, Mary Matalin, who was President Bush's political advisor, admitted, "The way they jujitsued the Flowers fiasco gave us the heebie-jeebies."[21] The Bush campaign was also worried because the Flowers scandal opened the door to questions about their own candidate's personal life.

FROM COLD WAR TO CULTURE WAR

At the height of the Cold War, undermining the commander in chief by reporting a story about his sex life would have been considered tantamount to treason. Without the existential threat of the Soviet Union, the president by the early 1990s was no longer glorified as defender of the free world and no longer protected by the press. It was no coincidence that the first president of the post–Cold War era, George H. W. Bush, became the first sitting president since Thomas Jefferson to be engulfed in a full-blown sex scandal.

Rumors that Bush was carrying on an affair with longtime aide Jennifer Fitzgerald had been rattling around DC since he was vice president, but the press ignored the story.[22] Hillary Clinton injected the Fitzgerald affair into the 1992 campaign during off-the-record remarks to *Vanity Fair*'s Gail Sheehy. Hillary was venting to Sheehy about "Bush and his carrying on, all of which is apparently well known in Washington." She complained that "the establishment" media chose to focus on Gennifer Flowers while ignoring "the other Jennifer." *Vanity Fair* published Hillary's off-the-record remarks, which were repeated in other publications under headlines like "Hillary's Revenge," "Hillary Goes Tabloid" and "Bill's Wife Dishes the Dirt."[23]

Bush tried to ignore the controversy, but during an August 11, 1992, press conference with Israeli prime minister Yitzhak Rabin, a CNN reporter asked the president about a front page *New York Post* story on Fitzgerald, "The Bush Affair." "I'm not going to take any sleazy questions like that from CNN," the president snapped. "I am very disappointed that you would ask such a question of me, and I will not respond to it. I think it's—I'm outraged. But, nevertheless, in this kind of screwy climate that we're in, why, I expect it. But I don't like it, and I'm not going to respond other than to say it's a lie." Bush had hoped to use his press conference with Rabin to highlight his foreign policy expertise in contrast to Governor Clinton's inexperience. Instead, the evening news broadcasts were filled with clips of Bush's irate reaction to the affair question. "We wish we didn't have to deal with this," *CBS Evening News* executive producer Erik Sorenson shrugged, "but our viewers are hearing it all day. We sort of have a *responsibility* to address it."[24]

Bush immediately deployed his son George W. to tell the press, "The answer to the 'A' question is a big N-O."[25] But the Fitzgerald story survived Bush's denial and even became a topic of a roundtable discussion on *The McLaughlin Group*. Before an Oval Office interview on August 12, the president felt the need to explicitly warn *Dateline NBC* reporter Stone Phillips not to inquire about his personal life. Phillips flouted the commander in chief's request and asked point blank, "Have you ever had an affair?" Bush was flabbergasted by the reporter's impudence, "I'm not going to take any sleaze questions. I gave you a little warning. You see, you're perpetuating the sleaze by even asking it in the Oval Office, and I don't think you ought to do that, and I'm not going to answer that question."[26]

Bush had entered politics in the mid-1960s; he did not understand that in the post–Cold War world the presidential press conference and the Oval Office had lost much of their majesty. The press now regarded the personal life of the president as fair game, just like celebrities and members of the British royal family who had been generating a steady supply of sex-filled news stories for over a decade.

The end of the Cold War had deprived the Republican Party of its long-standing edge on the national security issue and left the GOP looking for a new defining crusade. Despite the Fitzgerald scandal, the Republicans chose family values as the theme for their 1992 national convention in Houston.

Beginning in the 1970s televangelists had built media empires by whooping up followers against abortion, gay rights, feminists and other evils of the sexual revolution. Religion-based political groups like the Moral Majority pushed moral issues into the forefront of American political debate in the 1980s. The Clintons seemed the perfect targets for a family values crusade. Bill had his "bimbo eruptions" and Hillary was a career woman who promised to play a nontraditional advisory role in a Clinton administration. In the eyes of the Republican base, the Clintons embodied moral relativism and the Baby Boomer ethos of "Do it if it feels good." An interviewer asked a Bush supporter, "Why do you hate Bill Clinton?" The answer: "He's a womanizing, Elvis-loving, non-inhaling, truth-shading, war-protesting, draft-dodging, abortion-protecting, gay-promoting, gun-hating baby boomer. That's why."[27]

Bush's defeated challenger for the Republican nomination, Pat Buchanan, declared a culture war at the 1992 GOP convention: "The agenda Clinton and Clinton would impose on America, abortion on demand, a litmus test for the Supreme Court, homosexual rights, discrimination against religious schools, women in combat units—that's change all right. That's not the kind of change America needs, its not the kind of change America wants, and it is not the kind of change we can abide in a nation that we still call God's country." With clamorous cheers rebounding around the Astrodome, Buchanan thundered, "There is a religious war going on in this country for the soul of America. It is a cultural war as critical to the kind of nation we shall be as the Cold War itself. And in that struggle for the soul of America, Clinton and Clinton are on the other side and George Bush is on our side."[28] The last time a presidential campaign accused an opposing candidate and his wife of threatening the moral fiber of the nation was John Quincy Adams's 1828 campaign against Rachel and Andrew Jackson.

Known as the "Hate-fest in Houston," the 1992 Republican convention exposed a dramatic change in American politics. Elections were bitter in Kennedy's era, but the leadership of both parties honored the outcomes and the losers became "the loyal opposition." After Clinton won the election, conservative activists saw the new president as a usurper who had somehow hoodwinked the American public. The Christian Coalition called the inauguration of William Jefferson Clinton "a repudiation of our forefathers' covenant with God."[29]

From the start of the Clinton presidency in 1993, influential conservatives were determined to bring him down and restore morality to the White House. "I was up against a group of people who, while they claim they have great values and worship God, in fact worship power," Clinton recalled. "And that they would do or say anything, and that they really thought that we were illegitimate occupiers of their natural throne in Washington DC, and that anything they said or did against any of us was okay."[30]

Plenty of Americans had also hated Kennedy, but Congress in the 1960s was still a bastion of moderation, with members of both parties committed to preventing the whims of the masses from threatening the stability of the Republic. By the 1990s, thanks to gerrymandering, few congressmen in either party needed to worry about appealing to the center. The main threat to incumbents came from primary challenges by party extremists. Moderation, compromise and respect for the office of the president were no longer political virtues in the legislative branch.

The congressional old boys club was also dead. In Kennedy's day, Republicans and Democrats fought each other tooth and nail on the floor of Congress, but afterward they'd hit the bars together, get drunk and chase skirts. A lot of trust was built up between political opponents who knew each other's private secrets. The arrival of large numbers of women and evangelicals on Capitol Hill put an end to the frat house atmosphere and the traditional male bonding rituals that facilitated bipartisanship. The notion that politics was a war for the American soul also precluded compromise. Even when Clinton tried to appeal to the Right by supporting conservative legislation like banking deregulation, welfare reform and the 1996 Defense of Marriage Act, he was still viewed as the spawn of Satan.

FOLLOW THE HONEY

From the moment Clinton took the oath of office, congressional Republicans and many journalists were looking to expose a big White House scandal. Instead, they uncovered a string of trivial scandals, none of which rose to the level of high crimes but together gave the impression of a White House mired in conspiracy and cover-up. As Ben Franklin said, the press "can strike while the iron is hot," but it can also "heat it by continually striking."[31] Clinton's scandals generated some extra heat because they always seemed to have a sexual dimension.

The Whitewater scandal began in the 1980s when an old friend of the Clintons, Jim McDougal, convinced the Arkansas governor and his wife to invest $20,000 in a resort complex in the Ozarks near the White River. The Whitewater Project failed to attract buyers and the Clintons lost their investment, but two complicating factors raised eyebrows. Bill allegedly had an affair with McDougal's wife, Susan. And the McDougals' savings and loan, Madison Guaranty, retained Hillary as its lawyer even though her law firm also represented the Federal Deposit Insurance Corporation in recovering lost deposits from Madison when it failed in the late 1980s.

The *Washington Post*'s Michael Isikoff fed the scandal by reporting the questionable claims of David Hale, a shady, recently indicted Arkansas businessman, who accused Clinton of pressuring him to lend Susan McDougal $200,000 in 1986. Clinton's alleged affair with Susan provided the motive and gave the boring financial scandal enough heat to generate a media frenzy. In Clinton's first year in office congressional Republicans were already demanding an independent counsel to investigate Whitewater. Clinton could not believe it: "I had the lowest net worth of any president in modern history. Everybody who knew anything about me knew I wouldn't take a nickel to see the cow jump over the moon. They knew that whatever else was wrong with me, that I was scrupulously financially honest. And you know, it was never real. It was all about the narcotic of scandal."[32]

The Whitewater scandal gained added steam when longtime Clinton friend and White House counsel Vince Foster committed suicide in the summer of 1993 after being relentlessly hounded in the press for his involvement in the so-called Travelgate scandal. Foster had been Hillary's mentor at the Rose Law firm. When he became White House counsel he openly worried about rumors that he had had an affair with Hillary back in Little Rock.[33] In the wake of his suicide, the *New York Post* reported that Foster rented a "secret apartment hideaway" in Virginia where he allegedly entertained the First Lady. Right-wing radio hosts began suggesting that Hillary blew Foster's brains out in a cover-up.[34]

Televangelist Pat Robertson asked his *700 Club* viewers, "Suicide or murder? That's the ominous question surfacing in the Whitewater swell of controversy concerning Vincent Foster's mysterious death."[35] Rush Limbaugh repeated "claims that Vince Foster was murdered in an apartment owned by Hillary Clinton."[36] Bill Clinton later recalled, "I heard a lot of the right-wing talk show people . . . and all the sleazy stuff they said. They didn't give a rip that he had killed himself or that his family was miserable or that they could break the hearts [of Foster's friends and family]. It was just another weapon to slug us with, to demonize us with."[37]

Jack Kennedy never had to contend with talk radio hosts who filled hours of airtime every day with random callers offering up rumors. Only 2 radio stations had talk formats in 1960; by 1995 there were 1,130, and nearly 70 percent of talk radio listeners were conservative. Rush Limbaugh alone had 20 million listeners and was broadcast on 659 radio stations. That kind of power influenced the leadership of the Republican Party. Senate minority leader Bob Dole, who hoped to challenge Clinton for the presidency in 1996, began referring to Foster's death as an "alleged suicide." House minority whip Newt Gingrich dismissed the results of an FBI investigation into Foster's suicide that found no wrongdoing, saying, "There's a lot there that is weird."[38]

Jack Kennedy also did not have to contend with privately financed right-wing magazines like the *American Spectator*, largely funded by Clinton-hating billionaire Richard Mellon Scaife. *American Spectator* ran a January 1994 article claiming that when Clinton was governor he used state troopers on his security detail to coordinate his sexual trysts. The author was David Brock, a 31-year-old closeted homosexual who had become a darling of the Right after he penned the hatchet-job book *The Real Anita Hill.*

Brock later admitted that he was a "self-loathing" homosexual who desperately feared being outed. He figured that if he could score a big hit on Clinton, *American Spectator* would award him with a permanent staff position and he could come out.[39] Like the early American scandalmonger James Callender, Brock didn't care about journalistic ethics; he just wanted to please his financial patron. "I threw in every last titillating morsel and dirty quote the troopers served up," Brock recalled. "With my gonzo spirit on overdrive I tossed it all into the piece, [including] details that had no conceivable news value."[40] Brock claimed that Hillary was "intimately involved with the late Vincent Foster" and that the troopers saw them groping each other and "open-mouth kissing." Even the troopers were appalled by the liberties Brock took with their tales.[41] Despite the dubious journalistic merit of the *American Spectator* article, CNN used it as the basis for a report on what it dubbed Troopergate. *Washington Post* columnist Richard Harwood was appalled by how quickly a poorly sourced story in a little-known right-wing periodical could become national news. "We keep dishing the dirt because that's what readers want," Harwood wrote. "The media are about as likely to abandon the weather report as to abandon sex."[42]

Troopergate erupted at the same time the Clintons were trying to pass health care reform. Congress was poised to pass a modified version of Hillary's plan that would have covered 91 percent of the population rather than the universal coverage that the Clintons had promised.[43] The president's advisors wanted to accept Congress's compromise proposal, but Hillary urged her husband to threaten a veto if Congress dared to modify her plan. Senior presidential advisor David Gergen blamed Troopergate for his boss's decision to follow his wife's poor advice. "Watching him in that time it was very much like watching a golden retriever that has pooped on the rug and just curls up and keeps his head down," Gergen recalled. "I think it put him in a situation where on healthcare he never challenged it in a way he ordinarily would have, had he been under a different psychological situation."[44] After Clinton announced that he would veto Congress's version of health care reform, Hillary's plan failed to pass, and health care reform had to wait for almost two decades.

Troopergate also fed the increasingly heated demands for an independent counsel to investigate Whitewater.[45] Clinton's advisors suggested that the president and First Lady clear the air by handing over to the press their records on Whitewater and on Hillary's work at the Rose Law firm.[46] "What I should have done," the president later admitted, "is release the records, resist the prosecutor, give an extensive briefing to all the Democrats who wanted it, and ask for their support."[47] But Hillary adamantly refused to hand over the records of her legal work. Once again, thanks to Troopergate the president found himself in no position to pressure his wife to do anything.[48] When the Clintons refused to disclose their Whitewater records, even the *New York Times* accused the White House of engaging in a cover-up, and the establishment press joined the Republicans in demanding a special prosecutor.

There was no special prosecutor in Kennedy's era; the U.S. attorney general was solely responsible for investigating criminal allegations against the president. Robert Kennedy did more than ignore accusations against his brother—he squashed them. After Watergate, Congress created in 1978 the position of independent counsel, a special prosecutor with unlimited subpoena power to investigate criminal activity in the White House. In principle, the independent counsel seemed to be a good way to check the so-called imperial presidency. In practice, special prosecutors tended to overreach. The first independent counsel investigation, in 1979, was against Jimmy Carter's chief of staff, Hamilton Jordan, for snorting cocaine at Studio 54. The second independent counsel investigation was of Carter's campaign manager for also using cocaine. No charges were filed in either case.[49]

Under pressure from the media and congressional Republicans, Clinton made the worst blunder of his career when in 1994 he gave U.S. attorney general Janet Reno authority to appoint an independent counsel to investigate Whitewater. Reno chose moderate Republican Robert Fiske, who kept his investigation focused on the banking issues and within six months began wrapping things up.[50] The *Wall Street Journal* editorial page and the *New York Times* columnist William Safire immediately accused Fiske of complicity in a White House cover-up.[51] The three-judge panel that controlled the independent counsel then decided to replace Fiske with Ken Starr. Clinton knew

Starr's appointment meant trouble: "They're on a crusade. God has ordained them to crush the infidels. That's the way they look at it. . . . Ken Starr was their errand boy. And he danced to their tune, just as hard as he could dance."[52]

Starr's original plan was to indict Jim and Susan McDougal and then pressure them into testifying against the Clintons. The problem was that Jim died of a heart attack in prison and Susan refused to testify against Clinton. So Starr began investigating Clinton's personal life under the guise of trying to discover pillow talk about Whitewater. He ordered FBI agents to question troopers about 15 extramarital affairs that Clinton allegedly had as governor. One of the troopers told the *Washington Post*, "I was left with the impression that [the FBI] wanted to show he was a womanizer. All they wanted to talk about was women."[53] Once Starr moved from following the money to following the honey, he was bound to find something on Bill Clinton.

In the year before the 1994 midterm elections, the press ran more news stories about Whitewater than on Clinton's domestic agenda.[54] That November, the Republicans won both houses of Congress for the first time in 40 years. With control of the House of Representatives, Republicans had the power to impeach the president, and they were determined to find a way to use it. Incoming House Speaker Newt Gingrich announced his plans to have 20 congressional committees simultaneously investigating the Clinton administration, which he called "the enemy of normal Americans."[55] Gingrich's committees were soon investigating Whitewater, Travelgate, Filegate, Vince Foster's suicide and Troopergate.[56]

Meanwhile, Brock's Troopergate article in *American Spectator* set off another chain of events that would shape history. The article briefly mentioned that a young woman, identified only as Paula, attracted Governor Clinton's attention at an event in Little Rock's Excelsior Hotel on May 8, 1991. Clinton allegedly ordered a trooper to approach Paula and invite her up to a room where he was waiting. "After her encounter with Clinton, which lasted no more than an hour as the trooper stood by in the hall," Brock panted, "the trooper said Paula told him she was available to be Clinton's regular girlfriend if he so desired."[57] The woman in the article was Paula Corbin, who had subsequently married a failed movie actor named Steve Jones. Encouraged by her financially strapped husband, in May 1994 Paula Jones slapped the president with a $700,000 sexual harassment lawsuit.

Jones claimed that in the hotel room Clinton "began pulling me over like he has done this a million times and grabs me and pulls me over to him to the windowsill and tries to kiss me and just didn't ask me or nothing." According to Jones, Clinton pulled his pants down, sat down on the couch and asked, "Would you kiss it for me?" Paula protested, "I'm not that kind of girl!" and left the room.[58] Paula's sister Charlotte gave a different version of the story, "She just said he'd invited her up to the hotel room and that while she was up there, he asked her to do oral sex and she refused. She was excited; she was in no way upset."[59]

There were serious problems with Jones's claims, including the fact that Clinton was not in the hotel at the time she said their encounter occurred. But her problematic timeline did not stop the *Washington Post*'s Michael Isikoff from pursuing her story. Like his college heroes, Woodward and Bernstein, Isikoff appeared out to nail a president, one way or another.[60]

Since the 1960s, the feminist movement and public awareness about sexual harassment had changed the rules of behavior between men and women. What had been considered a "pass" or "flirting" in Kennedy's day had become grounds for a lawsuit by the 1990s. In the wake of Jones's accusations, the National Organization for Women (NOW) declared, "Sexual harassers are everywhere—in high public positions, in executive suites, and even in pulpits, . . . every Paula Jones deserves to be heard, no matter how old she is and how long ago the incident occurred, no matter what kind of accent she has or how much money she makes, and no matter whom she associates with."[61] While during the Cold War, no lawyer with any credibility would have sued the president over sex, now sexual harassment laws offered Paula Jones a legal avenue to avenge whatever happened in Clinton's hotel room. A conservative organization called the Rutherford Institute paid the way, funding her flimsy case's legal bills all the way to the Supreme Court.

To buttress her allegations, Jones said she could identify a peculiar bend to Clinton's penis.[62] The press speculated that the president suffered from a condition known as Peyronie's disease, which causes plaque or hard lumps to form on the penis and gives it a crooked shape when erect. Talk about the president's penis became so widespread that on October 10, 1997, Clinton's lawyer Bob Bennett went on CBS's *Face the Nation* and assured the American public that "in terms of size, shape, direction, whatever the devious mind wants to concoct, the president is a normal man."[63] Bennett then had his client undergo an examination that found no sign of curvature.[64] The conservative *Washington Times* broke the story about the president's unusual medical inspection on October 15 but added, "Definitive diagnosis is possible only when an erection is induced . . . and it was learned that this was not done at Mr. Clinton's examination."[65] Conservative media outlets then began claiming that Clinton must have undergone surgery to hide the problem.[66] Needless to say, the press in JFK's era never would have discussed the commander in chief's boner.

Since the foundation of the Republic, no one had ever been able to bring a civil suit against a sitting president because there was an assumption that national security depended on the chief executive being free of distraction. The Supreme Court even ruled in 1982 that a sitting president had immunity from civil suits relating to his official duties. But the end of the Cold War diminished popular anxiety over distractions to the president. In January 1997, the Supreme Court unanimously ruled in *Jones v. Clinton* that the president was not immune from civil suits related to his private conduct before he took office.[67] Clinton called the ruling "one of the most naïve decisions in the history of the Supreme Court."[68] The *New York Post* ran a gleeful headline, "Grin and Bare It," and stated that since Jones observed "distinguishing characteristics" on the president's genitals, she should "go into a deposition and ask the president to drop his pants."[69] With Congress, Ken Starr, Michael Isikoff and Paula Jones's well-funded legal team all peeping into Clinton's personal life, by 1997 the stage was set for someone to uncover his ongoing fling with Monica Lewinsky.

PRESIDENTIAL KNEEPADS

Monica Lewinsky would not have gone to Washington in the summer of 1995 had the 22-year-old not been having an affair with an older man in Los Angeles named Andy Bleiler, a married, ponytailed theater technician at her former high school in Beverly Hills. In a desperate attempt to split them up, her mother asked a friend who was a big Democratic contributor to get

Lewinsky a White House internship.[70] According to Bleiler's wife, Lewinsky spitefully announced that she was heading to Washington with her "presidential kneepads."[71]

Newt Gingrich was indirectly responsible for Bill and Lewinsky's first hookup in November 1995. He tried to force Clinton to make Medicare cuts by halting funding for the entire federal government. The resulting government shutdown left the White House with a skeleton staff and everyone in the West Wing working overtime, from the president down to the interns. On the night of November 15, a small group of interns were answering the phones in the chief of staff's office when Clinton walked in. Lewinsky looked up and noticed the president smiling at her. Over the next few hours, Clinton wandered down the hallway toward Lewinsky's desk so often another intern joked, "He must have a crush on Monica."[72]

Later that evening, Lewinsky happened to walk past the inner office of the West Wing and spotted Clinton by himself; she playfully lifted the jacket of her blue pantsuit to flash the straps of her thong and her bare upper rump. She later recalled that this "subtle, flirtatious gesture" elicited "an appreciate look" from the president. A few minutes later, Clinton beckoned her into his study, where they kissed. Lewinsky remembered "a softness and tenderness about him, his eyes were very soul-searching, very wanting, very needing and very loving. There was, too, a sadness about him that I hadn't expected to see."[73] They went back to work, and a few hours later, the president returned to summon the intern back to his darkened study.

Two nights later, Lewinsky performed oral sex on Clinton while he talked on the telephone with two members of Congress. He stopped her as he approached climax; he had somehow convinced himself that oral sex wasn't cheating if it ceased before completion.[74] As she left the room, Clinton tugged at the pink intern pass hanging from her neck: "This could be a problem," he said.[75]

For the next year and a half, Monica and Bill continued their clandestine hookups, which, by Ken Starr's sweaty count, totaled 9 physical encounters and 15 phone-sex conversations. Except for two occasions, Clinton was careful not to allow Lewinsky to bring him to a climax—often finishing himself off in a wastepaper basket or sink. On one occasion, they embraced afterward and Clinton left two tiny spots on Lewinsky's size 12, blue Gap dress.[76] That night, the one piece of evidence that eventually proved the president had a sexual relationship with an intern wound up in a heap at the back of Lewinsky's closet.

Of all the willing women in Washington, why Lewinsky? She was not particularly smart, beautiful or sexy. She was no Ellen Rometsch. She did, however, possess a youthful spirit that charmed the lonely president. "We enjoyed talking with each other and being with each other. We were very affectionate," Lewinsky recalled. "We would tell jokes. We would talk about our childhoods, talk about current events. I was always telling him my stupid ideas about what I thought should be done in the administration, or different views of things. I think back on it and he always made me smile when I was with him. . . . He was sunshine."[77] Clinton mused to Lewinsky about settling down with her after he left the White House and gave her gifts like *Leaves of Grass,* Walt Whitman's poems of unspeakable erotic love. Monica dreamed that one day Bill would dump Hillary and they would be free to tell the world about their storybook romance.

Like Alexander Hamilton with Maria Reynolds, Clinton fell into a foolish relationship due to a combination of lust and vanity. He felt entitled to a little extramarital sex. After all, he was the president of the world's only superpower, he was waging a wearying battle to defend Medicare from Newt Gingrich, and he was building a bridge to the twenty-first century. For all he had done and was doing for his country he deserved Lewinsky and more.

As is often the case, the sexual thrill died for Clinton within a few months of their first hookup. But he could not break off the relationship. "I formed an opinion early in 1996," he later said, "that she would talk about it. Not because Monica Lewinsky is a bad person. She's basically a good girl . . . but I knew that the minute there was no longer any contact, she would talk about this. She would have to. She couldn't help it. It was part of her psyche."[78] Even as the Supreme Court was preparing to hand down its Paula Jones verdict in the spring of 1997, Clinton continued to see Lewinsky, partly because he enjoyed her, partly because he feared her. Like Hamilton, Clinton made the calculated decision to keep up the relationship and risk the chance of discovery rather than break it off and definitely get caught. Keeping Lewinsky happy, however, did not keep her quiet; she gave her mother, her aunt and several friends regular updates on her affair with the president from November 1995 until March 1997.

As with past presidential mistresses, for example, Nan Brittan and Lucy Mercer, the Secret Service guards were well aware of Lewinsky's covert White House visits. When she showed up at the front gates on weekends, guards amused themselves by betting on how many minutes it would take before their computers flashed that the president was leaving the residence for the West Wing.[79] Harold Ickes and a uniformed Secret Service officer once entered the Oval Office while Clinton was in the adjoining study receiving a "Lewinsky" during a telephone conversation with political consultant Dick Morris. As in a door-slamming scene in a French farce, Ickes bellowed, "Mr. President!" Clinton pulled up his pants and rushed out one door while Lewinsky stole out the other.[80]

A Secret Service officer complained in April 1996 to deputy chief of staff Evelyn Lieberman, a close friend of Hillary's, about Lewinsky's visits. Lieberman immediately transferred Lewinsky to a job at the Defense Department. Had Lewinsky been transferred to the State Department or any other government office, America probably would have never heard of Monica Lewinsky. Unfortunately, at the Pentagon, the lovesick young intern began spilling her heart to a nosy 47-year-old coworker named Linda Tripp.

Tripp had previously worked in the White House under George Bush and Bill Clinton. Even before Lewinsky arrived at the Pentagon, she was in discussions with a New York literary agent to write a tell-all book about Vince Foster's death and Clinton's rampant flirting in the West Wing. Tripp scrapped the project after realizing she was not going to get a big enough book advance to risk her government job. As soon as Lewinsky shared her tale of presidential forbidden love, Tripp was back on the phone with her literary agent, Lucianne Goldberg.

Goldberg's motto in life was "I love dish. I live for dish."[81] She specialized in representing writers whom reputable agents wouldn't touch, one being detective Mark Fuhrman of O. J. Simpson fame. She began her career as a scandalmonger during the 1972 election when she worked for Nixon's dirty tricks operation as a mole in Democrat George McGovern's campaign. She said she kept Nixon apprised of "who was sleeping with who, what the Secret Service men were doing with the stewardesses, who was smoking pot on the plane—that sort of thing."[82] Goldberg claimed that every night her memos were driven over to the White House: "What Nixon really wanted to hear was the dirty jokes."[83]

Goldberg explained to Tripp that the problem with trying to sell a book about a love affair between a president and an intern was that no publisher would believe it. She advised Tripp to get evidence by recording Lewinsky talking about her affair. Like a two-bit J. Edgar Hoover, Tripp used a $100 Radio Shack recording device to secretly tape dozens of phone conversations with Lewinsky.[84] Goldberg meanwhile consulted with her client Mark Fuhrman about how to collect a DNA sample from the blue Gap dress. On Goldberg's advice, Tripp convinced Lewinsky not to wash the dress, and the two older women plotted to sneak into Lewinsky's apartment to swipe it.[85] Tripp and Goldberg hatched a plan that would throw a young woman, full of life and love, to the wolves. Lewinsky was no innocent, but at least she had a heart and a soul.

Destroying the life of a young woman was not enough for Goldberg, who also used Lewinsky to take down the Democratic president. On her literary agent's advice, in November 1997 Tripp tipped off Paula Jones's lawyers about Lewinsky. Jones's attorneys put Lewinsky and Tripp on their witness list to show a pattern of Clinton sexual activity with underlings. Goldberg also had Tripp tell Michael Isikoff about Lewinsky.[86] Isikoff, now at *Newsweek,* had quit the *Washington Post* because his editors refused to print his scandalous stories about the president and Paula Jones. Goldberg knew Isikoff would run with the Lewinsky story. Her plan was to have Isikoff take the initial heat for exposing the scandal and then have Tripp publish the book that filled in the details.[87] As her plot began to unfold, Goldberg exclaimed, "My tabloid heart beats loud!"[88]

On Goldberg's advice, Tripp also tipped off Ken Starr's office about Lewinsky on January 4, 1998. After failing to find any criminal evidence in the Whitewater investigation, the special prosecutors saw Lewinsky as their last chance to catch the president in a criminal act—even if it hadn't happened yet. Clinton was scheduled to testify in a deposition for the Jones lawsuit, about Lewinsky and other women on January 17. Starr's team knew he was going to lie about sex with the intern and quickly came up with a plan to trap the president.[89] On January 13, they put a body wire on Tripp and had her engage Monica in a conversation over lunch about lying in an affidavit for the Jones case. Lewinsky was also recorded talking about how Clinton's friend Vernon Jordan helped her get a job in New York.

With evidence of perjury and conspiracy, Starr's team had Tripp schedule a second lunch date with Lewinsky at the Pentagon City Mall on January 16, the day before Clinton's deposition. FBI agents and six prosecutors swooped down on Lewinsky on her way to the food court and escorted her up to a room at the Ritz Carlton. A prosecutor told Lewinsky that she faced charges for perjury, obstruction of justice, subornation of perjury, witness tampering and conspiracy; altogether she could expect to serve 27 years in prison, and her mother might also see jail time. She could avoid prosecution, however, if she wore a wire and recorded incriminating conversations with Clinton's secretary Betty Currie, Vernon Jordan and the president. Lewinsky had the presence of mind to immediately ask to speak to her attorney. Starr's team, however, knew her attorney would pull her out of the room, and she might then warn Clinton not to lie when he was deposed by Jones's attorneys the next day.[90] So the prosecutors delayed calling her attorney's office until 5:23, by which time her lawyer had left for the weekend. When Lewinsky asked to call her mother for advice, a prosecutor sneered, "You're twenty-four, you're smart, you're old enough. You don't need to call your mommy."[91] Starr's team held Lewinsky in the hotel room for the next several hours waiting for her mother to travel down from New York to collect her emotionally distraught daughter. As the hours passed, the frightened, humiliated young woman thought about hurling herself out the window in an attempt to save Clinton.[92]

If there is any hero in this saga, it's Monica Lewinsky, who withstood hours of badgering by FBI agents and prosecutors yet steadfastly refused to entrap the president. Had Lewinsky worn a wire and caught Clinton on tape suborning perjury, it is hard to imagine he would have survived politically. The 24-year-old might have jeopardized Clinton's presidency, but she also saved it.

Over a dozen Clinton enemies knew the president was walking into a legal trap when he showed up for his Paula Jones deposition the next morning, and they all rejoiced when he said under oath that he did not have sexual relations with Monica Lewinsky.

The day Clinton was deposed, Isikoff was prepared to run with his juicy scoop about the president and the intern, but *Newsweek*'s editors decided not to jeopardize the presidency over sex and spiked his story. Isikoff pleaded with his editors, "Human lives are not at stake here. The national security isn't hanging in the balance. Why the hell shouldn't we publish this?"[93] Bitter and disappointed, Isikoff informed Goldberg that his story was not going to run after all. Goldberg still wanted to get the Lewinsky story out, so she leaked it to Matt Drudge, a 31-year-old blogger who lived in a $600-per-month apartment in Los Angeles.[94]

Dubbing himself "a modern day Walter Winchell," Drudge had skipped college and worked in a CBS gift shop before launching the Drudge Report in 1995. Unlike the *Newsweek* editors, the blogger felt no qualms about destroying a presidency over sex. In the early morning hours of January 19, 1998, the Drudge Report blared the headline, "NEWSWEEK KILLS STORY ON WHITE HOUSE INTERN BLOCKBUSTER REPORT: 23-YEAR-OLD, FORMER WHITE HOUSE INTERN, SEX RELATIONS WITH PRESIDENT."

After breaking the Lewinsky story, the Drudge Report's viewership skyrocketed from hundreds to millions. Drudge became a media celebrity and made the talk show circuit wearing his trademark Walter Winchell fedora. Speaking at the National Press Club in Washington, Drudge pronounced the death of establishment journalism. The public has "a hunger for unedited information. We have entered an era vibrating with the din of small voices. Every citizen can be a reporter. The Net gives as much voice to a computer geek like me as to a CEO or a Speaker of the House. We all become equal. Now with a modem, anyone can follow the world and report on the world—no middle man, no Big Brother."[95] In the Internet age, the media establishment could no longer filter the news and tell the masses what they needed to know. Now people could get what they wanted to know with the click of a mouse.[96] Like his hero Walter Winchell, Drudge was both the herald of a new era of American journalism and a throwback to the early American scandalmongers.

It took the old media establishment a few days to catch up with the Drudge Report. But once that happened, few members of the press could resist hyperventilating over Lewinsky. Competing cable news programs filled the 24-hour-news cycle with endless lineups of pundits claiming the intern sex scandal would bring down the president. ABC News veteran Sam Don-aldson predicted, "Mr. Clinton, if he's not telling the truth and the evidence shows that, will resign, perhaps this week." ABC's George Will pronounced the Clinton presidency "dead, deader really than Woodrow Wilson's was after he had a stroke." Former Clinton advisor-turned-ABC-commentator George Stephanopoulos raised the possibility of impeachment: "Is he telling the truth, the whole truth, and nothing but the truth? If he is, he can survive. If he isn't, he can't."[97]

Political consultant Dick Morris, who had been ousted from the 1996 Clinton reelection campaign over his own sex scandal, called the besieged president. "It occurred to me that I may be the only sex addict you know," Morris offered, "and maybe I can help you." "Ever since I was elected," Clin-ton sighed, "I've tried to shut my body down, I mean, sexually, and sometimes I just failed."[98] As with all of Clinton's political dilemmas, Morris's solution was to take a poll to figure out what to do.[99] Morris found that a majority thought Clinton should be impeached if he lied under oath and 35 percent thought he should go to jail. "They're just too shocked by this. It's just too new, it's just too raw," he explained to the president.[100] On the basis of Mor-ris's poll, the president formulated a strategy: lie, stonewall and survive long enough for the public to get over the shock.[101]

A week after Drudge posted the Lewinsky story, Clinton finally broke his silence on the matter, at the end of a January 26, 1998, press conference on child care. In a declaration that would go down in the annals of history, he huffed, "I want to say one thing to the American people. I want you to listen to me. I'm going to say this again. I did not have sexual relations with that woman . . . Miss Lewinsky. I never told anybody to lie, not a single time ever. These accusations are false. And I need to go back to work for the American people."[102] The next day Hillary Clinton channeled Betsy Hamilton during the Reynolds affair, and she dismissed the scandal as a plot by lying scoundrels to destroy her husband's good work. "Look at the very people who are in-volved," she told *Today Show* host Matt Lauer. "The great story here, for any-body who is willing to find it and write about it and explain it, is this vast *right-wing conspiracy* that has been conspiring against my husband since the day he announced for president."[103] Although the pundits dismissed Hillary's vast right-wing conspiracy theory as a political smoke screen, history has shown that she was totally right.

Bill Clinton may be known as the Comeback Kid, but Hillary's performance on the *Today Show* began one of the most remarkable political comebacks in history. Before the Lewinsky scandal, Hillary was very unpopular with the public, who found her too pushy, too involved in policy, too aggressive. She was the most slandered First Lady since Dolley Madison. But once she assumed the traditional role of the victimized but dutiful wife standing by her man, à la Tammy Wynette, she suddenly became enormously popular. When New York senator Daniel Patrick Moynihan announced he was giving up his Senate seat a year later, Congressman Charles Rangel urged the popular First Lady to run for senator in a state she had never lived in.

The rest of the world was baffled by the Lewinsky scandal, which the French dubbed *Le Zippergate*. Anne-Elisabeth Moutet, bureau chief for *European* magazine in London, wrote at the time, "It looked pretty ridiculous" to Europeans, who asked, "Why doesn't he have a normal relationship, with a nice, elegant, clever mistress who won't talk?" "We do not talk about politicians' private lives," Moutet sniffed. "President Francois Mitterrand had lots of mistresses and two regular mistresses, and every journalist in town, myself included, knew all about them, and we had the telephone numbers and we knew about the kids and everything. And we never wrote it. It was perfectly understood that nobody will back you up. The public will hate you to kingdom come. Do not talk about politicians' private lives."[104] Moutet added, "Besides, the French like their leaders to have a sex drive." Popular Russian daily *Komsomolskaya Pravda* accurately predicted "the next American president will be a closed and sullen prude. This is the lesson from the long-suffering Bill Clinton." An American reporter in the Netherlands reported that when CNN used the word "historic" to describe the scandal, his Dutch friends asked, "What sort of history do Americans learn in school?"

Philippine president Joseph Estrada, known for having numerous affairs while fathering 10 children with his wife, joked, "Clinton and I both have sex scandals—he has the scandals and I just have sex."

While the American debate over Monicagate focused on issues of privacy and morality, the world press was concerned about how the scandal was weakening the presidency. "We don't always agree with the Americans," said a French TV analyst, "but we don't win a thing when the world's leading power is sunk in the mire of scandal and low comedy. It's not good for democracy." Singapore's *Straits Times* fretted, "There is no doubt that a weakened presidency, its energy to deal with global issues sapped, is bad news for the world." "Even if Clinton survives, his presidency is already dead," lamented the Washington correspondent for Italy's *La Repubblica.* "The forecasts for autumn aren't good: tempest over Washington, rain on all of us."

Iraq's most influential newspaper, *Babel,* accused Lewinsky of being a Mossad agent in a plot to unseat Clinton and install Vice President Gore, "known for his pro-Zionist stand." But some foreign commentators admired the fact that America could put its leader on trial for sex. Jordan's *al-Arab al-Yawm* newspaper wrote, "In Third World countries, governed by demigods who have come to power on the backs of tanks and usurped power, no power on earth can bring the ruler, who considers himself the envoy of the divine power, to the courtroom until after he has fallen." A Chinese pedicab driver assured an American reporter that the Lewinsky scandal was "a great moment in American history. It shows two things—that Clinton can be exposed as a liar in front of everybody and that your country won't collapse because of it. This could never happen in China."[105]

The U.S. public's reaction to Monicagate was closer to the blasé European press than America's frantic opinion makers. A week after the Lewinsky story broke, a *Washington Post* poll found Clinton's job approval rating at 67 percent, the highest of his presidency. The *Post* poll also found that even though a majority believed "something had happened" with Lewinsky, a majority thought Clinton's political enemies were "conspiring" to bring down the president. Two-thirds said they thought Clinton should stay in office even if an affair was proved. An ABC News/*Washington Post* survey found 56 percent thought the affair "was not an important issue."[106] Once the shock of the revelation passed, Clinton's poll numbers went even higher. By March 1998 his popular-approval rating soared to over 70 percent, while only 11 percent had a favorable view of Ken Starr. Clinton's strategy of stonewalling until the public got sick of the scandal worked.[107] Clinton told a friend, "The lie saved me."[108]

The president was on a trip to Africa in April 1998 when he heard that Judge Susan Webber Wright had dismissed the Paula Jones lawsuit. He figured he was out of the woods because his alleged perjury about Lewinsky had occurred in the Jones case. Fox News cameras peeping into his hotel room caught the president smoking a celebratory cigar and pounding a drum given to him during the trip. Clinton's celebration was woefully premature. An undeterred Ken Starr declared, "You cannot defile the temple of justice."[109] On July 28, Starr cut a deal with Lewinsky to testify under oath about her sexual activities with the president and to hand over the blue dress. In less than 24 hours the FBI determined that the whitish stains were positive for semen.[110]

Another major difference between Kennedy's and Clinton's eras was that J. Edgar Hoover was no longer running the FBI. As long as presidents gave Hoover what he wanted, the FBI director was always ready to shut down a brewing presidential scandal by intimidating journalists, publishers and congressmen. After Hoover's death, revelations about how presidents used the FBI to spy on political rivals led to reforms that gave the FBI director a greater degree of independence from the president. Now the FBI director served for a set tenure and could be fired by a president only for specific cause. When Clinton was looking for a new FBI director in 1993, he joked that it was going to be "hard to fill Hoover's pumps." He was right. His choice was Louis Freeh, a 41-year-old federal judge whom Clinton called a "boy scout."

"My job is not to make people happy," Freeh announced. "Or please them or be a loyal subordinate when that conflicts with what I think my job is."[111] Freeh's colleagues knew that Clinton's sexual infidelities outraged the devout Catholic FBI director, who embraced the Lewinsky investigation with determined fervor and assisted Ken Starr at every turn.[112] Deputy chief of staff John Podesta recalled that around the White House "Freeh's first name became 'Fucking' as in 'Fucking Freeh has screwed us again!'"[113] "That bastard is trying to sting us!" the president raged.[114] The head of the Secret Service, Lew Merletti, was furious that the FBI was spending so much time assisting Ken Starr when "what they should have been investigating was terrorism.

Chasing down Monica Lewinsky. A lot of good that did for us."[115] Clinton's head of counterterrorism, Richard Clarke, said, "Freeh should have spent his time fixing the mess that the FBI had become, an organization of fifty-six princedoms [independent field offices] without any modern information technology to support them. He might have spent some time hunting for terrorists in the United States, where al-Qaeda and its affiliates had put down roots, where many terrorist organizations were illegally raising money." Clarke said Clinton "should have fired Freeh and just taken the shit it would have caused."[116] But Freeh had become such a darling of the Right that if Clinton had fired his dangerously incompetent FBI director, he would have created yet another scandal.[117]

Once the FBI matched the semen on Lewinsky's dress with a blood sample from the president, Clinton had no choice but to finally come clean in testimony before Starr's grand jury. On August 17, 1998, the grand jury watched a closed circuit television feed of Clinton's four-hour deposition taken in the White House Map Room. In the same room where Franklin Roosevelt marked allied advances against the Axis powers, Clinton had to answer such questions as, "If Monica Lewinsky says that you ejaculated into her mouth on two occasions in the Oval Office area, would she be lying? . . . If Monica Lewinsky says that on several occasions you had her give oral sex, made her stop, and then ejaculated into the sink in the bathroom off the Oval Office, would she be lying? . . . If Monica Lewinsky says that you masturbated into a trashcan in your secretary's office, would she be lying? . . . If Monica Lewinsky says that you had phone sex with her, would she be lying? . . . If Monica Lewinsky says that you used a cigar as a sexual aid with her in the Oval Office area, would she be lying?"[118]

Clinton admitted that he had "inappropriate intimate physical contact" with Lewinsky, but stuck by his statement under oath in the Paula Jones deposition that he did not have sexual relations with her. It all depended on the definition of sexual relations, which the judge defined as "contact with the genitalia, anus, groin, breast, inner thigh, or buttocks of any person with an intent to arouse or gratify the sexual desire of any person." "If the deponent is the person who has oral sex performed on him," Clinton argued, "then contact is not with anything on that list, but with the lips of another person." One of the special prosecutors pointed out that Clinton's lawyer had assured the judge in the Paula Jones case that "there is no sex of any kind in any manner, shape, or form" between Clinton and Lewinsky. Clinton smirked and replied, "It depends on what the meaning of 'is' is . . . if 'is' means 'is and never has been,' that is one thing. If it means 'there is none,' that was a completely true statement."[119] With Lewinsky's testimony and Clinton's dodgy grand jury performance, Ken Starr had enough to accuse Clinton of perjury and obstruction of justice, and the congressional Republicans could finally get their wish: the impeachment of William Jefferson Clinton.

ENTER LARRY FLYNT

Even Ken Starr realized it was going to be impossible to eject Clinton from office through impeachment. By the fall of 1998 the public seemed to accept that their president lied under oath but made an allowance because he was lying about sex. The Republican majority in the House could impeach the president; but the Senate would never reach the two-thirds majority necessary to convict Clinton and remove him from office. Starr's last hope to eject the president from office was to produce a report with so many revolting details about the president's behavior that the public would demand his resignation.[120] On September 11, 1998, Starr's office released a 452-page report that included details such as "the President inserted a cigar into [Lewinsky's] vagina and then put the cigar in his mouth and said, 'It tastes good.'" Starr quoted Lewinsky verbatim: "We were kissing and he lifted my sweater and exposed my breasts and was fondling them with his hands and with his mouth."[121] Hundreds of newspapers posted the report on their websites, many displaying warnings like the *Denver Post*'s: "The following report contains material that readers may find offensive or objectionable."[122]

Starr's scheme worked with the press. In the wake of the public release of his report, over 65 major newspapers called on the president to resign. The *Los Angeles Times*, which had supported Clinton in the past, declared, "The picture of Clinton that now emerges is that of a middle-aged man with a pathetic inability to control his sexual fancies."[123] "Bill Clinton should resign," the *Philadelphia Inquirer* concluded. "He should resign because his repeated, reckless deceits have dishonored his presidency beyond repair."[124] "Character does matter, we've always known that," the *Pittsburgh Post-Gazette* contended. "A spontaneous and immediate resignation without histrionics is the only outcome that might salvage a measure of respect for [the president] and help the nation regain its moral bearings."[125]

Clinton's character mattered less to the American public than his economic record: a booming stock market, low unemployment, historically low inflation and higher household incomes across the economic spectrum. Crime under Clinton dropped for a record five years in a row while welfare rolls plummeted to their lowest levels in three decades.[126] Polls taken after the release of the Starr report revealed that Clinton's job-approval rating still hovered around 68 percent. A Gallup/CNN/*USA Today* poll asked, "Based on what you know at this point, do you think that Bill Clinton should or should not be impeached and removed from office?" and 66 percent said he "should not be." A *New York Times* poll found only 27 percent wanted to go forward with impeachment.[127]

If anyone was damaged by the Starr report it was the special prosecutor himself. Congressman John Conyers called Starr a "federally paid sex policeman."[128] The lawyer Alan Dershowitz dismissed the investigation as "sexual McCarthyism."

I called the Starr report "more depraved and scandalous" than anything Bill Clinton did.[129] I had already made history with the pink shot and two landmark Supreme Court free speech cases.[130] Now I decided to help save the president by fighting fire with fire. I knew the people on Capitol Hill were doing the same things they were trying to get Bill Clinton for. Hypocrisy never wins. So I took out a full-page ad in the *Washington Post* offering a million dollars to anyone who could supply "documentary evidence of illicit sexual relations" involving any member of Congress. Five days after Congress released the Starr report, *Salon* revealed that the leader of the House fight for impeachment, Congressman Henry Hyde, had engaged in an extramarital affair with a hairdresser back in the late 1960s. "Ugly times call for ugly tactics," a *Salon* editor explained.[131] Hyde turned out to be just one of many hypocrites on Capitol Hill.

Before the 1998 midterm election, Newt Gingrich allocated $10 million from the GOP war chest to highlight the Lewinsky scandal. He predicted that the Republicans would pick up 22 seats and told Clinton, "Mr. President we are going to run you out of town."[132] But that November, the American people rallied to their president and the Republicans lost four seats. For the first time since the Roosevelt administration, a party not occupying the White House failed to gain representatives in a midterm election. Two of Clinton's most fervent critics in the Senate lost their seats; Lauch Faircloth of North Carolina lost to John Edwards and Alphonse D'Amato lost to Chuck Schumer.

Facing a rebellion from the Republican caucus, Gingrich announced on November 6, 1998, that he would stand down as Speaker and resign from the House as well. After Gingrich left office he dumped his second wife and married a 27-year-old congressional aide, Callista Biesek, with whom he was carrying on an affair while he was waging his crusade against Clinton.[133]

When Congressman Bob Livingston was announced to replace Newt Gingrich as Speaker of the House in December 1998, I reported that Livingston engaged in numerous affairs, including one with a staff member. Livingston tried to deflect the charges by calling me a "bottom feeder." "Well, that's right," I replied. "But look what I found when I got down there." Years later Clinton told an interviewer, "The interesting thing was, Larry Flynt turned out to be a better guy than Ken Starr. I mean basically, the story was that Mrs. Livingston went to him and pleaded with him not to release any more details. And [he agreed to that after] Livingston resigned from Congress."[134] On December 19, 1998, Livingston announced his affairs and his resignation, and a couple of hours later the House of Representatives passed two articles of impeachment against Clinton—an awkward start to impeachment proceedings over a sex scandal.[135]

Bob Barr, one of the House managers who presented the case against Clinton to the Senate, also fell victim to my antihypocrisy campaign. I released transcripts of Barr's 1985 divorce proceeding in which Barr refused to answer whether he had cheated on his second wife with his soon-to-be third wife.[136] The Senate had its share of hypocrites too. Speaking on NBC's *Meet the Press*, Senator Larry Craig declared, "The American people already know that Bill Clinton is a bad boy—a naughty boy. I'm going to speak out for the citizens of my state, who in the majority think that Bill Clinton is probably even a nasty, bad, naughty boy." Craig was arrested in 2007 and charged with soliciting sex from a male undercover cop in an airport men's room.

On February 12, 1999, Clinton was acquitted in the Senate by a vote of 55 to 45 on a perjury count and 50 to 50 on an obstruction of justice count. Senate majority leader Republican Trent Lott was dumbfounded: "There are only a couple of political things in my career that I still have not been able to understand. One is the fact that the American people apparently continued to support Clinton throughout this whole thing, knowing what he did, knowing what he said, knowing how he had demeaned the office. . . . I still think history needs to try to explain why the American people thought that all that was okay."[137]

What Lott, Gingrich and Starr did not understand was that there was indeed a culture war and they lost. Americans were no longer disgusted by talk of oral sex in the Oval Office. They knew that plenty of presidents had affairs, including some of the heroes of American history. By the 1990s the so-called Moral Majority found themselves badly outnumbered.[138] The real majority chose peace, prosperity and privacy over hypocrisy posing as moral purity. Clinton did not charm his way out of impeachment nor did the Republicans fail because they were "mean." The impeachment of Bill Clinton failed because Americans thought their president was doing a good job. When Clinton left office he had the highest sustained approval ratings of any president since his hero John F. Kennedy.[139]

9/11 AND MONICAGATE

After Clinton gave his humiliating testimony to the grand jury in August 1998, he reminded the American people in a national address that "even presidents have private lives. It is time to stop the pursuit of personal destruction. Now it is time, in fact past time to move on! We have important work to do, real problems to solve, real security matters to face."[140] The United States did indeed have real security matters to face. America had been hit with numerous terrorist attacks while Clinton was in office: the 1993 World Trade Center bombing, the Oklahoma City bombing, the Unabomber, the 1996 Khobar Towers attack in Saudi Arabia, the 1996 Atlanta Olympic games, al-Qaeda's 1998 attacks on two U.S. embassies in Africa and the 2000 attack on the warship USS *Cole*. The public did not know that Osama Bin Laden tried to assassinate Clinton on two separate visits to the Philippines and had plans to kill him on a visit to Pakistan. The same month Clinton was impeached, he received a classified report, dated December 4, 1998, titled "Bin Laden preparing to Hijack US Aircraft and Other Attacks." While the Lewinsky affair consumed America in the winter of 1998, Osama Bin Laden approved the attacks that would kill 3,000 people on September 11, 2001.

For decades to come, historians will ask whether the Monica Lewinsky scandal made 9/11 possible. The scandal certainly was a major distraction to the president. One advisor said that sometimes Clinton "was there, but he really wasn't there. Either he was tired or distracted."[141] In the middle of the Lewinsky scandal, top military and national security advisors competed with Clinton's lawyers for meeting time with the president.[142] The record does, however, show that Clinton was determined to kill Bin Laden during the final two years of his presidency. He urged the chairman of the Joint Chiefs Hugh Shelton to attack al-Qaeda with special forces: "You know, it would scare the shit out of al Qaeda if suddenly a bunch of black ninjas rappelled out of helicopters into the middle of their camp."[143] Shelton and secretary of defense William Cohen rebuffed such an operation as impractical.[144]

Two weeks before his grand jury testimony, Clinton split his time between preparing for his grilling over Lewinsky and planning cruise missile attacks on a Sudanese pharmaceuticals factory with financial ties to al-Qaeda and on a terrorist training camp in Afghanistan. When Clarke warned the attacks might bring to mind the recently released film *Wag the Dog*, in which a president distracts the public from a sex scandal by launching a phony war against Albania, Clinton snapped, "Do you all recommend that we strike? Fine. Don't give me political advice or personal advice about timing. That's my problem."[145] Despite Clinton's determination to kill Bin Laden, according to the 9/11 Commission the failure of the cruise missile attacks and concerns about being accused of wagging the dog chastened the White House and inhibited further combat operations against America's number-one enemy.[146]

Clinton is not the only one to blame for the Lewinsky scandal hamstringing the presidency during this crucial time. Gingrich and the Republicans needlessly prolonged the Monicagate distraction with their futile impeachment crusade. The media also bears blame for focusing for so long on the titillating yet trivial Lewinsky story. Ultimately, we ordinary Americans are to blame for allowing our leaders and ourselves to become diverted by a sexual sideshow rather than focusing on the mounting threat to American lives.

CONCLUSION

FULFILLING
THE PLEDGE

From the very beginning of the American Republic, our leaders' sex lives have shaped our nation's history, for better and for worse. Ben Franklin's well-earned reputation as a ladies' man aided his effort to secure France's military assistance during the Revolutionary War. On the other hand, James Buchanan's gay love affair with a slave owner made him a slavery apologist who encouraged secessionists on the eve of the Civil War. Franklin and Eleanor Roosevelt's affairs helped them become great leaders who guided America through the dark days of the Depression and World War II. At the same time, J. Edgar Hoover was using his sex files on America's power elite to torment his opponents and undermine the Constitution.

It is highly disturbing to know that the sex lives of our leaders have had such a dramatic impact on everything from economic policies to wars. After all, few forces are as powerful as the human sex drive. Both Robert Kennedy and Martin Luther King Jr. knew they were under FBI surveillance but continued to carry on affairs that jeopardized their careers and their crusades. Presidential flings changed the course of history regardless of whether they remained secret, like JFK's, or were exposed to the nation, like Bill Clinton's. When the human sex drive is combined with a political system that endows single individuals with the power to shape the history of the world on a whim, we have a potentially explosive situation. So what can we do to prevent something as volatile as sexual desire from affecting our public life? If history is any guide, the answer is absolutely nothing.

Americans must come to terms with a simple fact: since the dawn of the Republic, politicians have been screwing around, and they always will be. Why would brilliant men and women with grand ambitions and historic plans risk a lifetime of hard work for an hour of pleasure? The answer can be found in the essential connection between political ambition and sexual conquest. Psychologists have identified a risk-taking, sensation-seeking personality type that is attributed to low levels of monoamine oxidase A (MAOA), an enzyme that regulates important neurotransmitters like dopamine. People with lower MAOA have a greater tendency to put themselves in new, exhilarating situations even if they are dangerous. They are more easily bored by repetition and routine both in the workplace and in their personal lives. In general, men have lower MAOA than women, and young people have lower MAOA than old people. But certain individuals with especially low MAOA are neurologically drawn to risky thrills.[1] Such sensation-seekers are often attracted to political careers along with reckless sexual behavior. The same man who hungers for adoring crowds hanging on his every word will also tend to seek the thrill of extramarital sex.[2] Combine this psychological tendency with the manifold sexual opportunities open to even the lowliest politician, and what do you think is going to happen? Ironically, the same biochemical drive that impels a politician to dedicate his life to winning the presidency will also get him impeached over sex with an intern.

The nature of our democratic government breeds risk-taking, promiscuous leaders. "We love charismatic people, the 'micro-messiahs,'" says University of Washington political scientist John Gastil. "We favor the candidates who are already concerned with projecting certainty and power and strength—and we cultivate those characteristics in people. We want a little bit of that sense that these people are special and different. Does that go to their heads? Of course it does."[3] A Fortune 500 CEO has to answer to a board of directors, but even a state assemblyman is an absolute master of his little universe. Every day he is surrounded by staff constantly telling him he is right about everything. When a politician gets caught in an affair, people often ask,

"Does this guy think the rules don't apply to him?" Well, that is exactly what he thinks. To get the sex out of politics, America would have to take the politicians out of government and create a political system like the old Soviet Union in which dutiful apparatchiks got to the top by quietly doing their bureaucratic jobs year after year. But who wants that?

We might not be able to prevent our leaders from being sexually reckless, but we can prevent their sex scandals from diverting our attention from the real problems at hand. We, the people, need to grow up and understand that our politicians are adults with intense sex drives. We need to be more like the Europeans, who just assume their leaders are promiscuous.[4] At the nationally televised funeral of French President François Mitterrand in 1996, the church procession was led by his wife—who was followed by his mistress and illegitimate daughter. Photos of Mitterrand's wife and mistress standing side by side at his gravesite appeared on the front pages of all the French newspapers. The French were outraged—not over the infidelity but over the violation of the dead president's privacy. Nicolas Sarkozy was elected president of France in 2007 even though he was widely known as a *chaud lapin,* or "hot bunny." Months after his election, the French shrugged with disinterest when Sarkozy divorced his second wife and married a new first lady of France, Carla Bruni, former model and ex-girlfriend to Mick Jagger, Eric Clapton, former French prime minister Laurent Fabius and many others. "I am a tamer of men, a cat, an Italian. . . . Monogamy bores me terribly," Bruni told *Le Figaro* in 2007. "I am monogamous from time to time but I prefer polygamy and polyandry."[5] Imagine if an American First Lady said that.

Look at the Italians' indifferent reaction to news in 2009 that their 72-year-old prime minister Silvio Berlusconi was having sex with numerous young women, including an 18-year-old lingerie model. When a prostitute released tapes of her romps with the married Italian PM, he didn't deny the sex; he denied that he had to pay for it. "I've never paid a woman," Berlusconi said. "I never understood where the satisfaction is when you're missing the pleasure of conquest."[6] Months later, Italian voters handed Berlusconi's party a landslide victory in the 2009 provincial elections. Berlusconi, the second-longest-serving prime minister in Italian history, finally got into political trouble in late 2010 only after a series of corruption and abuse of power scandals involving young women combined with Italy's failing economy.

If Americans adopted a more mature, European approach to the private lives of their leaders, we would be a lot less distracted by political sex scandals, and the nation would be on the road to a more mature approach to politics in general.

Moralism has poisoned the American political system since the late 1970s, when the Christian Right, led by Jerry Falwell's Moral Majority and later by James Dobson's Focus on the Family, began pushing moral issues to the forefront of the national political discussion. The Republican Party shrewdly took up fights against abortion, gay rights and sex education to pull ordinary Americans away from the Democratic Party. Working people were duped into believing that Republicans stood for Joe the Plumber and that Democrats catered to an immoral cultural elite. While everyone was distracted by debates about moral values, Ronald Reagan, Newt Gingrich and George W. Bush bulldozed financial regulations and social protections left over from the Progressive Era and the New Deal. The result was a disastrous transformation of the American economic system.

Between the late 1940s and the early 1970s, America experienced broad-based prosperity that saw incomes of all economic groups rise at roughly the same steady rate, more than 2.5 percent annually. But around 1979 top incomes began rising much faster while the middle class experienced slower growth and the lower class actually saw a decline in real wages. The rich got richer while the average American got the shaft. By 2007 the top 10 percent of American earners pulled in 49.7 percent of the nation's total wages, a proportion higher than any other year since 1917.[7] While income disparity reached Gilded Era proportions, deregulation of the banking industry further benefited the wealthy and turned the American financial system into a house of cards. When the system finally crashed in 2008, the government was forced to give the big banks a trillion-dollar bailout. While the seeds of our current economic crisis were being sown during the past few decades, the big domestic issues that grabbed the public's attention were abortion, Monica Lewinsky and gay marriage. It is no coincidence that America began adopting inequitable, self-defeating economic policies at the same time that moral issues began dominating the national political debate and distracting voters from what really matters.

Since moralism helped get us into this mess, we believe that ridding American politics of moralism is the first step to putting the national house in order. A recent spate of political sex scandals has begun the process by undercutting the notion that either party has a monopoly on family values. Democratic New Jersey governor Jim McGreevey resigned in 2004 after admitting an affair with a male underling. Two years later, Republican congressman Mark Foley of Florida, an outspoken opponent of child pornography and chairman of the House Caucus on Missing and Exploited Children, was caught sending sexually explicit texts about masturbation to teenage congressional pages. The following year, in 2007, Louisiana's Republican senator David Vitter was discovered on the client list of the DC Madam, Deborah Jeane Palfrey. Also in 2007, Republican senator Larry Craig of Idaho got caught playing footsie with an undercover cop in a Minneapolis airport bathroom stall. Democratic New York governor Elliot Spitzer resigned in 2008 after he was reported to have frequently engaged in unprotected sex with prostitutes, always while wearing his black socks. Then, in 2009, Americans watched South Carolina's Republican governor Mark Sanford cry his eyes out over his Argentinean mistress during a press conference. Later that year, GOP senator John Ensign of Nevada confessed an affair with the wife of his good friend, who was also his administrative aide. Former Democratic senator John Edwards admitted in January 2010 that he fathered a child with his mistress while he was running for president and his wife was recovering from cancer. A month later, Democratic New York congressman Eric Massa resigned after admitting he engaged in tickle fights with his male staffers and that he delighted in giving men "Massa Massages."

The funny thing is that the sheer number of revelations about politicians over such a short period has inured Americans to the shock of political sex scandals. While closeted politicians who get caught in compromising situations never really recover in the public eye, affairs with mistresses or even prostitutes are no longer a huge deal. Carl Paladino, the Tea Party candidate for governor of New York in 2010, admitted that a decade ago he fathered a love child with one of his employees. Paladino had introduced his three grown children to their young sibling, but for a decade he hid the secret of the child's birth from his wife. Only after he decided to run for governor did he tell his wife about his 10-year-old daughter.[8] Although the story of Paladino's unconventional personal life was widely reported in New York, he won the Republican Party gubernatorial nomination in a landslide. Even the whoremongering senator from Louisiana, David Vitter, routed his opponent in the 2010 Republican primary and won a landslide victory to reclaim his Senate seat. CNN meanwhile has given client number 9, Elliot Spitzer, his own primetime political talk show. The old line that a politician could survive a sex scandal unless he was caught in bed with a dead girl or a live boy has now become a fact in American life.

Throughout history we have seen how politicians have used sex to destroy their political enemies. Thomas Jefferson exposed Alexander Hamilton's affair with Maria Reynolds to foil his plans to modernize the banking system and industrialize the economy. Joe McCarthy went after pinks and pansies in the Truman administration to halt 20 years of Democratic rule in the White House. J. Edgar Hoover collected dirt on every powerful person in America and tried to destroy Martin Luther King Jr. In our own time, Newt Gingrich and the House Republicans sabotaged Bill Clinton's presidency with a futile impeachment fight about Monica Lewinsky. In each of these historical examples, the accusers were eventually exposed for being guilty of their own sexual indiscretions. As Hamilton once said, "How often the hypocrite goes from stage to stage of public fame, under false array, and how often when men attained the last object of their wishes, they change from that which they seemed to be."[9]

Today's new moralistic crusade against homosexuals and gay rights certainly has its fair share of hypocrites. Ted Haggard, the leader of the National Association of Evangelicals (NAE), was a leading voice against gay rights until 2006 when a gay escort and masseur, Mike Jones, alleged that Haggard responded to his ad on the website Rentboy.com and repeatedly paid for sex and crystal meth over a three-year period. "I needed to expose what was happening," Jones explained. "You can't say one thing and do another. There are consequences to your actions."[10] Haggard resigned from NAE and underwent three weeks of counseling, after which his pastor pronounced him "completely heterosexual."[11] Another fan of Rentboy.com was 61-year-old Reverend George Rekers, a psychologist and founder of the antigay Family Research Council. Rekers was the "scientific" advisor to the National Association for Research and Therapy of Homosexuality, which champions the "gay cure," converting homosexuals to heterosexuality. In April 2010 the *Miami New Times* caught Rekers returning from a 10-day European vacation with gay escort Jo-vanni Roman. Rekers admitted he found Roman on Rentboy.com but claimed he did not notice that Roman's profile boasted about his "smooth, sweet, tight ass" and his "perfectly built, nine inch cock (uncut)." Rekers tried to explain that he innocently hired Roman to accompany him to Europe just to "carry my luggage."[12]

Americans need to adopt one simple rule: Don't trust anyone who dedicates his or her life to stomping out other people's consensual sexual activities—it is pretty much guaranteed that lurking behind all the antisex zealotry are deep-seated sexual issues. What our straight readers need to do is follow the examples of Franklin Roosevelt and John Kennedy, who were both so secure in their heterosexuality that they did not discriminate against their openly gay friends.

We urge our gay readers, particularly the young ones, to take heart from the examples of Frederick von Steuben, Abraham Lincoln and Eleanor Roosevelt, who all enjoyed intimate relationships with people of the same sex. These three heroes stepped up to help save America when it was on the brink of destruction, and now America needs you. The old judgments are dying; you have the opportunity to not only live openly but also fight proudly to make the United States a more perfect union. We know it is not easy to defy convention and stand up to discrimination, but keep in mind that time is on your side.

America now averages one political sex scandal every six months. Fortunately, this steady stream of political sex scandals has begun to counteract three decades of moralistic propaganda. It has become harder and harder for conservative politicians to beat the drum of moral values when their closeted and adulterous colleagues are being constantly outed. How many more Ted Haggards, David Vitters, Larry Craigs and Mark Sanfords will it take before the American public sees the family values trope for what it is—a cynical attempt to distract voters from what really matters: securing economic prosperity, protecting American lives and making sound decisions about war and peace. Only then can we start confronting our nation's real problems. As soon as Americans finally realize that we really do live in one nation, under sex, we will be able to fulfill the promise of the Pledge of Allegiance and achieve liberty and justice for all.

NOTES

INTRODUCTION

1. Gore Vidal, *Palimpsest: A Memoir* (London: Andre Deutsch, 1995), 147.

CHAPTER 1: FOUNDING FLIRTS AND FORNICATORS

1. William Seale, *The President's House: A History* (Washington, DC: White House Historical Association with National Geographic Society, 1986), 1:66.
2. Andrew Burstein, *Jefferson's Secrets: Death and Desire at Monticello* (New York: Basic Books, 2005), 151.
3. Stacy Schiff, *A Great Improvisation: Franklin, France, and the Birth of America* (New York: Holt, 2005), 2.
4. Walter Isaacson, *Benjamin Franklin: An American Life* (New York: Simon & Schuster, 2003), 326.
5. John Adams to Abigail Adams, quoted in Schiff, 52.
6. Schiff, 52.
7. Jon Kukla, *Mr. Jefferson's Women* (New York: Knopf, 2007), 153.
8. J. P. Brissot de Warville, *New Travels in the United States of America, 1788* (New York: T. and J. Swords, 1795), quoted in Kukla, 153.
9. Kukla, 153. Jefferson complained that "the manners of the nation allow women to visit among all persons in office, to solicit the affairs of the husband, family or friends, and their solicitations bid defiance to laws and regulations." He also noted, "Our good ladies have been too wise to wrinkle their foreheads with politics." Kukla, 155–156.
10. Edmund S. Morgan, *Benjamin Franklin* (New Haven, CT: Yale Univ. Press, 2002), 3; Claude-Anne Lopez, *Mon Cher Papa: Franklin and the Ladies of Paris* (New Haven, CT: Yale Univ. Press, 1966), 20; David Schoenbrun, *Triumph in Paris: The Exploits of Benjamin Franklin* (New York: Harper & Row, 1976), 60.
11. Eric Burns, *Infamous Scribblers: The Founding Fathers and the Rowdy Beginnings of American Journalism* (New York: Public Affairs, 2006), 86–87.
12. *American Weekly Mercury,* 4 Feb. 1729; Isaacson, 61.
13. "Busy-Body," *American Weekly Mercury,* 4 Feb. 1729, quoted in Isaacson, 62.
14. *Pennsylvania Gazette,* 17 June 1731.
15. Ibid., 24 June 1731.
16. Franklin, "Speech of Polly Baker," *General Advertiser,* 15 Apr. 1747, quoted in H. W. Brands, *The First American: The Life and Times of Benjamin Franklin* (New York: Anchor Books, 2000), 569.
17. Isaacson, 121.
18. *The Works of Thomas Jefferson* (New York: Putnam, 1905), 12:111.
19. *Pennsylvania Gazette,* 7 Sept. 1731, quoted in Isaacson, 70.
20. *Pennsylvania Gazette,* 3 July 1731; Isaacson, 69.
21. Ben Franklin, "Advice to a Young Man on the Choice of a Mistress," 25 June 1754.
22. Jeffrey Pasley, *The Tyranny of the Printers: Newspaper Politics in the Early Republic* (Charlottesville: Univ. of Virginia Press, 2001), 52.
23. Burns, 93.
24. Benjamin Franklin, *The Autobiography of Benjamin Franklin* (London: J. Parson's, 1793), quoted in Brands, 108.
25. George Roberts to Robert Grafton, 9 October 1763, quoted in David Freeman Hawke, *Benjamin Franklin* (Old Saybrook, CT: Konecky & Konecky, 1976), 38.
26. Isaacson, 140–145.
27. Brands, 108.
28. Hawke, 38.
29. Isaacson, 216.
30. Benjamin Franklin, *Poor Richard's Almanac,* 1738.
31. Claude-Anne Lopez, "Why He Was a Babe Magnet," *Time,* 7 July 2003.
32. Isaacson, 243.
33. Thomas Jefferson to James Madison, 14 Feb. 1783, quoted in Hawke, 29.
34. Ronald W. Clark, *Benjamin Franklin: A Biography* (New York: Random House, 1983), 28.
35. John Adams to Abigail Adams, 25 Apr. 1778, quoted in Schiff, 160.
36. Isaacson, 330.
37. Lopez, "Why He Was a Babe Magnet."

38. Benjamin Franklin to Elizabeth Partridge, 11 October 1779, quoted in Clark, 311.
39. Adams Papers, quoted in Brands, 548.
40. Isaacson, 2.
41. Benjamin Franklin to Sally Franklin, 3 June 1779, quoted in Isaacson, 327.
42. Isaacson, 327.
43. Schiff, 3; Isaacson, 328.
44. Isaacson, 359.
45. Schiff, 176–177.
46. Benjamin Franklin to Madame Brillon, 27 July 1778, quoted in Isaacson, 360.
47. Madame Brillon to Benjamin Franklin, 3 Mar. 1778, quoted in Isaacson, 358.
48. Madame Brillon to Benjamin Franklin, Dec. 1778, quoted in Isaacson, 362.
49. Madame Brillon to Benjamin Franklin, 27 July 1778, quoted in Isaacson, 359.
50. Madame Brillon to Benjamin Franklin, 1778, quoted in Isaacson, 359–360.
51. Schiff, 179.
52. John Adams diary, quoted in Lopez *Mon Cher Papa: Franklin and the Ladies of Paris,* 42; Isaacson, 359 – 362; L.H. Butterfield ed., *The Diary and Autobiography of John Adams* (Cambridge: Harvard University Press, 1961) Vol 4, 46.
53. Andre Morellet, *Memoires inedits,* 2 vols. (Paris: Baudouin, 1823), 1:55.
54. Lopez, *Mon Cher Papa: Franklin and the Ladies of Paris,* 67.
55. Lopez, *Mon Cher Papa: Franklin and the Ladies of Paris,* 84.
56. Morellet, 1:141.
57. Isaacson, 364.
58. Schiff, 232.
59. John Adams, quoted in Brands, 557.
60. Brands, 562; Clark, 311.
61. Schiff, 404.
62. Anonymous letter to the prince of Hohenzollern-Hechingen, quoted in William Benemann, *Male-Male Intimacy in Early America* (New York: Harrington Park Press, 2006), 97.
63. Benemann, 96.
64. Schiff, 90.
65. Isaacson, 341.
66. Benemann, 100–113.
67. John Adams to Abigail Adams, 9 Jan. 1797, in John Kaminski, ed., *The Founders on the Founders: Word Portraits from the American Revolutionary Era* (Charlottesville: Univ. of Virginia Press, 2008), 200.
68. Thomas Fleming, *The Intimate Lives of the Founding Fathers* (New York: Smithsonian Books, 2009), 224–228.
69. Burns, 294.
70. Alexander Hamilton, "The Reynolds Pamphlet," Aug. 1797, quoted in Chernow, 364.
71. Willard Sterne Randall, *George Washington: A Life* (New York: Holt, 1997), 406.
72. Hamilton, "The Reynolds Pamphlet," quoted in Chernow, 364.
73. Alexander Hamilton to Elizabeth Hamilton, 21 Aug. 1791, quoted in Ron Chernow, *Alexander Hamilton* (New York: Penguin, 2004), 367.
74. Burns, 300.
75. Hamilton, "The Reynolds Pamphlet."
76. Chernow, 368–370.
77. Hamilton, "The Reynolds Pamphlet."
78. Thomas Jefferson, Papers of Thomas Jefferson, 18:635, quoted in Chernow, 415.
79. Burns, 304.
80. Ibid., 302.
81. Fleming, 239.
82. Burns, 308.
83. Thomas Callender, *History of the United States for the Year 1796,* 204.
84. Fleming, 243; Randall, 420.
85. Hamilton, "The Reynolds Pamphlet," quoted in Chernow, 533.
86. Callender, quoted in Chernow, 535.
87. *Aurora General Advertiser,* 19 Sept. 1797.
88. Chernow, 539.
89. Joseph Ellis, *Founding Brothers: The Revolutionary Generation* (New York: Knopf, 2000), 198.
90. Fleming, 310.
91. Burns, 356.
92. Ellis, 201.
93. James Callender, *Richmond Recorder,* 1 Sept. 1802.
94. Burns, 385.
95. Abigail Adams to Thomas Jefferson, 1 July 1804, quoted in Kukla, 150.
96. Kukla, 84.
97. Isaac Jefferson, quoted in Chernow, 315.
98. Kukla, 120.
99. Memoirs of Madison Hemings as told to S. F. Wetmore originally published as "Life among the Lowly, No. 1," *Pike County (Ohio) Republican,* 13 March 1873.
100. "Madison Hemings Memoir, as told to S. F. Wetmore."
101. Kukla, 135.
102. Clarence E. Walker, *Mongrel Nation: The America Begotten by Thomas Jefferson and Sally Hemings* (Charlottesville: Univ. of Virginia Press, 2009), 39–41.
103. Kukla, 115; Chernow, 512.
104. F. A. F. La Rochefoucauld-Liancourt, *Voyage dan les Etats-Unis d'Amerique* (Paris, 1798–1799), quoted in Kukla, 138.
105. Henry S. Randall to James Parton, 1 June 1868, quoted in Kukla, 119.
106. John Hartwell Cocke diary, quoted in Kukla, 119.
107. Burstein, 148.
108. Adams, quoted in Chernow, 664.
109. *Richmond Recorder,* 17 Nov. 1802.
110. John Walker's statement, 1805, quoted in Kukla, 55.
111. Ibid.
112. Thomas Paine, quoted in Fleming, 311.
113. Thomas Jefferson to Robert Smith, 1805 as quoted in Kukla, 53–56.

114. Thomas Jefferson to John Walker, 13 Apr. 1803 in Appendix A, Kukla, 190.
115. Harry Croswell, *The Wasp*, quoted in Burns 389.
116. Ibid.
117. *Richmond Examiner*, 25 Sept. 1802.
118. Burns, 389–394; Chernow, 664.
119. Alexander Hamilton, quoted in Chernow, 669.
120. Thomas Pickering to William Coleman, 11 Sept. 1827, quoted in Chernow, 670.
121. Burns, 390–394.
122. Gary Wills, *James Madison* (New York: Time Books, 2002), 5–6.
123. Fleming, 356.
124. Washington Irving, quoted in Alice Curtis Desmond, *Glamorous Dolley Madison* (New York: Dodd, Mead, 1946), 175.
125. Catherine Coles to Dolley Todd (Madison), 1 June 1794, quoted in Catherine Allgor, *A Perfect Union: Dolley Madison and the Creation of the American Nation* (New York: Holt, 2006), 28.
126. Allgor, 132.
127. Fleming, 332.
128. Allgor, 132.
129. Anthony Merry to Lord Hawkesbury, 6 Dec. 1804, quoted in Allgor, 85.
130. Colonel Andre de Bronne, quoted in Richard N. Cote, *Strength and Honor: The Life of Dolley Madison* (Mt. Pleasant, SC: Corinthian Books, 2005), 221.
131. Fleming, 378; Allgor, 95.
132. Allgor, 78–101.
133. Samuel Latham Mitchill to Catherine Akerly Mitchill, 23 Nov. 1807, quoted in Allgor, 122.
134. Allgor, 127.
135. Ibid., 266.
136. Fleming, 381.
137. Allgor, 134 (italics in original).
138. Allgor, 133.
139. Charles Pickney, quoted in Allgor, 137.
140. Jack N. Rakove, *James Madison and the Creation of the American Republic* (New York: Pearson Longman, 2007), 178.
141. Francis Few diary, 11 October 1808, quoted in Allgor, 249.
142. Allgor, 250.
143. Paul Zall, *Dolley Madison* (Huntington, NY: Nova History, 2001), 47.
144. Elizabeth Brown Harner to Dolley Madison, 27 Nov. 1812, quoted in Allgor, 253.
145. Fleming, 383.
146. Allgor, 247.
147. Ibid., 255.
148. Zall, 52.
149. Zall, 32.
150. Allgor, 212.
151. Washington Irving, quoted in Desmond, 175.
152. Zall, 55.
153. Ibid., 47.
154. Ibid., 53.
155. Allgor, 153.
156. Ibid., 279.
157. Ibid., 253–254.
158. George Robert Gleig, *A History of the Campaigns of the British at Washington and New Orleans* (1826), reprinted in Henry Steele Commager and Allan Nevins, eds., *The Heritage of America* (Boston: Little, Brown and Company, 1939.).
159. Fleming, 393.
160. Zall, 66.
161. Fleming, 295.
162. Ibid., 395.
163. Allgor, 254.
164. Fleming, 398.
165. Zall, 67.
166. Ibid., 67.

CHAPTER 2: SEX AND THE CIVIL WAR

1. Julia Perkins Culter, *Life and Time of Ephraim Cutler* (Cincinnati, OH: Robert Clarke, 1890), 189.
2. Lynn Hudson Parsons, *The Birth of Modern Politics: Andrew Jackson, John Quincy Adams and the Election of 1828* (New York: Oxford Univ. Press, 2009), 7.
3. Charles Francis Adams ed., *Memoirs of John Quincy Adams: Comprising Portions of His Diary 1794–1845*, diary entry 1 January 1825 (Philadelphia: J.B. Lippincott & Co. 1876) vol. 6, 457.
4. *Cincinnati Gazette*, 1828; quoted in Robert V. Remini, *John Quincy Adams* (Times Books: New York, 2002), 120.
5. Robert V. Remini, *Andrew Jackson and the Course of American Freedom* (Baltimore: Johns Hopkins Univ. Press, 1998), 119.
6. Charles Hammond, *View of General Jackson's Domestic Relations, in Reference to His Fitness for the Presidency* (Cincinnati, OH, 1828), 15.
7. John F. Marszalek, *The Petticoat Affair: Manners, Mutiny, and Sex in Andrew Jackson's White House* (Baton Rouge: Louisiana State Univ. Press, 1997), 8.
8. *Daily National Journal*, 26 Mar. 1827, quoted in Norma Basch, "Marriage, Morals and Politics in the Election of 1828," *Journal of American History* 80, no. 3. (Dec. 1993): 890–918.
9. Basch.
10. Alexis de Tocqueville. *Democracy in America*, ed. Bruce Frohen (Chicago: University of Chicago Press, 2000), 70.
11. Tocqueville, 145.
12. *Albany Argus*, 2 July 1844.
13. *Daily National Journal*, 14 Oct. 1828.
14. *We the People*, 12 April 1828.
15. Basch.
16. *Albany Argus*, 2 July 1844, p. 2, quoted in John H. Summers, "What Happened to Sex Scandals? Politics and Peccadilloes, Jefferson to Kennedy," *Journal of American History* 87, no. 3 (Dec. 2000).
17. Basch.

18. *Daily National Journal,* 24 June 1828, quoted in Basch.

19. Hammond, quoted in Basch.

20. *Frankfort Argus,* 18 Apr. 1827.

21. Hammond, quoted in Basch.

22. *Political Extracts from a Leading Adams Paper, The Massachusetts Journal,* ed. and pub. David L. Child (Boston, 1828), 10, 13, quoted in Basch.

23. *Correspondence of Andrew Jackson,* ed. John Spencer Bassett, 3:354 quoted in H. W. Brands, *Andrew Jackson: His Life and Times* (New York: Doubleday, 2005), 401.

24. Summers. 831.

25. Ibid. 832.

26. Remini, *John Quincy Adams,* 120.

27. Ibid., 119.

28. Eaton, quoted in Robert V. Remini, *Andrew Jackson and the Course of American Freedom, 1822–1832* (New York: Harper & Row, 1981), 2:149.

29. Remini, *Andrew Jackson,* 155.

30. Quoted in Jody C. Baumgartner and Peter L. Francia, *Conventional Wisdom and American Elections* (New York: Rowman & Littlefield, 2008), 70.

31. Andrew Jackson to Rachel Jackson, 27 Feb. 1824, Charles Norton Owen Collection; Remini, *Andrew Jackson,* 161.

32. John F. Marszalek, *The Petticoat Affair: Manners, Mutiny, and Sex in Andrew Jackson's White House* (Baton Rouge: Louisiana State Univ. Press, 1997), 28.

33. *Female Friend,* quoted in Queena Pollack, *Peggy Eaton: Democracy's Mistress* (New York: Minton, Balch, 1931), 15.

34. Brands, 424.

35. Marszalek, *The Petticoat Affair,* 43.

36. Remini, *Andrew Jackson.* 162.

37. Louis McLane to James A. Bayard, 19 February 1829, Bayard Papers quoted in Remini, *Andrew Jackson,* 162.

38. Meade Minnigerode, *Some American Ladies* (Freeport, NY: Books for Free Libraries, 1926), 252.

39. Andrew Jackson to John McLemore, 3 May 1829, *Correspondence of Andrew Jackson,* 4:31, quoted in Brands, 423.

40. Minnigerode, 260.

41. Marszalek, *The Petticoat Affair,* 52–57.

42. Ted Widmer, *Martin Van Buren* (New York: Times Books, 2005), 79.

43. Andrew Jackson to John McLemore, April 1829 (no day given), *Correspondence of Andrew Jackson,* 4:21, quoted in Brands, 424.

44. Marszalek, *The Petticoat Affair,* 79.

45. Ibid., 84.

46. Andrew Jackson to Ezra Stiles Ely, 23 March 1829.

47. Marszalek, *The Petticoat Affair,* 102.

48. Ibid., 171.

49. Ibid., 172.

50. Andrew Jackson to John McLemore, 24 Nov. 1829, Jackson, *Correspondence of Andrew Jackson,*

4:88–89; Richard B. Latner, *The Presidency of Andrew Jackson: White House Politics 1829–1837* (Athens: Univ. of Georgia Press, 1979), 62.

51. Brands, 424.

52. John Niven, *Martin Van Buren: The Romantic Age of American Politics* (New York: Oxford Univ. Press, 1983), 249–250.

53. Minnigerode, 268.

54. Martin Van Buren to Jesse Hoyt, 13 April 1829.

55. Andrew Jackson to John Overton, December 31, 1829, *Correspondence of Andrew Jackson,* 4:108–109, quoted in Brands, 425.

56. Charles Francis Adams ed., *Memoirs of John Quincy Adams: Comprising Portions of His Diary 1794–1845,* diary entry 6 February 1830 (Philadelphia: J.B. Lippincott & Co. 1876) vol. 8, 185.

57. Marszalek, *The Petticoat Affair,* 163.

58. Latner, 64.

59. Ibid., 143.

60. James Parton, *Life of Andrew Jackson* (New York: Mason Brothers, 1860), 287.

61. Marszalek, *The Petticoat Affair,* 228–236; *Washington Star,* 4 May 1901.

62. C-SPAN Survey of Presidential Leadership, 2009; Ranking of the Presidents by Scholarly Mean Score, Federalist Society and *Wall Street Journal,* 2005; Times Presidential Rankings, *Times Online,* 2008. http://www.timesonline.co .uk/tol/news/world/us_and_americas/us_elections/ article5048771.ece.

63. Jean Baker, *James Buchanan: The American Presidents Series: The 15th President, 1857–1861* (New York: Times Books, 2004), 22.

64. Baker, 19–26.

65. Ibid., 25.

66. Aaron V. Brown to Mrs. James K. Polk, 14 January 1844, *Polk Papers,* Library of Congress.

67. Baker, 26.

68. Baker, 25.

69. James W. Loewen, *Lies Across America* (New York: New Press, 1999), 367.

70. James Buchanan to Mrs. James J. Roosevelt, 13 May 1844; reprinted in George Curtis Ticknor, *The Life of James Buchanan: Fifteenth President of the United States* (New York: Harper & Brothers, 1883), vol. 1, 519.

71. Baker, 57.

72. Jonathan Ned Katz, *Love Stories: Sex between Men before Homosexuality* (Chicago: Univ. of Chicago Press, 2001), 105–106.

73. Katz, 273.

74. Baker, 20.

75. Birkner, 21.

76. Baker, 138.

77. Frederick Moore Binder, *James Buchanan and the American Empire* (Selinsgrove, PA: Susquehanna Univ. Press, 1994), 77.

78. *Chicago Tribune,* "An Incident in the Life of James Buchanan," 26 June 1868.

79. James Buchanan, quoted in Henry Graff, ed., *The Presidents: A Reference History* (New York: Scribner, 2002) 194.

80. *Dred Scott v. Sanford,* U.S. Supreme Court, 1857.

81. James Buchanan's Third Annual Message to Congress, 19 Dec. 1859.

82. *New York Times,* "Death of James Buchanan, ex-President of the United States," 2 June 1868.

83. *Chicago Tribune,* "Death of James Buchanan," 2 June 1868.

84. Baker, 152.

85. John Esten Cooke, *Mohun; or, The Last Days of Lee and His Paladins. Final Memoirs of a Staff Officer Serving in Virginia* (New York: F.J. Huntington and Co., 1869) 412.

86. *Chicago Tribune,* "Death of James Buchanan," 2 June 1868.

87. Joshua Wolf Shenk, *Lincoln's Melancholy: How Depression Challenged a President and Fueled His Greatness* (New York: Mariner Books, 2006).

88. Quoted in David Herbert Donald, *We Are Lincoln Men: Abraham Lincoln and His Friends* (New York: Simon & Schuster, 2003), 20.

89. Lincoln's boss Abner Ellis called him "a verry shy Man of Ladies." Michael Burlingame, *The Inner World of Abraham Lincoln* (Chicago: Univ. of Illinois Press, 1995), 123. Anna Roby said Abe "didn't like girls much," finding them "too frivolous," and Lincoln's cousin Sophie Hanks reported that he "didn't like the girls company." Michael Burlingame, *Abraham Lincoln: A Life* (Baltimore: Johns Hopkins Univ. Press, 2008), 41–42. Jason Duncan could "not recollect of his ever paying his addresses to any young lady." Abe's friend N. W. Brandon said, "It seemed as if he cared but little for them." David Turnham confirmed that "he did not seem to seek the company of the girls," and John D. Johnston speculated that Abe "didn't take much truck with the girls" because "he was too busy studying." Dennis Franklin Johnston, son of John D. Johnston, paraphrasing what his father told him, *Los Angeles Times,* 12 Feb. 1929, pt. 2.

90. *The Collected Works of Abraham Lincoln,* ed. Roy P. Basler (New Brunswick, NJ: Rutgers Univ. Press, 1953–55), 1:118–119, quoted in Donald, 23.

91. Abraham Lincoln to Mrs. Orville H. Browning, 1 April 1838, quoted in C. A. Tripp, *The Intimate World of Abraham Lincoln* (New York: Free Press, 2005), 96–99.

92. Abraham Lincoln to Mrs. Orville H. Browning, 1 April 1838, quoted in Tripp, 96–99.

93. James H. Matheny's account to William Herndon, 3 May 1866, quoted in Douglas L. Wilson and Rodney O. Davis, eds., *Herndon's Informants: Letters, Interviews, and Statements about Abraham Lincoln* (Chicago: Univ. of Illinois Press, 1997), 251.

94. Burlingame, *Abraham Lincoln,* 199.

95. Tripp, 175.

96. Thomas Stackpole, the White House steward, told this to Ward Hill Lamon. Lamon interview with William H. Herndon [1865–1866], *Herndon's Informants,* 467; Burlingame, *Abraham Lincoln,* 202.

97. Quoted in Tripp, 47.

98. Quoted in Wilson and Davis, 17–18.

99. John G. Nocolay and John Hay, *Abraham Lincoln: A History* (New York: Century, 1890), 1:194.

100. Joshua Speed to Josiah Gilbert Holland, June 22 1865, quoted in Katz, 5.

101. George McGovern, *Abraham Lincoln: The American Presidents Series* (New York: Times Books, 2009), 24.

102. Carl Sandburg, *The Prairie Years,* vol. 1 (New York: Scribner, 1924).

103. Doris Kearns Goodwin, *Team of Rivals: The Political Genius of Abraham Lincoln* (New York: Simon & Schuster, 2005), 99.

104. *Herndon's Informants,* 197; Joshua F. Speed, *Reminiscences of Abraham Lincoln and Notes of a Visit to California* (Louisville, KY: John P. Morton, 1884), 39; quoted in Donald, 44.

105. Quoted in Katz, 18.

106. James C. Conkling to Mercy Levering, 24 Jan. 1841, quoted in Tripp, 132.

107. Ninian W Edwards interview with William Herndon, 22 September 1865, quoted in Schenk, 51.

108. McGovern, 27.

109. Abraham Lincoln to Joshua Speed, 13 Feb. 1842, quoted in Tripp, 263.

110. Katz, 19.

111. Abraham Lincoln to Joshua Speed, 25 Feb. 1842, quoted in Tripp, 140.

112. Katz, 19.

113. Abraham Lincoln to Joshua Speed, 5 Oct. 1842, quoted in Tripp, 140; italics added.

114. Donald explains why the Coleman story is discredited in *We Are Lincoln Men,* 20–23.

115. Speed interview with Herndon, 5 Jan. 1889 quoted in Burlingame, *Abraham Lincoln,* 199.

116. Jerrold M. Packard, *The Lincolns in the White House* (New York: St. Martin's Press, 2005), 139.

117. Ibid., 140.

118. For details of Lincoln's relationship with Derickson, see Tripp, 1–21.

119. David Derickson, "Recollections of Lincoln," centennial edition *Meadville (PA) Tribune Republican,* 12 May 1888.

120. H. S. Huidekoper, "On Guard at the White House," *National Magazine,* Feb. 1909, 510–512.

121. Virginia Woodbury Fox diary, 16 Nov. 1862, Levi Woodbury Papers, Library of Congress. Quoted in Tripp 1.

122. Donald, 143.

123. Thomas Chamberlin, *History of the One Hundred and Fiftieth Regiment, Pennsylvania Volunteers, Second Regiment, Bucktail Brigade* (Philadelphia: F. McManus Jr., 1905), 31.

124. Donald, 143–146.

125. Virginia Woodbury Fox diary, 16 Nov. 1862, Levi Woodbury Papers, Library of Congress. Quoted in Tripp 1.

126. Daniel Mark Epstein, *The Lincolns: Portrait of a Marriage* (New York: Ballantine, 2008), 377.

127. Joshua Speed to William Herndon, 7 February 1866 quoted in Shenk 288–289.

128. Ibid.

CHAPTER 3: AFFAIRS OF STATE

1. Laton McCartney, *The Teapot Dome Scandal: How Big Oil Bought the Harding White House and Tried to Steal the Country* (New York: Random House, 2008), 40.

2. Woodrow Wilson (WW) to Ellen A. Wilson (EAW), 22 Dec. 1883, quoted in Phyllis Lee Levin, *Edith and Woodrow: The Wilson White House* (New York: Scribner, 2001), 20.

3. Irwin H. Hoover (IHH) papers, quoted in Levin, 74.

4. WW to EAW, 11 October 1883, quoted in Levin, 52.

5. Helen Bones to Arthur C. Walworth, 1 and 19 Jan. 1950, quoted in Levin, 126–127.

6. Donald Hoffman, *Mark Twain in Paradise: His Voyages to Bermuda* (Columbia: Univ. of Missouri Press, 2006), 107.

7. Ellen Maury Slayden, *Washington Wife* (New York: Harper & Row, 1963), 199–200.

8. Sina Dubovoy, *Ellen A. Wilson: The Woman Who Made a President* (New York: Nova History, 2004), 177.

9. Dubovoy, 178.

10. Ibid., 178.

11. Levin, 124.

12. August Heckscher, *Woodrow Wilson* (New York: Scribner, 1991), 174.

13. Heckscher, 252–253.

14. Lewis L. Gould, *Four Hats in the Ring: The 1912 Election and the Birth of Modern American Politics* (Lawrence: Univ. Press of Kansas, 2008), 78.

15. H. W. Brands, *Woodrow Wilson* (New York: Times Books, 2003), 63.

16. W. Barksdale Maynard, *Woodrow Wilson: Princeton to the Presidency* (New Haven, CT: Yale Univ. Press, 2008), 264.

17. Dubovoy, 180.

18. John Milton Cooper, *Woodrow Wilson: A Biography* (New York: Knopf, 2009), 100; Tom Shachtman, *Edith and Woodrow: A Presidential Romance* (New York: Putnam, 1981), 26.

19. Heckscher, 174.

20. John H. Summers, "What Happened to Sex Scandals? Politics and Peccadilloes, Jefferson to Kennedy," *Journal of American History* 87, no. 3, Dec. 2000.

21. Levin, 41.

22. Maynard, 265.

23. WW to Mary Allen Hulbert Peck (MAHP), 29 Sept. 1912, quoted in James D. Startt, *Woodrow Wilson and the Press: Prelude to the Presidency* (New York: Palgrave Macmillan, 2004).

24. Gould, 162.

25. *Buffalo Evening Telegraph,* 21 July 1884.

26. Ibid.

27. Summers, 834.

28. *Independent,* 4 Sept. 1884, in *American Press Opinion,* ed. Alan Nevins, 2:372; *Woman's Journal,* 4 Oct. 1884, p. 320; ibid., 9 Aug. 1884, p. 253, quoted in Summers, 833–834.

29. *Judge,* 27 Sept. 1884. Courtesy Library of Congress, #LC-USZ62–34246.

30. Quoted in Summers, 834.

31. Summers, 834.

32. Summers, 834.

33. Harvey, Yale lecture Mar. 1908, in Harvey, *Journalism, Politics, and the University* (1908), quoted in Summers, 844.

34. The Statutes of California and Amendments to the Codes Passed at the Thirty-Third Session of the Legislature, 1899 (Sacramento, 1899).

35. Herbert Croly, *The Promise of American Life* (1911; Cambridge, MA, 1965), 74.

36. Summers.833.

37. WW to Edith B. Galt (EBG), 3 June 1915, quoted in Levin, 85.

38. Carey Grayson to EBG, 15 Aug. 1914, quoted in Levin, 49.

39. Levin 52.

40. Edith Wilson, *My Memoir* (Indianapolis: Bobbs-Merill, 1939) 53–56.

41. Ibid.

42. Irwin H. Hoover papers, quoted in Levin, 52–53.

43. Shachtman, 108.

44. W. Barksdale Maynard, *Woodrow Wilson: Princeton to the Presidency* (New Haven, CT: Yale Univ. Press, 2008), 305.

45. WW to EBG, 27 May 1915, Edith B. Galt Wilson (EBGW) papers, quoted in Levin, 74–75.

46. Ibid., 9 June 1915, EBGW papers, quoted in Levin, 74–75.

47. Ibid., 27 May 1915, EBGW papers, quoted in Levin, 74–75.

48. EBG to WW, 18 June 1915, quoted in Levin, 74–75.

49. *Town Topics,* 5 August 1915.

50. James Strachey, ed. *The Standard Edition of the Complete Papers of Sigmund Freud* (London: The Hogarth Press and the Institute of Psychoanalysis, 1957).

51. WW to EBG, quoted in Levin, 109.

52. Levin, 79; Shachtman, 87.

53. Shachtman, 87.

54. WW to EBG, 9 PM, 11 May 1915, quoted in Levin, 79–80.

55. WW to EBG, 28 May 1915, quoted in Shachtman, 93; WW to EBG, 29 May 1915, quoted in Levin, 83.

56. WW to EBG, 1 June 1915, quoted in Levin, 83.

57. WW to EBG, 3 June 1915, quoted in Levin, 84.

58. EBG to WW, 7 June 1915, quoted in Levin, 84

59. Ibid.

60. EBG to WW, 4 Aug. 1915, quoted in Levin, 99.

61. WW to EBG, 15 Aug. 1915, quoted in Levin, 103.

62. Ibid., 14 Aug. 1915, quoted in Levin, 104.
63. Ibid., 7 June 1915, quoted in Levin, 85.
64. EBG to WW, 9 June 1915, quoted in Levin, 86.
65. WW to EBG, 12 June 1915, quoted in Levin, 86.
66. EBG to WW, 17 Sept. 1915, quoted in Levin, 112.
67. Ibid., 21 July 1915, quoted in Levin, 99.
68. WW to EBG, 21 July 1915, quoted in Levin, 99.
69. Ibid., 20 July 1915, quoted in Levin, 99.
70. Shachtman, 94.
71. Edward House diary, 24 June 1915, quoted in Levin, 96.
72. Levin, 97.
73. Ibid., 109;
74. Maynard, 306; Levin, 110; Heckscher, 354.
75. WW to EBG, 18 Sept. 1915, quoted in Levin, 113.
76. EBG to WW, 18 Sept. 1915, quoted in Levin, 113.
77. WW to EBG, 19 Sept. 1915, quoted in Levin, 113.
78. EBG to WW, 19 Sept. 1915, quoted in Levin, 113.
79. WW, "Analysis of the Statement of Admission," 20 Sept. 1915.
80. EBG to WW, 22 Sept. 1915, quoted in Levin, 115.
81. Shachtman, 136.
82. Warren G. Harding (WGH) to Carrie Phillips (CP), 11 Dec. 1915, quoted in James David Robenalt, *The Harding Affair: Love and Espionage during the Great War* (New York: Palgrave Macmillan, 2009), 157.
83. Maynard, 308–309; Leonard Baker, *Brandeis and Frankfurter: A Dual Biography* (New York: Harper & Row, 1984).
84. Memorandum of James W. Gerard to Ray Stannard Baker, quoted in Levin, 166.
85. Levin, 176.
86. WW speech in Arthur Link, ed., *The Papers of Woodrow Wilson* (Princeton NJ: Princeton University Press, 1966–1994) 4 Sept.–5 Nov. 1919, p. 63.
87. Edith Wilson, *My Memoir* (New York: Bobbs-Merrill, 1939).
88. Levin, 344.
89. Ibid., 338.
90. Ibid., 338–339; Bert E. Park, a neurologist, made his conclusions in 1990.
91. Edith Wilson, *My Memoir* (New York: The Bobbs Merrill Company, 1939), 289.
92. IHH papers, quoted in Levin, 338.
93. Levin, 340.
94. *New York Times,* 7 October 1919.
95. Edith Wilson, 289.
96. Levin, 338.
97. Ibid., 351.
98. Ike Hoover, quoted in Levin, 351.
99. McCartney, 33.
100. "The facts about President Wilson's illness," IHH papers, quoted in Levin, 389.
101. Levin, 390.
102. Shachtman, 212.
103. Levin, 430.
104. Shachtman, 222.
105. Ray Stannard Baker diary, 23 Jan. 1920, quoted in Levin, 433.
106. Levin, 433.
107. Ibid., 436.
108. *New York Times,* 21 Mar. 1920.
109. Robenalt, 340.
110. Levin, 437.
111. Ibid., 428.
112. Edith Wilson, *My Memoir,* 303.
113. Canton, Ohio, *Daily News,* 2 March 1920.
114. *Collier's,* quoted in *Harvey's Weekly,* 20 Mar. 1920.
115. *London Daily Mail,* 22 February 1920.
116. Arthur S. Link, *Washington Post,* 25 Nov. 1990.
117. WGH to CP, quoted in Carl Sferrazza Anthony, *Florence Harding: The First Lady, the Jazz Age, and the Death of America's Most Scandalous President* (New York: Morrow, 1998), 89.
118. Anthony, 82.
119. WGH to Carrie Phillips, 16 September 1913, quoted in Robenalt, 100.
120. Phillip G. Payne, *Dead Last: The Public Memory of Warren G. Harding's Scandalous Legacy* (Athens: Ohio Univ. Press, 2009), 5.
121. William Allen White, *Autobiography,* quoted in Payne, 129.
122. Anthony, 70.
123. Ibid., 82.
124. McCartney, 40.
125. WGH to CP, 2 Jan. 1913.
126. Anthony, 115.
127. Katherine Sibley, *First Lady Florence Harding: Behind the Tragedy and Controversy* (Lawrence: Univ. Press of Kansas, 2009), 39; Francis Russell, *The Shadow of Blooming Grove: Warren G. Harding in His Times* (New York: McGraw-Hill, 1968), 281.
128. Anthony, 145; Russell, 296; Robenalt, 310.
129. Robenalt, 310–311.
130. Report of Leonard M. Stern, 11 Mar. 1918, National Archives, quoted in Robenalt, 314.
131. WGH to CP, 14 June 1918, quoted in Robenalt, 324.
132. "Harding as Senator Befriended Woman Suspected as a Spy," *New York Times,* 13 Apr. 1931.
133. Robenalt, 316–317.
134. Samuel Hopkins Adams, *Incredible Era: The Life and Times of Warren Gamaliel Harding* (Boston: Houghton Mifflin, 1939), 103.
135. Anthony, 107.
136. Ibid., 90.
137. Quoted in Payne, 133.
138. Nan Britton, *The President's Daughter* (New York: Elizabeth Ann Guild, 1927), Charles Mee, *The Ohio Gang: The World of Warren G. Harding* (New York: Henry Holt & Co.1983) 72–73.
139. Anthony, 14.
140. Britton, *The President's Daughter,* quoted in Mee, 74.
141. Britton, *The President's Daughter,* quoted in Russell, 292.
142. Mee, 75.
143. Britton, *The President's Daughter,* 68–76, quoted in Payne, 136.

144. Britton, *The President's Daughter*, 77–130, quoted in Payne 136.

145. Robenalt, 324.

146. Anthony, 181–184.

147. WGH letter to CP, fully quoted in Anthony, 181–184.

148. Anthony, 185.

149. McCartney, 18–25.

150. H. L. Mencken, "Politics," in *Civilization in the United States: An Inquiry by Thirty Americans*, ed. Harold E. Stearns (New York, 1922), 21; H. L. Mencken, "Saturnalia," *Baltimore Sun*, 18 July 1927, p. 15.

151. George Harvey, quoted in Adams, 155.

152. A contemporary account of the 1920 Republican convention is M. R. Werner, *Privileged Characters: Teapot Dome Scandal* (New York: Robert M. McBride, 1935), 15.

153. McCartney, 25–26.

154. Anthony, 199.

155. Summers. 851.

156. William Estabrook Chancellor, *President Warren Gamaliel Harding: President of the United States* (Dayton OH: Sentinel Press, 1922), quoted in Anthony, 201.

157. William Allen White, *Masks in a Pageant* (New York: Macmillan, 1928), 409.

158. Russell, 402.

159. Anthony, 256.

160. Russell, 401

161. Francis W. Durbin to James M. Cox, 30 Sept. 1927, quoted in Robenalt, 351–352.

162. Britton, *The President's Daughter*, 102 quoted in Anthony, 210.

163. Mee, 115.

164. Nathan Miller, *New World Coming: The 1920s and the Making of Modern America* (New York: Da Capo Press, 2003), 88.

165. Maury Klein, *Rainbow's End: The Crash of 1929* (Oxford: Oxford Univ. Press, 2001), 81.

166. McCartney, 25.

167. Britton, *The President's Daughter*, quoted in Mee, 115.

168. Russell, 467.

169. Gaston B. Means, *The Strange Death of President Harding* (New York: Guild Publishing Company, 1930).

170. Payne, 154.

171. Quoted in Summers, 850.

172. *New York Times*, 3 Sept. 1927, quoted in Summers.

173. *Congressional Record*, 70th Cong., 1st sess., 26 Jan. 1928, p. 2077.

174. Richard Washburn Child, "Sh—They Say the President," *Collier's*, 12 Feb. 1927, pp. 8, 42, quoted in Summers.

CHAPTER 4: THE BALLAD OF FRANKLIN AND ELEANOR

1. Geoffrey C. Ward, *A First-Class Temperament: The Emergence of Franklin Roosevelt* (New York: Harper & Row, 1989), 382.

2. Doris Kearns Goodwin, *No Ordinary Time: Franklin and Eleanor Roosevelt: The Home Front in World War II* (New York: Simon & Shuster, 1994). 93.

3. James Roosevelt, *My Parents: A Differing View* (New York: Playboy Press, 1976), 18.

4. Peter Collier with David Horowitz, *The Roosevelts: An American Saga* (New York: Simon & Schuster, 1994), 87.

5. Michael Teague, *Mrs. L: Conversations with Alice Roosevelt Longworth* (New York: Doubleday, 1981), 158.

6. Joseph Persico, *Franklin and Lucy: President Roosevelt, Mrs. Rutherfurd and the Other Remarkable Women in His Life* (New York: Random House, 2008), 52.

7. Persico, 66.

8. Nathan Miller, *FDR: An Intimate History* (Lanham, MD: Madison Books, 1983), 153.

9. Collier, 219.

10. Blanch Wiesen Cook, *Eleanor Roosevelt* (New York: Viking, 1992), Cook, 1:27.

11. Elliot Roosevelt, *The Roosevelts of Hyde Park: An Untold Story* (New York: Putnam, 1973), quoted in Jean Edward Smith, *FDR* (New York: Random House, 2007), 151.

12. James Roosevelt, 17.

13. Persico, 84.

14. Arthur C. Murray, *At Close Quarters* (London: John Murray, 1946), 85.

15. FDR Papers as Assistant Secretary of the Navy, 1913–1920, Franklin D. Roosevelt Library, Hyde Park, New York, quoted in Persico, 90.

16. Elliot Roosevelt, 82.

17. Persico, 93.

18. Ibid., 100.

19. Quoted in Joseph P. Lash, *Love, Eleanor: Eleanor Roosevelt and Her Friends* (Garden City, NY: Doubleday, 1982), 69.

20. Teague, 157–158.

21. Smith, 151–153.

22. Henry Brandon, "A Talk with an 83-year-old Enfant-Terrible," *New York Times Magazine*, 6 Aug. 1967.

23. Quoted in James MacGregor Burns and Susan Dunn, *The Three Roosevelts: Patrician Leaders Who Transformed America* (New York: Atlantic Monthly Press, 2001), 155.

24. Persico, 127.

25. Eleanor Roosevelt to Joseph Lash, 1943, quoted in Lash, 66.

26. Burns and Dunn, 156.

27. Persico, 125.

28. Cook, 231; Goodwin, 20.

29. Persico, 127.

30. Joseph Lash interview with Anna Roosevelt Halsted, 29 Oct. 1968, papers of Joseph Lash, Roosevelt Library, quoted in Persico, 127.

31. Elliot Roosevelt interview, 20 June 1979, Eleanor Roosevelt papers, Franklin D. Roosevelt Library. Hyde Park, New York.

32. James Roosevelt, 101.

33. Eleanor Roosevelt, quoted in Lash, 70.
34. Smith, 163.
35. Lucy Mercer to Anna Roosevelt, quoted in Goodwin, 631–632.
36. Joseph Alsop, *FDR: A Centenary Remembrance* (New York: Viking, 1982) quoted in Persico, 365.
37. Fulton Oursler, quoted in Smith, 206.
38. Smith, 185.
39. Persico, 165.
40. Ibid., 159.
41. Missy LeHand to Francis Perkins, quoted in Goodwin, 116.
42. Persico, 165.
43. Goodwin, 36.
44. Ibid., 119.
45. Ward, 13.
46. Persico, 172.
47. Ibid., 165.
48. Ward, 710.
49. Missy LeHand to Franklin Roosevelt, letters, Franklin D. Roosevelt Papers, Family, Business, and Personal, Franklin D. Roosevelt Library; Goodwin, 35.
50. H. W. Brands, *Traitor to His Class: The Privileged Life of Franklin Delano Roosevelt* (New York: Doubleday, 2008), 180.
51. Dorothy Schiff papers, New York Public Library, quoted in Persico, 165–166.
52. James Roosevelt, 108.
53. Collier, 291.
54. Smith, 217.
55. Goodwin, 116–117.
56. Miller, 221.
57. Eleanor Roosevelt (ER) to FDR, 2 Oct. 1928, quoted in Miller, 222.
58. FDR to Frederic A. Delano, 8 Oct. 1928, quoted in Miller, 222.
59. Persico, 202.
60. Ibid., 367.
61. Ibid., 188.
62. Betty Houchin Winfield, *FDR and the News Media* (Urbana: Univ. of Illinois Press, 1990), 61.
63. Persico, 221.
64. Summers, "What Happened to Sex Scandals? Politics and Peccadilloes, Jefferson to Kennedy," *Journal of American History* 87, no. 3 (Dec. 2000).
65. Persico, 197.
66. James Roosevelt, quoted in Persico, 367.
67. Smith, 199.
68. Eleanor Roosevelt, *This Is My Story* (New York: Harper & Brothers, 1937), 325.
69. Goodwin, 207–208.
70. Rodger Streitmatter, *Empty Without You: The Intimate Letters of Eleanor Roosevelt and Lorena Hickok* (New York: Free Press, 1998), xx.
71. Eleanor Roosevelt diary 1925, quoted in Streitmatter, xix.
72. Eleanor Roosevelt, *This Is My Story*, 32.
73. Smith, 199.
74. Cook, 322.
75. Goodwin, 207; Persico, 158–159.
76. Persico, 177.
77. ER to Marion Dickerman, 27 August 1925, in *It Seems to Me: Selected Letters of Eleanor Roosevelt*, ed. Leonard C. Schulp and Donald W. Whisenhunt (Lexington: Univ. of Kentucky Press, 2001), 23.
78. Eleanor Roosevelt to Marion Dickerman, 5 Feb. 1926. Dickerman papers, Franklin D. Roosevelt Library.
79. Cook, 531.
80. Goodwin, 208.
81. Elliot Roosevelt, quoted in Persico, 177.
82. Kenneth S. Davis, *Invincible Summer: An Intimate Portrait of the Roosevelts Based on the Recollections of Marion Dickerman* (New York: Atheneum, 1974), 17.
83. Ibid., 35.
84. FDR to Elliot Brown, 5 August 1925, Franklin D. Roosevelt Library.
85. Smith, 214.
86. Cook, 333–334.
87. Sara Roosevelt, quoted in Jan Potker, *Sara and Eleanor* (New York: St. Martin's, 2004), 237.
88. Sara Roosevelt to FDR, quoted in Smith, 215.
89. Quoted in Streitmatter, 2.
90. Streitmatter, xix.
91. Smith, 219.
92. Persico, 176.
93. Ibid., 176.
94. Ibid., 184.
95. Ibid., 185.
96. Ibid., 186, 205.
97. Goodwin, 219.
98. Quoted in Streitmatter, 4.
99. Interview with Katherine Beebe Pinkham Harris by Shirley Biagi, Women in Journalism oral history project of the Washington Press Club Foundation, 22 Feb. 1989 to 19 Sept. 1990, Oral History Collection, Columbia University, New York City, 56, 114.
100. Ibid.
101. Quotes from Hickok letters and chapters from her autobiography in Hickok papers, Franklin Roosevelt Library, quoted in Cook, 482.
102. Cook, 482–489.
103. Goodwin, 220.
104. Hickok Associated Press copy, Sept. 1932, Hickok papers; Hickok, "'First Lady' Won't Give Statement," 9 Nov. 1932; "She'll Be Just Mrs. Roosevelt," 10 Nov. 1932; "New First Lady Even Tempered," 12 Nov. 1932.
105. Streitmatter, 8.
106. ER to Lorena Hickok (LH), 7 Mar. 1933, quoted in Persico, 203.
107. Ibid., 5 Mar. 1933, quoted in Streitmatter, 16.
108. Ibid., 6 Mar. 1933, quoted in Streitmatter, 17.
109. Ibid., 9 Mar. 1933, quoted in Streitmatter, 22.
110. Ibid., 11 Mar. 1933, quoted in Streitmatter, 25.
111. Persico, 230.
112. ER to LH, 25 Nov. 1933, quoted in Streitmatter, xxi.
113. LH to ER, 5 Dec. 1933, quoted in Streitmatter, 52.

114. LH to ER, 22 Jan. 1934, quoted in Streitmatter, 68.
115. LH to Anna Roosevelt Halsted, 9 June 1966, quoted in Streitmatter, xxii.
116. Persico, 214.
117. Lillian Parks, *The Roosevelts: A Family in Turmoil* (New York: Prentice Hall, 1981), 17.
118. Parks, 205–206.
119. Ibid., 5.
120. Hickok, unpublished manuscript, Papers of Lorena Hickok, Box 14, Franklin D. Roosevelt Library.
121. ER to LH, 18 Apr. 1943, quoted in Streitmatter, xxi.
122. ER to LH, Oct. 1936, quoted in Smith, 402.
123. Streitmatter, xxiv.
124. Ibid.
125. Persico, 218.
126. *Newsweek*, 9 Nov. 1942.
127. LH to ER, 26 Oct. 1942, Hickok Papers.
128. Quoted in Goodwin, 383.
129. William D. Hasset, *Off the Record with FDR* (New Brunswick, NJ: Rutgers Univ. Press, 1958), 200.
130. Lash, 116; Persico, 211.
131. Goodwin, 222.
132. Goodwin, 222.
133. Streitmatter, xxiii.
134. Persico, 208.
135. Streitmatter, 126.
136. Eleanor to Hickok, 27 Nov. 1933, quoted in Cook, 2:194.
137. "Relief," *Time*, 19 Feb. 1934, quoted in Streitmatter, 83.
138. Hickok to Katheryn Godwin, 18 Feb. 1934, quoted in Streitmatter, 84.
139. Lillian Parks quoted in Persico, 208.
140. Ibid.
141. Goodwin, 223.
142. Ibid.
143. Streitmatter, 125.
144. LH to ER, 15 August 1934 quoted in Goodwin, 224.
145. ER to LH, 23 Dec. 1933, quoted in Streitmatter, xxvii.
146. Goodwin, 224.
147. ER to LH, 4 Feb. 1934, quoted in Streitmatter, xxvii.
148. LH to ER, 11 Nov. 1940, quoted in Streitmatter, xxviii.
149. ER to LH, 6 June 1934, quoted in Cook, 200.
150. Goodwin, 339.
151. Persico, 219.
152. Ibid.
153. Smith, 494.
154. Parks, 184.
155. Ibid., 177.
156. Goodwin, 119.
157. Persico, 220.
158. Goodwin, 20.
159. Persico, 226.
160. Goodwin, 120.
161. *Newsweek*, 12 Aug. 1933, quoted in Goodwin, 119.
162. Goodwin, 120.
163. Ibid., 242.
164. Persico, 230.
165. Ibid., 216.
166. Miller, 493–494.
167. J. B. West with Mary Lynn Kotz, *Upstairs at the White House* (New York: Coward, McCann & Geoghegan, 1973), 26.
168. Persico, 250.
169. Ibid., 293.
170. Ibid., 302.
171. Goodwin, 520.
172. Winfield, 182.
173. Goodwin, 117.
174. Persico, 255.
175. Goodwin, 535.
176. Elliot Roosevelt, interview in Goodwin, 245.
177. Elliot Janeway, interview in Goodwin, 245.
178. Goodwin, 246.
179. Missy's friend Barbara Curtis, quoted in Goodwin, 534.
180. Persico, 304.
181. Smith, 622.
182. Miller, 493.
183. Persico, 356.
184. Margaret Suckley, Oral History, Franklin Roosevelt Library, quoted in Goodwin, 602.
185. Persico, 341.
186. Ibid., 345.
187. Ibid., 348.
188. Daisy Suckley diary, quoted in Persico, 285.
189. Carl Rowen, *Boston Globe*, 14 Oct. 1962.
190. Persico, 362.
191. Ward, 416.
192. Persico, 362.

CHAPTER 5: AMERICA'S SEX CZAR

1. Senator Estes Kefauver said from the early 1950s on Hoover's power over Congress gave him "more power than the president." Anthony Summers, *Official and Confidential: The Secret Life of J. Edgar Hoover* (New York: Putnam, 1993), 192.
2. Richard Hack, *Puppet Master: The Secret Life of J. Edgar Hoover* (Beverly Hills, CA: Phoenix Books, 2007), 247.
3. Summers, *Official and Confidential,* 29.
4. Summers, *Official and Confidential,* 38.
5. Director J. Edgar Hoover to All Special Agents in Charge, SAC Letter #512, 24 Mar. 1925, FBI 66–04-X92; Strictly Confidential Bureau Bulletin no 37, Series 1946, 10 July 1946, FBI 66–03–759; Athan Theoharis, *J. Edgar Hoover, Sex, and Crime* (Chicago: Ivan R. Dee, 1995), 63.
6. Ibid., 65–66.
7. Ibid., 66.
8. Confidential Memo, FBI Director J. Edgar Hoover, 24 Aug. 1936.

9. Richard Powers, *Secrecy and Power: The Life of J. Edgar Hoover* (New York: Free Press, 1987), 228–233.

10. Curt Gentry, *J. Edgar Hoover: The Man and His Secrets* (New York: Norton, 1991), 207.

11. Summers, *Official and Confidential*, 107–113.

12. Gentry, 283.

13. Hack, 245.

14. Gentry, 237.

15. R. J. C. Butow, "The FDR Tapes," *American Heritage*, Feb./Mar. 1982; Gentry, 227–228. FDR sent Hoover a letter on 14 June 1940, thanking him for the "many interesting and valuable reports that you have made to me regarding the fast moving situations of the last few months. You have done and are doing a wonderful job, and I want you to know of my gratification and appreciation." Edward Ennis, a senior aide to FDR's attorney general thought everyone in Washington was cowed by Hoover's relationship with the president and an "even deeper fear that he had files on everybody." Summers, *Official and Confidential*, 112.

16. Hack, 225.

17. Gentry, 308.

18. Hack, 226; Theoharis, *J. Edgar Hoover, Sex, and Crime*, 32.

19. Hack, 226.

20. Summers, *Official and Confidential*, 142.

21. Ibid.

22. Gentry, 301.

23. Eleanor Roosevelt to J. Edgar Hoover, 26 Jan. 1941, quoted in Gentry, 299.

24. Louis B. Nichols interview in Gentry, 301.

25. Hack, 238.

26. Summers, *Official and Confidential*, 143.

27. Gentry, 302–303.

28. FBI Liaison Agent George Burton to FBI Assistant Director D. Milton Ladd, 31 Dec. 1943.

29. Do Not File Memo, FBI Liaison Agent George Burton to FBI Assistant Director D. Milton Ladd, 31 Dec. 1943.

30. Do Not File Memo, FBI Liaison Agent George Burton to FBI Assistant Director D. Milton Ladd, 31 Dec. 1943; Joseph Lash, *Love, Eleanor: Eleanor Roosevelt and Her Friends* (Garden City, NY: Doubleday, 1982), 461; Hack, 236; Summers, *Official and Confidential*, 146.

31. Summers, *Official and Confidential*, 147; Powers, 266; Gentry, 306.

32. Summers, *Official and Confidential*, 105.

33. Ibid., 197.

34. Theoharis, *J. Edgar Hoover, Sex, and Crime*, 72.

35. Norman Koch, an FBI fingerprint specialist, said his colleagues often complained about "spending all their time investigating public official number so-and-so rather than Public Enemy Number One. They were digging into the background of anyone who might pose the slightest danger to the Director, and the idea was to find anything that could be used as leverage should any of these

36. Athan Theoharis, *From the Secret Files of J. Edgar Hoover* (Chicago: Ivan R. Dee, 1991).

37. Letter, Washington SAC James Gale to FBI Director J. Edgar Hoover, 12 Aug. 1960.

38. Letter, Washington SC Joseph Purvis to FBI Director J. Edgar Hoover, 25 Aug. 1965.

39. Summers, *Official and Confidential*, 200.

40. FBI assistant director William Sullivan recalled, "The moment [Hoover] would get something on a Senator he would send one of the errand boys up and advise the Senator that we're in the course of an investigation and by chance happened to come up with this—we realized you'd want to know. . . . Well, Jesus, what does that tell the Senator? From that time on, the Senator's right in his pocket." From Theoharis, *J. Edgar Hoover, Sex, and Crime*, 72.

41. Summers, *Official and Confidential*, 197.

42. Ibid., 202.

43. Ibid., 53.

44. Ibid., 197.

45. Athan Theoharis, *From the Secret Files of J. Edgar Hoover*, 4.

46. Summers, *Official and Confidential*, 198.

47. Ibid., 207–208.

48. Theoharis, *J. Edgar Hoover, Sex, and Crime*, 80.

49. Summers, *Official and Confidential*, 115.

50. Douglas FBI File 94–33476, quoted in Summers, *Official and Confidential*, 205.

51. Robert H. Jackson, *The Supreme Court in the American System of Government* (New York: Harper Torchbook, 1963), 70–71.

52. Hack, 405; Gentry, 233.

53. Gentry, 388.

54. Letter, Los Angeles SAC Richard Hood to FBI Director, 14 May 1947, FBI 61–7582–1468.

55. Gentry, 384.

56. Ibid., 385.

57. Hack, 196.

58. Burton Hersh, *Bobby and J. Edgar: The Historic Face-Off between the Kennedys and J. Edgar Hoover That Transformed America* (New York: Basic Books, 2007), 146.

59. Hack, 125.

60. Summers, *Official and Confidential*, 77.

61. Powers, 314.

62. Ibid., 173.

63. Summers, *Official and Confidential*, 78.

64. Powers, 171.

65. "Crime: Policeman's Lot," *Time*, 11 Mar. 1940.

66. Powers, 315.

67. Hack, 233.

68. Powers, 172.

69. Summers, *Official and Confidential*, 83.

70. Ibid., 93.

71. Theoharis, *J. Edgar Hoover, Sex, and Crime*, 23.

72. FBI veteran Joe Wickman explained, "We had communication saying he wanted us to deny any of those allegations that might come in, and how.

A report had to be made in every case. He wanted to know who said what." Summers, *Official and Confidential*, 93.

73. Personal and Confidential Do Not File Memo, FBI Assistant Director Robert Hendon to FBI Assistant Director Clyde Tolson, 30 June 1943.

74. Memo, FBI Assistant Director Louis Nichols to FBI Associate Director Clyde Tolson, 20 June 1951.

75. Ibid., 22 June 1951.

76. Personal and Confidential letter, Conroy to Hoover, 30 Oct. 1944.

77. Gentry, 240.

78. Personal and Confidential Letter, SAC Louisville M. W. McFarlin to FBI Director J. Edgar Hoover, 14 July 1944.

79. Airtel, SAC Birmingham to FBI Director, 11 June 1970.

80. Theoharis, *J. Edgar Hoover, Sex, and Crime*, 38.

81. Quoted in Hack, 140.

82. Powers, 185.

83. Summers, *Official and Confidential*, 32.

84. Ibid., 95.

85. "Employment of Homosexuals and other Sex Perverts in Government," 1950 Interim Report submitted to the Committee on Expenditures in the Executive Departments by its Subcommittee on Investigations pursuant to S. Res. 280 (81st Congress).

86. Theoharis, *J. Edgar Hoover, Sex, and Crime*, 103.

87. Theoharis, *J. Edgar Hoover, Sex, and Crime*, 24.

88. Unnamed former Hoover aide, interview in Gentry, 413.

89. David Halberstam, *The Fifties* (New York: Ballantine, 1994), 50.

90. Hersh, 110.

91. Joe McCarthy Speech, Wheeling, West Virginia, 9 Feb. 1950.

92. Haynes Johnson, *Age of Anxiety: McCarthyism to Terrorism* (New York: Harcourt Books, 2005), 147.

93. John O'Donnell, quoted in David K. Johnson, *The Lavender Scare: The Cold War Persecution of Gays and Lesbians in the Federal Government* (Chicago: Univ. of Chicago Press, 2004), 71.

94. Johnson, *The Lavender Scare*, 31.

95. Ibid., 20.

96. "The Aberrants" *The Washington Post*, 17 March 1950.

97. Edwin R. Bayley, *Joe McCarthy and the Press* (Madison: Univ. of Wisconsin Press, 1981), 161.

98. Bayley, 161.

99. Mark Feldstein, *Poisoning the Press: Richard Nixon, Jack Anderson, and the Rise of Washington's Scandal Culture* (New York: Farrar, Straus and Giroux, 2010) 42.

100. Former Hoover aide, interview in Gentry, 379.

101. Theoharis and John Stuart Cox, *The Boss: J. Edgar Hoover and the Great American Inquisition* (Philadelphia: Temple Univ. Press, 1988), 283

102. Gentry, 381. Powers, 321.

103. Gentry, 378.

104. Informal Memo, New York SAC Edward Scheidt to FBI Director Hoover, 17 Apr. 1952.

105. Informal Memo, FBI Assistant Director D. Milton Ladd to FBI Director, 24 June 1952; Theoharis, *J. Edgar Hoover, Sex, and Crime*, 106; Summers, *Official and Confidential*, 181–182.

106. Informal Memo, FBI Supervisor William Cleveland to FBI Assistant Director Courtney Evans, 31 Oct. 1964.

107. "How that Stevenson Rumor Started," *Confidential*, Aug. 1953; Henry E. Scott, *Shocking True Story: The Rise and Fall of* Confidential, *"America's Most Scandalous Scandal Magazine"* (New York: Pantheon, 2010).

108. Gentry, 402.

109. Johnson, *The Lavender Scare*, 121.

110. Gentry, 403.

111. Hack, 296.

112. Johnson, *The Lavender Scare*, 77.

113. Ibid., 76.

114. Theoharis and Cox, 289.

115. Gentry, 433.

116. Gentry, 434

117. Feldstein, 35.

118. "The Tenacious Muckraker," *Time*, 12 Sept. 1969.

119. Feldstein, 38; Theoharis and Cox, 291.

120. *Time*, "Querulous Quaker," 13 December 1948.

121. Hack, 280.

122. Hersh, 141–142.

123. Andrea Friedman, "The Smearing of Joe McCarthy: The Lavender Scare, Gossip, and Cold War Politics," *American Quarterly* 57, no. 4 (Dec. 2005): 1105–1129.

124. Hersh, 117.

125. Hack, 258.

126. David M. Oshinsky, *A Conspiracy So Immense: The World of Joe McCarthy* (New York: Free Press, 1983), 256.

127. Oshinsky, 256.

128. Hack, 261.

129. Oshinsky, 279.

130. Friedman. "The Smearing of Joe McCarthy" 1105–1129.

131. Hack, 287.

132. Ellen Schrecker, *The Age of McCarthyism: A Brief History with Documents* (Boston: Bedford/St. Martin's, 2002), 74.

133. Oshinsky, 400.

134. *New York Times*, 13 Mar. 1954.

135. Oshinsky, 417.

136. Oshinsky, 422.

137. Hearings before the Special Subcommittee on Investigations of the Committee on Government Operations, Special Senate Investigation on Charges and Counter Charges Involving: Secretary of the Army Robert T. Stevens, John G. Adams, H. Struve Hensel, and Senator Joseph McCarthy, Roy M. Cohn and Francis P. Carr (Army-McCarthy Hearings), 1954.

138. Friedman. "The Smearing of Joe McCarthy" 1105–1129.

139. Drew Pearson, Washington Merry-Go-Round, 1 April 1954.

140. Drew Pearson, Washington Merry-Go-Round, 5 June 1954.

141. William Benton to John Howe, 23 March 1954, William Benton Papers, Wisconsin State Historical Society, Madison, WI. Quoted in Oshinsky, 311.

142. Oshinsky, 452; italics in original.

143. Bayley, 204; italics in original.

144. Friedman.

145. Hersh, 149.

146. Bayley, 208.

147. Oshinsky, 443.

148. Hack, 288.

149. Summers, *Official and Confidential,* 191.

150. Informal Memo, FBI Assistant Director Louis Nichols to FBI Associate Director Clyde Tolson, 13 May 1955.

151. Kay Summersby Morgan, *Past Remembering: My Love Affair with Dwight David Eisenhower* (Simon & Schuster: New York, 1976), 14.

152. Informal Memo, FBI Assistant Director Louis Nichols to FBI Associate Director Clyde Tolson, 23 Sept. 1955.

153. Ibid., 28 Sept. 1955.

154. Summersby, 14.

155. Ibid.

156. Summers, *Official and Confidential,* 254–258.

157. Theoharis, *J. Edgar Hoover, Sex, and Crime,* 40.

158. Summers, *Official and Confidential,* 253–256.

159. Theoharis, *J. Edgar Hoover, Sex, and Crime,* 15.

160. Summers, *Official and Confidential,* 13.

161. When Hoover and Clyde took road trips together, agents went ahead and inspected every gas station toilet along the way to make sure they were tidy enough for the finicky director. Summers, *Official and Confidential,* 221; Hack, 181.

162. Summers, *Official and Confidential,* 222–223.

163. Ibid., 13.

164. Ibid., 223.

165. Hersh, 161.

166. Ibid., 156.

167. Hack, 252.

168. "At headquarters," recalled former FBI agent William Turner, "there wasn't even a section working on organized crime. In the field, what we did get on top mobsters was just dropped into the General Investigative Intelligence file—to be forgotten." Millions of Americans watched Senator Estes Kefauver hold nationally televised Senate hearings on organized crime in 1951. After gathering testimony from 800 witnesses, including several Mafia kingpins, the Kefauver committee concluded that there was indeed "a nationwide crime syndicate known as the mafia." Hoover not only failed to act on the Senate's findings but he also tried to prevent the committee from being formed in the first place. Reporter Jack Anderson said, "[Kefauver] told me the FBI tried to block it. . . . Hoover knew that if the public got alarmed about organized crime, the job would go to the FBI. And he didn't want the job." Kefauver's assistant counsel Joseph Nellis said, "We had a long series of meetings with [Hoover] off the record, at which he told us, 'We don't know anything about the Mafia or families in New York. We haven't followed this.' He told us what we were learning about the mafia wasn't true, but we didn't believe him." Instead of assisting Kefauver, Hoover gathered dirt on him and forbade agents to meet with the senator. Hoover also refused requests for the FBI to protect Kefauver Committee witnesses—even after two were murdered. Hoover's refusal to acknowledge the existence of a national Mob syndicate became impossible after November 14, 1957, when a New York State police sergeant discovered a conference of more than 60 Mafia dons at Joe "The Barber" Barbara's country home in the upstate New York town of Apalachin. Police raided the house and arrested dozens of mobsters. FBI deputy director William Sullivan put together a report on Apalachin and distributed 25 copies to law enforcement officials in various government departments. Hoover dismissed the report as "baloney," recalled every copy and had them destroyed. Hersh, 160. In the wake of Apalachin, the U.S. attorney general created a special program to go after Mafia figures. Richard Oglive, who served as the Justice Department official in charge of the Midwest in the 1950s and later became governor of Illinois, said, "Hoover was very cool to the whole idea of the Attorney General's special group. He ordered that the FBI files, containing the very information we needed on organized crime, were to be closed to us." Hersh, 164.

169. Powers, 333.

170. Summers, *Official and Confidential,* 259.

171. Ibid., 227–228.

172. Powers, 335.

173. Hersh, 16.

174. Summers, *Official and Confidential,* 241–243.

175. Ibid., 244–245.

176. Theoharis, *J. Edgar Hoover, Sex, and Crime,* 46.

177. Summers, *Official and Confidential,* 5.

178. Ibid., 203.

179. Sam Tanenhaus, *Whittaker Chambers: A Biography* (New York: Random House, 1998), 231.

180. Memo, FBI Director J. Edgar Hoover to FBI Assistant Director Clyde Tolson, William Sullivan, Thomas Bishop, Charles Brennan, and Alex Rosen, 25 Nov. 1970, 4:32 PM.

181. "Tapes Show Nixon Feared Hoover," *New York Times,* 5 June 1991; italics added.

182. John M. Crewdson, "FBI Investigated Hong Kong Woman Friend of Nixon in '60s to Determine if She Was Foreign Agent," *New York Times,* 22 June 1976.

183. Summers, *Official and Confidential,* 371–376.

184. Barbara Wilkins, "Marianna Liu Admits She Knew Nixon in Hong Kong, but Says There Was

No Spying and No Romance," *People* 6, no. 14 (4 Oct. 1976); Anthony Summers, *The Arrogance of Power: The Secret World of Richard Nixon* (New York: Viking, 2000), 268–270.

185. Summers, *Official and Confidential*, 371–376.
186. Rick Perlstein, *Nixonland: The Rise of a President and the Fracturing of America* (New York: Scribner, 2008), 654.
187. Hack, 9.
188. Hack, 21.
189. Gentry, 42.

CHAPTER 6: THE NUDE FRONTIER

1. Don Van Natta Jr., *First off the Tee: Presidential Hackers, Duffers, and Cheaters from Taft to Bush* (New York: PublicAffairs, 2003), 47.
2. Gore Vidal, *Palimpsest: A Memoir* (New York: Penguin Books, 1996), 380.
3. James Bacon interview in Seymour M. Hersh, *The Dark Side of Camelot* (New York: Little, Brown, 1997), 107.
4. Sally Bedell Smith, *Grace and Power: The Private World of the Kennedy White House* (New York: Random House, 2004), 159.
5. "Jack Kennedy's Other Women," *Time*, 29 Dec. 1975.
6. John H. Summers, "What Happened to Sex Scandals? Politics and Peccadilloes, Jefferson to Kennedy," *Journal of American History* 87, no. 3 (Dec. 2000).
7. Anthony Summers, *Official and Confidential: The Secret Life of J. Edgar Hoover* (New York: Putnam, 1993), 270.
8. Richard Reeves, *President Kennedy: Profile in Power* (New York: Simon & Schuster, 1994), 288.
9. Inga Arvad, *Washington Times-Herald*, 27 Nov. 1941, quoted in Hersh, *The Dark Side of Camelot*, 83.
10. Nigel Hamilton, *JFK: Reckless Youth* (New York: Random House, 1992), 423.
11. Hamilton, 433.
12. Ibid., 434.
13. FBI Memo, SAC Washington S. K. McKee to FBI Director, 12 Dec. 1941; FBI Memo, FBI Assistant Director D. Milton Ladd to FBI Director, 17 Jan. 1942; FBI Memo, FBI Director J. Edgar Hoover to Attorney General Francis Biddle, 21 Jan. 1942.
14. Arvad Memoir (1945), quoted in Hamilton, 431–432.
15. FBI Memo, FBI Director J. Edgar Hoover to Attorney General Francis Biddle, 21 Jan. 1942.
16. Hersh, 84.
17. Walter Winchell, syndicated column, 12 Jan. 1942, quoted in Hersh, *The Dark Side of Camelot*, 83.
18. Robert Donovan Oral History, John F. Kennedy Presidential Library, Boston.
19. Personal and Confidential Report of Special Agent Savannah Office to Washington Office, 9 Feb. 1942 (italics in original).
20. Gentry, 469; Hersh, *The Dark Side of Camelot*, 83.
21. Henry James, interview with Nigel Hamilton, 489.
22. Dallek, 85.
23. Hamilton, 494.
24. Summers, 266; italics in original.
25. Langdon Marvin, interview in C. David Heymann, *Bobby and Jackie: A Love Story* (New York: Atria Books, 2009), 25–26.
26. Theodore H. White, *The Making of the President, 1960* (New York: Atheneum, 1961), 288–290.
27. Quoted in Dallek, 285.
28. Quoted in Hersh, *The Dark Side of Camelot*, 297.
29. Evan Thomas, *Robert Kennedy* (New York: Simon & Schuster, 2000), 167.
30. Campbell, quoted in Hersh, *The Dark Side of Camelot*, 299–300.
31. Hersh, *The Dark Side of Camelot*, 135–136.
32. Ibid., 303.
33. Hersh, 303.
34. Campbell's account of delivering the satchel to Giancana was confirmed by Martin E. Underwood in a 1997 interview with Seymour Hersh. Underwood, who worked for the Kennedy campaign, told Hersh he was sent to trail Campbell on her overnight train ride. Underwood said he saw Campbell hand Giancana the satchel. Hersh, *The Dark Side of Camelot*, 304–305.
35. Ibid., 306.
36. Ibid., 310.
37. Gentry, 472.
38. Hersh, *The Dark Side of Camelot*, 307.
39. Ibid., 307.
40. Thomas, 166.
41. Hersh, *The Dark Side of Camelot*, 312.
42. David Talbot, *Brothers: The Hidden History of the Kennedy Years* (New York: Free Press, 2007), 139.
43. Hersh, *The Dark Side of Camelot*, 314.
44. Judith Campbell Exner, *My Story* (New York: Grove Press, 1977), quoted in Hersh, *The Dark Side of Camelot*, 316.
45. Hersh, *The Dark Side of Camelot*, 323.
46. Ibid., 295, 317.
47. G. Milton Kelly, "TFX Plane Award on High Bid Draws Fire of Senators," *Washington Post*, 7 Mar. 1963.
48. "Controversy over the TFX," *Washington Post*, 8 Mar. 1963, p. A16.
49. "Jack Kennedy's Other Women," *Time*, 29 Dec. 1975.
50. Hersh, *The Dark Side of Camelot*, 237–238.
51. C. David Heymann, *Bobby and Jackie: A Love Story* (New York: Atria Books, 2009), 182.
52. Susan Sklover, interview with C. David Heymann, *Bobby and Jackie* 28–29.
53. C. David Heymann, *A Woman Named Jackie: An Intimate Biography* (New York: Signet, 1991), 371.
54. Cari Beauchamp, "It Happened at the Hôtel du Cap," *Vanity Fair*, Mar. 2009.
55. Smith, 358.

56. John F. Kennedy, American University Commencement Address, 10 June 1963.

57. Benjamin C. Bradlee, *Conversations with Kennedy* (New York: Norton, 1984), 230.

58. FBI Operation Bowtie file, quoted in Hersh, *The Dark Side of Camelot*, 391.

59. Hersh, *The Dark Side of Camelot*, 391.

60. Hoover to RFK, 18 June 1963, http://foia.fbi.gov/foiaindex/bowtie.htm; italics added.

61. Branch, 836.

62. Ibid., 837.

63. Arthur Schlesinger Jr., *Robert Kennedy and His Times* (New York: Ballantine, 1978), 384; Branch, 837–838; italics added.

64. "High US Aide Implicated in V-Girl Scandal," *New York Journal American*, 29 June 1963, p. A1.

65. Hersh, *The Dark Side of Camelot*, 397.

66. FBI Bowtie file, Evans to Belmont, 2 July 1963.

67. Dallek, 636.

68. C. David Heymann, *A Woman Named Jackie* (New York: Lyle Stuart, 1989), 373.

69. Heymann, *A Woman Named Jackie*, 373.

70. Burton Hersh, *Bobby and J. Edgar: The Historic Face-Off between the Kennedys and J. Edgar Hoover that Transformed America* (Basic Books: New York, 2007), 364.

71. *Danville Virginia Register*, 2 July 1963.

72. Dallek, 636.

73. Burton Hersh, interview with author David Eisenbach, June 2008.

74. Baker, interview, 30 May 2005, in Hersh, *Bobby and J. Edgar*, 366.

75. Hersh, *The Dark Side of Camelot*, 400.

76. Bobby Baker interview in Evans, 263.

77. Thomas, 265.

78. Clark Mollenhoff, "US Expels Girl Linked to Officials," *Des Moines Register*, 26 Oct. 1963.

79. Branch, 912.

80. "Hill Probe May Take Profumo-Type Twist," *Washington Post*, 27 Oct. 1963, p. A2.

81. Evelyn Lincoln, diary, 28 Oct. 1963, quoted in Dallek, 637.

82. FBI Memo, Rosen to Belmont, 26 Oct. 1963, quoted in Thomas, 265.

83. FBI Memo, 28 Oct. 1963. National Archives, College Park, MD.

84. Thomas, 276–268; Hersh, *The Dark Side of Camelot*, 403–405; Dallek, 638; Hersh, *Bobby and J. Edgar*, 367–368.

85. Thomas, 268; Dallek, 637; Hersh, *The Dark Side of Camelot*, 401.

86. Drew Pearson, "Senate to Keep Lid on Sex Rollicks," *Washington Post*, 2 Nov. 1963.

87. Hoover to Assistant Directors, 28 Oct. 1963, FBI Ellen Rometsch Files.

88. Bradlee, quoted in Summers, *Official and Confidential*, 313.

89. MLK FBI File, Memo from William Sullivan to Alan Belmont, 30 Aug. 1963.

90. MLK FBI File, J. Edgar Hoover note on UPI press release announcing King's honor, 29 Dec. 1963.

91. Hersh, *The Dark Side of Camelot*, 401; Dallek, 637.

92. Church Committee Report, bk. 3, p. 159, quoted in Michael Friedly and David Gallen, *Martin Luther King Jr.: The FBI File* (New York: Carroll & Graf, 1993), 39.

93. Taylor Branch, *Parting the Waters: America in the King Years, 1954–63* (New York: Simon & Schuster, 1988), 911–912; Taylor Branch, "Affairs of State," *Washington Post*, 30 Oct. 1988; Talbot, 142; Evans, 264.

94. Branch, 908.

95. Friedly and Gallen, 39.

96. FBI Memo Sullivan to Belmont, 24 Dec. 1963. National Archives, College Park, MD.

97. Friedly and Gallen, 66.

98. Ibid., 39.

99. David Garrow, *The FBI and Martin Luther King: From "Solo" to Memphis* (New York: Norton, 1981); Summers, *Official and Confidential*, 354.

100. MLK FBI File, Memo from William Sullivan to Alan Belmont, 27 Jan. 1964.

101. MLK FBI File, Memo from Frederick Baumgardner to William Sullivan, 4 Mar. 1964.

102. Ibid., 31 Aug. 1964.

103. Friedly and Gallen, 42.

104. MLK FBI File, Memo from Frederick Baumgardner to William Sullivan, 30 Nov. 1964.

105. Friedly and Gallen, 48.

106. Anonymous Letter (drafted by FBI) to MLK, 21 Nov. 1964, quoted in David Garrow, *Bearing the Cross: Martin Luther King, Jr., and the Southern Christian Leadership Conference* (New York: Harper Perennial, 1999), 373.

107. Hersh, *Bobby and J. Edgar*, 376.

108. Church Committee Report, bk. 3, p. 159, quoted in Friedly and Gallen, 49.

109. Friedly and Gallen, 49.

110. Friedly and Gallen, 49; Garrow, 134.

111. Friedly and Gallen, 49; Garrow, 134.

112. Feldstein, 88.

113. Eugene Patterson, "Sweet Lies Soothe Hoover," *Atlanta Constitution*, 31 Mar. 1976.

114. Hersh, *Bobby and J. Edgar*, 379.

115. Taylor Branch, *Pillar of Fire: America in the King Years 1963–1965* (New York: Simon & Schuster, 1998), 556.

116. Unnamed agent, quoted in William W. Turner, *Hoover's FBI*, rev. ed. (1970; repr., New York: Thunder's Mouth Press, 1993).

CHAPTER 7: SEX, DEATH AND THE KENNEDYS

1. "The Nation: Jack Kennedy's Other Women," *Time*, 29 Dec. 1975.

2. C. David Heymann, *Bobby and Jackie: A Love Story* (New York: Atria Books, 2009), 28.

3. Christopher Anderson, *Jack and Jackie: Portrait of an American Marriage* (New York: Morrow, 1996), 60.

4. George Smathers, interview in Anderson, 60.

5. Paul F. Healy, "The Senate's Gay Young Bachelor," *Saturday Evening Post,* 13 June 1953.
6. Sarah Bradford, *America's Queen: The Life of Jacqueline Kennedy Onassis* (New York: Penguin Books, 2000), 13.
7. Lee Radziwill, interview in Bradford, 13.
8. Barbara Leaming, *Mrs. Kennedy: The Missing History of the Kennedy Years* (New York: Free Press, 2001), 15.
9. Bradford, 206.
10. Anderson, 330.
11. Bradford, 209.
12. Heymann, *Bobby and Jackie,* 28.
13. Bradford, 207.
14. Anderson, 211.
15. Ibid., 329; italics in original.
16. Lester David, *Jacqueline Kennedy Onassis: A Portrait of Her Private Years* (New York: Birch Lane Press, 1994), 15.
17. Tony Bradlee interview in Sally Bedell Smith, *Grace and Power: The Private World of the Kennedy White House* (New York: Random House, 2004) 162.
18. George Smathers, interview, quoted in Anderson, 167.
19. Bradford, 108.
20. Anderson, 167.
21. Richard Reeves, *President Kennedy: Profile of Power* (New York: Simon & Schuster, 1993), 668.
22. Anderson, 168.
23. George Smathers, interview, in Edward Klein, *All Too Human: The Love Story of Jack and Jackie Kennedy* (Pocket Books: New York, 1996), 215.
24. Anderson, 168–169.
25. Bradford, 108.
26. Anderson, 171; Klein, *All Too Human,* 219.
27. Bradford, 111.
28. Heymann, *Bobby and Jackie,* 24.
29. Bill Walton, interview, in Heymann, *Bobby and Jackie,* 25.
30. George Smathers, interview, in Anderson, 336–337.
31. Anderson, 337.
32. Anderson, 337–338, Leaming, 215.
33. "The Press: Paparazzi on the Prowl," *Time,* 17 Apr. 1961.
34. George Ball, interview in Klein, *All Too Human,* 316.
35. Leaming, 216.
36. Klein, *All Too Human,* 317.
37. Carl Sferrazza Anthony, *As We Remember Her: Jacqueline Kennedy Onassis in the Words of Her Family and Friends* (New York: Harper Collins, 1997), 101.
38. Maria Callas, interview in Peter Evans, *Nemesis: Aristotle Onassis, Jackie O, and the Love Triangle that Brought Down the Kennedys* (New York: Harper Collins, 2004), 111.
39. Bradford, 326.
40. Ibid., 254.
41. Evans, 70.
42. Ibid., 72.
43. Ibid., 66–67.
44. Ibid., 96.
45. Richard Burton, interview in Evans, 101.
46. Evelyn Lincoln, interview in Evans, 76.
47. Evans, 77.
48. Yannis Georgakis, chairman of Olympic Airways, interview in Evans, 78.
49. Anderson, 356.
50. Suzanne Roosevelt, interview in Bradford, 255.
51. Evans, 95–96.
52. Constantine Gratsos, interview in Evans, 97.
53. Evans, 96.
54. Ibid., 99–100.
55. Klein, *All Too Human,* 337.
56. Evans, 113.
57. Christina Onassis, interview in Evans, 105.
58. Edward Klein, *Just Jackie: Her Private Years* (New York: Ballantine, 1998), 165.
59. Evans, 107.
60. Ibid., 106–107.
61. David Binder, "Mrs. Kennedy Lands in Athens to Begin Two-Week Vacation," *New York Times,* 2 Oct. 1963.
62. Leaming, 314.
63. Bradford, 257.
64. Drew Pearson, "First Lady's Cruise Causes Stir," *Washington Post,* 17 Oct. 1963.
65. "Bolton Renews Attack of Cruise," *Washington Post,* 17 Oct. 1963.
66. Evelyn Lincoln, interview in Evans, 101–102.
67. Evans, 103.
68. Ibid., 107, 104.
69. Anderson, 356.
70. Evans, 107.
71. Benjamin C. Bradlee, *Conversations with Kennedy* (New York: Norton, 1984).
72. Coates Redmon, interview in Bradford, 258.
73. Evelyn Lincoln, interview in Anderson, 357.
74. Evans, 110.
75. Costa Gratsos, interview in Evans, 111.
76. Evelyn Lincoln, interview in Evans, 112–113.
77. Leaming, 211.
78. Bradlee, 219.
79. Anderson, 49.
80. Heymann, *Bobby and Jackie,* 14.
81. Bradford, 257.
82. Constantine Gratsos, interview in Evans, 117.
83. Edward Klein, *Just Jackie,* 167.
84. Theodore White, interview in Heymann, *Bobby and Jackie,* 37.
85. Theodore H. White, *In Search of History: A Personal Adventure* (New York: Harper & Row, 1978), 524 (italics added).
86. Art Buchwald, interview in Heymann, *Bobby and Jackie,* 38–39.
87. Evans, 121.
88. Pierre Salinger, interview in Heymann, *Bobby and Jackie,* 54.
89. Charles Spalding, interview in Heymann, *Bobby and Jackie,* 58.
90. Arthur Schlesinger Jr., interview in Heymann, *Bobby and Jackie,* 61.

91. Johnny Meyer, interview in Evans, 125.
92. Gore Vidal, *Palimpsest: A Memoir* (London: Andre Deutsch, 1995), 311.
93. Heymann, *Bobby and Jackie,* 115.
94. Mary Harrington, interview in Heymann, *Bobby and Jackie,* 82–83.
95. Morton Downey Jr., interview in Heymann, *Bobby and Jackie,* 88.
96. Truman Capote, interview with Lester Persky, quoted in Heymann, *Bobby and Jackie,* 113–114.
97. Franklin Roosevelt Jr., interview in Heymann, *Bobby and Jackie,* 77.
98. The *New York Express* commented that RFK and Jackie were "being seen together all the time." The *New York Post* quoted one of Bobby's secretaries saying Jackie called his office "every day." Heymann, *Bobby and Jackie,* 61–62.
99. Bradford, 304.
100. Klein, *Just Jackie: Her Private Years* (New York: Ballantine Books, 1998), 68–69.
101. Marlon Brando, draft of autobiography, quoted in Heymann, *Bobby and Jackie,* 55–56.
102. Bradford, 320.
103. Ibid., 296.
104. Heymann, *Bobby and Jackie,* 62.
105. Courtney Evans interview in Heymann, *Bobby and Jackie,* 69.
106. Heymann, *Bobby and Jackie,* 68.
107. Ibid., 50–51.
108. George Smathers, interview in Heymann, *Bobby and Jackie,* 117–118.
109. Johnny Meyer, interview in Heymann, *Bobby and Jackie,* 120.
110. Ibid., 115.
111. Lilly Lawrence, interview in Heymann, *Bobby and Jackie,* 124.
112. Larry Rivers, interview in Heymann, *Bobby and Jackie,* 119.
113. Art Buchwald, interview in Heymann, *Bobby and Jackie,* 141.
114. Jack Newfield, interview in Heymann, *Bobby and Jackie,* 139–140.
115. Arthur Schlesinger, quoted in Evan Thomas, *Robert Kennedy* (New York: Simon & Schuster, 2000), 361; Johnny Meyer, interview in Heymann, *Bobby and Jackie,* 140–141.
116. Bradford, 329.
117. Constantine Gratsos, interview in Heymann, *Bobby and Jackie,* 143.
118. Heymann, *Bobby and Jackie,* 143.
119. Heymann, *Bobby and Jackie,* 144.
120. J. Randy Taraborrelli, *Jackie, Ethel and Joan: Women of Camelot* (New York: Rose Books, 2000), 321; italics added.
121. Pierre Salinger, interview in Heymann, *Bobby and Jackie,* 155.
122. Vidal, 392.
123. Heymann, *Bobby and Jackie,* 155–156.
124. Eugene McCarthy, *Up 'Til Now: A Memoir* (San Diego, CA: Harcourt Brace Jovanovich, 1987), 196.
125. Feldstein, 90–91.
126. Richard Goodwin, interview in Bradford, 331.
127. Heymann, *Bobby and Jackie,* 175–176; Evans, 187–188.
128. Heymann, *Bobby and Jackie,* 179; Evans, 199.
129. David, 92.
130. David, 103.
131. Yannis Georgakis, interview in Evans, 208.
132. Evans, 249.
133. Heymann, *Bobby and Jackie,* 181.
134. Ibid., 181.
135. Jenna Russell, "Conflicted Ambitions, Then, Chappaquiddick," *Boston Globe,* 17 Feb. 2009.
136. "Dinis Says Blood on Mary Jo's Body," *Boston Herald Traveler,* 16 Sept. 1969.
137. Senate Intelligence Committee Report, quoted in William Safire, "The President's Friend," *New York Times,* 4 October 1999.

CHAPTER 8: THE FULL BILL CLINTON

1. David Maraniss, *First in His Class: A Biography of Bill Clinton* (New York: Simon & Schuster, 1995), 18–20.
2. Nigel Hamilton, *Bill Clinton: Mastering the Presidency* (New York: Public Affairs, 2007), 540.
3. Bernie Lewinsky, interview in Ken Gormley, *The Death of American Virtue: Clinton vs. Starr* (New York: Crown, 2010), 236.
4. Gormley, 235.
5. Sally Quinn, "Tabloid Politics, the Clintons and the Way We Now Scrutinize Our Potential Presidents," *Washington Post,* 26 Jan. 1992; Burton Hersh, *Bobby and J. Edgar: The Historic Face-Off between the Kennedys and J. Edgar Hoover that Transformed America* (Basic Books: New York, 2007), 361.
6. Quinn, "Tabloid politics."
7. Christopher Anderson, *Jack and Jackie: Portrait of an American Marriage* (New York: Morrow, 1996), 253.
8. Gennifer Flowers, *Passion and Betrayal* (DelMar, CA: Emery Dalton, 1995) 32.
9. Nigel Hamilton, *Bill Clinton: An American Journey* (New York: Random House, 2003), 217.
10. Joe Klein, *The Natural: The Misunderstood Presidency of Bill Clinton* (New York: Doubleday, 2002), 100.
11. A 1997 Pew poll found 3 percent of Americans "always" trust the government, while 59 percent do "sometimes." "How American's View Government: Deconstructing Distrust," Pew Poll, 10 March 1998, http//people-press.org/report/95/.
12. Hamilton, *An American Journey,* 452.
13. Bill Clinton, *My Life* (New York: Knopf, 2004), 332.
14. "My 12-Year Affair with Bill Clinton," *Star,* 23 Jan. 1992, 1.
15. Hamilton, *An American Journey,* 597.
16. Mary Matalin and James Carville, *All's Fair* (New York: Simon & Schuster, 1995), 107.
17. Hewitt, quoted in Matalin and Carville, 107.
18. Bill and Hillary Clinton, *60 Minutes* interview, quoted in Hamilton, 617.

19. Hamilton, *An American Journey*, 623–624.

20. Hamilton, *An American Journey*, 618.

21. Matalin and Carville, 117.

22. "Bush Angrily Denounces Report of Extramarital Affair as 'a Lie,'" *Washington Post*, 12 Aug. 1992.

23. Deborah Sontag, "Candidate's Wife; Hillary Clinton: Speaking about Rumors," *New York Times*, 5 Apr. 1992.

24. James Gerstenzang, "President Denounces as a Lie Paper's Story about Romantic Affair," *Los Angeles Times*, 12 Aug. 1992; "Bush Angrily Denounces Report of Extramarital Affair as 'a Lie,'" *Washington Post*, 12 Aug. 1992 (emphasis added).

25. William Poundstone, *Gaming the Vote: Why Elections Aren't Fair (and What We Can Do about It)* (New York: Hill and Wang, 2008), 104.

26. "Bush Angrily Denies a Report of an Affair," *New York Times*, 12 Aug. 1992.

27. Steven M. Gillon, *The Pact: Bill Clinton, Newt Gingrich and the Rivalry that Defined a Generation* (Oxford: Oxford Univ. Press, 2008), 274.

28. Patrick Buchanan, speech to the 1992 Republican National Convention, Houston, Texas, 17 Aug. 1992.

29. Joe Conason and Gene Lyons, *The Hunting of the President: The Ten Year Campaign to Destroy Bill and Hillary Clinton* (New York: St. Martin's, 2000), 139.

30. Gormley, 90.

31. Franklin, quoted in Burns, 134.

32. Gormley, 39.

33. Gormley, 69.

34. Russell Watson, "Vince Foster's Suicide: The Rumor Mill Churns," *Newsweek*, 21 Mar. 1994.

35. Watson.

36. Gormley, 108.

37. Ibid., 89.

38. Conason and Lyons, 129.

39. Hamilton, 248.

40. David Brock, *Blinded by the Right* (New York: Crown, 2002), 146.

41. Hamilton, 240.

42. Quoted in Gormley, 115.

43. John F. Harris, *The Survivor: Bill Clinton in the White House* (New York: Random House, 2005), 117.

44. Quoted in Harris, 115.

45. Gormley, 91–92.

46. Klein, 117.

47. Clinton, 547.

48. Hamilton, 267.

49. Klein, 94–95.

50. Gormley, 110.

51. Conason and Lyons, 128.

52. Gormley, 151.

53. Bob Woodward and Susan Schmidt, "Starr Probes Clinton's Personal Life," *Washington Post*, 25 June 1997.

54. Alicia C. Sheppard, "The Second Time Around: The Media Coverage of the Whitewater Development Corp. Scandal," *American Journalism Review*, 1 June 1994.

55. Conason and Lyons, 174.

56. Gormley, 276.

57. David Brock, "Living with the Clintons," *American Spectator*, Jan. 1994.

58. Gormley, 181.

59. Charlotte Corbin Brown, interview in Rudy Maxa, "The Devil in Paula Jones," *Penthouse*, Jan. 1995, 107–109.

60. Michael Isikoff, *Uncovering Clinton: A Reporter's Story* (New York: Crown, 1999), 8.

61. "Statement of NOW President Patricia Ireland Calling for a Fair Treatment of Jones' Suit," NOW press release, 6 May 1994.

62. Gillon, 125.

63. Stuart Taylor Jr., "At War in Jones vs. Clinton," *Newsweek*, 27 Oct. 1997.

64. Harris, 293–294.

65. Frank Murray, "Is This the President's Distinguishing Characteristic?" *Washington Times*, 15 Oct. 1997.

66. Gormley, 256.

67. Ibid., 173.

68. Bill Clinton, interview in Gormley, 253.

69. Rita Delfiner, "Paula's Lawyer Wants Private Peek at Prez," *New York Post*, 28 May 1997.

70. Hamilton, *Mastering the Presidency*, 532–533.

71. Ibid., 606.

72. Monica Lewinsky, grand jury testimony, 6 Aug. 1998.

73. Andrew Morton, *Monica's Story* (New York: St. Martin's, 1999), 65.

74. Hamilton, *Mastering the Presidency*, 540.

75. Harris, 223–224.

76. Gormley, 533.

77. Monica Lewinsky, grand jury testimony, 6 Aug. 1998.

78. Conason and Lyons, 215.

79. Gormley, 238.

80. "Starr Report," 9 Sept. 1998, 102, U.S. Government Printing Office.

81. Conason and Lyons, 328.

82. Ibid., 325.

83. Isikoff, 192.

84. Gormley, 473.

85. Conason and Lyons, 337.

86. Isikoff, 237.

87. Ibid., 189.

88. Gormley, 302–307.

89. Isikoff, 297.

90. Gormley, 359.

91. Conason and Lyons, 349.

92. Monica Lewinsky, interview in Gormley, 361.

93. Isikoff, 334.

94. Harris, 303; Isikoff, 340.

95. Matt Drudge, speech to the National Press Club on Media and the Internet, 2 June 1998.

96. Gormley, 530–531.

97. Sam Donaldson, George Will and George Stephanopoulos on *This Week*, ABC, 25 Jan. 1998.

98. Dick Morris, grand jury testimony, 18 Aug. 1998, quoted in Harris, 307.

99. The Clinton White House spent more money on polling than all previous administrations combined. Klein, 7.

100. Klein, 174.

101. Gillon, 226.

102. Bill Clinton, press conference, 26 Jan. 1998.

103. Hillary Clinton, *Today Show*, NBC, 27 Jan. 1998; italics added.

104. Anne-Elisabeth Moutet, "Le Zippergate," *Pittsburgh Post-Gazette*, 1 Mar. 1998.

105. Charles Trueheart, "Speech Drew a World of Opinions," *Washington Post*, 19 Aug. 1998.

106. Richard Morin and Claudia Deane, "White House Sex Allegations Don't Trouble Most People," *Washington Post*, 26 Jan. 1998.

107. Harris, 330.

108. Ibid., 342.

109. Gormley, 477.

110. Ibid., 524.

111. Jerry Seper, "Freeh Won't Quit as FBI Director" *Washington Times*, 17 Dec. 1997.

112. Harris, 115.

113. Ibid., 277.

114. Ibid., 275.

115. Gormley, 667–668.

116. Harris, 408.

117. Hamilton, *Mastering the Presidency*, 619.

118. Gormley, 541.

119. "Testimony of William Jefferson Clinton before the Grand Jury Empaneled for Independent Counsel Kenneth Starr," 17 Aug. 1998.

120. Harris, 350.

121. Hamilton, *Mastering the Presidency*, 588.

122. Gormley, 574.

123. Quoted in Gormley, 575.

124. "Time to Resign," *Philadelphia Inquirer*, 13 Sept. 1998.

125. Editorial, *Pittsburgh Post-Gazette*, 13 Sept. 1998.

126. Klein, 13.

127. Gillon, 243.

128. Gormley, 595.

129. Ibid., 4.

130. In *Keeton v. Hustler Magazine* (1984) the United States Supreme Court ruled that a state could assert personal jurisdiction over the publisher of a national magazine that published an allegedly defamous article about a resident of another state. In *Hustler Magazine, Inc. v. Falwell* (1988), the United States Supreme Court unanimously held that the First Amendment prohibits awarding damages to public figures to compensate for emotional distress intentionally inflicted upon them.

131. Gillon, 242.

132. Harris, 334.

133. John H. Richardson, "Newt Gingrich, the Indispensable Republican," *Esquire*, September 2010.

134. Gormley, 4–7.

135. Ibid., 625.

136. Ibid., 626.

137. Ibid., 646.

138. Conason and Lyons, 372.

139. Klein, 179.

140. Bill Clinton, Statement on His Testimony before the Grand Jury, 17 Aug. 1998, printed in *New York Times*, "Testing of a President in his Own Words," 18 August 1998.

141. Harris, 327.

142. Gormley, 542.

143. *9/11 Commission Report: Final Report of the National Commission on Terrorist Attacks upon the United States* (New York: Norton, 2004), 189.

144. Harris, 401–407.

145. Richard Clarke, *Against All Enemies: Inside America's War on Terror* (New York: Free Press, 2004), 188–189.

146. *9/11 Commission Report*, 118.

CONCLUSION: FULFILLING THE PLEDGE

1. Marvin Zuckerman, "Are You a Risk Taker?" *Psychology Today*, 1 Nov. 2000.

2. "The Cheating Man's Brain," *Newsweek*, 12 March 2008.

3. Ibid.

4. Anne-Elisabeth Moutet, "Le Zippergate," *Pittsburgh Post-Gazette*, 1 Mar. 1998.

5. Angelique Chrisafis, "I Am a Cat, a Tamer of Men," *Guardian*, 18 Jan. 2008.

6. Nick Squires, "Silvio Berlusconi Triumphs in Italy's Elections Despite Allegations," *London Telegraph*, 23 June 2009.

7. Emmanuel Saez and Thomas Piketty, "Income Inequality in America, 1913–1998," *Quarterly Journal of Economics*, 2003, updated 2007.

8. Kenneth Lovett, "New York State Gubernatorial Hopeful Carl Paladino Has 10-year-old Love Child," *New York Daily News*, 5 Apr. 2010; Maureen Callahan, "Tea for Three: The Candidate, His Wife and His Mistress," *New York Post*, 26 Sept. 2010.

9. Alexander Hamilton, quoted in Ron Chernow, *Alexander Hamilton* (New York: Penguin, 2004), 669.

10. Fernando Quintero, "Accuser Recounts Trysts with 'Art,'" *Rocky Mountain News*, 3 Nov. 2006.

11. Neela Banerjee, "Ousted Pastor 'Completely Heterosexual,'" *New York Times*, 7 Feb. 2007.

12. Sandhya Somashekhar, "Family Research Council Founder Hires a Rentboy," *Washington Post*, 5 May 2010; Brandon K. Thorp and Penn Bullock, "Christian Right Leader George Rekers takes Vacation with 'Rent Boy,'" *Miami New Times*, 6 May 2010; Brandon K. Thorp and Penn Bullock, "How George Alan Rekers and His Rent Boy Got Busted by New Times," *Miami New Times*, 13 May 2010.

INDEX